ACOUSTIC
GUITARS

ACOUSTIC
GUITARS

THE ILLUSTRATED ENCYCLOPEDIA

CHARTWELL
BOOKS

Inspiring | Educating | Creating | Entertaining

Brimming with creative inspiration, how-to projects, and useful information to enrich your everyday life, Quarto Knows is a favorite destination for those pursuing their interests and passions. Visit our site and dig deeper with our books into your area of interest: Quarto Creates, Quarto Cooks, Quarto Homes, Quarto Lives, Quarto Drives, Quarto Explores, Quarto Gifts, or Quarto Kids.

ISBN-13: 978-0-7858-3571-4

Printed in China

contents

contents

introduction

The golden age of the acoustic guitar is upon us, and *Acoustic Guitars: The Illustrated Encyclopedia* is a celebration of the incredible variety of the most popular musical instrument in the western world.

Guitarists today have the great privilege of access to more styles and grades of guitars than ever before available, at prices to suit every budget. The vintage market continues to thrive, of course, but even more significant is the way that newer makers have adapted the classic designs to carve fresh and, very often, improved instruments from the old templates. Never have so many skilled craftsmen built so many top-grade instruments – and the roster of respected guitar-makers grows yearly as former apprentices graduate to mastery of their craft.

In this book you'll find virtually every maker or brand of acoustic guitar. Some are from the past, others very much of the present. This is no foolish attempt to be complete, and no doubt some will find a few omissions, for which we apologise. But what you hold is the biggest, most comprehensive survey of the acoustic guitar ever published, and of that we are certainly proud. The guitars themselves are given star treatment in an array of remarkable photographs, alongside a wide-ranging selection of musicians seen cradling, playing, fondling, and generally enjoying the company of their hollowbody friends. We've also displayed for you a stunning collection of period and contemporary ads, catalogs, and photographs from guitar brands ancient and modern. And the experienced team of writers we've assembled to tell you the stories of these acoustic guitars – flat-tops, archtops, resonators, Hawaiians, electros and all – is without rival.

In the world of the steel-string flat-top acoustic guitar, not only have major names like Gibson and Martin recovered the quality and cachet of earlier days, but a long list of smaller makers has risen to match them and, at times, even surpass them in the custom work that more and more guitarists appreciate and are eager to commission. The bluegrass picker of 1939 would have had a Martin dreadnought, a Gibson jumbo, or maybe an Epiphone to choose from when he wanted a quality flat-top. Today, he or she can also test-drive a Santa Cruz, Bourgeois, Collings, Gallagher, Froggy Bottom, Taylor, Lowden, or any of a number of others before spending a cent.

Meanwhile, guitars at the entry level are better than ever. A North American or European instrument made from all-solid woods can be bought at a lower price – in real terms – than ever before, while veneer-constructed 'beginner guitars' are more playable and durable. Guitars at the high end of the price spectrum are at the top of their game, too, with a good dozen or more makers achieving degrees of artistry – and consistency – barely dreamt of in the past.

Along with this blossoming of makes and models has come a heightened awareness of design and materials on the part of the player. The skilled steel-string fingerstylist understands the differences in timbre produced by a rosewood versus a mahogany back; jazz players study the response and projection offered by parallel-braced and X-braced tops; classical musicians

> " What I am trying to do is to achieve in the present what will be the guitar of the future. And if I can't achieve that, then I'll try to find a way that might be a guide to others yet to come. "
>
> MANUEL CONTRERAS

weigh up the warm and 'played in' voice of cedar against the yielding and full-frequency voice of spruce.

This book makes no comprehensive attempt to instruct in the art of guitar-making, but where relevant does discuss materials and build techniques used by luthiers working today and in the past. With this knowledge comes power. Guitarists are better than ever equipped to fine-tune their own sound before they have even put fingers to strings. A broad range of skilled builders are willing to cater for their desires, matching koa to mahogany to ebony to spruce to maple to oak to rosewood … in an infinity of potential ratios and designs. Many of those guitars are displayed in these pages. Some are creations of great beauty; a few are even works of art, by any definition.

The acoustic guitar has weathered the dawn of amplification and the electric guitar, the slowdown of production during the war years, and the dark days of the synthesizer and the electronic-music boom of the early 1980s. The instrument is now more valued and enjoyed than ever before. It is undoubtedly here to stay – a voice for all seasons, all moods, all music.

> " Some guitar-makers think that they have made a guitar superior to all others, but I do not think I have as yet produced the best guitar ever made. So far, there is no equivalent to a Stradivarius among guitar makers, but one day I hope to produce the exceptional guitar. "
>
> PAULINO BERNABÉ

Sada-Yairi ad c1975 *Kazuo Yairi's cousin Sada produced instruments with the Sada-Yairi brand.*

A L V A R E Z

Alvarez is the brand name used originally on acoustic guitars imported from Japan to the US by St Louis Music beginning in 1965. Sourced from various factories, including K. Yairi, Alvarez guitars aimed at beginners to intermediate, with some better models nearing the quality of the more upscale Alvarez-Yairi line.

The range launched with the typical laminated dreadnoughts, but in the 1970s Alvarez fueled the 'copy era' with classicals, dreadnoughts, and folk and jumbo models based on Martin and Gibson designs, many with adjustable saddles. Many were made by Terada in Nagoya, Japan. By 1978 the line had become quite diverse, with cutaway dreadnoughts, three-piece jacaranda and maple backs, black finishes, tree-of-life inlays, and some solid-top models.

In 1979 Alvarez introduced its Artist line of original-style classicals, folks, and dreadnoughts. By 1982 student-grade guitars were offered in the Regent line, better models carried the Artist name, and progressive cutaway full and thin-body acoustic-electrics were Fusions, with some very nice Diamond Anniversary models. In around 1984 production of lower-grade guitars began shifting to Samick in Korea. In the mid

1980s Alvarez introduced a Bi-Phonic pickup with stereo bass and treble output and EQ systems. In the early 1990s even more upscale Professional, Elegance and Exotic models were added, including the f-hole Bluesman dreadnought. A wide range of designs continues to provide a budget alternative to the flagship Japanese Alvarez-Yairi line.

A L V A R E Z - Y A I R I

Alvarez-Yairi guitars are top-of-the-line instruments either made by or under the supervision of Kazuo Yairi in Japan, for sale in the US by St Louis Music. K. Yairi also markets similar instruments under his own name for European and other markets. Featuring top-grade materials and impressive attention to detail, they are highly valued by collectors and have been played by a long list of pros, including Jeff Baxter, Pat Simmons, and Mike McDonald of the Doobie Brothers; Roy Clark; John Cougar Mellencamp; Jerry Garcia and Bob Weir of the Grateful Dead; Carlos Santana; Ani Difranco; Warren Haynes; David Crosby; Graham Nash; Felicia Collins; Chris Cagle; Carly Simon and many others.

Alvarez Artist Missouri nine-String 1981 (*left*) This dreadnought, Model No. 5058, follows the form of the traditional 12-string, but excludes the octave-high strings from the three bass strings.

Alvarez-Yairi Model 5011 1972 (*right*) This hand-made cedar-top classical guitar typifies the value-for-money nylon-string offerings of Alvarez in the early 1970s.

Alvarez-Yairi ad 1973 (*left*) The company's declaration that "the herringbone is back" shows the importer is willing to pit Japanese craftsmanship against the obvious Martin associations.

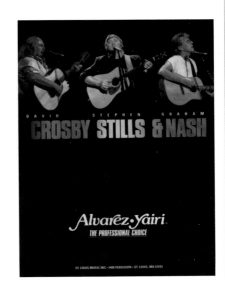

Kazuo Yairi learned lutherie from his father and opened a small factory in Kani-City, Gifu, in 1935. His reputation grew, and in 1965 his path crossed with that of St Louis Music (SLM). SLM had been founded in St Louis, Missouri, in 1922 by violinist Bernard Kornblum. A major regional distributor, by the late 1930s SLM was selling its own Custom Kraft guitars made primarily by Kay. In around 1965, Bernard's son Gene went to Japan, where he was introduced to Yairi. SLM became the exclusive US distributor of Yairi guitars in 1966, relaying its own market expertise and design input back to the builder. The deal included Alvarez-Yairi guitars, supervised and signed by Yairi, and Alvarez By Yairi models made by his workers. These were all produced in Japan and received a final check and set up in St Louis.

Early Alvarez-Yairi guitars included upscale Martin-inspired DY dreadnoughts, FY orchestras, and CY classicals with solid tops. By the mid 1970s limited production dreadnoughts had three-piece backs, very fancy timbers, and loads of pearl and

K. Yairi AR300 1983 (left) *This small-bodied, steel-string flat-top with its distinctive rounded headstock was hand-built by company founder and master luthier Kazuo Yairi.*

Alvarez-Yairi Classical 1989 (right) *A typical example of the later Alvarez-Yairi nylon-string models from the Japanese factory.*

Chris Smithers 2001 (above) *Singer/songwriter Smithers accompanies himself on an Alvarez-Yairi SY88 thinline electro-acoustic.*

Alvarez-Yairi ad 1989 *Alvarez-Yairi further solidified their association with quality US-built acoustics like those of Martin by securing this endorsement from Crosby Stills & Nash in the late 1980s.*

The Flaming Lips 2001
Singer/guitarist Wayne Coyne of alt-rockers The Flaming Lips puts his Alvarez 12-string to work in an absorbing acoustic moment.

abalone trim, including tree-of-life inlays. Classicals favored cedar and came with distinctively bright floral rosettes or carved headstocks. A cutaway Wellington dreadnought joined the list by 1978.

Yairi himself built many Alvarez and Alvarez-Yairi prototypes during this period, almost all encrusted with elaborate inlays and sporting experimental bracing, bridges, and headstock designs, most of which never made it to production.

In 1978 Alvarez-Yairi introduced a new truss-rod that extended all the way through the neck. By 1979, some of the earlier gaudier design elements were replaced by a more restrained look, though figured exotic woods and abalone inlays continued to be a trademark. The old Martin-style head was given distinctive notches at the corners.

By around 1982 the Alvarez-Yairi line began introducing a number of new features. One was a cool CY132C with a truncated lower body that joined the neck at the 14th fret. Another fascinating model was the DY92 with a new tulip-shaped head and a rounded lute back. The Express line also appeared, offering cutaway dreadnought acoustic-electrics with new colorburst finishes, thinner bodies, arched backs, and new tapered heads (these would later get the tulip shape, too). A more conventional looking thin-bodied acoustic-electric classical was offered a year later. Swept along

by the acoustic-electric boom, Alvarez-Yairi featured Bi-Phonic pickups with stereo bass/treble output by 1985. Signature dreadnoughts – signed by K. Yairi on the lower bout – also debuted, drenched in understated elegance. The only fingerboard inlays were a pearl snowflake and diagonal abalone line at the octave. Also in 1985 a few 12/6 doublenecks were made, as well as some nine-string models, basically a 12-string without the doubled basses. In 1988 a new 'direct-coupled' bridge was introduced, with the pin section separated from the bridge and saddle.

In the early 1990s Alvarez-Yairi continued to innovate. Other different bridge shapes began to be used, recalling Yairi's earlier prototypes. In 1991 the Virtuosos appeared – the GY1 cutaway dreadnought for Jerry Garcia and the WY1 cutaway grand concert for Bob Weir. Following these – and working with Garcia again – Alvarez-Yairi debuted the tree-of-life inlaid DY99 Virtuoso Custom and plainer DY98 Graphite, both with solid graphite necks built by Modulus Graphite. A new System 500 EQ system was also adopted.

Also by 1991, if not before, K. Yairi was promoting his own brand outside of the US. Most of these were the same guitars as were being sold as Alvarez-Yairi, including the direct-coupled bridge, lots of dreadnoughts, classicals, and the

Alvarez ad 1999 *Independent-minded singer/songwriter and self-proclaimed 'righteous babe' Ani DiFranco is a long-time devotee of Alvarez-Yairi guitars.*

Sada-Yairi Model 726 1975 (left) *Sada was Yairi founder Kazuo's cousin, and although they had separate workshops they did apparently have some business associations and their guitars are often loosely associated. S. Yairi guitars, such as this classical example – and others in the ad on page 10 – are less common than models with the Alvarez-Yairi or K. Yairi brands.*

Aria HF A588 1969 (right) *A typical budget-priced Japanese-made Aria classical guitar of the late 1960s.*

Expresses (several with a unique curved six-in-line head). However, as one might guess, many featured far more inlay work, many with K. Yairi's logo, a cherub with a bow, and one with a full Japanese figure. Unlike the line marketed in the US, elsewhere K. Yairi still offered models more closely inspired by Martin and Gibson, as well as a full line of small-bodied 'parlor' guitars, including one with pearl-and-black-mastic trim, a scrolled violin-style head, and a 19th-century style mustache bridge.

Alvarez-Yairi's future was fairly well set by this time, yet new models continued to arrive. In 1994 two dreadnoughts in maple and koa appeared with new 'swoosh' bridges made of graphite, along with the first jumbos since the 1970s. In 1996 a jumbo-sized baritone guitar debuted. A year later the company built a Virtuoso 12-string for David Crosby, and two new cutaway models with dramatically swept-back horns debuted. In K. Yairi's own promotions of the mid 1980s he described his guitars as "works of art." It wasn't hype.

ANDERSEN

Steven Andersen is considered to be one of the premier archtop guitar builders in America. He built his first guitar in 1973 while he was still in high school, and in 1978

went to work with Nick Kukich, who owned the Franklin Guitar Co. In 1980 he started his own workshop, where he made flat-top steel-string guitars and carved top mandolins. In 1986 Andersen moved to Seattle, where he started building archtops after repairing a number of classic Gibsons, Strombergs, and D'Angelicos.

Andersen's guitars are characterized by clean, modern lines and meticulous attention to detail. His traditional models include the Emerald City, the Metropolitan, and the Streamline. He also makes an unusual model called the Little Archie, which has a 14" body and an oval soundhole in the upper bout on the bass side.

ARIA

One of the quieter guitar giants, Aria pioneered many innovations in Japanese guitar-making and has been a steady provider of very good beginner and intermediate level guitars since 1960.

Aria was created by classical guitarist Shiro Arai, whose inspiration was to improve the quality of classical guitars in Japan. In 1960 Arai began working with the Ryoji Matsuoka Guitar Company to make better domestic classical guitars. In the winter of 1963, exploring export markets, Arai brought some Masaru Kohno classicals

Aria catalog 2002 *This catalog page displaying the Elecord range declares that "these models incorporate Fishman matrix Pickups and electronics," further emphasizing the importance of the electro-acoustic market to Aria.*

Aria SPE Sandpiper 12-String 1998 (left) *The evolving Sandpiper range has long been a popular line from Aria. This 12-string example is an electro-acoustic model with under-saddle pickup and onboard preamp.*

Aria AW-130 1998 (right) *This budget-priced dreadnought made in China partners a solid spruce top with laminated mahogany back and sides.*

to the US. They disintegrated in heated hotel rooms because the wood wasn't seasoned to withstand climate differences, and Arai took this knowledge back to Japan. In 1964 Arai purchased several factories and began making his own solid-topped classical and laminated-top steel-stringed guitars. Until production shifted to supplier factories, Aria also did work producing some guitars with other companies' brand names.

In 1967 Arai and his engineers developed one of the earliest versions of the modern piezo transducer that attached to an internal body brace. Refinements a year later led to perhaps the first in-bridge piezo pickup, which appeared on Aria and Conn acoustics for a few years.

In the early 1970s Aria, like other Japanese companies, built acoustic guitars that imitated models by Martin and Gibson. In 1975, however, Aria changed its primary brand name to Aria Pro II, and more original work was just down the road – though the most notable acoustic of this period was probably a dreadnought fully bound with abalone trim and a full tree-of-life pearl fingerboard inlay.

In around 1977 Aria's acoustic lines exploded with a range of new offerings, and many of its popular lines debuted. Early versions still used the Aria Pro II brand name,

but by the end of the decade Aria reverted to using Aria only for acoustics. These guitars included laminated six-string and 12-string dreadnoughts, folk and classical guitars with laminated tops, and either maple, mahogany or rosewood bodies in traditional Gibson and Martin styles, with a mix of natural and sunburst finishes. A few cheaper models had bolt-on necks.

The more upscale PW Series included more copies – including some of lesser-imitated Guild guitars – with fancier trim and some solid tops. A Handcrafted series featured fancier timbers, solid tops, and abalone trim, and were endorsed by Ricky Hirsch of the Gregg Allman Band. Aria's better classicals were designated AC and included laminated and solid tops, depending on the grade. Aria's Maestro Hand Crafted Classics were better, and curiously finished inside to protect against moisture. Arai also distributed hand-made guitars by Kohno and M. Sakurai.

In 1979 Aria introduced its SW Series dreadnoughts, and the following year the downscale LW Series of folk and dreadnought models joined them. Aria returned to acoustic-electrics with its Elecord Series of full and thin-body cutaway jumbo-shaped guitars in 1981, and the following year the long-lived budget Ariana brand debuted. By the mid 1980s Aria was also producing the LJ Series of jumbo-shaped guitars. Like

Aria NXG 1998 (left) *Aria's take on the semi-solid nylon-string electro format pioneered by Gibson has a solid spruce top with offset soundhole and bolt-on neck.*

Aria SP99 Sandpiper 1999 (center) *A six-string Sandpiper built a year after the 12-string pictured opposite. Note the pearloid tuner buttons and elaborate headstock logo.*

Aria AMS-04 1999 (far right) *This folk-sized guitar from Aria's Meister Series was designed by German luthier Stephan Schmitz and built in China. Another budget offering, it features a solid spruce top but laminated rosewood back and sides.*

Aria catalog 2002 *The cover of this Aria brochure seeks to establish period-Americana associations in the minds of potential buyers.*

Marc Bolan and Ringo Starr c1972 (*above*) *The former Beatle and T. Rex mainman Bolan laugh it up on film with an invisible piano and an Aria 'copy' of a Gibson Hummingbird. Like other Japanese makers, Aria spent much of their effort copying popular US models during the late 1960s and into the early '70s.*

Art & Lutherie AA85 2002 (*left*) *This translucent green dreadnought is a 'Wild Cherry' example of the model from Canadian maker Art & Lutherie, known for its good-quality yet affordable guitars.*

Ashborn 1855 (*right*) *James Ashborn of Wolcottville, Connecticut, was one of America's biggest guitar builders before the Civil War. The guitar here is outwardly similar – though not identical – to the much better known Martins of the period.*

Aria ASP-930 2000 (*above*) *A millennial take on the ongoing Sandpiper theme, this time with more subdued headstock inlays.*

everyone else, Aria found it increasingly difficult to sell Japanese-made guitars profitably by the mid '80s, and in 1985 began to source acoustics from Korea. The AC prefix changed to AK at that time.

Particularly noteworthy is a line of acoustic and acoustic-electrics from 1993 called the Sandpipers, with Baroque-style soundhole roses or fancy rosettes. Around this same time Aria briefly offered several classy CE acoustic-electric classicals and a pretty AF Series modeled after Martin's OM, with retro slotted heads, and some with flamed maple tops.

In 1994 Aria took the bold step of opening a factory in, of all places, Spain, and for a few years produced some high quality yet affordable classical guitars there under the revived AC Series umbrella. In recent years Aria's acoustics have been made at several factories in Korea and elsewhere in Asia, like almost every other company selling guitars in the lower price ranges.

ART & LUTHERIE

Art & Lutherie, another product of Robert Godin's LaSiDo company in Quebec, was originally conceived as a good-value, entry-level line that would feature all-Canadian tonewoods (and optional electronics). Upon their debut in 1994, Art & Lutherie guitars shared LaSiDo design features, including laminated wild cherry, bolt-on necks, and lacquer finishes. Initial Art & Lutheries were dreadnoughts with maple necks, walnut fingerboards and bridges (rosewood was used later), and either natural solid cedar or spruce tops, or colored finishes over laminated cherry tops. Around 1996 the Ami model debuted, a parlor guitar with full-scale fingerboard, intended as a child's guitar but often used a travel or blues guitar. By 2017, the Art & Lutherie lines were divided into Americana dreadnoughts, Legacy folk instruments, and Roadhouse parlor guitars.

ASHBORN

Before the Civil War, one of the largest guitar factories in America was run by James Ashborn in Wolcottville, Connecticut. Born in England, Ashborn (with John Hungerford) began to make guitars in the late 1840s, selling to the big New York music publishers Firth, Pond & Company (later J. Firth Sons) and William Hall & Son, whose labels Ashborn's instruments usually carry. Featuring a robust tone for their size, most were small gut-string parlor guitars with fan-braced spruce tops in a variety of grades, with different woods (often laminated over spruce) and decoration.

Ayers DS 2002 (*left*) *By using minimal decoration and a satin finish on the DS, Ayers has managed to offer an all-solid-woods guitar (spruce and mahogany) at an affordable price.*

Ayers ad 2002 (*above*) *The Australia-designed, Vietnam-built Ayers brand clearly seeks to establish a calm, quiet confidence among potential buyers with its laidback, new-age-leaning approach to promotion.*

Ayers ACSM-E 2002 (*right*) *This cutaway grand auditorium model features a gloss finish and onboard Fishman pickup with preamp.*

AVALON

Many had special patented wooden spindle peg tuners. In 1864 Ashborn was elected state senator and ended his guitar-making.

AVALON

Avalon appeared in early 2002 – not just as a new brand within the Lowden guitar stable, but as the new holding-company name for the whole operation. Slightly confusingly, this respected Northern Irish maker still trades under the Lowden Guitar Co. moniker, although this changed at the end of 2003 when the company formally ended its relationship with its original founder George Lowden and became Avalon Guitars in all respects.

Avalon's initial marketing thrust has been to target the more affordable professional sector (roughly $1,250 to $2,250), achieving cost economies – where possible – through standardization of jigs, cosmetics, and gloss lacquering involving far fewer coats. A new double-X/part-A bracing pattern, common to all models, has also been incorporated.

The launch line-up, solid timbers throughout, was ostensibly vast – over 40 models – but this boils down to three designs: D dreadnought, A auditorium and S

smaller-bodied concert, the model numbers completed by wood options (cedar or spruce, mahogany or rosewood), along with the expected cutaway, electro, and 12-string variants.

As anticipated, build and sound quality have proved excellent – the latter subtly different to Lowdens, perhaps sparklier and more American in character – and Avalons have received plaudits from the press as a result. Approximately 700 were sold during 2002, the best seller being the spruce/rosewood A200CE cutaway auditorium electro.

Avalon divided its line in 2003 into two: the UK-made models were called the Gold series, and a low/mid-price line of Silver models was added, which were built in Korea. The following year, Avalon split with Lowden, and the firm now produces its own instruments from its base in Newtonards, Northern Ireland.

AYERS

Ayers had its international launch in 2002, representing an unusual tie-up involving three countries. Designer-cum-production consultant (and coiner of the Oz-evocative name) is established Australian luthier Gerard Gilet; the company, Ayers Music,

Benedetto Anima e Corpo seven-String 2003 *This hand-built 18" archtop guitar is not only a stunning instrument in its own right, it is a new piece of jazz guitar history. At the request of client Bill Doyle, over the course of six years Bob Benedetto tracked down as many jazz-guitar stars as he could find to sign the inside back of the instrument (see inset picture). The tally had reached 80 by the time Benedetto completed the guitar; among the signatories are Howard Alden, Jimmy Bruno, Frank Vignola, Johnny Smith, Herb Ellis, Les Paul, George Benson, Bucky Pizzarelli, Tal Farlow, and Martin Taylor.*

Howard Alden 2001 (below)
A signed shot of jazz guitarist Alden, from the Benedetto archive. Alden used this acoustic La Venezia model to record his acclaimed 1997 CD, Take Your Pick.

operates out of Taiwan, but production is sourced from Vietnam, not a country hitherto known for its acoustic-making prowess. The brand-dedicated Saigon factory is nonetheless achieving consistant high quality starting from near-budget prices. An important marketing plus is that the line-up – based on dreadnought, auditorium, and slot-head grand concert designs – features all-solid-timbers throughout. Cutaway electro versions are offered in the dreadnought and auditorium series.

AYLWARD

Rob Aylward is perhaps best known for his Selmer/Maccaferri-style guitars, but also builds a full line of fretted instruments including banjos, dulcimers, mandolins, and flat-top steel-string, classical, and archtop guitars.

Of his specialty instrument, he builds both oval-hole and D-shaped soundhole Selmer-style guitars with the slightly larger body pioneered by Favino in the 1950s. Aylward studied Musical Instrument Technology for four years at London's Guildhall University with Herbert Schwartz and the classical guitar maker Michael Gee. He doesn't offer any standard models as such, preferring instead to build each instrument to the client's specifications.

BELTONA

Steve Evans and Bill Johnson started building metal-bodied resonator instruments in England under the Beltona name in 1990. Their first guitars were based on the National tri-cone and Style O single-cone designs of the late 1920s, but they soon expanded the line to include instruments of their own design, such as the Electro Resonator with cutaway, and a metal mandolin with an F-5 shape. They have since added a full range of ukuleles and tenor guitars to the line. In 1998 Evans returned to his native New Zealand, but he and Johnson still continue to offer the metal-bodied instruments. In 2000 Beltona took a radical new step and introduced a line of resonator instruments with fiberglass bodies, and metal was discontinued in 2002.

BENEDETTO

Robert Benedetto emerged in the 1990s as the most successful of a new wave of independent makers, as evidenced by an artist-endorsement list that ranges from jazz players Jimmy Bruno, Bucky Pizzarelli and Kenny Burrell to such mainstream pop artists as Andy Summers and Earl Klugh.

Through the styling of his instruments, as well as through an instructional book and

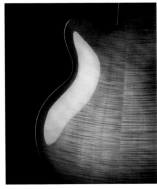

Benedeto La Venezia 2003 (left) *An earlier collaboration with guitarist Chuck Wayne led to this elegant, minimalist model joining the regular Benedetto line.*

Benedetto La Cremona Fiorita late 1990s (below) *One of a series of experimental guitars, this one made for Skot Koenig, with floral-pattern soundholes.*

Benedetto promo shots *These artful photographs of Benedetto archtops display and highlight the breathtaking woodworking skills of this master luthier.*

video, Benedetto led a modern school of archtop design characterized by the use of wood instead of metal or plastic for tailpieces, pickguards, and bindings, along with a general tendency to simplify, if not minimalize, the ornate, traditional style of D'Angelico and D'Aquisto.

Benedetto began making guitars in 1968 in New Jersey and has relocated to Florida (1976), Pennsylvania (1990), and Plant City, Florida (since 1999). Unlike other archtop makers, he went back to the original inspiration for the archtop design – violins – and has made over 50 violin-family instruments. His violin work would result in his introduction of violin finishes, such as oil-varnish, spirit varnish, and French polish, to the world of archtop guitars.

His first standardized guitar model, the Cremona, was introduced in 1972, and showed signs of his designs to come with an inlay-free fingerboard, ebony tailpiece, and a sleek, narrow pickguard shape. Other features, however, such as the large, flared peghead, remained in the D'Angelico tradition.

His next model, the Fratello, appeared in 1980 and gave a stronger nod to conventional ornamentation, with pearl block fingerboard markers and fancy pearl inlay on the headstock and tailpiece.

Benedetto 'Pine Guitar' c1992
To prove a point about the importance of craftsmanship over materials, Bob Benedetto built this guitar entirely from what many would consider to be 'inferior' tonewoods. It has a two-piece top carved from flatsawn 2"x10" construction-grade pine, a two-piece back carved from unmatched maple, and sides and neck of plain maple. The guitar is riddled with small knots, weather checking, and discoloration but, declares the maker himself, "sounds and plays as good as any made from expensive tonewoods."

Bernabé 1992 *Spanish luthier Paulino Bernabé, a former apprentice to famed Spanish guitar-maker José Ramirez III, is said to have built this beautiful classical guitar for himself, though he later sold it to its present owner. Note the flamed-maple headstock facing, and the further use of attractive European maple on the instrument's sides and back (far left and opposite page), something not often seen on classical guitars.*

Through the 1980s, Benedetto straddled tradition and modernism with the Cremona and Fratello. There was also an early version of the Limelite (1980-84) that was simply a small Cremona (16" wide).

In 1989, a new model, the Manhattan, still showed elements of both schools, with a dearth of ornamental inlay (except for the headstock logo) but with multi-ply binding everywhere – on the top, back, fingerboard and peghead.

By the end of the decade, his guitars were commanding higher prices than those of any other living archtop maker except James D'Aquisto, and he had established his own signature features, among them a semi-opaque 'honey blonde' finish, headstock veneers of exotic, highly figured woods, and solid ebony tailpieces. He had also become the leading maker of seven-string archtops, which were favored by many of his jazz-playing clients.

Benedetto hit his stride as an influential maker with the introduction during 1993 of the La Venezia model. It was based on a guitar he had built more than ten years earlier, working with jazz guitarist Chuck Wayne (a veteran of George Shearing's group), and it took the all-wood/minimalist concept to a new level, with no inlay, no binding, and no pickguard. A year later, Benedetto made the first of several experimental guitars, which had floral-pattern soundhole openings as well as some other non-traditional appointments.

Benedetto solidified his status as the leader of the new archtop makers in 1994 by publishing what remians at the time of writing the only comprehensive book on his specialist subject, *Making An Archtop Guitar*. He followed this in 1996 with a nine-and-a-half-hour video course entitled *Archtop Design And Construction*, and then in 2002 contributed the chapter on Archtop Acoustics to the book *Guitar: A Complete Guide For The Player*.

In 1999, Benedetto was hired by the Fender company to consult on its Guild line of archtops (Fender had acquired Guild in 1995), at which time Benedetto agreed to cut his own guitarmaking back to the occasional custom instrument.

The agreement led to Fender building Benedetto guitars under his supervision, at first at the Guild custom shop and later at the Fender plant. This lasted until 2006. Howard Paul joined Benedetto that year, back at his own workshop, and by 2017 a team of six more makers were producing an expanded line of Benedetto models, namely the Bambino, Benny, Bravo, Cremona, Gypsy, and La Venezia, as well as a signature instrument for Pat Martino.

Bohmann Grand Concert c1896 (*near right*) *A steel-string flat-top made by self-proclaimed 'World's Greatest Instrument Maker' Joseph Bohmann of Chicago.*

Back (*far right*) *Note the attractive, highly figured wood used for the back of this Bohmann flat-top.*

Bernabé back (*left*) *This rear view of the classical guitar seen on the opposite page highlights Bernabé's use of finely flamed maple.*

B E R N A B É

The guitars of Paulino Bernabé are in the Spanish tradition without being enslaved by it. Bernabé began as a cabinet-maker and a student of the guitar – he learnt from a pupil of Francisco Tárrega – before turning to guitar-making in the Ramírez workshop in Madrid. There, as head artisan, he imposed new standards of craftsmanship, inaugurating a golden age in which the company managed to combine quality and quantity. But in 1969, rejecting further mechanization, Bernabé established his own business, hand-building instruments with an emphasis on power and projection for concert use.

To this end, he constantly adjusted his strutting techniques and experimented with unusual woods, including pear and sandalwood. All of which means that Bernabé's guitars tend to be very individual. In 1972 he built a ten-string instrument for Narciso Yepes, perhaps the best-known of his customers.

Bernabé died in 2007, and his son, also called Paulino, continued the business in a workshop in the north of Madrid. Today, he produces numerous models that range from the Royal, for which he uses wood at least 40 years old, down to a student model with a laminated back.

Bohmann Harp Guitar c1910
The body of this bizarrely Gothic-looking harp guitar has an unusual, almost organic 'swollen' look to it, even better appreciated in the side view (left). Harp guitars were surprisingly popular in the early part of the last century, but this one has a far more extreme look than most.

B O H M A N N

With a label reading "World's Greatest Instrument Maker, Chicago, Illinois," Joseph Bohmann was not shy, and indeed had a standing bet that no one could top him. Having won eight international prizes between 1888 and 1904, he had evidence to support his boast, too. Born in 1848 in Neumarkt, Bohemia, Bohmann emigrated to Chicago and established American Musical Industry in 1878, becoming an early supplier to Sears. Bohmann offered 12 grades of guitars in a rosewood and figured maple combination (and rosewood alone), in standard, concert, and grand-concert sizes, with increasingly elaborate decoration, although he also made birch guitars with fancy faux finishes. His guitars were noted for playability and tone, with many innovations, including triple, cross-grained laminates to prevent cracking, special patented back-mounted tuners, X-bracing, very thin necks, and special bridge posts that appear to be intended to relieve the tension of increasingly popular silk and steel strings. Bohmann also made some huge guitars for the time, with 14" and 15" lower bouts. Harp guitars and unusual experimental guitars with odd string configurations were other specialties of Bohmann's shop. Bohmann was succeeded by his son, and Bohmann's American Musical Industry was still in business as late as 1926.

B O L I N

Professor Georg Bolin was a Swedish luthier born in 1912 who learned cabinetmaking from the famous furniture designer Carl Malmsten. But Bolin's tastes shifted to the musical, and eventually he took up classical guitar making.

His clients were mostly classical masters, including the legendary Andrés Segovia. Bolin's best known design is probably the 11-string alto guitar – tuned a third above the guitar, and with five extra bass strings – designed for playing renaissance lute music on a guitar-type instrument.

In addition to the guitars he built by hand under his own name, Bolin designed guitars for Levin and Landola, spent much time doing acoustics research, and fostered a great number of Scandinavian luthiers. He died in 1993. (Note: Georg should not to be confused with US luthier John Bolin.)

B O U R G E O I S

Maine luthier Dana Bourgeois built his first guitar while still a college student. By using what he learned from guitar repair work and from books such as Irving Sloan's *Classic Guitar Construction*, he entered luthierie full-time in 1978. During the 1980s,

Bourgeois OMC 1998 (*left*) *This cutaway OM-bodied flat-top from Maine guitar-maker Dana Bourgeois has a subtle yet distinctive abalone soundhole ring and miniature diamond-shaped position markers.*

Bourgeois Vintage OM 2002 (*right*) *A more traditional take on the classic 'orchestra model' shape.*

Bourgeois catalog 2003 *The understated elegance of many of the high-end models made by Bourgeois is highlighted in this promotional shot.*

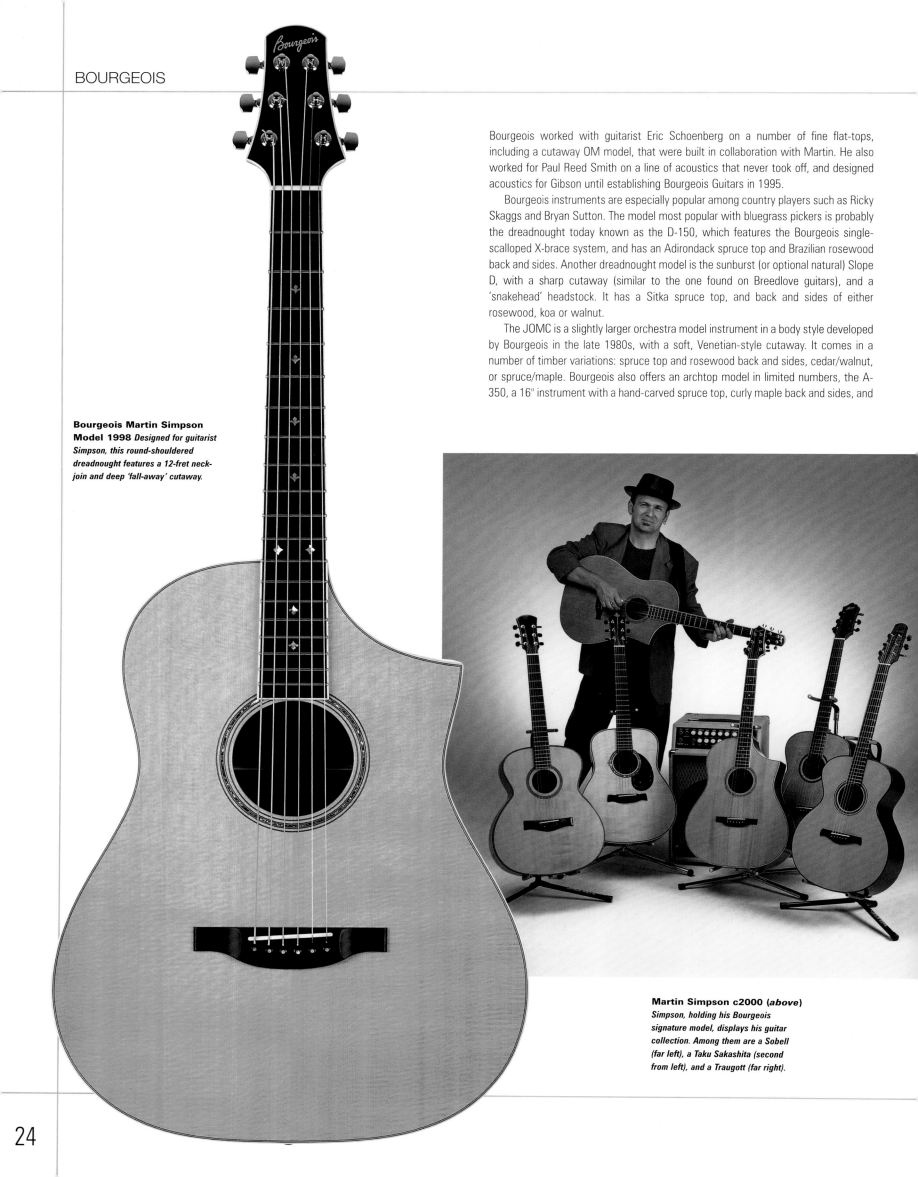

Bourgeois worked with guitarist Eric Schoenberg on a number of fine flat-tops, including a cutaway OM model, that were built in collaboration with Martin. He also worked for Paul Reed Smith on a line of acoustics that never took off, and designed acoustics for Gibson until establishing Bourgeois Guitars in 1995.

Bourgeois instruments are especially popular among country players such as Ricky Skaggs and Bryan Sutton. The model most popular with bluegrass pickers is probably the dreadnought today known as the D-150, which features the Bourgeois single-scalloped X-brace system, and has an Adirondack spruce top and Brazilian rosewood back and sides. Another dreadnought model is the sunburst (or optional natural) Slope D, with a sharp cutaway (similar to the one found on Breedlove guitars), and a 'snakehead' headstock. It has a Sitka spruce top, and back and sides of either rosewood, koa or walnut.

The JOMC is a slightly larger orchestra model instrument in a body style developed by Bourgeois in the late 1980s, with a soft, Venetian-style cutaway. It comes in a number of timber variations: spruce top and rosewood back and sides, cedar/walnut, or spruce/maple. Bourgeois also offers an archtop model in limited numbers, the A-350, a 16" instrument with a hand-carved spruce top, curly maple back and sides, and

Bourgeois Martin Simpson Model 1998 *Designed for guitarist Simpson, this round-shouldered dreadnought features a 12-fret neck-join and deep 'fall-away' cutaway.*

Martin Simpson c2000 (above)
Simpson, holding his Bourgeois signature model, displays his guitar collection. Among them are a Sobell (far left), a Taku Sakashita (second from left), and a Traugott (far right).

a three-piece maple neck with a snakehead headstock. Pickguard, tailpiece and fretboard are all cut from ebony, and the instrument has a light violin finish.

In the year 2000, Bourgeois and Patrick Theimer formed Pantheon Guitars to act as distributor for Bourgeois as well as Charles Fox guitars. Prior to joining Pantheon, Dana Bourgeois had built over 1,000 guitars. Today, he is considered one of the foremost world authorities on the voicing, selection and utilization of tonewoods.

B O Z O

Bozo Podunavac learned to build fretted instruments in the late 1940s in what was then Yugoslavia. He emigrated to the United States in 1959, and got a job repairing instruments at a music shop in Chicago. In 1964 he started making guitars – at first based on the dreadnought body shape – which he sold under the name Bozo (pronounced *bo-zho*). In 1968 he developed an unusual variation with a large lower bout and a smaller, squarer upper bout that he dubbed the Bell Western. Podunavac offered the Bell Western in six and 12-string versions, which were usually heavily ornamented with pearl and abalone inlays and lots of fancy purfling. Bozo guitars became quite popular in the 1970s after Leo Kottke started performing with them. In

Bozo Chicagoan 1996 (*left*)
This Bozo archtop – commissioned for Scott Chinery's 'Blue Guitars' collection – may look more rhinestone cowboy meets Turkish bazaar than 'Chicago' to many eyes, but it's a prime example of guitar-maker Podunavac's exquisite way with decorative inlays.

Bozo Requinto c1996 (*right*)
The requinto is an acoustic lead guitar played in Mariachi bands, and is distinctive for having a neck/body join at the 16th fret and, typically, a small body. This one is just 13.5" wide.

Bozo ad 1977 (*left*) *Folk fingerstylist and 12-string devotee Leo Kottke promotes elaborately decorative Bozo flat-tops of the late 1970s.*

the mid-1970s Podunavac moved to southern California, where he opened a guitar making school. In the late 1970s he licensed his designs to the Japanese luthier Kazuo Yairi, who produced a few hundred guitars in Asia, mostly made with laminated back and sides. (The Japanese made Bozos are easy to spot because the serial number on the neck block is preceded by a B.)

Padunavac stopped building guitars in the early 1980s due to illness, though he took up his work again in the mid 1990s. By 2003 he was building just a handful of Bell Westerns and the occasional archtop every year. He died in 2015.

BREEDLOVE

Breedlove is one of the most renowned quality manufacturers of the late 20th century. The company was founded in Tumalo, Oregon, in 1990 by Steve Henderson and Larry Breedlove — who had both previously worked for Taylor — with the intention of merging traditional luthiers' skills with modern technology. Today, older brother Kim Breedlove is also involved in the company.

With a firm dedication to 'green' issues, Breedlove Guitars focuses on using harvested alternatives to endangered rainforest timber and alternative tonewoods such as myrtlewood and walnut. Many Breedlove guitar bodies display radical exterior designs, and their custom inlay work can compete with most. Breedlove stresses the importance of its unique bracing, and voices the tops before as well as after bracing. All Breedlove guitars also feature the patented JLD bridge system, a lever device that counterbalances string tension on the top of the guitar by applying pressure on the tailblock. At the opposite end, headstocks are designed so that the strings break less sharply from the nut toward the tuner posts, as Breedlove claims that sharp angles here cause loss of sustain.

The first Breedlove line was the shallow-body C-10 series, still produced, with a distinctive assymmetrical headstock and an equally off-balance 'mustache' bridge that could have found inspiration from Salvador Dali's upper lip. The C-12 has the signature sharp cutaway while the C-15 has a rounded, Venetian cutaway. The assymmetry comes in even larger helpings on the distinctive CM, an award-winning orchestra-size guitar with upper body angles that owe more to futuristic electrics such as Gibson's Moderne than to traditional flat-tops.

Near the top of the 2017 line were the Masterclass and Exotic series, along with further models in several more series, including the Honduran-mahogany Frontier,

Breedlove SC20 1996 (*right*)
Breedlove designed the S series to be the 'hot rods' of its guitar line. This grand concert-sized model features a solid spruce top with ebony peghead overlay and fingerboard.

Brook Torridge 1999 (far right) *Brook has become known for its use of 'reclaimed' and sometimes unusual timbers. This 00-sized flat-top features a spruce top with wide herringbone binding, while the back and sides are made of solid mahogany salvaged from an old bank counter.*

Brook catalog 2009 (*above*), ad 2004 (*top right*) *These promos highlight Breedlove's distinctive CM body shape, an unusual asymmetrical design claimed to provide both bass and treble tones with more energy.*

Mark Eitzel 2000 (*opposite*) *The former American Music Club mainman, now a solo artist, accompanies his eclectic alt-pop stylings on a Brook Torridge.*

beginner-friendly Discovery, Brazilian-rosewood Journey, sound-profiled Premier, light-body USA, and workhorse Stage. Breedlove steel-string guitars can all be delivered in 12-string versions, and it also offers a couple of nylon-string models.

Madonna, although not primarily famous for her guitar-playing skills, has chosen to pose with a Breedlove guitar on several occasions.

BRINK

Garrett Brink was a Grand Rapids, Michigan, violin-maker of considerable regard, who dabbled in other stringed instruments including ukuleles and guitars – including Hawaiians – in the late 1920s and early 1930s. Brink's koa acoustic lap steels show the influence of his violin background – inlaid purfling, "pigeon-blood" varnish, and pins securing the bridge to the top and the top and back to internal blocks. His Hawaiians mix features and dimensions borrowed from Weissenborn and the deeper-body (Weissenborn-made) Kona Hawaiians. A significant appropriation from Weissenborn was X-bracing, leaving these two makers (and of course, Martin) virtually alone among Hawaiian guitar builders in the use of this sonic advantage. Brink's characteristic sound is tighter than Weissenborn's creations but equally pleasing.

BROOK

Having learned their skills working with Andy Manson, one of the UK's most respected luthiers, Simon Smidmore and Andy Petherick set up Brook Guitars in 1995, working out of Manson's former workshop in rural Devon.

Their first instruments were the 00-size Torridge and the medium-bodied Taw, which remain best sellers from the catalog. As of 2003, the range, all named after rivers in England's west country, comprises around 14 standard models – from the tiny Kit travel guitar to the Okement super-jumbo, Otter acoustic bass, and the hand-carved Exe jazz archtop. Alongside all this, they have continued to build A.B. Manson flat-tops under license.

With a four-strong production team, Brook's annual output averages 120 instruments, and such has been the growth in demand that virtually all are made to order, with a lead-time of around six months for stock models.

Doubtless helped initially by the Manson connection – and their own considerable abilities – commissions from pro players come in regularly. Jethro Tull's Martin Barre owns a Bovey travel guitar, while Ian Anderson has a Creedy parlor, the model also chosen by meisterpicker Adrian Legg. The members of Portishead-singer Beth

Gibbons's spin-off band, Rustin Man, have three Taws between them, singer-songwriter and former American Music Club frontman Mark Eitzel plays a Torridge, and Tim 'Hey Joe' Rose played a Teign dreadnought before his death in 2002.

Often working with naturally harvested woods and searching for reclaimed timbers, Brook is always experimenting. Recent projects have included baritone and resonator Tavy jumbos, bolt-on neck options for Taw and Torridge, and various "half-banjo, half-bouzouki things." Finely-wrought headstock inlays are a custom speciality.

C A M P E L L O N E

Providence, Rhode Island, luthier Mark Campellone is representative of the new breed of American archtop makers that has taken the heritage from D'Angelico and Stromberg into the 21st century.

After having studied guitar at Berklee and worked as a pro musician and guitar repairman, Campellone built his first archtop guitar in 1988. Campellone's guitars are inspired by the huge 18" orchestra models of the 1930s and '40s, and come in four series: Standard, DeLuxe, Special, and Artist Cameo. All guitars are made from the finest wood and have tailpieces of brass and ebony.

Brook Clyst 2002 (far left) *A body width of 13¾" – roughly Martin 0 size – puts this 12-fret, slot-head model between the smaller Creedy and the larger Lyn in the Brook catalog.*

Campellone Special 1995 (left) *This extremely ornate though otherwise fairly traditional archtop by Mark Campellone features an impressive abalone pickguard and custom-order blue finish.*

Brook catalog *Four Brook models posed along one of the Devon rivers that give them their names, plus a 12-string Tamar, grace this catalog page.*

CARVIN

Carvin, a leading Californian mail order manufacturer of musical equipment, began in 1946 as Kiesel Electronics, founded by Lowell Kiesel. Three years later, the name Carvin was made up from the names of Kiesel's sons Carson (who today is president of the company) and Gavin.

Emphasis over the years has been on electronic equipment such as instrument amplifiers and PA systems, and on electric guitars and basses, but in 1994 Carvin launched its first electro-acoustic guitar: the AC175. It had a semi-hollow body with a piezo bridge and the rather unusual choice of maple for the top (later changed to spruce or optional koa).

Two years later, a new electro-acoustic entered the catalog, the AC275 Jumbo, smaller than a dreadnought but more traditional in shape than the AC175, which owed more to Carvin's solidbodies. The electro-acoustic AE185 that followed sported quilted maple or flamed koa with matching headstock. It had dual outputs for piezo and magnetic pickups.

The AC275 was also joined by a 12-string version. Over the years, Carvin's electro-acoustics have also been offered in optional translucent colours – blue, red, and so

on, which have further enhanced their 'modern' image. In 1999 the top-of-the-line AC375 was introduced, a hollowbody thinline acoustic-electric with a Fishman transducer system, and controls mounted on the upper bout to allow the braced top to vibrate freely.

Ex-Starship guitarist Craig Chaquico – rocker-turned-jazzer and a Carvin endorser of years past – performs with an AC375. A year later came Carvin's first nylon-string electric-acoustic, the thin-bodied CL450, with a distinctive red cedar top.

In 2001 Carvin finally offered a fully acoustic guitar line, the Cobalt series, made in Korea, with seven different solid-wood-top models. In 2015 the Carvin guitar company was renamed Kiesel Guitars, and the only acoustic guitars in the line were a small number of electro-acoustic models.

COLLINGS

Collings Guitars of Austin, Texas, is probably the most progressive of America's mid-size guitar companies when it comes to construction methods, yet the instruments it builds are highly traditional in appearance and always pay respectful homage to the originals they emulate. Whether it's a D2H, patterned after a 1930s Martin D-28, or

Collings Baby 2001 (left) *With the new popularity of 'parlor' guitars, many flat-top makers – Collings included – have introduced their own variations on the small-bodied theme, often calling them 'baby' guitars.*

Collings Custom 1996 (center) *Despite the intensity of its color, this Collings archtop radiates a certain understated elegance aided by its matching ebony tailpiece, bridge, pickguard, fingerboard, and headstock facing. The art deco look of the 'flying chips' position markers and headstock inlay is an unusual custom touch.*

Collings 000-2H 1998 (above) *This mid-sized, vintage-styled Collings flat-top features slotted headstock and 12-fret join, with wood herringbone binding (hence the 'H' suffix) around its solid sitka spruce top.*

a 16" archtop design derived from a 1920s Gibson L-5, each model is distinctly a Collings from headstock to tailblock. Rather than building copies, Collings instead uses classic instruments and designs from America's 'Golden Era' of guitar-making as little more than stylistic templates.

Bill Collings left an aimless five-year stint as a pre-med student at Ohio University to work in a machine shop when still in his early 20s. While employed there, he grew fascinated by the banjos of the great jazz age and decided to build one. With that success under his belt he went on to build a mandolin, and from there approached guitar-making. By 1975 Collings had moved to Houston, Texas, where he repaired and built guitars out of one room in a two-room apartment. It was while working in that setting in 1978 that he met Lyle Lovett, who immediately ordered a guitar. Lovett has been Collings's biggest supporter and endorser ever since, using that early example of Bill's work almost exclusively for over a decade before adding other Collings instruments to his tool kit.

After building about 50 guitars in Houston, in 1980 Bill headed west for Southern California but only got as far as Austin. He shared space with mandolin builder Tom Ellis until 1984, when he

Collings OM2-H (*far left*) *Like its other flat-tops, Collings's take on the traditional Martin OM shape uses a mortoise-and-tenon neck joint. Bill Collings, like many other contemporary high-end builders, reasons an eventual neck reset is inevitable on a resonant, lightly braced guitar, and builds his instruments to make such work routine and untraumatic, when necessary.*

Collings CJSB Lyle Lovett Model 1999 (*left*) *This signature model for long-time devotee Lovett is a 'jumbo'-shaped flat-top in vintage sunburst finish.*

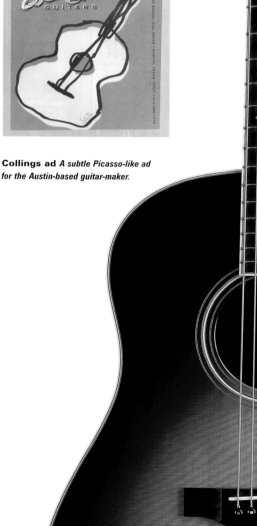

Collings ad *A subtle Picasso-like ad for the Austin-based guitar-maker.*

moved in with former Fender Custom Shop head Mike Stevens on Austin's East Side. Collings went solo again in 1986, working out of his garage for the next two years. In 1987 serial numbers were added, but the first 200 or so instruments have no number, although many are dated on the underside of the top. Throughout these early years he was called upon to repair, and often salvage from the dead, many used and vintage acoustic guitars, and it was this experience that gave him insight into how to build a more stable and roadworthy instrument.

One of Collings's realizations was that building a guitar strong enough to withstand string tension without needing a neck reset after ten years was not enough. By using a mortise-and-tenon neck joint held in place with two hidden bolts, Collings was able to reset the neck on one of his own guitars in a matter of minutes, without disturbing any glue joints. While bolt-on necks done with a simple butt joint were common, especially from high-production guitar companies, Collings's neck joint was more sophisticated, and his use of a bolted neck in a high-priced steel-string gave the concept some much-needed credibility.

In 1988 Collings began to focus upon guitar-building more exclusively, prompting a move to a 1,000-square-foot space near downtown Austin, just a few blocks from that city's fabled club district. One of his first employees was Bruce Van Wart, a former boat builder from Boston who is still with the company and serves as shop foreman. In 1989, Collings met guitar dealer George Gruhn at a Dallas guitar show, and a limited run of 21 guitars of Gruhn's design was the result. These were a round-shouldered dreadnought and a 16" jumbo, marked "Gruhn" on the headstock. Also in 1989 came the first sales of regular Collings dreadnoughts through a few retailers.

Around this same time a slightly different strain of Collings guitars was begun for John Holman of Dallas, who advertised as Baldy Brothers. Holman had the rights to the use of the name of legendary bluegrass flatpicker Clarence White, and for the next decade Collings built a variety of large-soundhole 'CW' dreadnought models that were sold exclusively by Holman. These guitars evolved into the Collings Winfield models of today, which display the same features derived from White's highly modified 1935 Martin D-28, now owned by Tony Rice.

By 1989 Collings was primarily making big guitars: square-shouldered dreadnoughts, plus the round-shoulder D (Collings Jumbo, or CJ) and the 16" jumbo (SJ). The smaller sizes for fingerstyle players soon followed, including the OM and a smaller model called the C-10, based on the shape of Gibson's L-00. A larger version

of the same shape, called the C-100, was discontinued in the mid 1990s. The OM, C-10, and SJ models are offered with optional cutaways.

In early 1992 Collings purchased a 3,200 square-foot building southwest of Austin, just inside the Travis county line. This space was doubled in 1995, then enlarged again a few years later. The early 1990s also brought a wider array of guitar shapes, while the decorative features of standard Collings models remained much the same. Twelve-fret D models (DS) had been part of the company's repertoire for some time, but Collings was also one of the first builders to offer a 12-fret 000 shape (1991), followed soon after by a 12-fret 00 with short-scale neck. One of the most outstanding Collings creations has been the Baby, a smaller-than-0-size guitar (12" wide) with 14-fret neck and 24" scale. Although the cost is the same as for the full-sized dreadnought with similar features, the Collings Baby has sold well, finding favor with Keith Richards, Joni Mitchell, Joan Baez, and other performers who appreciate a small guitar that doesn't sound like one.

Collings Style 1 is severely plain, usually with a mahogany body, tortoiseshell celluloid binding and simple dots on the fretboard much like a Martin Style 18. Style 2 is more like a Style 28 Martin, with ivoroid binding and either black and white lines or herringbone (2H) around the top edge. Style 3 is not directly related to any historical model, and features ivoroid binding on the neck and headstock as well as the body, with a blank fretboard, abalone rosette and backstrip of colorful marquetry. This style is the basis for most custom orders, with inlays, special finishes, and pearl bordering added. Tom Ellis, who maintains his own shop, is responsible for all inlay work with the exception of pearl bordering on the body.

For guitars not based on old Martin models, Collings styles are divided into regular and deluxe, with the latter version including binding on the fretboard and headstock. Much of Collings's production is custom order, and all body shapes are available in a wide range of woods, including mahogany, rosewood, maple, and koa for the backs and sides, with tops of Sitka, Englemann, European or Adirondack spruce, as well as red cedar. Brazilian rosewood is a popular option, especially on the square-shouldered D and the OM models.

With eight different body shapes – more than most larger guitar companies offer – and a wide range of optional woods, bindings, and inlay sets, the Collings shop has an unusually diverse selection of guitar types in production at any given time, especially for a company its size. Although CNC (computer numeric control) milling

**Collings C10 1998 (*left*) The
C10 – based roughly on Gibson's L-00
of the 1920s – looks like a compact
instrument, but its 15"-wide body is
designed for a surprisingly full voice.**

**Collings D3 2001 (*right*)
Collings is a favorite among many
bluegrass flat-pickers, and their
dreadnought models – like this D3 –
are considered some of the best
current-make guitars available.**

**Collings OM2-H 2000 (*left*) This
OM2-H's vintage sunburst finish gives
it a distinctly different look from the
natural-topped example on page 30.**

Patti Griffin c1998 (*below*)
*Singer/songwriter Griffin exemplifies
the diversity of Collings players.*

COLLINGS

machines are now used when making the numerous parts that go into a guitar, the Collings shop has always been outfitted with many specialized tools and fixtures, most of them designed and built by Collings himself. From his earliest days as a guitar-maker, the accuracy of even the smallest parts has been an obsession, and this high regard for tooling shows in the finished instruments. Most guitar manufacturers rely on quick hand sanding to round off sharp edges left by machining, primarily to make finishing easier. At Collings more man-hours are spent preserving these edges and angles with fine sanding done by hand, and they are then further emphasized with a thin gloss finish.

When archtop guitars began to command big prices in the late 1980s, many flat-top builders rushed to include them in their repertoire, hoping to get a piece of the action enjoyed by Jimmy D'Aquisto, John Monteleone, Bob Benedetto, and a few other recognized builders. Bill Collings had been bitten by the archtop bug in the early 1980s, long before his production of flat-top models took off. By the mid 1980s Collings was already building both 17" and 18" archtop models, with Lyle Lovett once again the first to use a Collings archtop onstage. Despite rave reviews, only a few archtops have been built each year, partly because they are built by Bill himself.

In 1999 Collings began building A-style mandolins with carved tops and backs (MT1 and MT2), and the success of these models prompted introduction of an F-style mandolin (MF5) in the summer of 2002. At the winter trade show in 2003, Collings unveiled a pair of 16" non-cutaway archtop guitars (AT16), with the body shape based on early Gibson L-5 models of the 1920s. Unlike the earlier, and larger, cutaway models, these new Collings archtops are much lower in price. Thanks to thin, careful graduation of both the back and the soundboard, the Collings 16" archtop has a warm, balanced response that may prove appealing to guitarists who haven't felt compelled to make the switch, and pay the high price, to play an acoustic archtop.

In 2005, Collings opened a new 27,000-square-foot plant, which included CNC machines for more consistent (and safer) production. A year later, Collings added electric instruments to its catalog and in 2009 introduced concert and tenor ukuleles. In 2014, Collings had a new sister brand, Waterloo, that aimed to capture the tone and character of some of the best Depression-era vintage acoustics. Despite all this expansion, when it comes to the details, the Collings shop still has the feel of a small band of guitar-makers working on highly individualized instruments. Sadly Bill Collings died in 2017.

CONTRERAS

Of all the Spanish makers, Manuel Contreras has found the most radical solutions to the classical guitar's perennial problems with volume and sustain. And yet, throughout his career he continued to produce a traditional 1a model, just like Ramírez, in whose workshops he began his career. He was there for three years, leaving in 1962, at which point he began to build the first instruments issued under his own name. All are large, traditionally fan-strutted models. But Contreras was a restless experimenter with form and function.

A conversation with a customer, Celedonio Romero, led him to build, in 1974, the first of his double-top guitars. Despite this name, really these instruments are double-back guitars, since the second top, which resonates in sympathy with the first, is placed in front of the instrument's back. Contreras immediately built three more of similar design, for each of the Romero sons. The model, which has a conventional appearance, remains in production.

Then in 1983 a discussion with the Uruguayan player Abel Carlevaro led to a more visually arresting experiment. The Carlevaro model had a one-sided waist, no normal soundhole, and double sides and back. It performed well, but was heavy.

Collings ASB 2001 (left) This sunburst 00-size model has a 12-fret neck join, a slotted headstock, and a top made from highly prized Adirondack spruce.

Collings C10C 2000 (right) An optional cutaway (hence the C suffix) brings this otherwise very traditional, medium-sized flat-top right up into the 21st century.

Collings ad 2012 (above left) Rodney Crowell is featured in this on-the-road snap with his well-traveled 1993 Collings C10 Deluxe.

Manuel Contreras died in 1994. His son Pablo, known as Manuel Contreras II, took over, but he, too, died in 2011. The firm now continues headed by Victoria Velasco, who has worked at Contreras since 1989, and together with a team of guitar-makers built up over recent years she produces a range of models.

CORT
(KINGSTON, EMPERADOR, CORTEZ)

Today, the mass-production guitar-making world is centered in Korea, and one of its most significant manufacturers is Cort, which produces reasonably priced acoustics of excellent quality. This did not come about by chance, nor did it happen overnight. Cort was founded in 1973 when American instrument wholesaler Jack Westheimer hooked up with Yung H. Park to build a factory in Korea that would provide a cost-effective alternative to Japanese sources. Westheimer had already been a pioneer of using Japanese manufacturers to produce his Teisco/Teisco del Rey electrics and Kingston, Cortez, and Emperador acoustics, beginning around 1959.

Kingston was Westheimer's budget brand for beginners, while Emperador and Cortez were more upscale brands, all made in Japan. The Cortez models were

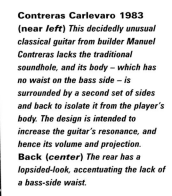

Contreras Carlevaro 1983 (near *left*) *This decidedly unusual classical guitar from builder Manuel Contreras lacks the traditional soundhole, and its body – which has no waist on the bass side – is surrounded by a second set of sides and back to isolate it from the player's body. The design is intended to increase the guitar's resonance, and hence its volume and projection.*
Back (*center*) *The rear has a lopsided-look, accentuating the lack of a bass-side waist.*

Collings SJ 2016 (*far left*) *This model is the Collings version of the Jumbo-style acoustic, typically with more treble clarity and midrange crunch than a dreadnought.*

generally the best quality Japan was producing at the time. By the time the 'copy era' arrived in the 1970s, Cortez guitars included very fancy hybrids of the Martin D-35/45 and the Gibson J-200, often sporting pearloid and abalonoid trim. All Cortez guitars were made in Japan until the brand finally disappeared around 1986.

By the early 1970s, however, the price of Japanese guitars was climbing, due to rising costs and unfavorable exchange rates. The conditions inspired Westheimer to travel to Korea and open the Cort enterprise (shortened from Cortez) with Park. Kingston production was shifted to the new factory and was used to improve the quality of the work. Other brands made by Cort in the later 1970s included Conn, Lotus, and Arbor. Around 1977, Cort felt quality had reached a level such that it could begin to use its own name, though all models still featured plywood tops at this time.

The company continued to improve quality and to grow, but its great leap forward came in 1994 with the introduction of its Earth series of acoustics, with solid spruce or cedar tops and scalloped bracing. Consisting of OM, dreadnought, and classical styles, these were initially modeled after Martin guitars, but as the '90s progressed Cort guitars acquired their own distinctive styling. Better models feature fancy pearl and abalone inlays. By 1999 the Earths expanded into 12-string and parlor models.

Also in 1999, Cort introduced a second line of dreadnoughts, the NTL series, with a more Gibson Jumbo-inspired styling. These also featured solid tops with premium timbers, scalloped bracing, and relatively deluxe appointments, even including a handmade Custom Shop model. In 2000 these were joined by models with Fishman pickup systems and both a fretted and fretless acoustic-electric bass.

Cort continues to make excellent guitars for many other brands, but now those carrying the company name have gained respect in their own right.

CRAFTER

In many ways, Crafter mirrors the growth of the Korean guitar-making industry. Started by HyunKwon Park in a small Seoul workshop in 1968, the company, under the Sungeum name, initially produced classical guitars for the domestic market. After the brand-change to Crafter in the late '70s, two factory moves over the years, and the promotion of Park's son Injae to company president in 1986, Crafter grew to produce an impressive 60,000 instruments in 2001. These covered a wide range of acoustic and electro-acoustic styles, which sold in more than 30 countries. One of the best sellers in the UK, Crafter's biggest single market, is the FX550EQ cutaway

Kingston V-4 Mockingbird 1970 (far *left*) *This playfully-named copy of a Gibson Hummingbird was built by Cort before the company began putting its own name on the logo. Note the orange-stained flame maple veneer on the guitar's back (far left).*

Cortez J6000 1976 (*left*) *This fancy dreadnought is a decent-quality Japanese-built approximation of the Martin D-45.*

bowlback electro. Keen pricing and well-loaded cosmetics are Crafter hallmarks, and while in earlier days sound quality didn't always live up to visual promise, the caliber of performance (and timbers) has continued to improve, helping explain the brand's international success.

Damon Johnson (Thin Lizzy, Alice Cooper) and Keri Kelli (Night Ranger, Slash) are namechecked among Crafter's user roster, along with a number of South American solo artists like Flavio Lemos and Leonardo Amuedo.

CROMWELL

The Cromwell name appeared from 1935-39, mostly on archtops, most of them distinguishable either by a line of binding material running down the center of the fingerboard or by large 'dot' fingerboard inlays, or both. A number of mail-order companies distributed Cromwells, including Grossman, Richter & Phillips, and Continental, but the instruments were all made by Gibson.

Like Gibson's Kalamazoo guitars, and all of the other Gibson budget and contract brands, Cromwells lacked the truss-rod in the neck that all Gibson-brand guitars had. The Cromwells shared other features with Kalamazoo models of the same period,

Cort Earth 1200 2002 (near right) An elaborately inlaid contemporary Cort dreadnought.

Crafter ad 2013 (center) The Twin Bird was Crafter's 35th anniversary model, with fancy bird inlays on the body and fingerboard.

Crafter CTS-155C 2000 (far right) A Korean-built modern-styled classical guitar from the budget-range Crafter brand.

such as their 'rooftop' pointed peghead shape and their Gibson body shapes and sizes. The most commonly seen Cromwells are the three most expensive archtops, all of which are 16" wide with mahogany back and sides, a feature found on only one 16" Kalamazoo model and not at all in the Gibson line until after World War II. (The Gibson standard was maple back and sides.)

The higher-end Cromwell archtop models have the bindings and pearl inlays of expensive guitars, but in fact in the way that they were constructed and their inherent quality they are comparable to Gibson's contemporary mid-line L-50 model.

D'ANGELICO

John D'Angelico was the most highly respected individual maker of traditional archtop guitars. Although he was not an innovator — aside from the cosmetic features that distinguish his instruments, the progression of his designs followed those of the Gibson company — and his craftsmanship was not always exemplary, by the late 1930s his instruments nevertheless set a standard of performance by which all other archtops are judged, even today. He did essentially the same thing that Gibson, Epiphone, Gretsch, and the other leading guitar companies did — he just did it better.

Born in New York in 1905, D'Angelico became an apprentice in the instrument shop of his uncle, a Mr. Ciani, at age nine, and he took it over when his uncle died. Supervising a group of 15 workers did not suit him, however, and he opened his own shop in 1932. For the next 32 years he handbuilt guitars (and some mandolins) with never more than two helpers.

D'Angelico started off copying the original f-hole archtop, the Gibson L-5. Designed by Gibson's Lloyd Loar in 1922, the L-5 was 16" wide with parallel 'tone bar' bracing.

Crafter catalog 2002 (top of page) *These pages from the Korean maker's catalog display their ornate 33 Series and 24 Series guitars, each of which includes solid spruce top and onboard electronics.*

D'Angelico L-5-Style 1933 (near right) *The New York luthier's earliest designs were near-direct copies of Gibson's Lloyd Loar-era L-5.*

D'Angelico New Yorker 1939 (far right) *This early non-cutaway New Yorker shows how D'Angelico's own style has emerged. D'Angelico's records say this was built for a client named Joe Senacorin.*

D'Angelico developed his own pickguard shape, with a small 'stairstep' on the outer edge, and he engraved his name in a large piece of mother-of-pearl in the headstock, but otherwise his guitars looked very much like the Gibson, right down to the dip in the center of the headstock.

Gibson 'advanced' the size of the L-5 in 1934 to 17" and also introduced the fancier, 18" Super 400 model that same year. D'Angelico (as well as the rest of the guitar industry) followed suit, with 17" and 18" models appearing by 1936 – the year that he began using model names.

His least expensive model was the Style A, with 17"-wide body. The instrument generally featured pearl block inlay, parallel bracing, and a peghead with a rounded peaked top. Style B was the same size, also with block inlay and parallel bracing, but with the ornamental headstock that would become an instant identifier of a D'Angelico guitar.

Many Italian-style 'bowlback' mandolins of the 19th century had an ornamental cutout near the top of the headstock, and D'Angelico adapted the concept so that the cutout opened at the top of the headstock in a 'broken scroll pediment' design. Within the cutout, he placed a small button or 'ornamental cupola.' Just below the cutout,

D'Angelico Special 1949 (*left*)
This unusual model with an oval soundhole is believed to be the biggest guitar that D'Angelico ever built, with a body width of nearly 19 inches. It has a huge sound, too, though one that is more raw and less refined than the typical D'Angelico.

D'Angelico Excel Cutaway 1955 (*right*) *Note the cupola-topped, 'flared' headstock on this mid-period Excel. In stark contrast to the oval-holed Special on this page, this guitar has a more refined sound than the average D'Angelico.*

he inlaid his name in a flowing script style, and on a small banner underlining his name he engraved "New York."

Models A and B only lasted until 1945 and 1948, respectively, having been surpassed in demand by the two models for which D'Angelico is best known: the 17" Excel and the 18" New Yorker. Both of these models appeared for the first time from the maker's workshop in New York City during 1936, and both had X-braced tops. Again D'Angelico was following the lead of the Gibson company, which had switched to X bracing in 1934. Gibson returned to parallel bracing on its top models in 1939, but D'Angelico stayed with the X.

Since many of D'Angelico's guitars were made to the personal preferences of individual customers, there is much variation in specifications. He began offering cutaway bodies on both models in 1947, again following the example of Gibson, which had introduced cutaways in 1939.

The typical New Yorker is easily recognizable by its large deco-style peghead inlay that suggests the stair-step design of a New York skyscraper building. The motif is repeated across the guitar, in the gold-plated tuner buttons, the truss-rod cover, the outer edge of the pickguard, and even the heavy, harp-shaped tailpiece. The pearl block fingerboard inlays of the New Yorker are slashed diagonally with one or two lines to create what some collectors call 'split block markers.' The top and peghead are heavily bound with multiple layers, and the fingerboard and f-holes are also bound.

The Excel is only slightly less ornate. The peghead inlay looks something like a military medal, and the pearl blocks in the fingerboard usually do not have a diagonal slash, but it still has the appearance of a formidable instrument. Beginning in 1943, D'Angelico also made the Excel-sized guitar with New Yorker style ornamentation, which he called the Excel Special.

D'Angelico's guitars sounded great, looked great and were sturdy instruments – a combination of qualities that made them highly desirable to professional musicians. By the late 1930s his advertisements listed an impressive group of players. If the guitarists' names are no longer familiar to you, then the bands and artists that they played for might well be: Chick Robertson with Joe Venuti, John Truhart with Ella Fitzgerald, Eddie Asherman with Xavier Cugat, Roc Hillman with Jimmy Dorsey, Tony Colucci with the NBC staff orchestra.

D'Angelico made two guitars – an Excel in 1946 and then an Excel cutaway in 1948 – for jazz great Oscar Moore, best known for his work with the Nat King Cole

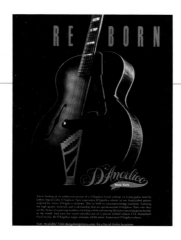

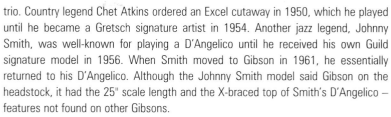

Neil Young mid 1970s (*below*)
The often grungy, occasionally folky Neil Young is associated with Gibson and Martin flat-tops – but here he employs an uncharacteristic D'Angelico New Yorker in a live acoustic performance, proving they're not just jazz boxes.

D'Angelico ad 2013 (*above*) *An announcement from the revived D'Angelico brand.*

trio. Country legend Chet Atkins ordered an Excel cutaway in 1950, which he played until he became a Gretsch signature artist in 1954. Another jazz legend, Johnny Smith, was well-known for playing a D'Angelico until he received his own Guild signature model in 1956. When Smith moved to Gibson in 1961, he essentially returned to his D'Angelico. Although the Johnny Smith model said Gibson on the headstock, it had the 25" scale length and the X-braced top of Smith's D'Angelico – features not found on other Gibsons.

D'Angelico had two assistants, one of whom, Vincent 'Jimmy' DiSerio, is virtually unknown now in guitar circles. He worked in the shop from 1932-60 and then left for a job with the Favilla guitar company. The other assistant, James L. D'Aquisto, joined D'Angelico in 1952 and would go on to become a legendary archtop maker in his own right, as well as a design innovator.

D'Angelico suffered a heart attack in 1959 and died in 1964 at age 59. He made a total of 1,164 numbered guitars, the last ten of which were finished by D'Aquisto. His Excel and New Yorker models, particularly the cutaway examples, are considered by many as the epitome of the classic era of the archtop guitar. In recent years the brand was revived and has appeared on a line of imported and US-made models.

D'Angelico NY2 2002 (*left*)
This small-bodied D'Angelico reissue is built in Japan, and carries a pressed arched top of solid spruce, rather than John D'Angelico's laboriously hand-carved top.

D'Angelico's workshop 1957 (*right*) *These rare photos show John D'Angelico (far left in the top photo) working on the design and construction of a special-order guitar for nightclub performer Peter Girardi (in the dark suit). The result is the incredible, one-off 'Teardrop' guitar shown on the following page.*

D'AQUISTO

James L. D'Aquisto began his career making guitars in the style of his mentor, John D'Angelico, and as he developed his own distinctive style, he achieved the same reputation D'Angelico had enjoyed, as the premier maker of traditional f-hole archtops.

However, D'Aquisto would eventually undergo the most radical metamorphosis of any guitar maker, as he left tradition behind and pushed archtop design into a style that is best described by the name he gave one of his models: Avant Garde. The guitars he made near the end of his life would not be recognizable as coming from the same maker as those from his early years.

D'Aquisto was born in 1935 in Brooklyn, New York, into a musical Italian family. He was a 17-year-old aspiring jazz guitarist in 1951 when he visited John D'Angelico's shop and accepted an invitation to work there. The shop was closed temporarily in 1959 when D'Angelico parted ways with his longtime assistant, Vincent DiSerio, and after D'Aquisto was unable to find work in the Favilla guitar factory, he convinced D'Angelico to reopen. When D'Angelico died in 1964, D'Aquisto bought the business and, after struggling through a bad business arrangement, he picked up where

D'Angelico New Yorker Cutaway Special 'Teardrop' 1957 *Believed for years to be no more than a rumor, this teardrop-shaped D'Angelico archtop is a one-off built for Peter Girardi – who wanted an instrument that would make audiences remember him – and is widely considered the most prestigious vintage guitar in existence.*

Back (*far left*) *A back view of this guitar emphasizes its smooth, flowing lines and the select figured maple used in its construction.*

Peter Girardi 1957 *D'Angelico's customer examines the neck of his guitar, still in progress.*

D'Angelico had left off – literally. He finished ten guitars that D'Angelico had started, and as those instruments were seen and heard by musicians, he became accepted as D'Angelico's successor. He moved from Brooklyn to a series of towns on Long Island (east of New York City): Huntington in 1966, Farmingdale in1973, and finally to Greenport in 1977.

Although D'Aquisto kept D'Angelico's model names – Excel for 17″ guitars, New Yorker for 18″ – he quickly incorporated his own designs. The headstock inlay on his New Yorker was a large scroll instead of the skyscraper figure of a D'Angelico. By 1967 he had taken the 'notch' out of the center of his f-holes so that they were now elongated S-holes. At the same time he changed the cutout at the top of the headstock from D'Angelico's flattened 'broken scroll' to a circular shape.

Having cosmetically distinguished his guitars from his mentor's, D'Aquisto then began making changes that would improve their sound. As a player – which D'Angelico was not – D'Aquisto was not only able to fine-tune the tone and feel of his instruments to suit his customers, he was also able to accurately assess the results of his experimentation with various aspects of guitar construction and design, particularly the bridge, tailpiece, and soundholes.

One tenet of D'Aquisto's emerging philosophy was that non-wood materials, such as pearl, plastic and metal, did not contribute to the tone of a guitar, and therefore should be eliminated. By 1969 he had done away with the ornamental inlay on the bridge. By 1973 the metal tailpiece had been replaced with an ebony unit. He also changed the pickguard material from celluloid to ebony and gave it a sleek, elongated shape. The modernistic look began to carry over to other features as well, as he removed layers of plastic binding and the large pearl fingerboard inlays that had been standard fare on high-quality archtops since the early 1930s. His New Yorker Classic of 1985 represented the fulfillment of his all-wood quest, with wood binding, wood headstock veneer, and no pearl inlay.

By the mid 1980s D'Aquisto was firmly established as the leading independent guitar maker, and also as one of the most versatile. He had built a variety of guitars, including oval-hole archtops, seven-strings, 12-strings, steel-string flat-tops, nylon-string classicals, and even hollow and solidbody electrics. His archtops were in the hands of many notable players, ranging from jazzmen Joe Pass and Jim Hall through to pop star Paul Simon.

In 1987, with his Avant Garde archtop model, he began focusing on soundholes,

James D'Aquisto mid 1980s
The builder in his workshop, holding a guitar near completion. Note how the headstock has evolved from the D'Angelico-inspired shape of the guitars on this page.

D'Aquisto New Yorker 1968
(*left*) *This example from the early career of James D'Aquisto shows how the guitar-maker's work was influenced by – though subtly different from – his mentor, John D'Angelico.*

D'Aquisto New Yorker Oval Hole 1973 (*right*) *At this point D'Aquisto's own style is emerging, though it remains overtly traditional, despite the less-seen oval soundhole. D'Aquisto felt the oval soundhole compressed the sound somewhat like a squeezed garden hose, and made it come out more powerfully.*

D'AQUISTO

which aside from his S-shaped design had remained virtually unchanged since Gibson introduced the f-hole archtop in 1922. The Avant Garde featured two oversized holes with an elongated triangular shape. His next model, the Solo, had similar soundholes, except that they were in two segments (for a total of four holes), and it featured an enlarged headstock cutout. His Centura model also had the large headstock cutout, with beveled veneers to simulate binding – a forgotten traditional technique that was popular on 'jazz' banjos of the 1920s.

At the beginning of 1995 D'Aquisto took his soundhole experimentation to a new level with his Advance model, which featured large elliptical holes, plus a set of inserts that the player could put into the soundholes in various combinations to achieve as many as 18 different tonal shadings.

Whether D'Aquisto's vision for the future of archtop guitar design was still developing or fully realized will never be known, for he died in 1995, just a few months after finishing the Advance.

DE JONGE

Like a surprising number of accomplished builders, Sergei De Jonge got his start making classical guitars in 1970 when he apprenticed with Jean Larrivée in Canada. In 1971 he studied with Patt Lister, an innovative luthier who was experimenting with a lattice-braced top on his classical guitars. De Jonge set up his own shop in 1972, where he built classical guitars and a few steel-string flat-tops until 1986, when he decided to retire from building. After six years away from lutherie, he took up the craft again in 1992, and at the same time began to teach his 13-year-old daughter Joshia and his 11-year-old son Sagen how to make guitars. Both children have continued to build instruments, and they are both earning reputations as fine luthiers in their own right. All of the De Jonge family luthiers build classical guitars, most with a lattice-style bracing system that was devised by Sergei and Sagen and was based in part on Patt Lister's designs. Sergei also builds the occasional steel-string guitar. From 2003, his teenaged sons Rubin and Alan were building guitars as well.

D'Aquisto New Yorker Special 1978 (left) *Note the S-shaped soundholes and ebony tailpiece that by this time were an important part of the D'Aquisto design.*

D'Aquisto Classical 1982 (right) *D'Aquisto built even fewer flat-top guitars for nylon strings than for steel, so this is now considered to be an exceedingly rare instrument.*

D'Aquisto ads (top of page) *These ads for New Yorker and Centura models show the coexistence of D'Aquisto's traditional and more futuristic designs, respectively.*

D'Aquisto Flat-Top Delux 1977 (above) *James D'Aquisto made far fewer flat-tops than archtops, but was a builder keen to try his hand in a range of genres. His flair for quiet elegance comes through even on this relatively simple instrument.*

DEL VECCHIO

Brazilian maker Del Vecchio is best known for its resophonic Brazilian rosewood guitar, the Dinâmico, introduced in 1938. Founder Angelo Del Vecchio emigrated from Sicily to São Paolo in 1900 and opened his first lutherie shop in 1902. In the 1940s, his sons Francisco and Salvador took over the business, and since 1968 grandson Angelo Sergio Del Vecchio has run the family enterprise.

The sound of the Del Vecchio Dinâmico was heard worldwide when the group Los Indios Tabajaras hit with 'Maria Elena' in 1962. Although the guitars have had some wider popularity – especially among Nashville session players – Del Vecchios are a rare sight, since the company never formally exported its instruments, apparently being content with domestic sales (which have been good: the operation has expanded steadily since grandpa Angelo's days).

Most players feel the Dinâmico, unlike other resophonics, sounds best with nylon or silk/steel strings. It has also been suggested that what Del Vecchios offer in tone, they lack in sturdiness. Del Vecchio manufactures a full range of guitars, including Spanish, flat-top roundhole and f-hole models, and Brazilian folk instruments such as cavaquinhos. Dinâmicos are also available with a magnetic pickup.

D'Aquisto Solo 1992 (*left*)
The Solo was the flagship model of D'Aquisto's later career. This example was once owned by noted guitar collector Scott Chinery, who declared it his "favorite guitar in the whole world." At the time, Chinery owned more than 350 of the most significant guitars ever built.

Back (*far left*) *Note the stunning flamed maple used for the Solo's back.*

D'Aquisto Advance 1994 (*right*) *Collector Scott Chinery commissioned this distinctly modernistic guitar from D'Aquisto, asking him to "show me what an archtop is going to be like a hundred years from now." The tailpiece can be adjusted to alter string length and break angle, and the soundholes have movable baffles designed to create tonal variations.*

Dell'Arte catalog c2002 *The Dell'Arte company's catalog cover illustrates its emphasis on Selmer Maccaferri-style guitars.*

DELL'ARTE

Dell'Arte is best known for its Selmer/Maccaferri style guitars, but the company also makes flat-top steel strings, archtops, and a highly regarded reproduction of the Stella 12-string made famous by Leadbelly. Alain Cola, a guitarist who grew up in France playing Gypsy jazz, founded the company in 1997. Cola was not a luthier himself, so for the first two years of production he had the guitars made in Mexico to his specifications. He stopped Mexican production of the instruments in 1999 when he became partners with John Kinnard, a guitar maker who previously had worked for Taylor Guitars. Even though they are made in California, Dell'Arte instruments have nonetheless gained a following among some of Europe's finest Gypsy jazz guitarists; along with its standard line, the company offers models endorsed by Angelo Debarre and Robin Nolan.

DI MAURO

Antoine Di Mauro was born in 1900 in Italy, where he trained as a luthier from an early age. He moved to Paris in 1932 and quickly set up shop as a guitar-maker. He initially made gut-strung classical guitars and mandolins, but when Selmer's new Maccaferri-designed guitar became popular, he started making less expensive versions of it. He also built archtops, Hawaiian steel guitars, mandolins, harp guitars, tenor guitars, and banjos. The most famous Di Mauro model was the Chorus Special, which had a Selmer body shape with two f-holes. The Chorus Special was first made in 1942 and remained in the catalog until the company closed. In 1947 Antoine's son Joseph began working at the small factory, and he eventually took over in 1975 when his father died. Joseph ran the company until he closed it down upon his retirement in 1993. In six decades of business the Di Mauro company produced thousands of guitars, but since it didn't keep records, the exact number is unknown.

DITSON
(HAYNES/BAY STATE/TILTON)

Ditson is best known as the company that sold Martin's first dreadnoughts from 1917 until its stores closed in 1930, but it was actually a major player in the early American

Ditson Model 261 c1906 (*left*) *Like many guitars of its day, this model sold by Oliver Ditson is in fact a flat-top, but uses a separate bridge and tailpiece. This particular arrangement applies less stress to the top of the guitar than today's more common integral pin bridge.*

Dobro No. 55 1930 (*near right*) *Originally named for its $55 price, the 55 typifies the spartan – but now highly desirable – Dobro resonator guitar, particularly when compared to the style of its chief rival, National.*

Back (*above*) *Note the highly figured laminated wood of this Dobro.*

guitar scene, producing generally high-quality parlor guitars. Founded in Boston in 1834 by Oliver Ditson (1811-88), Ditson established several subsidiaries in the 1860s that also went on to make guitars, such as Church, and Lyon & Healy.

In 1865 Ditson opened the John C. Haynes Co, an instrument distribution company headed by Haynes, a firm partner and later president. By the 1880s Haynes was manufacturing William B. Tilton's Gold Medal Guitars featuring the Tilton Improvement, an internal wooden reinforcement rod (later featured on New York-made Celebrated Benary brand guitars).

The Haynes Excelsior guitar line was launched in 1885, made under the supervision of former C. Bruno luthier Pehr A. Anderberg and offering upscale parlor guitars in a range of sizes and with varying amounts of trim, some quite luxurious. By 1889 the Bay State brand was in existence, consisting of a range of humbler models, including faux-finished birch guitars, for both gut and steel strings.

Around 1900 the Haynes operation rejoined its parent and guitars became Ditson, sold through its stores and others.

Ditson continued to make guitars, including the more upscale Conquest and Empire lines, until sometime after 1910.

DOBRO

In the late 1920s, the Dobro company introduced the type of resonator guitar that today is most often heard contributing a blues-influenced, slide-guitar sound to bluegrass music. The typical Dobro has a wood body and a single resonator cone that opens toward the top of the instrument (the opposite of the cone configuration on a National resonator guitar).

Although the Dobro is usually held and played 'Hawaiian style' in the lap with a metal slide, practically all Dobro music today is more heavily influenced by blues than by Hawaiian music. That was not true, however, at the invention of the Dobro.

The Dobro grew out of a disagreement between John Dopyera (pronounced Do-PEER-uh), a Los Angeles inventor, and his brothers, several of whom were his partners in the National company. Dopyera had started National in 1926 and had developed a revolutionary new guitar design built around three 'resonators' – spun aluminum cones that acted much like the cones in an audio speaker. National's tri-cone design produced a significantly higher volume than a conventional flat-top guitar, and the company further distinguished the tone of its guitars by putting the cones into a body that was made of 'German silver,' a nickel alloy. In 1927, the guitar was not

Dobro No. 100 1935 (*right*)
The eight legs of the Dobro 'spider' bridge are partly visible through this example's body plate. The design differentiates the Dobro further from National's tri-cone or biscuit-bridge single-cone designs.

The Wranglers c1930 (*left*) *Far more than the National, the wood-bodied Dobro found its way into the emerging bluegrass scene, as seen here with the overtly western-themed Wranglers ('The Sheriff' – far right – clearly enjoying that haunting, atmospheric reso sound immensely).*

the universally popular instrument that it is today. The tenor banjo still overshadowed the guitar as the preferred rhythm instrument in the Dixieland jazz bands of the day. The guitar's stronghold was in Hawaiian music, and the lap-style guitarists were the players most desperately in need of greater volume. They immediately adopted the new, louder Nationals.

In the meantime, John Dopyera and his brothers had taken on additional partners, and a disagreement erupted, the nature of which remains unknown. The result was that John left in 1928 (although he didn't officially resign until 1929) and immediately embarked on a new resonator guitar venture.

John Dopyera created a less expensive instrument by making the body of laminated wood and using a single resonator cone rather than three. So as not to infringe on National's patents, he turned the cone upside down, so that it fit into a guitar body like a bowl, with its rim resting on the top of the guitar. He devised an eight-armed aluminum 'spider' to distribute the vibration of the strings from the bridge, which was mounted in the center of the spider, to the edges of the cone. The new design was the opposite of the National resonator system, but the effect was the same: a louder guitar. Dopyera apparently was not completely at odds with his

Back (*above*) *A rear view of the No. 62 reveals one of the typically elaborate engravings sandblasted onto the backs of the guitars. This one is known among collectors as 'The Spanish Dancer.'*

Dobro No. M/16/S c1934 (*left*) *Best known for their wood-bodied resonators, Dobro also began to make metal-bodied guitars in Los Angeles in 1934. The M/16, with a nickel-alloy body and elaborate engraving, was the company's top LA-made metal guitar.*

Dobro No. 62 c1934 (*right*) *This is another Los Angeles-made metal-bodied Dobro.*

Dickey Betts c1973 (*below*) The Allman Brothers guitarist is probably best known for his work on a Gibson Les Paul or – more recently – PRS electric, but the Dobro sound suited the band's mellower musings.

brothers because he named his new guitars Dobro, combining the words Dopyera and Brothers. Introduced in 1928 or '29, Dobro's initial three models were priced at $45, $55, and $65. Even the most expensive one was barely more than half the cost of National's cheapest tri-cone model, the $125 Style 1.

National quickly responded with its own single-cone guitars, bringing the price down as low as $32.50. Responding now to the onset of the Great Depression as well as the competition from National, Dobro brought the price of its cheapest model down even lower, to $27.50.

Competition may have been heated, but the wounds of the 1928 split healed quickly and the two companies merged to form the National-Dobro company in 1933.

By 1930, the Dobro line had expanded from the initial three models to a total of eight, all available with round neck for standard play or square neck (with raised strings) for Hawaiian style. Few of the models had names; they were delineated by price. The standard models, Nos. 45 and 55, were made of unspecified wood (typically birch) and sold for $45 and $55, respectively. No. 65 featured an ornate design that was achieved by sandblasting the pattern into the wood body. No. 85 sported ribbon-grained mahogany and an engraved coverplate (the name for the

ornamental plate that covers the resonator and spider). Nos. 106, 126, 156, and 206 were progressively fancier instruments that sported walnut bodies.

The model nomenclature led to confusion when prices changed but model specifications didn't. They became more confusing when, in 1933, Dobro licensed the brand to the Regal company of Chicago, and Dobros were made both by Regal and by National-Dobro in California. Regal introduced three new models: No. 27, with birch, maple or mahogany body; No. 37, with mahogany body; and No. 45, with mahogany body and spruce top, which was obviously quite different from the earlier Dobro-made No. 45. In addition, Regal made a limited number of Dobros with metal bodies. Although Dobro is best-known for woodbody guitars, and National for metalbodies, both brands offered both wood and metalbody models. Dobros were always distinguished, however, by their 'spider' resonator system.

The resonator guitars were a godsend to Hawaiian players, but their reign was shortlived. The electric Hawaiian guitar – invented by yet another ousted former National partner – appeared in 1932 and Hawaiian players soon began plugging in. Although National-Dobro made acoustic resonator guitars through 1939, the instruments were passé after 1935.

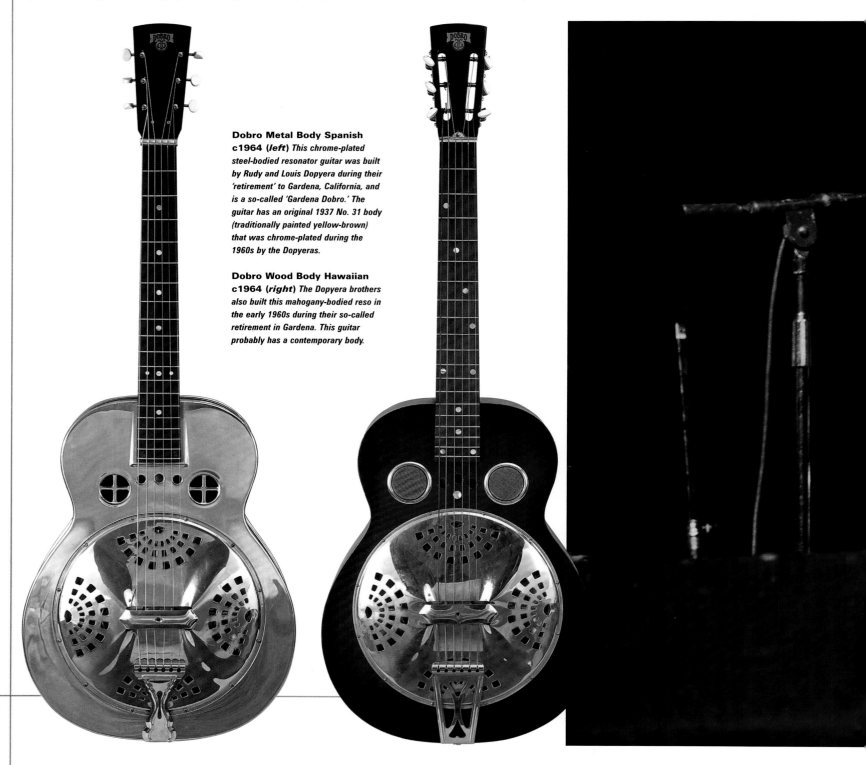

Dobro Metal Body Spanish c1964 (left) *This chrome-plated steel-bodied resonator guitar was built by Rudy and Louis Dopyera during their 'retirement' to Gardena, California, and is a so-called 'Gardena Dobro.' The guitar has an original 1937 No. 31 body (traditionally painted yellow-brown) that was chrome-plated during the 1960s by the Dopyeras.*

Dobro Wood Body Hawaiian c1964 (right) *The Dopyera brothers also built this mahogany-bodied reso in the early 1960s during their so-called retirement in Gardena. This guitar probably has a contemporary body.*

Adrian Belew (*below*) *The King
Crimson member and solo artist is known
for his ability to produce unearthly noises
from an electric guitar. In the acoustic
realm, a Dobro suits his style well.*

DOBRO

One can hear National tri-cone and single-cone metalbody models on numerous 1930s Hawaiian and blues recordings, respectively, but the Dobro is seldom heard – a surprising circumstance in light of the fact that the supply of vintage Dobros today suggests that Dobros sold as well as, or better than, the National models. Be that as it may, the Dobro all but died out in the 1930s.

Musically, the Dobro owes its existence today to Cliff Carlisle (whose brother Jumping Bill Carlisle is still an active performer on the Grand Ole Opry). Carlisle's blues-influenced Dobro licks can be heard on records by Jimmie Rodgers, the Father of Country Music.

The Dobro still might have been forgotten had it not been for Beecher 'Pete' Kirby, better known as Bashful Brother Oswald in the band of Roy Acuff, the biggest country star of the late 1930s. Ironically, the musician whom Kirby replaced in 1939, 'Cousin Jody,' played electric Hawaiian guitar. Kirby played an acoustic Dobro – usually a spruce-top Style 45 model – with a strong Hawaiian influence. One of his best-known solo numbers, 'Dobro Chimes,' was an adaptation of the standard 'Maui Chimes.' He maintained the same style in Opry performances right up to his death in 2001.

Although Kirby could not be called a highly influential Dobro player, his importance in maintaining awareness of the Dobro cannot be understated. For more than 15 years, he was virtually the only professional Dobro player in existence. By virtue of his weekly Opry appearances with Acuff, which often included his solo on Acuff's hit 'Wabash Cannonball,' the sound of Kirby's Dobro reached into millions of homes across the southern and eastern states.

In 1957 a Dobro player named Burkett 'Buck' Graves left the regionally popular Wilma Lee and Stony Cooper and joined the premier bluegrass band, Flatt and Scruggs, adopting the persona of 'Uncle Josh.' Graves had been playing Dobro since 1942, influenced primarily by Cliff Carlisle. He even owned one of Carlisle's old instruments, a No. 37 model. Graves combined blues licks with high-speed Scruggs-style finger rolls, thereby inventing the concept of bluegrass Dobro.

Although the Dobro was not, and still isn't, an absolutely essential element to the bluegrass sound, Josh Graves's work with Flatt and Scruggs established a home for the instrument in bluegrass. Hundreds of thousands of country, folk, and bluegrass fans watching Flatt and Scruggs's syndicated TV show in the 1960s heard Lester Flatt introduce Uncle Josh on the 'old hound dog guitar' – the nickname for the Dobro. By the time Flatt and Scruggs parted ways in 1969, Graves had created a repertoire for

the instrument and inspired a new generation of Dobroists. On the corporate side, Dobro had ceased to exist when the National-Dobro company changed its name to Valco in 1943. After World War II, Valco made no Dobros but retained rights to the name. However, in response to the Dobro's emergence in bluegrass, Ed and Rudy Dopyera, John's brothers, began making instruments in 1962 under the DB Original brand. They regained the right to use the Dobro name in 1964 and made instruments under the Dobro brand for two years, before selling the Dobro name to Semie Moseley, a noted electric guitar maker.

The Dopyeras had changed the look of the Dobro in 1965, making the screen on the upper-bout soundholes look more like a sieve and the resonator cover more like the hubcap on an automobile. The Dobros made by Mosrite (Moseley's company) retained that look over a wide range of styles. Most models were offered with the regular Dobro spider resonator system or the inverted-cone 'biscuit' system (the bridge was mounted in a round piece of wood, about the size of a biscuit) that had previously only been found on Nationals. Some Mosrites sported electric guitar bodies and some, like the Uncle Josh model, were more traditionally acoustic in design, but most were offered with an optional magnetic pickup. When Mosrite went

into bankruptcy in 1970 and lost the Dobro name, a few instruments appeared under the Mobro brand.

In the meantime, the Dopyeras continued to make Dobro-type guitars under various brands, including Replica 66 in 1966, Hound Dog from 1967-70, and Dopera's Original from 1970-71 (the brand an intentional misspelling of the family name).

In 1970, Dopyera family members reacquired the Dobro brand and formed the Original Musical Instrument company in Huntington Beach, California. The standard model was, and still is, No. 60, made with a body of 3-ply laminated maple, available in roundneck or squareneck. With Valco/National going out of business by the late 1960s, no one was making guitars with the National type 'biscuit' resonator, so OMI began designing new guitars – woodbody and even engraved metalbody models – in the style of the Nationals of the 1930s.

In the 1970s, Josh Graves continued to bring wider exposure to the Dobro through his work with the genre-crossing Earl Scruggs Revue. In the bluegrass world, the eclectic repertoire of The Seldom Scene, a Washington, DC-based group, provided the perfect musical vehicle for Mike Auldridge to introduce a more lyrical, melodic Dobro style. At the same time, in another DC-area group, The Country Gentlemen,

Dobro No. 33 c1990s (*left*) This round-necked metal-body model has the 'biscuit' bridge more often associated with National resonator guitars.

Dobro F60 2002 (*right*) A Gibson-made Dobro of the traditional style, with 'spider' bridge.

Eric Clapton c2000 (*below*) *According to Clapton authority Saiichi Sugiyama, Slowhand's 'Dobro' has been assembled from an altered but vintage 1930s body and a recently fitted neck. Note the elaborate inlays, which include a skull at the 14th fret.*

DUNN

Jerry Douglas had taken a similar approach. By the early 1980s, as a member of The Whites, a country group, Douglas introduced mainstream country audiences to the smooth, fluid style that earned him the nickname 'Flux.' Douglas went on to perform with artists in various genres of popular music and to lead his own band. Along the way to becoming today's premier Dobro player, he set new standards for technique and repertoire, just as Josh Graves had done a generation earlier.

Gibson Guitar Corp acquired the Original Musical Instrument company in 1993, and two years later secured its domination of the bluegrass market by signing the best known Dobro players to endorsement agreements. In 1995 Dobro introduced signature models from Jerry Douglas, Al Perkins (of Emmylou Harris's Nash Ramblers), Josh Graves, Oswald Kirby, and Tom Swatzell (a noted teacher).

In 1997, Gibson moved Dobro production to Nashville and changed the name to Original Acoustic Instruments, bringing mandolin and banjo production under the same roof to form essentially a bluegrass manufacturing division. Since 1999, Dobros have been made in public view at Gibson's Bluegrass Showcase, located in the Nashville's Opry Mills retail complex. Since 2001, Dobros have been fitted exclusively with the spider resonator system.

Although John Dopyera's single-cone creation of 1928 almost died out in the 1930s and 1940s, it is firmly established now, as proven on the high-end by a growing number of individuals making custom resonator guitars and, on the low-end, by the availability of cheap Asian-made models. Still, Gibson's OAI, the descendant of the original company, remains not only the leading maker of Dobros but also, by virtue of its trademarked name, the only maker of a genuine Dobro.

DUNN

Another devotee of the Selmer/Maccaferri style, Michael Dunn began his career as a luthier in 1966 when he started a three-year apprenticeship with José Orti and José Ferrer in Spain. In the late 1960s he heard a Django Reinhardt record and became obsessed with Gypsy jazz, and the Selmer-style guitars used to play it. Dunn doesn't make exact replicas of the Selmer/Maccaferri instrument, opting instead to add his own personal twist to the classic designs, such as using exotic woods like blackwood and sapele and utilizing elaborate, multi-colored inlays. As of 2003 Dunn makes at least ten different models, including the Mystery Pacific, a 12-fret D-soundhole model with an internal resonator, and the Belleville, a 14-fret oval-soundhole model.

DUPONT

Maurice Dupont is best known outside of France for his accurate reproductions of Selmer/Maccaferri style guitars, although he also builds nylon-strings, archtops, and flat-top steel-string guitars. He constructed his first instrument, a lap dulcimer, when he was 18, and quickly went on to build an electric guitar, a banjo, and a hurdy-gurdy. In 1981 he settled in Cognac after a brief period working for a company called Camac, where he made wooden flutes, hurdy-gurdies, and psalters.

Dupont built his first Selmer-style guitar in the early 1980s, having learned the basic construction from his many visits to Jacques Favino's workshop in Paris, and from the handful of original Selmers he repaired. He also tracked down the original jigs and fixtures that Selmer used between 1932 and 1952 and from them he was able to learn the specific techniques that the maker used in order to build the guitars.

His first model was the MD-50, which was based on a Selmer Modèle Jazz similar to the one that Django Reinhardt played. Dupont replicated all of the distinctive Selmer features, including the laminated back and sides, walnut neck, and engraved headstock logo. Other reproductions soon followed, including the MC-50, which was based on the D-shaped-soundhole Modèle Orchestre, and the MCC-50, which was based on the nylon-string Modèle Concert. Dupont also made Selmer-style guitars out of solid woods like Indian rosewood, Brazilian rosewood, maple, mahogany, and other tropical hardwoods. As his reputation grew he began to take custom orders, and two of them – the 14-fret, D-soundhole with an internal resonator for John Jorgensen and the blue, 14-fret oval-hole with an arched back for the French guitarist Romane – have become part of the standard line.

Dupont also builds a complete line of classical guitars that range from relatively inexpensive student-grade instruments up beautifully crafted concert-grade guitars. Dupont builds two models of archtop – the cosmetically simple Excellence and the fancier Privelège – and a small assortment of flat-top steel strings.

By 2017 Dupont had a staff of a dozen or so workers who produce around 325 instruments a year. Most of these are built by hand, although Dupont experimented with making some components on a CNC machine he purchased back in the late 1990s. The machine is primarily used to carve the tops and pegheads for the *violas de gamba* that Dupont builds for the French school system. Recently much of Maurice Dupont's time has been taken up with running a company – and creating a new Larson Bros brand – but he does take the time to personally build the archtop guitars.

Michael Hedges (*above*) *The virtuoso, who died tragically young in a 1997 car accident, is seen here with a vintage Dyer. Hedges was one of few guitarists able to make the most of the harp guitar's extended range.*

D Y E R

The Dyer brand is probably most known for its association with harp guitars, but its importance lies more in the fact that it brought together guitars from several significant smaller guitar-makers than it does in any specific instruments. Despite the fact that Dyer labels claim that its guitars were "manufactured by..." it's unlikely that Dyer ever built any of its own guitars.

William John Dyer (born 1841) moved from London to Boston, where he became a music teacher, then relocated to Minnesota in 1869 and opened a music store with his brother C.E. Dyer. In 1871 the Dyers established W.J. Dyer & Bro in St Paul, expanding into Minneapolis in 1875. Two other brothers, S.H. and D.M. Dyer, joined them in 1889. Its principal lines were pianos and organs, but from around 1894 to 1909 or slightly later the Dyers used the brand name J.F. Stetson & Co. (perhaps an earlier local maker) on parlor guitars sourced primarily from Lyon & Healy and Harmony, though some were also made by the Larson brothers.

Probably around 1906 Dyer hooked up with the West Coast-based Norwegian immigrant Chris J. Knutsen to market a version of his patented Symphony Harp Guitar, a big flat-top with a large extension of the body above the neck outfitted with extra

Dyer Symphony Harp Guitar Style 7 c1920 (*left*) *Unlike many other harp guitars, the Dyers – built by Larson Brothers of Chicago – employ a long, hollow body extension, which contributes a reverberant sound.*

Dyer Symphony Harp Guitar Style 8 c1920 (*right*) *This similar but more elaborately decorated harp guitar was owned by noted collector Scott Chinery, who enthused: "This instrument is without question the best-sounding flat-top guitar that I've ever played or heard."*

bass strings. Knutsen (born 1862) grew up in Minnesota (Dyer country), moved to Washington Territory (later State) in the 1880s, and began making guitars. In 1896 he obtained a patent on a new design for a harp guitar. Dyer harp guitars had labels signed by Knutsen, but most, if not all, were built by the Larson brothers. Knutsen, a lone luthier, probably did not make any Dyers himself (also see the entry on Knutsen).

The Swedish luthiers Carl and August Larson took over the Maurer factory in Chicago in 1900, and by around 1904 were producing Stetsons and, later, Dyer harp guitars, among others. Since the Larsons never mounted full-scale factory production, all Larson Dyers were basically custom-made and are instantly recognizable as Larson creations. As with other Larson guitars, these Dyers featured 'stressed' (arched) tops and backs and were probably designed for steel strings.

After Knutsen's patent expired in 1912, the Larsons redesigned the Dyer harp guitar with an extension soundhole and a flat (not slotted) head. The Larsons appear to have made Dyer guitars until at least the 1920s. In 1925 founder William Dyer, the last surviving brother, died and the company was taken over by the next generation. The Dyer firm lasted at least until World War II. The brand was revived in 2014 at a workshop in South Pasadena, California, by Scott Holloway and Jim Worland.

EKO

If accordions had remained popular after the early 1950s squeezebox rage, there might never have been any EKO guitar, or any of a number of others. But they didn't – and it was pretty much a survival strategy that led Oliviero Pigini and Company of Recanati, Italy, into producing the EKO guitars that provided a budget alternative during the early days of the 1960s 'guitar boom' in the US and the UK.

EKOs aren't the sort of guitar to garner big-name endorsements (about the only name one can dredge up in this regard is that of Connie Stevens), though the pop band The Grass Roots did play them for a time, and Peter Sellers used one as 'clothes' in a nudist-camp scene in the movie *A Shot In The Dark*.

EKO guitars were actually developed around 1961 in conjunction with the LoDuca Brothers of Milwaukee, Wisconsin. Ace accordionists Tom and Guy LoDuca had built a sizeable music studio and instrument distribution network, which included accordions from Pigini, and had supplied Sears, Roebuck and Company. With a contract to provide Sears with acoustic guitars, LoDuca turned to Pigini. For about three years, early EKOs were therefore sold in the US as Silvertones.

A full EKO line was introduced in America and Britain in 1962, including Studio

EKO catalog c1967 *After the daily gunfight, a cowpoke of the old West liked nothing better than to kick back and strum a few licks on his EKO Ranger 12-string ... with onboard pickup, of course.*

EKO P12 Betty 1962 *(left)*
One of EKO's better quality small-bodied steel-string models.

EKO P2 Angela 1963 *(right)*
This one employs a floating bridge and trapeze tailpiece. Note also next to the nut the 'zero fret' (also on the P12), intended to equalize the tone between open and fretted strings.

steel-string flat-tops and Plectrum archtops. All EKO guitars of the 1960s employed zero frets and had arched backs. The Studios (Angela, Paola, Mina, and Betty) had laminated mahogany bodies and glued-on adjustable necks with slotted heads. Tops were either spruce or a novel brown-shaded African oak – indeed EKO was one of the few brands to employ oak for its tops. All were available with either moveable bridges and a trapeze tail or a pinless fixed bridge. The Plectrum archtops had bodies sporting a single round cutaway and solid headstocks. The Studio Jazz had the oak top, cat's eye soundholes, and either mahogany or maple body. The EKO Plectrum had a maple body and regular f-holes. These early guitars had lacquer finishes.

This beginner range of guitars continued for a few years. By 1965 EKO had replaced the adjustable set-neck with a bolt-on version reinforced by a non-adjustable T-bar, and added classicals in either mahogany or maple. Logos had migrated from plastic headstock plates to stencils on the upper shoulder. Just one oak-topped, bolt-neck acoustic archtop remained.

Around the same time, EKO introduced its first dreadnought with a spruce top, laminated mahogany body, batwing pickguard, pin bridge with adjustable saddle, and bolt-on neck with both a T-bar and adjustable truss-rod. A 12-string version was also available, as well as models with electromagnetic pickups at the end of the fingerboard. These dreadnoughts remained through the '60s, though by the brand's apex in 1967 they'd acquired the Ranger name. The 12-string Ranger 12 Electra now had block inlays, a bound fingerboard, and came with a maple body. Some Ranger 12s were made with the fixed bridge plus trapeze tails. By '67 finishes had changed to polyurethane 'dura-glos.'

EKO's flat-top line also got new names by 1967 (Coronado, Bolero, Riviera, Fiesta, Junior, and Petite), but were otherwise pretty much unchanged – with spruce or oak tops and mahogany or maple bodies.

Also about this time the EKOette line debuted, positioned as 'rental' models, including a couple with adjustable saddles, a new classical, and EKO's first all-mahogany guitar, with a solid French-curve headstock.

In around 1967 or '68 Oliviero Pigini, whose hobby was collecting sports cars and driving them fast, died in a car crash. Relations between the LoDucas and the EKO company were never as cozy afterward, though the link continued into the 1980s. The company received another blow when, around 1970, a repairman who was repairing one of the Roke electrics left a soldering iron on and a disastrous fire resulted,

EKO catalog 1969 (*left*) Promo material for the Ranger, Rio Bravo, and El Dorado models strummed by many a fledgling songwriter.

Epiphone Recording C c1929 (*left*) This early Epiphone flat-top may look more 'traditional,' but it is actually a far rarer example of this top-of-the-line Recording model, lacking the cutaway usually seen on such guitars at the time.

Epiphone Recording D c1928 (*right*) This model displays the more characteristic sloping cutaway of most A, B, C, D, and E models. Note the distinctive peghead – a throwback to Epiphone banjos.

EKO

The Five Spirits Of Rhythm 1935
(**below**) *Left to right: Douglas Daniels, Teddy Bunn with an Epiphone Deluxe Masterbilt model, Leo Watson, Virgil Scoggins, and Wilbur Daniels.*

destroying supplies of seasoned wood. Subsequent EKOs were built of inadequately seasoned timbers and suffered a marked decline in quality.

By around 1972 EKO added an expanded line of dreadnoughts, most in six and 12-string models, with or without pickup. Several variants on the Ranger were offered, in solid black or orange sunburst. The Rangers were joined by the upscale Rio Bravo, with bound fingerboard, block inlays, and a new heavy mustache pin bridge. There was also an E-85 in black, with double pickguards. Top of the line was the El Dorado, EKO's first set-neck acoustic since the early 1960s, with bow-tie pearl inlays, and elaborate mustache bridge. One jumbo folk guitar was also offered, the bolt-neck Navajo, with a Douglas fir top!

The standard-sized Studio line progressed through some cosmetic changes, notably the use of an orange pumpkin finish on the tops. Most interesting was a new flat-top with a single pointed cutaway. These acoustics made up the EKO line through the 1970s. Around 1975 EKO introduced the Marling brand, which also included bolt-neck standard and dreadnought guitars. But EKO found it hard to compete in the 1980s and went out of business in 1985. During the late 1990s there was a revival of the brand, and by 2017 EKO offered ten series of flat-top acoustic models.

EPIPHONE

The first name that usually comes to mind in connection with factory-made archtop guitars is Gibson, but during the 1930s heyday of acoustic jazz boxes you would be just as likely to find an Epiphone in the hands of jazz legends Carl Kress, Dick McDonough, and George Van Eps, or in the rhythm sections of popular big bands led by Kay Kyser, Jan Savitt or Will Osborne.

With often sumptuous appointments and excellent workmanship — and even a gigantic 18½" option on the Emperor model — Epiphone instruments were the choice of many professionals. Indeed, when Les Paul needed a guitar to dress up his early electric 'Log' experiments, he chose an Epiphone.

 dates its history back to 1873 in the famed Greek city of Sparta, when Anastasios Stathopoulo — born 1863 or '64 to a father in the lumber trade — began making instruments as an apprentice. Shortly thereafter the Stathopoulo family moved to Smyrna, Turkey, where Anastasios married and began a family.

Anastasios and his family emigrated to New York in 1903, where he established an instrument-making business, primarily making Greek-style lioutos and mandolins under the A. Stathopoulo label. Of his four sons and two daughters, three of them —

58

Epaminondas (better known as Epi, born 1893), Alkminie (Minnie, 1897), Orpheus (Orphie, 1899), and Frixo (1905) – would play significant roles in the subsequent Epiphone saga. Around 1911 or so, Anastasios was also making some parlor guitars. In 1915, Anastasios died and was succeeded by his eldest son Epi, who began to do business as The House Of Stathopoulo in 1917, incorporating under that name in 1923. In 1924 Epiphone Recording Series banjos were introduced, named for company president Epi. By this time all three Stathopoulo brothers were involved with the business. In 1928 the company was renamed the Epiphone Banjo Corporation.

Epiphone introduced its first line of production guitars, the Recording Series, during 1927. The Recordings had unusual asymmetrical bodies similar in spirit to the Venetian guitars that Stromberg-Voisinet (Kay) debuted in 1927, with a humped upper shoulder and a dramatically swept, pointed treble cutaway. These had engraved celluloid banjo-style heads and tuners and came as either flat-tops or archtops. A few

Epiphone Emperor 1942 (*left*)
A rare cutaway example of Epiphone's top-of-the-line archtop, launched in 1935 in response to Gibson's giant new Super 400, introduced the year before.

Epiphone Emperor 1949 (*right*) *This sunburst example is another guitar from Epiphone's heyday in New York. Production in the Big Apple ended in 1953, when the factory moved to Philadelphia.*

Epiphone catalog 1959 (*top of page*) *Promotional pages for Emperor, Deluxe, Triumph and Zenith archtops.*

Recording models had a Spanish shape. Accompanying these, Epiphone had a line of more conventional flat-top instruments that had rounded figure-eight bodies and regular heads and tuners.

By the 1930s guitars were rapidly replacing banjos in dance bands and Epiphone switched gears to meet the changing tastes of the day.

In 1931, the company revamped its range to offer a full range of advanced Masterbilt archtops, as well as the beginnings of its traditional flat-top line. The first

Nat King Cole Trio 1939 (*above*) *The great singer and pianist prepares for a session in the NBC studio, with guitarist Oscar Moore (playing a non-cutaway Emperor) and bassist Wesley Prince.*

Epiphone Madrid 1936 (*right***)** *This is the revamped large-body style for Epiphone's Madrid model, which earlier had carried the unusual feature of four extra f-holes around its body edge.*

Epiphone Emperor Cutaway 1954 (*left***)** *The flagship acoustic archtop of the mid 1950s.*

Epiphone catalog 1955 *Among Epi's noted supporters featured here are Carmen Mastren, Ike Isaacs, George Van Eps, Grady Martin, J.B. Brinkley, and Claude King of Ernest Tubbs & The Texas Troubadours.*

Masterbilts were excellent-quality guitars, with 14-fret necks, carved spruce tops, and solid sides and backs made of materials ranging from curly maple on the fancy grand auditorium (16⅜") De Luxe to walnut and mahogany on the humbler concert-sized (13⅝") Olympic model. The Masterbilts came in shaded (sunburst) finishes and included tenor and plectrum guitars.

Some of the new flat-tops also had f-holes, the Madrid actually sporting four of them! These quickly changed to round holes and came in 14-fret Spanish and 12-fret Hawaiian versions. The better Madrid and Navarre models featured a large auditorium body with round shoulders and thick waist, not unlike a later Harmony Sovereign, and a style often referred to as a 'round-shouldered' dreadnought. As early as 1932 better Epis featured neck reinforcement. While these were factory guitars, there was a lot of handwork involved, and often there's a great deal of variation in individual instruments' specifications.

In 1934 the auditorium flat-tops were joined by a new FT (flat top) series, folk style guitars with more of a Martin OM shape. The FT and archtop lines continued to expand as the 1930s progressed. The Masterbilts were a hit, and Epiphone had become a guitar company. In 1935 the company name was changed once more, to

Epiphone, Inc. With growing acceptance in the orchestra, guitarists wanted more volume. On the acoustic side this resulted in a kind of size escalation. In 1934 Gibson introduced its 18" Super 400. In 1935 Epiphone responded and also started adding inches, rolling out the 17⅜" Super De Luxe and spectacular 18½" Emperor.

During the Depression, Epiphone – like most other American manufacturers – also produced guitars for other companies. Some of these instruments carry brands such as Howard, and Sorrentino.

In 1937 Epi Stathopoulo applied for a new patent for an adjustable truss-rod, which was used on subsequent Epiphones. Also in that year, Epiphone introduced the distinctive Frequensator tailpiece, a two-part trapeze that added about three inches to the length of the bass strings behind the bridge, and was supposed to improve clarity and tone and eliminate dead spots. The following year Epiphone debuted its first classical guitars, the Concert, Alhambra, and Seville.

Epiphone was at this time a very traditional-looking maker by today's standards, but it took a step forward in the cosmetic stakes toward the end of the decade, when increasingly popular natural (blonde) finishes were made available alongside the traditional sunbursts. As to further modernity, in 1939 archtop rivals Gibson upped the

Epiphone FT-79 1944 (right)
This square-shouldered dreadnought appears to have been influenced by the seminal Martin design. A year after Gibson's takeover of Epiphone in 1957 the FT-79 would evolve into the Texan.

Epiphone catalog 1969 (center) *A selection of the range aimed at tapping the folk boom.*

Epiphone Frontier FT-110 early 1960s (far right) *A guitar from the upper-middle range of the Gibson-built Epiphone flat-top line.*

Epiphone ad 1994 *Heavy rockers Brother Cane prove uncharacteristic endorsers of the EJ-200.*

ante again, adding a cutaway to its Super 400. Epiphone was a little slower to respond this time, but introduced its first cutaway, the Soloist Emperor, in 1941.

Also debuting in 1941 were the FT 110 and 79 (numbers stood for prices) with a new square-shouldered dreadnought shape, recognizable today as the typical dreadnought body style. At that moment, however, World War II intervened and Epiphone production slowed to a trickle.

After the war, Epiphone tried to pick up where it had left off, but things weren't the same. Epi Stathopoula had died of leukemia in 1943 and Orphie and Frixo were left in charge. Theirs was not a harmonious relationship and management disagreements hampered the firm's success. In 1947 Frixo left the company, leaving Orphie in control.

Except for the new cutaway feature, acoustic guitars continued as before the war. By this time most archtops had laminated bodies. The rounded cutaway option introduced in 1941 now appeared on Epiphone's full line, with the change indicated by the name Regent. The Soloist Emperor, for example, became the Emperor Regent.

A small portion of Epiphone's post-war workforce was unionized, mostly younger employees. This group began to demand improved conditions, which Orphie was not inclined to grant. In late 1951 Epiphone workers staged a strike that closed down the factory. In 1952, rather than give in, Orphie moved equipment and supplies to Philadelphia. To raise cash, he gave exclusive distribution rights to Continental Music of Chicago. Most of the workers left behind in New York were hired at a new guitar factory called, appropriately enough, Guild.

Epiphone continued to build guitars in Philadelphia, and even introduced new models, including its first cutaway flat-top model, the FT De Luxe, introduced in 1954, but the company was unable to recover. In late 1956 Frixo decided to rejoin Epiphone and try to jump-start the business, but he died in January of 1957 before any revitalization could take hold.

Shortly thereafter Orphie Staphopoulo saw no other option but to offer Epiphone to its old arch-rival. Orphie contacted Ted McCarty of Gibson, who brokered the deal with Maurice Berlin, president of Chicago Musical Instruments (CMI), which owned Gibson. CMI purchased Epiphone and transported everything to Gibson's base in

Epiphone ad c1960s (right) *It's clear from the advertising strategy that Epiphone was gunning for the country & western market with the blatantly-named Texan.*

Epiphone Texan 1964 (main guitar) *A fine example of the company's round-shouldered dreadnought model.*

Epiphone ad c2002 (above) *Rock'n'swing proponent Duke Robillard squeezes out those double-stops on a contemporary Emperor Regent.*

T.Rex early 1970s (opposite page) *Percussionist Mickey Finn thumps a mock-crock guitar case while Marc Bolan warms up on a mid-bodied Epiphone Cortez of the late 1960s.*

Kalamazoo, Michigan. In 1958 a totally new Epiphone line debuted, positioned as a budget line under the flagship Gibson, a position it retains to this day.

By this time the market for acoustic archtops was pretty much gone. Gibson kept the principal Epiphone cutaway models, including the Emperor, Deluxe, Triumph, and Zenith, but dropped the rest. Epiphone flat-tops were consolidated into the older round-shouldered (Texan) and square-shouldered (Frontier) dreadnoughts, and folk models (Cortez, Caballero). Epiphone reintroduced classical guitars in 1961-63. With the folk revival in progress, more dreadnoughts joined the line in 1963 (Excellente, El Dorado, Troubadour), as well as the first 12-strings (Bard, Serenader). A Folkster appeared in 1966.

All of these Kalamazoo-made Epiphones lasted until the end of the 1960s, the last few shipping in 1970. By that time Gibson had begun planning to shift Epiphone production to Japan. In 1969 CMI – including Gibson and Epiphone – was purchased by ECL (the Ecuadorian Company Ltd.). The CMI name was then changed to Norlin. Shortly thereafter the first Japanese-made Epiphone guitars appeared.

Early 1970s Japanese-made Epiphones were a pale reflection of their predecessors. Gone were archtops. Flat-tops continued to be identified with the FT prefix and consisted of folk, dreadnought, and 12-string models, all with Gibson-style adjustable saddles. All but one dreadnought, however, the FT-155, had slim, fast, low-action bolt-on necks. Epiphone also offered a line of EC classicals, with set necks.

But Epiphone wasn't left to languish forever, and quality began to improve in the mid 1970s. By 1974 most models in the 100 series continued to have bolt-on necks, but some fancier 300 and 500-series set-neck models were offered, including the FT-550 and FT-565 12-string with three-piece jacaranda and maple backs. Also available was a nice blonde Super Jumbo model.

Epiphone acoustics continued to be made in Japan probably through the early 1980s. By around 1984 or so the Epiphone line was reflecting some of its earlier heritage. The big-bodied Emperor was back in a two-pickup acoustic-electric version with the old Frequensator tailpiece and either round or pointed cutaway. PR-series flat-tops included six and 12-string dreadnoughts and folk-style guitars, with either solid (with S suffix) or laminated spruce tops, all with glued-in necks. Most dreadnoughts were standard-issue, but there was also one round-shouldered model, like the good old days. Two classicals were offered, with solid or laminated cedar tops. By this time the Epiphone line included a pair of folk-style models with single

cutaways, one with a pickup system. These would foreshadow the future. Meanwhile, interest in keyboards and economic recession hurt the demand for guitars in the early 1980s. Norlin decided to get out of the business and in January 1986 sold Gibson and Epiphone to Henry Juszkiewicz, David Berryman, and Gary Zebrowski. Epiphone production shifted to Korea, with many models being sourced from Samick.

Lean years were again ahead for Epiphone, in terms of quality and model offerings. The late-1980s acoustic line was all Korean and consisted of a number of natural and black dreadnoughts and classicals, all but the top models made with laminated tops. There was also a black jumbo model in the catalog that was styled loosely after the old Gibson Everly Brothers with double pickguards – but the great archtops of the company's glory years were all gone.

In the early 1990s Jim Rosenberg was hired to rejuvenate the Epiphone brand. His efforts, combined with a dramatic increase in Korean quality, were wildly successful. Over the decade the Epiphone line increasingly evolved into budget copies of the more upscale American Gibson counterparts, and increasingly earned critical plaudits and greater acceptance in the market once again.

With the 'budget Gibson' tag again more firmly established, the first US-built

Epiphone AJ-15 2002 (*left*)
This Korean-made budget model was built with laminated top, back and sides – and proudly sports parent company Gibson's name on the truss-rod cover.

Epiphone AJ-30CE 1999 (*right*) *The traditional Epi round-shouldered dreadnought (or jumbo) shape is enhanced with modern specs here as suitable features are added: a gentle cutaway, an under-saddle pickup, and an onboard preamp.*

Epiphone ad 2006 (*top right*) *Country artist Gretchen Wilson is pictured in this promo with her custom Epiphone Masterbilt EF-500RA.*

fRoots magazine 2002 (*right*) *Singer-songwriter Souad Massi chooses an Epiphone John Lennon model for her cover shoot.*

Crystal Bowersox 2015 (*left*)
The singer-songwriter is pictured with her Epiphone FT-350 fitted with a Min-ETune self-tuning system.

guitars to carry the Epiphone brand name in more than 20 years emerged from Gibson's new Bozeman, Montana, workshop in 1993-94, in the form of limited-edition reissues of popular 1960s Epiphone acoustics.

By the late 1990s there was an almost bewildering array of Korean-made Epiphone acoustics. Dreadnoughts included both traditional square-shouldered and round-shouldered (Advanced Jumbo) dreadnoughts, increasingly with solid tops (including mahogany), some with cutaways. There were copies of the Gibson Dove and a Don Everly signature model; Venetian cutaway thin-body acoustic-electrics, including a Jeff 'Skunk' Baxter model; classicals, including cutaway models; and even spider and biscuit-bridge resonator guitars.

Among the most notable of the acoustic stable at this time was a John Lennon signature copy of the Gibson J-160E dreadnought he had played, with a single-coil pickup tucked under the end of the fingerboard. The acoustic bounty continued into the late 1990s, with noteworthy instruments including a series of special '125th Anniversary' Advanced Jumbo models, and a cutaway jumbo version of the Everly Brothers guitar with a piezo-electronic system that was developed in conjunction with Shadow. As the Epiphone company moved into the 21st Century, the emphasis on

Epiphone EJ-160E John Lennon Model 2000 (*left*) *A guitar that follows the form of Gibson's equally Beatled-up J-160E, Epiphone's Lennon model is one of its high-end modern offerings. Note the onboard pickup and controls, and Lennon's signature printed on the top along the bass-side edge of the fingerboard.*

Epiphone EL-00 2002 (*right*) *Gibson's L-00 body shape – a size that has seen a new popularity in recent years – is given an outing on this vintage-styled but contemporary Epiphone model.*

Epiphone AJ 500RC Cedar 2015 (far *right*) *Gibson's L-00 body shape – a size that has seen a new popularity in recent years – is given an outing on this vintage-styled but contemporary Epiphone model.*

copying Gibson acoustic models began to recede, although the basic direction remained the same.

New in 1991 was a flat-top series called the Orville, named for the original Gibson founder and with his distinctive paddle-shape headstock and star-and-crescent inlay. Also new were the PR models, which had Epi active EQs designed by Oberheim, an synth and electronics company that was now owned by Gibson.

US-made reissues of the Excellente, Fontier and Texan appeared in 1993, with regular versions of the first two introduced a few years later. A take on Gibson's Hummingbird was launched in 1994, and in '95 an Elvis J-200, the same year that a successful Epiphone moved to its own HQ buildings in Nashville, separate from the Gibson operation. Some Epis had been made in China since the 90s, in addition to the continuing Korean sources, but in 2002 the brand incorporated in China and opened a new plant in Qingdao.

Epiphone introduced more versions of Gibson classics in the early 2000s, adding a J-200, Dove, L-00 (EL-00), and J-45, and it reorganized the flat-top lines in 2003 and '04, with the square-shoulder dreadnought models changing names from the PR to the DR series, and the round-shoulder models remaining as AJs. There was also a

Epiphone 50th Anniversary 1964 Caballero 2014 (left) *Based on a 1960s Caballero model, with its small mahogany body, this recent update is fitted with a Shadow pre-amp and pickup system.*

Epiphone Don Everly SQ180 2006 (right) *Don's well-known Gibson J-180, complete with double pickguards and star inlays, was the inspiration for this Epi signature model.*

Epiphone ad 2015 (above right) *A classic image, here featuring a Masterbilt AJ500.*

Epiphone C-25 1999 (opposite page) *Not known for nylon-string guitars, Epiphone – like most acoustic makers – has always offered a few such models to maintain its presence.*

new style, which was similar to a Martin 000 and called the EF series, and there were Masterbilt top-of-the-line versions of many of these. A Paul McCartney Texan model appeared in 2005, and a Dave Navarro black Hummingbird-style flat-top, the E/A, in 2010. By 2017, Epiphone acoustics were being made in a number of locations, with results that were significantly improved and a long way from those humble beginnings back in Sparta.

ESPAÑA

España was a brand name used in the 1960s by the New York-based instrument importer Buegeleisen & Jacobsen on a line of low to medium-priced Spanish and flat-top guitars manufactured by the Finnish maker Landola. They were well built and offered good value for money. Despite the name, España guitars were, oddly, often marketed in ads that show the virtues of Finnish nature and traditions, such as backpacking. España decals may also have been put on guitars by other makers, but the bulk of them – electrics included – are Landolas.

ESTESO

The guitars built by Domingo Esteso date from the most Romantic era of Spanish guitar-making, and today they are sought after by both classical and flamenco enthusiasts.

Domingo Esteso was born in 1882, and joined the great Manuel Ramírez as a teenage apprentice. After Ramirez's death in 1916, Domingo Esteso set up shop on his own account, producing guitars for Manuel's widow, who sold them on to a company in Buenos Aires, Argentina.

The instruments are in the small-bodied, relatively lightweight style of the era, and use standard bracing. They generally produce a slightly soft, mellow tone. Some of the guitars are quite ornate.

When Esteso died, in 1937, his workshop was taken over by his three nephews, the brothers Faustino, Julian, and Mariano Conde. They traded first as Vda. y Sobrinos de Domingo Esteso (widow and nephews of Domingo Esteso). The Esteso inheritance is currently split between at least two firms in Madrid, trading as Conde Hermanos (Conde brothers) and Hermanos Conde.

David Bowie *A young Bowie in singer-songwriter mode with an España 12-string.*

E U P H O N O N

Euphonon guitars are among the least remembered yet most successful creations of Carl and August Larson and their Maurer & Co of Chicago. They were favored by many of WLS Radio's hottest stars and even Johnny Cash.

Euphonon replaced the Maurer brand around 1935 when the Larsons jumped on the increasingly popular 14-fret bandwagon. The guitars featured a new square-shouldered shape and a solid headstock, but otherwise had signature Larson construction. Bodies were mahogany, rosewood or figured maple. Student-grade models were built in the 13¾" size with ladder-braced tops, but better models had laminated, X-braced 'stressed' tops and larger sizes of 15" to 16", even 19". Many had typical Larson inlays, some fancy trim, but others sported more modern pearl blocks.

Toward the end of the 1930s Euphonon gained a dreadnought, with a body like a cross between a Martin and Gibson of that style. Some models had dark stained tops. Euphonon models with the Larsons' internal metal rod supports wore the Prairie State brand, and a few were shipped to Wack Sales Co in Milwaukee as Maurers. The Euphonon brand ceased in the early 1940s, but it was revived in 2013 with the launch of a new Larson Bros company at a workshop near Cognac in France.

Esteso 1934 (right) *This instrument by the great Spanish flamenco guitar-maker has a top of European spruce, with cypress back and sides.*

Esteso label (above) *Note the photo of Gypsy flamenco virtuoso Ramón Montoya glued to the back of this Esteso below the label, possibly placed there to inspire the guitar's original owner.*

Back and sides (left) *These views reveal the 'friction pegs' traditionally used on flamenco guitars.*

FAVINO

In a career that stretched from 1945 to 1981, Jacques Favino made hundreds of instruments, including violins, mandolins, archtop guitars, and flat-tops, but he is best known for his Selmer-style guitars. Favino's guitars were slightly deeper and a little wider across the lower bout, and many players prefer their slightly warmer tone to the brighter, snappier Selmers. In the late 1960s Jean Beuscher, the man who bought the remaining inventory of guitar parts from Selmer when it stopped producing guitars in 1952, commissioned Favino to build bodies for ten original necks. Favino did such a fine job that these guitars are occasionally sold as original Selmers.

Jacques Favino's son Jean-Pierre started working full time in the Paris workshop in 1973. When Jacques retired in 1981, Jean-Pierre took over the business and continued to produce guitars to the same high standards. In 1990 he closed the workshop in Paris and moved to a village in Castelbiague in the Pyrenees. These days he builds very few guitars a year. Most of them are in the Selmer style, but Jean-Pierre has also made some unusual instruments such as harp guitars, flat-tops with three soundholes, and the Modèle Verseau — a reversible guitar with two tops and both steel and nylon-strung necks.

FENDER

The history of the Fender Electric Instrument Co is a one-stop lesson in the vast gulf between the design and production of acoustic and solidbody-electric guitars. Fender's first acoustics were revolutionary for their day — they had slim, fast-action, bolt-on necks; six-a-side headstocks; adjustable-steel-saddle mustache bridges; oversized, screwed-on pickguards; and western cosmetics — but swiftly proved that not every revolution is a good thing.

Fender Manufacturing (later Fender Electric Instrument Co) was set up by former radio repairman Leo Fender in 1946 to build lap-steel guitars and amplifiers. As almost any guitarist will already know, the company became the most innovative and influential builder of solidbody electric guitars of the 1950s.

As Fender's success grew, its sales team was drooling for a bite of the acoustic guitar sector. A short-lived deal for exclusive distribution of a line of Regal-brand flat-tops built by Harmony in Chicago gave them a taste — but it seemed to make better business sense to exploit the increasing name recognition of the Fender logo.

In the early 1960s Leo hired former Gibson and Rickenbacker designer Roger Rossmeisl to oversee design and manufacture of flat-tops. The results had the

Euphonon c1936 (*left*) *This Larson-built guitar was made shortly after the Euphonon name replaced the Chicago company's Maurer brand.*

Euphonon c1941 (*left and above*) *This slightly later Euphonon emulates Martin's dreadnought shape and employs quality woods for both front and back. Note the fine bird's-eye maple of the guitar's back (above).*

69

Euphonon c1940 (right) This large-bodied flat-top subtly emulates Gibson's SJ-200, introduced three years before. Of anecdotal interest is the fact that this guitar has newspaper photographs of Django Reinhardt stuck inside the body; certain authorities have suggested it might once have been owned by Reinhardt himself.

The Kinks mid 1960s (opposite) Chief Kink Ray Davies (right) makes a fashion statement with his new Fender flat-top. Sadly, brother Dave's Gibson Flying V (far left) proved a far better investment.

outward shape and approximate body construction of traditional flat-tops, but included many 'innovations.' These first Fender-branded acoustics employed several features intended to secure their association with the successful electrics, most notably the heel-less bolt-on neck and metal backplate, which in turn necessitated a larger-than-usual neck block inside the guitar's body. The feature gave Fender's marketing team an angle to pitch to players who already liked the playing feel, but was more likely an effort to ease assembly-line production.

In late 1963 Fender launched its flagship King flat-top (renamed Kingman in 1966), a 15⅝" round-shouldered dreadnought with natural-finished spruce top and mahogany back and sides (other finishes and wood options were available in years to come). It was accompanied by the Concert, Folk, and nylon-string Classic models. Through the 1960s the flat-top series swelled to include the smaller-bodied Malibu, Newporter, and Redondo, the 15⅜" Palomino, and the 12-string Villager and Shenandoah. Fender also sold some Swedish-made Tarrega classical guitars from about 1963 until the end of the decade.

Rossmeisl put no lack of effort into his work, introducing a 'psychedelic' dyed-wood Wildwood version of the Kingman and a patented interior aluminum body

support rod in 1967 and '68 respectively, but Fender's first acoustics never caught on. Models were photographed in the hands of endorsees Johnny Cash and Rick Nelson, but to most guitarists these acoustics looked pretty homely, and sounded even worse. By the end of 1971, each of these models had been discontinued.

Leo Fender had sold his company to CBS in 1965. After designing an equally strange Fender archtop, 1969's LTD model, Rossmeisl finally left the company two years later and returned to Germany, where he died in 1979. Leo Fender died in 1991.

Throughout the 1970s Fender kept a presence in the acoustic market with the F-Series flat-tops built in Japan, along with some Harmony-built guitars. The Japanese guitars were still low-cost models, but were generally better value – and more traditionally styled – than their misguided Californian predecessors.

Hard times all around for the guitar in the early 1980s, and for CBS-Fender in particular, rendered any meaningful acoustic efforts dead in the water. Following a management buyout in 1985, a young and downsized Fender Musical Instruments concentrated on rebuilding its reputation in the electrics field. As it regained a solid footing, however, acoustics again became an attractive avenue for the '90s and into the new millennium. While they may have been less distinctive than their 1960s forerunners, most of the Korean-built Fender acoustics competed better in their price bracket than ever before. Lines like the Grand Series (prefix GC for grand concert, GA for grand auditorium, and GD for grand dreadnought), Mini Jumbos (JG), and Dreadnought Series (DG as opposed to the confusingly similar GD) made up the widest range yet of Fender acoustic offerings, including many affordable solid-top and even all-solid-woods versions, and of course cutaway and electro-acoustic options.

FENDER

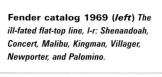

The Telecoustic and Stratacoustic thinline electros, however, did hark back to Fender's first own acoustic efforts. These guitars featured bolt-on necks, solid spruce tops on one-piece Tele and Strat-shaped fiberglas bodies, 'wobbly oval' soundholes, and Fishman Classic 4 electronics.

When Fender acquired Guild in 1995 it seemed the company had bought a way into quality acoustics, but by 2014 it had sold the brand on. A few years later, Fender's acoustic line included low and midprice Concert models, a few Parlor guitars, a good showing of Dreadnoughts and Triple-Os, and a new Paramount series of guitars with "premium materials and superior design."

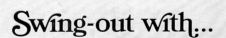

FLETA

Fleta instruments are highly sought-after guitars. Produced painstakingly in tiny quantities, their power and clarity have won over generations of concert players.

Ignacio Fleta had an individual approach to guitar-making. He trained first as a violin-maker in Barcelona, and when he turned to the guitar in the 1930s, he used a

Fender ad 1966 (above) *Some typical Fender mid-1960s publicity, with suitably hip tagline, continues to feed on the maker's success among the surf crowd as a T-Bird-load of groovy teens toy with their spanking new Fender acoustics. Let's hope they had some Fender electric guitars back home as well.*

Fender Palomino 1970 (right) *This model sat around the middle of Fender's acoustic line. Note the adjustable steel bridge saddles and heavy screwed-on pickguard – neither particularly tone-enhancing. The model vanished after just another year.*

Fender catalog 1969 (left) *The ill-fated flat-top line, l-r: Shenandoah, Concert, Malibu, Kingman, Villager, Newporter, and Palomino.*

Fender pricelist 1966-67 (above) *More of the apparently sure-fire girls-roadster-acoustics theme.*

distinctive technique: he built the soundbox first before attaching the neck. In appearance, however, his early instruments resembled those of Torres, which he knew well enough because he had repaired some in his workshop. But then, in 1955, he heard Segovia on the radio and dedicated himself seriously to making guitars, delivering the first to the maestro in 1957. At the same time, he moved away from the Torres model.

The new instruments used a distinctive strutting pattern designed to stiffen the treble side of the soundboard and produce a crisp, articulate sound at odds with much of the Spanish tradition. They also had their own, slightly plump look, thanks to broader dimensions in the waist and upper bout.

For many years, Fleta built the instruments in his apartment in the medieval heart of Barcelona, producing no more than 20 a year. His methods were idiosyncratic. He worked extensively on the soundboard, even filing and scraping inside the body after it was closed. Fleta soundboards can apparently display 20 different thicknesses as a result of the work they have undergone.

In the 1960s, Fleta made soundboards from the western red cedar introduced by Ramírez. Unlike spruce, cedar needs no playing in. Another departure from tradition was his willingness to use synthetic glue when he felt it was necessary. The bodies were finished in shellac and polished over the course of 15 days, while the tops were treated with Fleta's own patent varnish, which accounts for their distinctive orange hue.

By the time of his death, in 1977, the waiting list for an instrument had reached 15 years. That did not deter the Fleta enthusiasts, however. After Segovia came Alexandre Lagoya, John Williams, Alberto Ponce, Jorge Morel, Ichiro Suzuki, Carlos Bonell, Julian Byzantine, Nicola Hall and Slava Grigoryan. But when Williams moved on to newer makers, many followed his lead.

Fleta's sons Francisco and Gabriel joined him in the business, and the firm became known officially as Ignacio Fleta & Hijos (sons) in the 1960s. They continued the tradition after their father's death. Gabriel died in 2013 and his son Gabriel Jr continues the business today.

Fender ads mid 1970s (top of page) Promos for the Japanese-sourced Fender acoustics of 1974 (left) and Cumberland strings (right).

'Fleta Jazz Guitar' c1945 (right) Ignacio Fleta is said to have experimented toward the end of World War II with the construction of a few steel-string archtop guitars, of which this may be an example.

Fleta 1975 (left) Note the wider-than-usual waist of this Fleta classical guitar. It makes for a less elegant shape, but contributes to the design of a powerful concert guitar.

Back (above) The Fleta carries a richly hued back and sides of Indian rosewood, while the top (left) is of western red cedar.

F R A M U S

Framus guitars were made in Bavaria, Germany and are best remembered for their strong multi-laminate necks (and, on the company's electrics, some wildly exotic electronics). However, Framus – short for Franconian Musical Industry – began as a manufacturer of acoustic stringed instruments, and grew to be one of Europe's largest guitar-makers, producing many low to mid-grade flat-top and archtop guitars that fueled the 1960s guitar boom.

Framus was founded by Fred A. Wilfer, a Czechoslovakian immigrant who came to Erlangen in 1946. Wilfer opened a workshop and then recruited a community of some 70 Czech luthiers to make parts that were centrally assembled. In 1948 Framus consolidated into a single factory at Bubenreuth, then six years later built a bigger factory and acquired several other concerns, including its own sawmill in Austria for preparing spruce and maple, and a string-making factory.

Little information is available on the earliest Framus guitars, but they probably sported a rounded figure-eight shape recollecting many older European guitars. Precisely when Framus began making archtops is unknown, but they were probably in the company's line very early on. Single-cutaway models existed by the late 1950s,

Framus ad mid 1960s
Framus 12-strings of the folk-boom era.

and may have been available earlier. In the mid 1950s Wilfer met Fred C. Baas, who was attending the University of Heidelberg and whose father, William Baas, had started the Philadelphia Music Co. in 1939. As a result, in 1958 Philadelphia Music became the exclusive distributor of Framus guitars in the US, and around the same time Framus instruments were made available in the UK, imported through London-based distributor Dallas.

Soon the Framus line included a wide range of acoustics, including Student guitars with cute names such as Teenager and Sport, a number of Wander folk guitars, a huge range of classicals, and a large number of Plectrum (archtop) models, including the Missouri, Black Rose, and President – all quite fancy cutaway models. There was even a model endorsed by Josh White. Lower-grade models featured spruce and maple; better guitars used ribbon mahogany.

By 1963 the upscale models had super-thin, multi-laminated "Stiletto" necks. Framus also offered three lutes with either full or half bowl-backs, but outfitted with

Framus catalog 1960 (*left*)
These pages show the diverse Framus archtops available in Britain to power the early days of many a rock'n'roll combo.

Framus 5/98 King 1963 (*left*)
The body shape is a fairly standard, rounded jumbo, but the Framus flat-top's deep cutaway and multi-pointed pickguard make it distinctive. Note, too, the 'zero fret,' a mark of the breed.

Framus c1965 (*right*) *This small-bodied Framus was built in Bavaria. Note the string guide above the nut, made necessary by the strings' severe break-angle toward the sides of the instrument's headstock.*

guitar necks. These models continued to make up the Framus line – with minor changes – into the early 1960s.

In 1959 Framus expanded into Country and Western guitars with the Dix, a Gibson-style dreadnought, and the Doc Williams, a hefty 17" jumbo. These quickly grew to include more traditional square-shouldered dreadnoughts, including the famous sunburst Texan, and a cutaway jumbo called the King. Framus was also making a couple of slotted-head 12-strings by 1963, with a jumbo joining them the following year. Acoustic archtops were still offered, including the deluxe Florida, but with a diminished presence amid the other styles.

In 1965 the Framus acoustic line consolidated around its most popular models. Most steel-strings were now sunburst and had laminated tortoise 'batwing' pickguards. The only acoustic archtops left were the humble non-cutaway Studio model and a cutaway Sorella.

Quirky design trends took a firmer grip in 1967, when traditional pin bridges were replaced by large, pinless, rosewood mustache bridges with adjustable saddles, and headstocks became straight with string retainers. Models such as the Jumbo and a now zebra-wood Blue Ridge dreadnought got fancy pearl in black mastic rosettes and black-and-white marquetry trim. With the new bridges, these were pretty over-the-top looking guitars. Coolest (depending on your taste) was the Big 18, a 12/6 doubleneck dreadnought with the new fancy decoration. Also new was the Romance, a revival of the lute-guitar notion, with a pear-shaped body but flat back.

These esthetics defined Framus acoustics into the 1970s. The King cutaway jumbo returned by 1972 in a red sunburst with fancy inlays, and, consistent with the copy era, some models had engraved Gibson-style pickguards, but otherwise little was new. Framus found it increasingly difficult to compete with Asian exports and in 1977 closed its doors. The name was recently revived, including acoustic models.

FRANKLIN

Founded by luthier Nick Kukich, Franklin guitars were among the first to signal in the era of high-end, small-shop steel-strings. Kukich established the company (which, with the exception of an occasional apprentice, remained a one-man operation for most of its existence) in Franklin, Michigan, in 1976, and moved to Sandpoint, Idaho, shortly after – and it was here that he produced the majority of his guitars. Primarily known for OM-style guitars, Franklin is often credited for having significant impact in

Franklin SC270 1983 (right)
Nicholas Kukich completed this gently elegant 15" flat-top in Sandpoint, Idaho, on January 29 1983, and signed a handwritten note inside, adding the message: "A special one for J.C. Hecht. Thanks Chriss for helping thru hard times." A MIDI synthesiser-feed pickup has since been added: note the segmented bridge saddles.

Back (left) *The back and sides of this Franklin are made from highly figured solid koa.*

Froggy Bottom D Standard 1997 (right) *This dreadnought from the acclaimed Vermont-based guitar-maker has solid rosewood back and sides, a subtly cross-flecked spruce top, and a soundhole ring of herringbone-like colored wood inlays – a feature of this maker, along with the squatting-frog headstock inlay.*

the renewed interest in these instruments. John Renbourn and Stefan Grossman were Franklin's most famous advocates, and Grossman's vintage Stella 12-string as well as his Prairie State jumbo served as templates for the company's similarly designed models. Kukich moved to Seattle, Washington, then to Portland, Oregon, in the early 1990s, and later to Rocheport, Missouri.

FROGGY BOTTOM

Froggy Bottom was founded in 1970 by luthier Michael Millard, and has developed into one of the longest-running and most respected manufacturers of custom guitars. Millard learned the craft from Michael Gurian, and his early instruments shared many design traits with Gurian guitars, such as a pinned-mortise neck-joint (although currently-made Froggy Bottoms feature a bolt-on neck design). Although several apprentices moved through the Froggy Bottom shop, Millard worked mostly by himself until forming a partnership with Andy Mueller in 1994. Since then, the Chelsea, Vermont-based shop has employed up to four workers in addition to Millard and Mueller, producing about 125 guitars annually. Froggy Bottom offers flat-top steel-strings ranging from a small 12-fret Parlor to the baritone Model B. Although the company has a fixed line of models, its emphasis remains on custom orders, with choices including various woods, appointments, neck shape, and scale length. Froggy Bottom's ability to build a guitar to match individual players is underscored by the fact that its instruments are favored by guitarists as different as fingerstylist Will Ackermann, bluesman Paul Geremia, and pop star Duncan Sheik.

FURCH

This Czech Republic maker, headed by Frantisek Furch, began producing guitars (initially Ovation-influenced roundbacks) clandestinely in 1981, since private enterprise was illegal during the Communist era. After the 'Velvet Revolution' of 1989, however, the company was able to go legit and has made flourishing progress ever since, gaining a reputation for exacting quality across Europe and beyond. Since 1999 production has grown from 30 to 55 instruments per week. The line — covering traditional dreadnought, jumbo, grand auditorium, and OM styles — numbers well over

Froggy Bottom H12 Deluxe 2002 (*left*) *This evocative sunburst Froggy follows the approximate shape of Martin's pre-war 00, with a 12-fret neck and the maker's 'Deluxe' appointments, including gold Waverly tuners and abalone soundhole ring.*

Froggy Bottom ad c2002 (*above*) *A slot-head A12 breathes in that clean Vermont air.*

Furch D25-SR 2000 (*left*) *An all-solid-woods dreadnought model that exemplifies the quality work achieved by this Czech builder at relatively affordable prices.*

Furch F26 2001 (*above*) *Since becoming more widely available in western markets in the late 1990s, Furch guitars have made a name for themselves, in part thanks to artistically elaborate inlays, such as the original twist on the abalone tree-of-life motif seen on this flat-top jumbo.*

30 stock models (plus cutaway and electro options), from mid-price to high-ticket, graded by series according to timbers and cosmetics. The flagship 26-Series sports elaborate vine neck inlays.

Furch has also been a manufacturing source for some Stanford acoustics, a collaborative project started in 1997 with German acoustic-instrument distributor Pro Arte. Furch endorsers are mainly east European artists, but the list includes Kipper of Sting's band, and the Scorpions' Matthias Jabs, who also totes a custom-made Stanford D5 6/12 double-neck dreadnought electro.

FYLDE

Fylde is one of the most enduringly successful British acoustic brands, and at one time was the biggest. When in 1973 Roger Bucknall formed Fylde – named after the coast in north-west England where his first full-time workshop was – he had already been building guitars for years, with folk luminaries such as Gordon Giltrap, Martin Carthy, and Vin Garbutt among his pro-player clientele. Today that players roster reads like an A-list of international performers across many musical spheres, including Al DiMeola, Stanley Clarke, Arlen Roth, and Keith Richards. Bucknall's first design, the fingerstyle-

friendly Oberon, remains in the catalog today. Back in the late 1970s, having moved to Kirkham in Lancashire, Fylde was producing around 1,000 instruments a year, most models having Shakespearean names, like the still best-selling Orsino dreadnought and the small-bodied Ariel and Goodfellow.

In 1980, personal family tragedy and economic circumstances forced Bucknall to wind up the company, but he started again soon afterwards, and never made fewer than 100 guitars a year. Interestingly, his main money-earner through these difficult years was his 'sideline' of manufacturing snooker (pool) cues – a business he sold in 1992. Four years later Fylde moved its factory to Cumbria, where with a small team

Doves (*above*) *A Fylde flat-top for left-handed frontman Jimi Goodwin amid the alt-rockers' moody musings.*

Fylde Alchemist 2000 (*left*) *It may not be turning base matter to gold, but this jumbo-shaped cutaway converts a heap of solid wood into a toneful and artfully assembled flat-top.*

Fylde 'Single Malt' Alexander 2002 (*right*) *An example of the British maker's Alexander model from the 'Single Malt' series of guitars, made from discarded Scotch whisky barrels. Its top is solid Oregon pine, while back, sides and fingerboard are of American oak. The neck is a five-piece laminate of the two.*

produce around 300 instruments a year, which includes a line of mandolins, mandolas, and bouzoukis. One hallmark of Fylde guitars is the use of the zero fret – unusual to see on acoustic guitars, but always a friend of comfortable actions. The turn of the millennium saw new models – not least the cutaway jumbo Magician, the smaller Magician-influenced Alchemist, and the medium-bodied Alexander. This last model was also done in a 'Single Malt' special edition – as were the Ariel and the Touchstone mandolin – using American oak and Oregon pine from old whisky barrel staves and a washback fermenting vessel. Artist-model Fyldes include instruments for Eric Bibb, Gordon Giltrap and Ken Nicol.

GALLAGHER

Located in Wartrace, Tennessee, J.W. Gallagher & Son was one of the first small shops to successfully break into the steel-string flat-top market. Founded in 1965 by the late J.W. Gallagher, the company is now run by his son, Don Gallagher. Much of Gallagher's acceptance can be attributed to the fact that its dreadnought design has been used by flatpicking legend Doc Watson since the early '70s (and the company began offering a signature model in 1974), garnering much respect among bluegrass

players. However, while dreadnoughts such as the G-70 make up a large percentage of the approximately 75 guitars that the company builds each year, it also makes smaller body sizes, as well as a slope-shoulder signature model for Jim Hurst.

GARRISON

Garrison Guitars was launched in 2000, and has already become one of Canada's largest manufacturers of stringed instruments. Specializing in affordable steel-string flat-tops, the company's guitars are designed around a unique fiberglas bracing concept. Using projection-molding technology, the Griffiths Active Bracing System (named for the company's founder, Chris Griffiths) integrates the body's bracing, kerfing, and bridge-plate, as well as head and endblocks into a single component. A variety of solid tonewoods are then used to complete the instruments, which look just like 'regular' guitars on the outside. Currently, the company only offers a dreadnought size, with or without cutaways and optional electronics. Models range from the entry-

Giannini CraViola CRA6S 1970 (left) *The steel-string version of Brazilian maker Tranquillo Giannini's asymmetrical flat-top.*

Giannini Acoustic-Electric Classical 1977 (right) *A pair of magnetic pickups make this nylon-string guitar something of an oddity among a full and generally more conventional line of classicals offered by Giannini.*

Adam Cohen 1998 (far left) *Cohen thrums a CraViola 12-string ... with a few strings missing.*

Giannini ad 1974 (below left) *This promo highlights the CraViola's "more penetrating clearer sound that shades conventional guitars with overmastering timbre."*

level G-20 – which uses Canadian birch for its back and sides, along with a cedar top – to the top-of-the-line G-50. The firm was sold to Gibson in 2007, produced the shortlived Gibson Songmaker models, and later closed.

GAY

Like the technicolor, rhinestone-encrusted cowboy suits most famously associated with Nudie's Rodeo Tailors of Hollywood, Canadian Frank Gay (1920-1982) built gaudy guitars for several Grand Ole Opry stars of the 1950s. Good taste be damned. Gay's creations were big, loud (visually, anyway) and as exuberantly expansive as the Wild West. Gay – who was based in Edmonton, Alberta – used large blocks of pearl and abalone for edge trim, rococo cutout designs on headstocks, and stars' names (Johnny Horton, Carl Smith, Hank Snow, Faron Young and Webb Pierce) inlaid on the fingerboard, and his own on the pegheads. He favored highly figured maple bodies and broad expanses of black-white laminated pickguards and headstock overlays.

One surviving non-celebrity dreadnought eschews traditional bookmatched halves for top, back and sides, instead using multiple joined panels. As if his cowboy acoustics weren't enough to lock in his reputation for thinking outside the box, Gay (who was actually a fine classical player and teacher) was engaged by the artist ManWoman to do the luthierie work on three erotically-themed electric guitars that ManWoman designed. Underneath Gay's personal chàrm and the exuberance of his guitars were personal problems, including alcoholism. Gay had a reputation for uneven workmanship, which longtime friend ManWoman attributes to drinking bouts.

GIANNINI

The name Giannini most often conjures up visions of highly figured rosewood and the unusual CraViola guitars. Founded when Tranquillo Giannini began building handmade guitars in Sao Paulo, Brazil in 1900, Giannini was a major Brazilian manufacturer by the 1930s. With the folk revival of the 1960s, Giannini began exporting folk (auditorium), dreadnought and classical guitars. Most sported native jacaranda de bahia rosewood, and by the mid 1970s exotic woods such as pau ferro and later morado.

Most distinctive was the asymmetrical cutaway guitar from the late 1960s called the CraViola, including classical and 12-string versions. (Japanese Westbury-brand copies appeared in 1985.) Recent lines include the conventional Performance and Study series and a full range of classical models.

Doc Watson 1980s *The flatpicking virtuoso is a long-time endorser of Gallagher guitars.*

GIBSON

Orville Gibson invented the archtop guitar in the 1890s, and the company that bore his name went on to lead the development and refinement of the archtop as it is known today. In addition, when Gibson began making flat-top guitars in the late 1920s, the company quickly became one of the leading makers. The Gibson SJ-200 flat-top, introduced in the 1930s, is still the company's most famous acoustic, and it is the flagship of an acoustic line that now consists almost exclusively of flat-tops.

Orville Gibson was born in 1856 in the small settlement of Chateaugay in upstate New York, near the Canadian border. Some time in the 1880s he relocated to Kalamazoo, Michigan, and began building instruments while he supported himself with jobs in retail establishments and restaurants.

In designing his mandolins – which were the most popular fretted instruments of the day – and guitars, Orville subscribed to the belief that wood should be unstressed (unbent), and to that end he appropriated from the violin the concept of a top that was carved into an arched shape, which made it virtually self supporting and requiring very little bracing. His one and only patent, however, was granted for a mandolin that, ideally, would have had its rim, back and neck carved from a single piece of wood,

Gibson Style O 1916
Before the more familiar look of the L-5 and its descendants dominated the archtop world, the oval-holed Style O – introduced in 1903 – was Gibson's leading archtop. The elaborate scrolled upper horn and flat cutaway appeared by about 1907, but 'The Gibson' logo wasn't added to the model's headstock until after 1916.

Gibson Catalog c1908 *This page shows the L-1 in its original style, as seen from its debut in 1902.*

even though he admitted in his patent application that the design was impractical.

Orville's earliest surviving instrument is an unusual 10-string guitar-mandolin creation dated 1894. He also made a highly ornamented harp guitar, a large zither, and one guitar with an elaborate pearl butterfly inlaid into the top below the bridge, but these were apparently experimental showcase pieces for his work. The few other guitars and mandolins that survive are relatively plain instruments. The back and sides of the guitars were made of walnut, at a time when the vast majority of guitars (and mandolins, too) were made of rosewood. Orville carved out the back, but he left it flat across the middle – just the opposite of what the Gibson company would soon establish as the 'standard' carving pattern, which is rather flat around the rims and arched across the middle of the back. The tops were carved out of spruce and were not as highly arched as contemporary archtops. The headstocks had a rounded upper edge and were so wide that they are known today as 'paddle heads.' Some had a star-and-moon pearl inlay, the

significance of which in Orville's life is unknown. The guitars were finished with a dark brown, walnut stain.

After the arched top, the most radical new feature of Orville's guitars was their size, which was noticeably larger than those of his contemporaries. Orville's guitars measured as much as 18" across the lower bout at a time when Martin's largest size, the 00, was less than 14½" wide. Orville's instruments were also stronger – designed to withstand the pressure of steel strings, which were the standard strings on mandolin but not on the typical guitar of the 1890s. Although they may have lacked the brilliant tone of instruments designed to be played in a parlor, the power generated by these large bodies and steel strings made them especially appealing to professional musicians, who had to play for large crowds without amplification.

By 1902, demand for 'The Gibson' had increased beyond the manufacturing capacity of Orville's one-man shop. According to Gibson company lore, a music teacher from New York state wrote Orville asking for a price and delivery date for 100

Gibson L-Artist 1906 (*far right*) *The 'L' prefix on early Gibson archtops denotes round soundhole models, but 'Artist' was an unofficial name adopted by collectors to indicate instruments with more extravagant features than were standard, such as the fancy fingerboard inlays seen here.*

Gibson Style O 1905 (*center*) *The earliest form of the oval-soundholed Style O is readily identified by its 'paddle' headstock.*

Gibson Style O 1906 (*left*) *For a brief period around 1906, Gibson made its Style O model with this kind of enlarged 18" body.*

mandolins. Orville quoted a reasonable price but said the delivery time would be 100 years. The teacher, one Lewis A. Williams, was intrigued rather than put off by the reply, and he journeyed to Kalamazoo to join a group of businessmen — including a Kalamazoo music store owner and three local lawyers — who sought to capitalize on the booming demand for The Gibson. They bought the rights to Orville's name and his patent on November 10, 1902, through an agreement creating the Gibson Mandolin-Guitar Mfg. Co., Ltd. Orville was never a partner, but he was given stock in the company and hired as a consultant. He became disenchanted within a few months, however, and except for receiving a monthly stipend until his death in 1918, he was never again involved with the Gibson company.

The new company immediately published a catalog that included two lines of archtop guitars: the Style O series, with an oval soundhole, and the Style L with a conventional round hole. Style O was available in several degrees of ornamentation, ranging from the plain O and O-1 to the fancy O-3, which was bound in alternating pieces of white and green pearl. In addition, each level of ornamentation was offered in three sizes: 12", 13" or 16" wide. The Style L offering was organized in similar fashion. Curiously, the guitars (as well as the mandolins) were described as having

maple back and sides, but all surviving examples were made from Orville's choice of wood — walnut. Gibson would soon switch to birch, which is much closer to maple than walnut, but the changeover to maple wouldn't be complete until the early 1920s.

The first catalog also included two versions of what would become one of the dinosaurs of the guitar world, the harp guitar — an instrument with a standard guitar neck and an additional framework (or as some makers designed it, with the entire body extended) to accommodate a set of sub-bass strings. In theory, the harp guitar seemed like a good idea. There are many musical situations in which a guitarist could use a lower bass string: to play a full D chord, for example (the standard guitar's lowest string is tuned to E). Also, an open bass string — one that did not require fretting with the left hand — could be useful. The harp guitar provided these strings, as many as a dozen of them, usually tuned chromatically in half-steps, starting a few steps above the low E-string.

Gibson wasn't the only maker of harp guitars, but Gibson promoted them more heavily than any other maker. After the company's first catalog, subsequent catalogs always devoted the center spread to the Style U harp guitar (there had originally been a Style R as well). Lewis Williams, the original sales manager and one of the founding

Gibson Style U Harp Guitar 1906 (far right) *The ten sympathetic strings on the headstock extension of the so-called 'harp' guitar were designed to add bass accompaniment to the normal playing of the six-string neck, rather than to be played in the manner of an actual harp.*

O.H. Gibson 1898 (near right) *This guitar made by Orville Gibson himself illustrates the groundbreaking craftsmanship of the father of the archtop guitar. The one-piece carved top required no internal braces.*

Big Bill Broonzy c1935 (left) *Delta blues hollerer Broonzy poses with a Gibson Style O built between about 1918 and 1923.*

partners, wrote page after page of florid catalog prose on Gibson instruments, including a memorable essay on the harp guitar entitled *When gray hairs applaud, progress may well ask "What have I done amiss"* in which he compared the six-string guitar to the harpsichord and the harp guitar to the pianoforte.

Gibson's promotional efforts resulted in a fair number of harp guitars sold, but the instrument was large, unwieldy and expensive. It required what felt to a guitarist like an awkward stretch of the right hand to make use of the extra strings, and it never caught on. Gibson continued to catalog the harp guitar into the 1930s, but the last one was probably made in the early 1920s.

Two of the partners in the Gibson company were musicians – sales manager Williams, and Sylvo Reams, the music store owner who was Gibson's general manager. Williams was particularly active in improving designs, and the company's instruments almost immediately began to evolve. Among the first changes was an increase in the neck-set angle so that the bridge was raised, thereby increasing the pressure of the strings on the top and producing more volume. This also necessitated a separate tailpiece to anchor the strings. Orville had used a standard (flat-top style) bridge pin design, and the new Gibson tailpiece incorporated bridge pins in a

Gibson Style U Harp Guitar 1912 (left) This later, less elaborately decorated Style U shows changes to the designs of the bridge, tailpiece, and bass-string tuners when compared with the example on the previous page.

Gibson L-4 1924 (right) This 'snakehead' L-4 bears similarities to Gibson's first pre-scroll Style Os.

Duke Ellington Orchestra c1941 (opposite page) In this jam session from the early 1940s, Eddie Condon plays what appears to be a Gibson TG-7 four-string tenor guitar from the mid 1930s.

crosspiece of tortoiseshell-grained celluloid. Eventually the pins would be eliminated and ball-end strings would anchor through slots in the 'trapeze' tailpiece. Early models also had a pickguard inlaid into the top, but by 1908 an elevated pickguard had been developed and implemented. Through these first few years of the Gibson company, the O-series was distilled down to a single 16" model, and the L-series consisted only of the L-1 and L-3, both 13½" wide.

As the company's name suggests, Gibson's focus was on the most popular fretted instrument of the day – the mandolin. The company helped to create demand for its product by selling direct to mandolin teachers and setting up a sales force of 'teacher-agents,' bypassing traditional music stores. Gibson encouraged the formation of mandolin clubs and orchestras, even publishing musical arrangements and 'how-to' manuals for organizing a mandolin group. And if all the members of a group played Gibson instruments, Gibson would publish a photograph of the group in a catalog or advertisement under the caption "Every One a Gibson-ite."

In the grand Gibson vision, the guitar was a member of the mandolin family, and this association was nowhere so obvious as in the redesigned Style O model of 1908, which would be called the Style O Artist guitar within a few years. Still one of the most striking guitar designs ever conceived, the new Style O featured a scrolled upper bass bout, inspired by the scroll on Gibson's F-style mandolins (one of Orville's designs). The upper treble bout came straight out from the neck at a 90-degree angle and curled up slightly into a point. Earlier versions of the Style O had had the top filed down where the upper treble bout met the fingerboard, to provide easier access to the higher frets, but the Style O had the body 'cut away,' providing free access to the 15th fret at a time when most guitars had only 12 frets clear of the body. The modern 'cutaway' body shape wouldn't appear until the late 1930s, when the guitar had become the most popular fretted instrument and players truly needed the higher-fret access, but the Style O had it in 1908, providing function along with its stylish form.

Although some early Gibson-company guitars have survived measuring 18" across, the Style O was the largest catalogued model at 16", which was still a relatively large guitar by industry standards. Martin's new 000 body measured only 15" wide. In 1912, no doubt in response to a demand for a large Gibson without the fancy appointments and high price of the Style O Artist, Gibson introduced a 16" guitar with a standard, symmetrical body shape, calling it the L-4, even though it had the oval hole that had previously distinguished the O-series models from the L series.

Seger Ellis & His Embassy Orchestra 1929 (*below*) Eddie Lang plays an L-5 here, and had played an L-4 before it. Tommy and Jimmy Dorsey are also pictured (top row, far left and far right respectively).

The L-4 became the standard-bearer of Gibson's guitar line – the basic, representative, professional-quality Gibson – through the mandolin craze, through the tenor banjos of the Jazz Age, and into the early years of the guitar era. When tenor banjoists began switching over to guitar in the late 1920s, they did not reach for the f-hole archtops that would dominate the guitar world in the 1930s. Instead, they reached for an L-4. One of the first great guitarists of that period, Eddie Lang, is usually associated with Gibson's first f-hole model, the L-5, but a photo of Lang from 1927 with the Adrian Rollini band shows a banjo and an L-4. Similarly, photos of Duke Ellington's band in the late 1920s show Fred Guy sometimes holding a banjo, other times holding an L-4.

The L-4 was not a particularly fancy instrument. In fact, outside of the occasional custom instrument, no Gibson would qualify as fancy. A fleur-de-lis peghead inlay identified the highest level of guitars, the Style O and L-4. A bound fingerboard and a strip or two of marquetry encircling the soundhole were the only other signs of a high-end instrument. There were none of the ornamental pearl fingerboard-inlay patterns that had characterized expensive banjos and Italian-style mandolins at the turn of the century. And there was good reason for that, as Lewis Williams explained in prose in

Gibson HG-24 1929 (*right*) *The four f-holes and extra internal body wall on this short-lived model generate much interest, but its historical importance derives more from the fact that it is the first Gibson with a 16" body of dreadnought proportions and the neck joining at the 14th fret.*

Gibson L-5 1929 (*left*) *By early 1929 the L-5 had replaced its simple dot fingerboard markers with these pearl (or pearloid) blocks.*

VITAPHONE # 1504

a Gibson catalog that warned against erysipelas, an ugly skin condition. He noted that there was no glue yet invented that would affix pearl to ebony, so that fancy fingerboard inlays were doomed to fall out.

In the early 1920s photos of Hawaiian-style guitarists – with their instruments held in their lap – began to appear in catalogs. A craze for Hawaiian music had started in 1915 when the territory of Hawaii featured musicians at its pavilion at the Panama-Pacific Exposition in San Francisco. Hawaiian-style guitar playing required steel strings, and Gibson was the only major manufacturer at that time whose guitars were designed for steel strings. Gibson quickly offered Hawaiian kits, which included picks, a steel bar and a nut extender (to raise the strings higher off the fingerboard), but it would be the end of the decade before Gibson would design a guitar specifically for Hawaiian playing.

The rising popularity of Hawaiian music was certainly a factor in the slow but steady rise of the guitar, from out of the shadow of the mandolin and the tenor banjo, into the spotlight in the late 1920s. However, in the years immediately following World War I, Gibson needed more help than the demand for Hawaiian guitars could provide. Gibson had been, and still was, primarily a mandolin company, and the

Gibson L-C Century 1934
(*right*) *Along with the L-1 and L-00, the L-C was part of Gibson's line of L-style flat-tops of the 1930s, and was also the flat-top representative of the special Century models.*

The Carter Family 1928
(*below*) *Maybelle Carter – seated between A.P. and Sara – clutches the L-5 she moved up to when the group started having some success. Just the year before, she had still been playing her Gibson L-1.*

mandolin suddenly was dying. The new music was loud and raucous, and the mandolin was no part of it. A new instrument, the tenor banjo, was the favored child in the jazz bands that played the most popular music of the day, and Gibson didn't make a banjo. To make matters worse, Gibson's board of directors, which by the late 1910s included no musicians except for Williams (who was now general manager), carried on as if the company were still enjoying its prewar prosperity, distributing dividends on profits that no longer existed.

Under Williams' leadership, Gibson made several stabs in new directions. The first Gibson banjo was introduced in 1918, and it was decidedly inferior to those of the competition, who had been making banjos since the glory years of the minstrel or 'classic' banjo era of the late 1800s. In 1919, Gibson swallowed its pride and produced some inexpensive flat-top mandolins, to be sold exclusively to servicemen at military-post exchanges. Williams carefully worded the promotional material to explain that this mandolin was made by Gibson but it was 'not a Gibson.' With the mandolin came a footnote in Gibson guitar history: Gibson's first flat-top guitar. The GY or 'Army-Navy' model was essentially a plain, flat-top version of the lowest Gibson, the 13½" L-1. Although the Army-Navy mandolins are fairly common, the

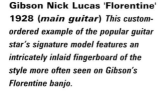

Gibson Nick Lucas 'Florentine' 1928 (*main guitar*) *This custom-ordered example of the popular guitar star's signature model features an intricately inlaid fingerboard of the style more often seen on Gibson's Florentine banjo.*

Transition Logo 1928–'34 (*above*) *The change varies according to model, but the famed logo slowly lost its 'The,' along with a little of its antiquated look.*

Gibson L-75 1932 (*right*) *The archtop representative of the Century line is an extremely rare bird; just two years later, the L-75 would become a far less ornate instrument.*

guitars are quite rare. In 1919 Williams apparently decided that Gibson should do what it did best, and that was to make mandolins – a decision that would ultimately have as profound an effect on the guitar world as it would on mandolins. He hired Lloyd A. Loar, a mandolin virtuoso who also had some new ideas for instrument design. Loar would hold various positions during his five-year tenure, but the most important one was that of 'acoustic engineer.' Williams' plan was for Loar to develop a new and improved mandolin – a whole family of mandolin instruments, actually, that would be so great as to rekindle interest in mandolins and revive the company. As always, Gibson thought of the guitar as a member of the mandolin family, so Loar's new Style 5 line included a guitar: the L-5. Interestingly, Loar also designed his mandocello, the K-5, with a guitar body. Except for its four pairs of strings, it is the same instrument as the L-5 guitar.

Loar's Style 5 Master Models debuted in 1922, complete with an extra label signed by Loar inside every guitar, saying that he had personally inspected the instrument. He had refined many features, the most obvious of which was the replacement of the traditional round or oval soundhole with a pair of violin-style f-holes – a logical advancement of Orville Gibson's original carved-top concept. With the f-holes came a pair of 'tone bars' – top braces that ran lengthwise in the manner of a violin tone bar. The headstock received a narrower, more elegant design. The finish – a dusky amber-to-brown sunburst – was called Cremona brown, a reference to the Italian home of Stradivarius violins. One element of fine violins that the early L-5s lacked, however, was a back of highly figured maple. Although a nice two-piece, book-matched back would eventually become a standard feature on archtop guitars, these first L-5s, like most of Gibson's guitars at the time, were constructed of birch. Within a short time, however, the changeover was made and Gibson used maple.

The L-5 sported two recent improvements that set Gibson apart from other makers: the adjustable truss-rod in the neck and the height-adjustable bridge. Ted McHugh, a longtime Gibson employee, and Lewis Williams collaborated on the height-adjustable bridge that appeared in late 1921. Gibson guitars had had moveable bridges since the early years of the company. This allowed for adjustments in string length, which made for better intonation, but there were still a number of reasons that players would want to adjust the height of the bridge: to lower it for easier play, to raise it to avoid string buzzing or achieve more volume, to move it up or down in response to changes in climate that affect playability. With a fixed-height bridge, the only solution was to have a new bridge made. Gibson's bridge solved the problem by mounting the bridge saddle (the part that the strings make contact with) on a simple pair of threaded rods. The simple turn of a nut on either end of the saddle raised it or lowered it.

McHugh alone invented the adjustable rod, and it debuted in late 1922. At low tension, it allowed the neck to bow slightly in response to the tension of the strings, which was the most desirable neck shape for keeping the strings low without buzzing against the frets. If the bow were too great, a small turn of a nut (accessible on the

Gibson L-10 Double-Neck 1936 (right) *An exceedingly rare beast, this L-10 with six-string and tenor necks was custom ordered by Art Pruneau, and is believed to be the only archtop double-neck that Gibson ever built, as well as their first f-hole guitar in a natural finish.*

Gibson L-12 1933 (left) *For its first two years, the L-12 was given delicately ornate headstock and fingerboard position marker inlays of a type not often associated with Gibson guitars. This example from the year after the model's debut has a 16"-wide body, but by 1934 it would be increased to 17".*

Alexis Korner 1961 (opposite) *The influential early British blues guitarist plays a Gibson L-1 at the Jazz Shows Club, 100 Oxford Street, London, with Bob Guthrie on drums and Little Brother Montgomery on piano and vocals.*

Benny Goodman 1940 (*below*)
*The bandleader shows off his two
guitarists: Charlie Christian with
electric ES-150 (left) and Arnold
Covarrubias with Super 400 (right).*

headstock with a small socket wrench) made a great difference in playability. The end of the rod was covered with a bell-shaped piece of celluloid, a shape that has since been trademarked by Gibson. With a few exceptions, the adjustable truss-rod has been installed in every guitar that Gibson has made since then.

These two patented adjustment features not only made unplayable or uncomfortably set up instruments once again playable, they also allowed players to set up their guitars to suit their personal preferences. Both inventions became industry standards. Virtually every major maker today uses some sort of neck adjustment system, and the height-adjustable bridge design is standard on all acoustic archtops.

Although the Loar-signed L-5 represented a monumental step forward in acoustic guitar design, it would never be as revered as Loar's F-5 mandolins, which are considered to be the finest carved-top mandolins ever made. The L-5 guitar still had a few refinements and improvements ahead, but those would have to wait until there was more interest in the guitar among musicians. In 1922, the year the L-5 appeared, a trumpeter named Louis Armstrong journeyed from New Orleans to Chicago – only 100 miles from Gibson in Kalamazoo – to join Joe 'King' Oliver's band. Armstrong's

Gibson Super 400 1935 (*left*)
*With its formidable 18"-wide body, the
Super 400 – introduced just a year
before this example was made – set
the standard for large-bodied archtop
guitars, and inspired many rival makers
to 'advance' their body sizes soon after.*

Gibson Super 400 1942 (*right*)
*By 1940 Gibson's premier archtop had
acquired both a wider upper bout and
parallel-bracing to replace its original
X-bracing. By the time production was
halted for the war in 1942, Gibson had
made 401 non-cutaway Super 400s in
sunburst, but this is one of only seven
natural-finish examples.*

New York 1939 (*below*) *Takin' five behind Harlem's Apollo Theater: Spirits Of Rhythm guitarist Teddy Bunn (left) cradles his Super 400 amid fellow players Al Norris and Ulysses Livingston (right).*

GIBSON

jazz music would rule the 1920s, and the tenor banjo reigned as the rhythm instrument of those first jazz bands. It was too strong a force to be slowed by Gibson's Style 5 mandolin family. With the commercial failure of the Style 5 models, Lewis Williams resigned in late 1923 and Loar followed at the end of 1924. Loar's efforts had not all been for nought, however. He had also designed a Style 5 banjo, and although it is not regarded today as a classic design, it brought Gibson banjos up to a professional level and allowed Gibson to be competitive in the banjo market for the first time.

Coincidentally, with the appearance of the L-5 in 1922 there came a distant sound of the future of the guitar. It probably went unnoticed in Kalamazoo, but in a recording studio in the New York area, a young musician named Nick Lucas was having a hard time keeping the sharp attack of his tenor banjo from making the stylus of a recording machine jump out of the grooves. To solve the problem, he switched to guitar. He was an accomplished guitarist, and he recorded a solo number called 'Pickin' The Guitar.' The tune sounds a little stilted to today's ears — more of a semi-classical piece than a hot guitar solo — but it was an omen for the guitar as well as for Gibson.

With the departure of Loar, Williams, and an interim general manager, Gibson's board appointed Guy Hart — an accountant who had joined the company as an in-house auditor — to the general manager's post. He had no musical background and was probably seen as a temporary caretaker, someone to keep an eye on the bottom line until an experienced manager could be found, but Hart would have the longest tenure of any head of Gibson, leading the company through the Depression and into a golden era of acoustic guitar design.

For Gibson, the beginning of the guitar era — when Gibson first began thinking of the guitar as an instrument with its own voice rather than as a member of the mandolin family — is marked by the lowliest of models. Throughout Gibson's history, there was no lower guitar, in the company's official opinion, than a flat-top, but in 1926 Gibson offered its first one (the GY Army-Navy flat-top of 1919 notwithstanding). The L-1, one of the company's original archtop models, had been discontinued in 1925, and the name was appropriated for the new flat-top.

The L-1 flat-top, like the archtop, was only 13½" wide and not very impressive. The top bracing on early examples varied from the lateral ("ladder") configuration of most cheap guitars to an H-pattern with two lengthwise braces and a cross-brace between the soundhole and the bridge. Gibson's goal seems to have been to keep the top from

pulling up, regardless of sound quality. The best indication of Gibson's disdain for the flat-top was the lack of a truss-rod in the earliest L-1s. Through no effort on Gibson's part, the L-1 would become famous a half-century later as the guitar that blues legend Robert Johnson held in a studio photograph from the mid 1930s. It has the circular lower body shape typical of Gibson's archtops – a shape that would later be copied for Gibson's most famous flat-top, the J-200.

Gibson introduced a second flat-top in 1926 that was even lowlier than the L-1. In place of the L-1's ebony fingerboard, this model had 'ebonized' or black-stained wood, probably pearwood. In nomenclature, there was nowhere to go but down, and the new model was dubbed the L-0. Within two years the L-0 was further distinguished from the L-1 by a mahogany top.

Gibson's new flat-tops were no doubt developed in response to the growing popularity of the guitar. Although Gibson pursued the banjo market aggressively in the late 1920s, introducing three fancy new models in 1927 and its all-time fanciest, the All American, in 1930, and although the rise of the guitar is generally assigned to the early 1930s, when the Dixieland jazz bands evolved into the big bands, the level of guitar activity was rising in the late 1920s. Lonnie Johnson, who set the standard for

Gibson Super 300 1952 (right)
After WWII, Gibson introduced the Super 300 at the same time as it brought back the Super 400. The former also had an 18" body, but was given less elaborate trim – including unbound f-holes, squared fingerboard end, and 'double parallelogram' position markers – and sold at a lower price to match.

Gibson Super 400C 1940 (left)
The cutaway version of the big archtop joined the line in 1939.

future waves of blues guitarists, had begun recording in 1925. Eddie Lang, who would become the first jazz guitar virtuoso, had made solo recordings as early as 1927. Hawaiian music received a boost from the new, higher-volume resonator guitars introduced by the National company in 1927. Also in 1927, the Victor company released the first recordings of the Carter Family and Jimmie Rodgers, establishing the foundation of country music. Maybelle Carter provided a distinctive solo guitar accompaniment for the Carter trio, starting on an L-1 but switching to an L-5 as soon as they had their first taste of success.

The guitar was making deep inroads into mainstream popular music, too, by the late 1920s, thanks in part to Nick Lucas. The man who had committed the first hot guitar solo to wax in 1922 had become one of the leading pop singers, known as 'crooners,' and he accompanied himself on guitar. Gibson had almost gone bankrupt trying to catch up to established banjo makers in the early 1920s, and there was formidable, established competition in the promising guitar market. Looking for an advantage, Gibson enlisted the endorsement of Nick Lucas, first making a custom guitar for him and then, in 1928, introducing an official Nick Lucas model, complete with a photo of the singing star on the label.

The original Lucas model was the same small size as the L-1 – 13½" across the body – but it was significantly deeper. Through the next five years, Gibson seemed to be unable to make up its mind about the Lucas model. It gained a wider body and had a variety of features, including archtop-style bridge and tailpiece, elevated pickguard, 12, 13 and finally 14-fret neck, and a body of maple, mahogany or rosewood. The deep body remained constant, however, and gave the Lucas a fuller tone than other smallbody flat-tops. The rosewood-body version with flat-top-style pin bridge (made for a short time in 1933) was especially powerful and may well be the finest smallbody flat-top Gibson ever made.

In 1929 Lucas appeared on the New York stage in the review *Gold Diggers Of Broadway*, performing his smash hit 'Tip Toe Through The Tulips' and accompanying himself on his Gibson Special, as Gibson called the signature model. The biggest recording star of the day played a Gibson. It was a dream come true for a guitar company, and Gibson immediately introduced the L-2 flat-top, which fell between the Lucas and L-1 in ornamentation.

Also in 1929, Gibson introduced a curious trio of Hawaiian models – curious not only because of their odd design but also because virtually all surviving examples are

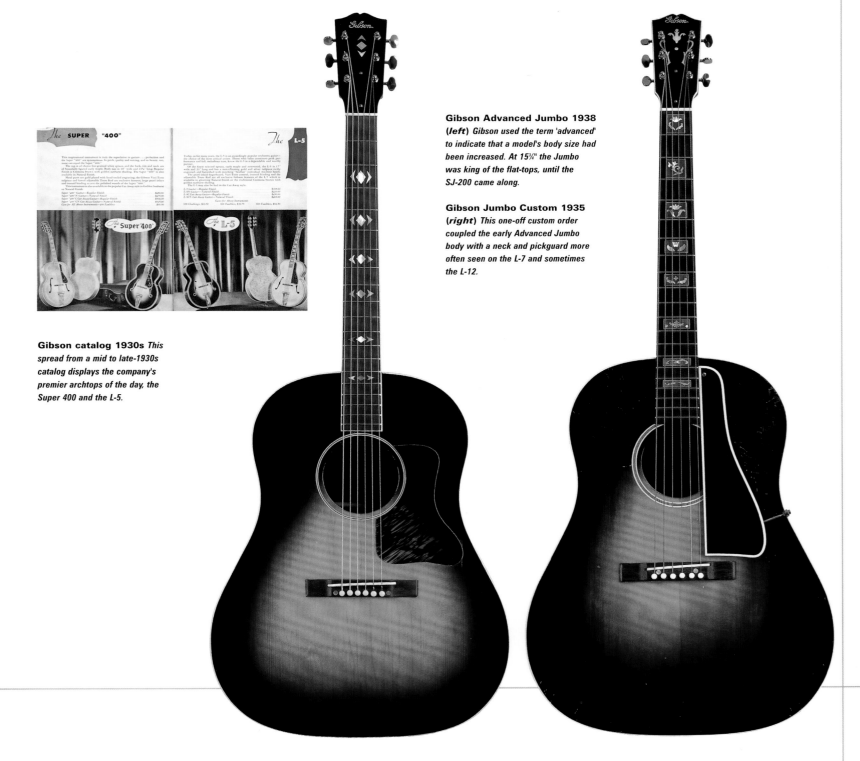

Gibson catalog 1930s *This spread from a mid to late-1930s catalog displays the company's premier archtops of the day, the Super 400 and the L-5.*

Gibson Advanced Jumbo 1938 (*left*) *Gibson used the term 'advanced' to indicate that a model's body size had been increased. At 15¾" the Jumbo was king of the flat-tops, until the SJ-200 came along.*

Gibson Jumbo Custom 1935 (*right*) *This one-off custom order coupled the early Advanced Jumbo body with a neck and pickguard more often seen on the L-7 and sometimes the L-12.*

set up for standard play rather than Hawaiian. The new HG models (HG for Hawaiian Guitar) had a flat top with a standard round soundhole and four additional f-holes in the top. Inside they had an inner baffle that followed the contour of the body to create almost a double-bodied instrument. Ironically, the f-holes and the baffle were the guitars' least noteworthy features, when viewed in the overall history of Gibson. The

most important features were their size and shape. They were larger than the existing Gibson flat-tops – two of them were 14¾" wide, the third was 16" wide – and all three had a new body shape, with a thicker waist than any other style of Gibson or of any other maker (except for some contract guitars Martin had made for the Ditson company more than a decade earlier). Although the HG series made only one catalog

SUPER JUMBO - 200

This "King of the flat tops" was created for professional entertainers who require an instrument with a full, rich, round tone and an unrivalled appearance.

Body size is 17" wide, and 21" long and 4½" deep. Back, rim and neck are beautifully figured curly maple with a fine spruce top. Finish is a lustrous cremona brown, highlighted and shaded to a radiant sunburst.

Rosewood fingerboard has artistic pearl inlays, celluloid-bound edges and side position marks. Brown celluloid guard-plate is elegantly decorated and etched with colored designs.

Other features include burnished gold plated Kluson Sealfast individual machine heads and specially designed pin bridge.

Requires No. 600 Faultless plush lined case.

SOUTHERNER JUMBO

An excellent instrument for the player desiring a deep, brilliant tone at a moderate price.

Body size 16" wide, 20¼" long and 4¼" deep. Back, rim and neck are selected mahogany with spruce top. Finished in a dark red mahogany with golden sunburst shading on top. Rosewood fingerboard has pearl inlays, is celluloid bound and marked for positions.

Equipped with individual machine heads and the Gibson Adjustable Truss Rod.

Requires No. 514 Faultless flannel lined or No. 118 Challenge case.

Gibson SJ-200 1937 (*left*) As it states on the headstock, this SJ-200 was 'Custom Built for Ray Whitley' the singing cowboy, and served as the prototype for the model, which was widely available just a year later.

Kitty Wells (*above*) The country singer posses with an unusual dreadnought-size Gibson that has features like the larger SJ-200.

appearance, the smaller models led the way for Gibson to increase the existing flat-tops to 14¾" wide, and the 16" model served as the prototype for Gibson's classic 'round-shouldered dreadnought' design.

With a selection of high-quality 14¾" flat-tops and a vision of the 16" guitars on the horizon, Gibson should have been off and running in its quest to capture the entire guitar market. However, the stock market crashed in October 1929, bringing on the Great Depression and changing Gibson's goal to mere survival. General manager Guy Hart had once worked for a woodworking company, and when Gibson's instrument sales plummeted, he had the workforce manufacture wooden toys. He also initiated production of cheaper guitars, which were either made under contract for distributors with other brand names or marketed by Gibson using the Kalamazoo brand, thereby maintaining the integrity and reputation of Gibson as a maker of high quality guitars.

The Depression did not stop people from making music, nor did it stop music from

Gibson J-200 1954 (*far right*) *Also known as the J-200 or Super Jumbo, this guitar has been Gibson's top-of-the-line flat-top throughout its long, distinguished career. Post-WWII models like this one were built with maple back and sides.*

Gibson SJ-100 1939 (*near right*) *Introduced the year after its upmarket brother, the short-lived SJ-100 featured mahogany back and sides rather than rosewood, had simple dot position markers, and featured a distinctive 'stair-step-sided' peghead.*

Lonnie Johnson 1946 *(opposite) Seen here with Blind John Davis, Johnson plays a latter-era J-100, which no longer features the distinctive 'stair-step' headstock.*

evolving. The Charleston – the wild, arm-swinging dance of the 1920s – gave way to the elegance of the fox trot or the rather more sophisticated abandonment of the jitterbug, as jazz bands became dance bands and the smoother, more versatile guitar began to replace the tenor banjo. The conventional flat-top guitar had a richer chordal capability than the four-string banjo, but it was not as adept at filling the banjo's rhythm role, simply because it was not as loud or as 'cutting' in tone.

Guitarists began to find that cutting tone in the maple-bodied L-5, Gibson's only f-hole model. In 1929 Gibson added a second f-hole model, the L-10. The L-5's dot inlays were changed to large pearl blocks, and the L-10 was given dots. (At this point, Gibson's nomenclature system, with higher numbers indicating more expensive guitars, was abandoned.) A year later, yet another f-hole model, the L-12, was introduced, featuring fingerboard inlay of delicate curlicues enclosed in the outline of

Gibson J-200 1952 (*right*) *This example was made with the scarce 'blonde' finish.*

Gibson J-45 c1947 (*left*) *This relatively cheaper model from Gibson's Jumbo line was aimed directly at one of the company's big competitors: the Martin dreadnought.*

a rectangle. In 1930, a fourth model, the L-7, joined the line, with varied-pattern fingerboard inlay and a fleur-de-lis on the headstock, a symbol that in earlier years had been reserved for the top-of-the-line models. All of the new Gibsons had maple back and sides, and all were 16" wide, like the L-5.

Gibson had invented the archtop guitar, and through 1930 it had the market for f-hole archtops all to itself. Suddenly, though not surprisingly, there was competition. Epiphone, a New York company that had been a leading banjo maker in the 1920s, launched a full-fledged attack on Gibson in 1931 with a full line of archtops called 'Masterbilt,' a name with an obvious similarity to Gibson's Master Model designation for the L-5. Epiphone introduced seven new models all at once, offering a variety of sizes – the largest being ⅜" larger than Gibson's 16-inchers – and a variety of woods, including maple, walnut and mahogany.

In the midst of the Depression, with Gibson's survival in doubt, the company did not immediately rise to the challenge posed by Epiphone, except to add two smaller, 14¾" archtops to the line in 1932: the f-hole L-75 and the roundhole L-50 (soon to have f-holes). Both had stubby bodies, shorter than any of the 14¾" flat-tops that had recently appeared.

Gibson's counter-attack came in 1934, and with it came an improvement to the guitar's relatively low volume (compared to the tenor banjo). In one sweeping move, Gibson 'advanced' the body sizes of all of the 16" archtops to 17". The smaller models would be advanced to 16" the following year, and two more 14¾" models, the L-30 and L-37, would be added at the same time.

The larger bodies took care of the volume issue. To take care of competition and to establish Gibson once and for all as the leading maker of archtops, Gibson advanced the body size yet another inch – using one of the 18" Style O guitars of the early 1900s as a template – and introduced a new model called the Super 400. The model name corresponded to its price of $400, which was almost twice as much as the L-5's early-1930s price of $225. The Super 400 backed up its high price with such features as a five-piece pearl inlay on the headstock forming a split diamond, with the motif repeated in three pearl pieces on the back of the headstock; large pearl

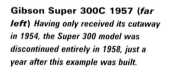

Gibson Super 300C 1957 (far left) *Having only received its cutaway in 1954, the Super 300 model was discontinued entirely in 1958, just a year after this example was built.*

Gibson L-5CT 1958 (near left) *This unusual acoustic thinline model was first made in March 1958 for comedian 'Lonesome' George Gobel, but was discontinued from the line just three years later.*

Bill Haley 1958 (above) *Although the music itself sounded radically different at the time, the Super 400 – and other big-bodied Gibson archtops – made the transition from jazz to jive in the hands of the first rock'n'rollers.*

**Gibson Super 400C-WR 1977
(left)** *For its first 42 years, the Super 400 was available only in sunburst or blonde (natural), but in 1976 Gibson offered the model in two more colors: wine red, as seen here, and ebony. The more opaque colors were introduced to use up stocks of plainer wood that was less visually impressive under the transparent finishes.*

Gibson Super 400CN-WAL 1968 (right) *This otherwise standard-looking Super 400's maple back and sides were given a rare walnut stain at the factory, which explains the 'WAL' suffix.*

Larry Coryell c1969 (above) *The young jazz-fusion guitarist lets rip on a Super 400C with floating pickup.*

block fingerboard inlays, split diagonally with one or two lines; engraved tuner buttons; a huge Y-shaped metal tailpiece and multiple layers of binding everywhere. A leather-covered case with its own protective canvas case cover was included in the price.

Epiphone responded with its own advanced body sizes and an even larger new model. Through the remainder of the 1930s Gibson would have Epiphone trying to top every move, and that competition inspired two more improvements. In 1939 Gibson introduced a rounded cutaway on the L-5 and Super 400, designating them Premier models. Also in 1939, natural ('blonde') finish became an official option on both models (although natural-finish examples exist before that date).

By that point, the electric guitar had gained a foothold, and the acoustic archtop had reached the end of its evolution. Only four Gibson models would survive World War II: the Super 400, L-5, L-7 and L-50. The L-7C (C for cutaway body) and the L-50 last appeared in 1970, and Gibson offered the last acoustic L-5C and Super 400C in 1981.However, the decline of the acoustic archtop by no means meant a similar decline of interest in acoustic guitars. It only indicated a shift in player preference to flat-top models, and Gibson had been steadily improving and refining its flat-top line all along the way.

The demand for increased volume that led to the advanced-body archtops had the same effect on flat-tops. The Martin company introduced a new 16" body with the thick-waisted design that became known as 'dreadnought' in 1931. In 1934, the same year that Gibson advanced its archtop bodies, Gibson appropriated the shape of its largest HG (Hawaiian) model of 1929 and introduced it as the Jumbo.

The Jumbo was noteworthy for the depth of its mahogany body, which was near-uniform – like that of the Nick Lucas – and well over four inches from neck heel to endpin (the standard, then as now, was to make the body shallower toward the neck). At the same time, the new body size was introduced on a pair of Hawaiian guitar models endorsed by Roy Smeck, a virtuoso instrumentalist known as 'The Wizard of the Strings.'

Perhaps the most enduring effect of the Jumbo, which was only produced for two years, was the confusion it started in the area of flat-top body nomenclature. Gibson would continue to use 'jumbo' for all its 16" flat-tops, regardless of body shape, while

Gibson catalogs *Another bird-themed flat-top, the Dove, is featured on the cover of the promotional material (left), while Gibson flaunts the diversity of its folk instrument range on the cover (above left).*

Gibson Hummingbird 1960 *(left and above) At 16¼" the Hummingbird was big for a square-shouldered dreadnought. The rear shot (above) shows its mahogany back.*

ACOUSTIC Series

PRE-OWNERS MANUAL

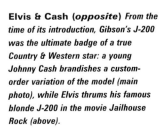

Elvis & Cash (opposite) *From the time of its introduction, Gibson's J-200 was the ultimate badge of a true Country & Western star: a young Johnny Cash brandishes a custom-order variation of the model (main photo), while Elvis thrums his famous blonde J-200 in the movie Jailhouse Rock (above).*

GIBSON EVERLY BROTHERS FLAT TOP JUMBO

the rest of the guitar world came to describe the shape of Gibson's Jumbo and all subsequent similar model as 'round-shouldered dreadnoughts' (to distinguish them from Martin's 'square-shouldered' shape), reserving the 'jumbo' term for later flat-tops with a large circular lower bout.

The Jumbo was succeeded in late 1936 by a pair of dreadnoughts, the J-35 and the Advanced Jumbo. The J-35 became Gibson's basic, mahogany-body dreadnought of the prewar era. The Advanced Jumbo did not represent an advance in size, rather in material. Its rosewood back and sides represented a first for Gibson – a nod to flat-top tradition – and gave it a richness of tone to go with its power. Consequently it is often cited as Gibson's finest prewar large-body flat-top.

Although Gibson was doing well enough with its flat-top line, particularly the smaller-bodied L-1, L-0 and L-00, the competition began to garner attention, right in Gibson's backyard. In Chicago, radio station WLS aired a Barn Dance program with

The Everly Brothers late 1950s (*main photo, right*) *Don and Phil Everly were playing J-200s long before Gibson approached them about an endorsement model.*

Gibson Everly Brothers 1963 (*right*) *The popular singing duo's model (also detailed in the catalog, top of page) is easily identified by its large double pickguards (smaller on later models), star position markers, and enlarged bridge, the latter feature designed by their father, guitarist Ike Everly. The brothers are seen (above) playing Everly models on a TV set.*

country & western artists, and many of them played flat-tops made by the Larson Brothers of Chicago. One of these artists, Gene Autry, had Martin make him a fancy version of their new dreadnought with Autry's name inlaid in script on the fingerboard (it was the first D-45). Gibson's attempt to suppress the archtop competition with the Super 400 had been successful, and in late 1937 the company made a similar move in the flat-top arena, starting with a 17" flat-top made for singing-cowboy movie star Ray Whitley. Although it was labeled as an L-5 Special, the style officially appeared a year later as the Super Jumbo – a larged-bodied, highly ornamented flat-top that was initially available only as a custom order.

Catalog photos showed that Gibson had been busy lining up as many of the cowboy movie stars as possible to play the new model, including Tex Ritter, Gene Autry and Ray Corrigan. Their guitars were indeed customized, with rope-pattern binding and other Western appointments, but the model quickly became a standard catalog item called the Super Jumbo 200. Among its distinguishing features were rosewood back and sides, fancy 'crest' or 'pineapple top' fingerboard inlays, a pickguard engraved with Western floral images, and a bridge that outlined the shape of a moustache. Gibson's strategy worked even better with the SJ-200 than it had

George Harrison's J-160E 1962 (*left*) *Harrison's actual J-160E retains its original sunburst finish but bears the scars from an extra pickup added at the bridge side of the soundhole and later removed.*

John Lennon's J-160E 1964 (*left*) *Lennon and George Harrison each owned a '62 J-160E, and they were frequently swapped in the studio, but both were used on many classic recordings. Lennon stripped this replacement J-160E of a psychedelic finish in 1968, then added these caricatures of himself and Yoko during their second Bed In for peace in Montreal, Canada.*

106

with the Super 400. It quickly became a badge of identification for country singers, and it remains the flagship model of Gibson's flat-top-line.

World War II severely curtailed guitar production as Gibson retooled to make war products. The model line was trimmed to a few flat-tops and one acoustic archtop, and due to restrictions on metal content, none of them had a truss-rod. Even wartime conditions, however, did not stop Gibson from moving ahead with flat-tops. The small models were redesigned with a slightly different body, renamed LG (LG for little guitars) and introduced during the war. In the dreadnought line the J-35 was revamped and introduced as the J-45 with sunburst finish, the J-50 with natural top, and the Southerner Jumbo with fancier, double-parallelogram fingerboard inlays. These three dreadnought models became the workhorse guitars of the postwar years, among the most highly respected of any Gibson flat-tops. In 1944, in the midst of these new wartime model introductions, Gibson was purchased by Chicago Musical Instrument, one of the largest instrument distributors in the United States at the time. Their take-over introduced no changes, however, other than the change of Guy Hart's title to 'president.'

After the war, Gibson abandoned rosewood, traditionally considered to be the best

wood for flat-tops. All of the LG and dreadnought models had mahogany back and sides, and the SJ-200 (soon to be just J-200) went back into production with maple back and sides. A smaller, 16" guitar with the same circular lower body as the J-200 appeared in 1951. Called the J-185, it had the maple back and sides of the J-200. Through the 1950s, while the LGs and dreadnoughts accounted for the bulk of Gibson's acoustic sales, the J-200 kept the Gibson image in front of music audiences. It continued as the cowboy guitar, although it was more often held by artists who merely dressed as cowboys rather than rode horses – country artists. Gibson's ledger books from the 1950s list numerous J-200s specially made for such country stars as Eddy Arnold, the Wilburn Brothers, and Johnny Cash.

Early in the 1950s, Gibson appropriated two features from its archtop and electric lines to the flat-top line, but with limited success. The CF-100, a small body flat-top, debuted in 1951 sporting a cutaway with pointed bout. It was available with or without an electric pickup. Three years later a dreadnought body was fitted with a pickup and introduced as the J-160. Although neither model was very successful, the J-160 would achieve considerable fame for providing the acoustic guitar sound (despite its ladder bracing and generally inferior performance as an acoustic) on The

Beatles' early records. Competing primarily with Martin in the flat-top market of the 1950s, Gibson maintained its own distinguishable body styles until late in the decade, when Gibson president Ted McCarty (who had joined Gibson in 1948) used Gibson's 1957 purchase of Epiphone as an opportunity to compete head-on with Martin's square-shouldered dreadnoughts. In his instructions for a new Epi line, McCarty included two flat-top 'jumbos,' one of which was described with these words: "Copy Martin D'naught size."

The square-shouldered Martin design appeared in the new Epi line of 1958 as the Frontier model, with a true-to-Gibson maple body, but two years later it moved into the Gibson line, with a mahogany body. Named the Hummingbird, it was moderately ornamented with an engraved pickguard featuring the image of the bird approaching a flower, plus double-parallelogram fingerboard inlays.

In the early 1960s, as folk music began to spur the demand for acoustic guitars, Gibson expanded the line with a pair of eye-catching new models. The Dove offered the square-shouldered dreadnought with a maple body, a pickguard inlaid with a pearl dove image, and an oversized bridge with abstract dove images inlaid in the bridge ends. The Everly Brothers was similar to the J-180 'jumbo' (non-dreadnought) body with a black finish, double oversized pickguards, and a pinless bridge designed by the Everlys' father, Ike Everly.

The rising popularity of acoustic guitars had an ironic effect on Gibson: the company began 'improving' features on guitars that did not need improving. Clearly (in hindsight, at least) the flat-top guitar, like the archtop, had reached the final stage of its evolution and perfection by World War II. Nevertheless, Gibson introduced a height-adjustable bridge saddle as an option in 1956, and it permeated the flat-top line in the early 1960s. In theory it was a good idea, but any advantages it provided in adjustability were more than offset by its negative affect on tone. The concept reached a ludicrous pinnacle in 1961, when the J-200 was fitted with Gibson's Tune-

o-matic bridge. Ted McCarty had designed the metal bridge, with overall height adjustment and individual string-length adjustments, for Gibson's electric solidbodies, where it remains the standard bridge design today, but its heavy weight killed the vibrations of the J-200 top.

The combination of higher production, unwise changes in specifications and increasing competition from cheap Japanese imports resulted in a slow deterioration of quality through the 1960s that picked up speed in the 1970s. One catalyst to Gibson's fall was the acquisition of the Chicago Musical Instrument Co. (Gibson's parent company) in 1970 by ECL, an Ecaudorian company that had no previous experience with musical instruments. The new company, renamed Norlin, would all but destroy Gibson in its 15 years of ownership, and warning signs appeared early in the acoustic line. In 1971 someone at Norlin apparently reasoned that if one X-brace was good (X-pattern top bracing had been the industry standard since C.F. Martin developed it in around 1850), then two Xs would be better. Gibson's new double-X bracing inhibited the vibration of the top, which had the effect of dulling the volume and the tone of its flat-tops.

Still confident that a century's worth of development and refinement of flat-top

Bob Dylan 1965 (*main photo*)
Dylan plays a Nick Lucas model during rehearsals for a BBC TV show at TV Theatre, Shepherds Bush, London.

Gibson Mark 53 1978 (*right*)
The jumbo-sized Mark Series, conceived by Michael Kasha and Richard Schneider, signaled the first significant new flat-top designs from Gibson in many years, and was plugged heavily in the promotional literature (above, opposite page). Despite the effort, the line was discontinued in 1979, just four years after its introduction.

Gibson C-O 1968 (*left*) *The bottom-of-the-line classical guitar.*

guitars had yet to produce the ultimate instrument, Norlin started from scratch. Possibly inspired by Ovation's recent success with a fiberglass-backed guitar designed by aviation engineers, Norlin hired designers Michael Kasha and Richard Schneider to re-create the flat-top using modern technology and scientific testing methods. The result of their research and development, the Mark series, appeared in 1975. On paper, the Marks held great promise, with a new bracing system, a new bridge design that featured a broader base on the bass side of the instrument, several bridge saddles, and even an easily removable pickguard. They may have passed all the laboratory tests, but the Marks failed the 'playing' test miserably.

Although Norlin continued trying to introduce new versions of the electric guitar in the late 1970s and early '80s, the company seems to have all but abandoned the acoustic line after the failure of the Marks. Besides new Chet Atkins electric nylon-string guitars, nothing of note happened in the early 1980s except mounting losses

and decreasing quality. Norlin had opened a Gibson facility in Nashville in '74 and closed Kalamazoo in 1984, moving all of Gibson to Nashville. By then Nashville was diverting resources to wood cases for chronometers in an effort to keep the doors open. Norlin had been steadily selling off musical instrument divisions, and the last of these, Gibson, was unloaded in 1986. The new bosses were graduates of Harvard Business School who had already turned around a near-bankrupt company in Oklahoma.

Led by Henry Juszkiewicz, the new owners slashed the management ranks and, in a risky move, raised the price of Gibsons. They justified the price increase by providing a higher quality guitar case and, more importantly, devoting more attention to quality control. According to company reports, they made Gibson profitable again within one month.

With Gibson back on its feet, Juszkiewicz bought the Flatiron mandolin company, based in Belgrade, Montana, in 1987. The obvious plan had been to acquire the

Gibson Chet Atkins CEC 1990 *(left) Introduced in 1982, the chambered-solidbody Chet Atkins model sparked a revolution in amplified classical guitar. Atkins – seen far left with a deluxe artist model – first conceived the design in an effort to preserve his fingernails, which were breaking on steel-string instruments.*

Gibson Chet Atkins SST 1987 *(right) Despite Chet's suffering digits, this steel-string model (also detailed in the catalog, below left) was introduced five years after the nylon version. Both remain in production at Gibson today.*

Gibson Advertisements (*right*) *In 1986 Gibson posed a J-200 on the front of a Rolls-Royce. Trying to tell us something? In 1994, B.B. King posed with a Bozeman-built L-00 'Blues King.'*

mandolin-making expertise of the Flatiron staff, but Juszkiewicz also wanted to relocate that staff to Nashville to revive Gibson's acoustic guitar line. However, the two key Flatiron figures, founder Steve Carlson and master luthier Ren Ferguson, refused to move to Nashville, so Gibson built a new acoustic guitar facility in Bozeman (near Belgrade).

Through the 1990s, Gibson attempted to reassert its reputation for innovation with new models that took advantage of improvements in acoustic guitar amplification. The Star introduced a pointed cutaway on a 16" jumbo body in 1991 and was followed the next year by three Starburst models. Also in 1992, a pair of EAS (Electric-Acoustic Starburst) models debuted, sporting a transducer pickup as standard equipment. The acoustic properties of the EAS models were of secondary importance, as indicated by a shallower body and an arched back of laminated maple. While these models were short-lived, the concept of a cutaway flat-top took hold in the Gibson line in the EC series of 1997. The Starburst bridge shape, with rounded ends to suggest a bird in flight, also survived – with an added point on the lower edge

Gibson J-50 1999 *Gibson strongly reasserted its reputation for quality acoustics through the 1990s, thanks largely to its new factory in Bozeman, Montana. This J-50, which harks back to a guitar of the early 1950s, is one example of the effort.*

Bill Withers 1973 *The man liked the sound of his Gibson – though many players disagreed with his opinion as the company moved through the 1970s.*

Gibson ads 1995 (*right*) The Montana acoustics continued to get heavy promotion, with endorsements from blues legend John Lee Hooker (below), country star Travis Tritt, and the late Buddy Holly (right) – the latter rock'n'roller long a major name-check for Fender.

John Lee Hooker and the Gibson Blues King Electro

– as the 'bird and beak' bridge on later models. In the dreadnought line, Gibson successfully introduced a rosewood square-shouldered model, the J-60, in 1992 to offer a respectable alternative to Martin's D-28. In 1997 a new style of 'thin-shouldered' dreadnought appeared (it was a fraction of an inch smaller across the shoulders and the waist) and evolved into several established cutaway models, although these lost their original CL (for Custom Line) model names. A line of no-frills models, dubbed the Working Man series, also gained acceptance due to their 'more affordable' prices.

While the Starbursts, EAS, EC, CL, and Working Man guitars gave Gibson a wide array of competitive flat-top models, the company was equally successful in its efforts to recapture the magic of vintage Gibsons with reissue versions of classic models. Although there were a number of variations, Gibson brought the basic J-200, J-45, Dove, and Hummingbird back to the specifications – and the quality – of their respective golden years. The legendary prewar rosewood dreadnought, the Advanced

Gibson Sheryl Crow 2000 (*left*) This signature model – put through its paces by the singer herself in the main photo, opposite – is a square-shouldered dreadnought based on Crow's own 1962 Gibson Country Western model.

Gibson J-45 1966 (*right*) This vintage flat-top – minus the tone-deadening adjustable saddle - is an original example of the type of guitar players wanted to see again from Gibson through the 1980s and '90s.

Gibson 60s Dove Reissue 2000 (*left*) Another run around the block for the bird-bejeweled flat-top.

Gibson SJ-200 'Western Classic' 2001 (*right*) Bozeman offers yet another take on Gibson's self-proclaimed 'king of country rhythm' instrument.

Sheryl Crow (*above*) Pictured on-stage with the signature Gibson based on her old Country Western.

Jumbo, was reintroduced with a series of limited runs, beginning in 1990, continuing through the decade, and finally going into regular production in 2002. The smallbody L-00 came back in 1991, was renamed the Blues King, and then after a few years out of production returned in 1999 as the L-00.

Gibson also added the names of recording artists to enhance new versions of classic models. A 1960s version of the Country & Western model (basically a natural finish Southerner Jumbo) reappeared as the Sheryl Crow model in 2001. The World War II version of the Southerner Jumbo was reissued in 1997 as the Hank Williams Jr. model and again in 2003 as the Woody Guthrie model. And the original Gibson signature guitar, the Nick Lucas, made a short return to the Gibson line in 1991, and then came back in 1999.

Gibson began promoting the J-200 as 'The King of the Flat-Tops,' and the J-200 line became a veritable kingdom, with over 30 different models offered in the 1990s. Additional offshoots included the trimmed-down J-150 and J-100 Xtra, the fancier J-250, J-1000, J-1500 and J-2000, and artist versions, including two Elvis models.

In the midst of Gibson's revival of past models, two acoustic archtops reappeared. Gibson's Custom division had been making a few Citations and Le Grandes (formerly the Johnny Smith), which were constructed as acoustic archtops but always sold with a floating pickup. In 1995 the Custom Shop introduced Gibson's first true acoustic archtop in 15 years: a reproduction of the 1934 L-5 (the 16" version). In 2003, Gibson Montana ventured into the acoustic archtop arena for the first time with an L-7 cutaway instrument, based on a late-1940s version of the 17" model. In 2007, Gibson bought Garrison, helping to create the shortlived Songmaker models, but the operation was closed later.

By 2017, Gibson offered one main series of acoustic models, the Songwriters. Gibson said its Songwriter series was at the heart of its square-shoulder dreadnought line. The Songwriter Deluxe Studio was introduced in 2003 as the basis of the line, with traditional materials, bracing and shape. There was a cutaway version, too, as well as higher-end versions, the Songwriter Deluxe Standard (in sunburst finish) and the shortlived Custom (fancier appointments). The company's other acoustics were grouped together as Limited Runs, and these included various J models, such as the

SJ-200 Birdseye, the J-35 Vintage Collectors Edition, the J-45 Rosewood Tonewood Edition, the J-185 Quilt Vine VS, and a couple of L models, the L-00 Mystic Rosewood and Acacia Special. Joining those were a number of takes on the venerable Hummingbird and Dove.

Among Gibson's late-2010s Artist models were a Bob Dylan SJ-200 Players Edition, an Elvis Costello modeled on a 1930s Century Of Progress flat-top, a John Hiatt J-45, the Woody Guthrie SJ that aimed to recreate Guthrie's 1945 Southern Jumbo, and a Jackson Browne based on a 1930s Roy Smeck model.

Today, Gibson continues to innovate and respond to new trends as best it can, such as the Emmylou Harris L-200, a small-body acoustic-electric with J200 trim that was introduced in 2002. At the same time, Gibson has recognized the value of its tradition, and it presents variations on the classic models – without abandoning the original versions. In recent years, Gibson acoustic guitars seem to be enjoying their highest reputation since the 1950s.

Gibson J-45 2002 (*left*) *The worthy, workaday J-45 is perhaps 'the' classic of Gibson's standard-sized Jumbos (often known as round-shouldered dreadnoughts), and a worthy Bozeman-built reissue.*

Gibson L-00 2016 (*right*) *Gibson's classic small-body acoustic was reissued in a special edition with acacia back and sides and a natural spruce top.*

Richard Ashcroft, Badly Drawn Boy, c2000 *Alternative British songsmiths Richard Ashcroft (opposite) and Badly Drawn Boy (top) reflected ongoing respect for Gibson.*

Gibson ad 2002 (*above*) *A variation on the guy-comes-into-a-bar joke was used for this J-series promo.*

115

GILBERT

John Gilbert was a tool-maker with Hewlett-Packard in Palo Alto, California, when a friend gave him A.P. Sharpe's famous book *Make Your Own Spanish Guitar*. He did exactly that, then built and repaired instruments as a hobby until making them his career from 1974.

His method was based on careful measurement, record-keeping, and experimentation, leading to guitars of great consistency and accuracy. Visually, the most striking characteristic of later Gilbert guitars is their unusual pin bridge, with the strings individually supported. In 1991, his son William joined the workshop, and John handed over to him in 1997, in order to concentrate on his line of machine heads. John Gilbert died in 2012.

GOODALL

The same fertile San Diego lutherie scene of the early 1970s that spawned Taylor and Breedlove guitars and banjo-makers Geoff Stelling and Greg Deering also gave rise to James Goodall. Goodall built his first guitar in 1972 and by 1978 his one-man operation was going full-time. He moved to Mendocino, California, in 1981 and then to Kailua-Kona, Hawaii, in 1992.

Goodall builds guitars with the unique body shapes he developed in San Diego in

Gilbert 1994 (*left*) *John Gilbert's son William joined him in the business in 1991, and has also signed the label of this fine hand-made classical guitar. Note the unusual bridge on this example: rather than the conventional one-piece saddle, it employs individual 'pin' saddles for each string.*

Back (*far left*) *A rear view shows the highly figured Indian rosewood back and sides which complement its western red cedar top.*

Gilbert c1990s (*right*) *Note the difference in soundhole rosette designs between this Gilbert and the example shown left.*

Back (*above*) *This guitar's rosewood back has a richer color, but displays less figuring in the grain than the guitar on the left.*

the early 1970s, as well as more Martin-like shapes he has dubbed the Traditional Series. In 2002 he introduced nylon-string guitars and baritones. His son Luke joined in 2004, and five years later they moved back to California, to Fort Bragg. By 2017 they offered thirteen sizes of guitar in five series.

GRAMMER

Country artist Billy Grammer helped found the R.G.&G. Co. in Nashville in 1965, with the goal of making the finest flat-top guitar that could be built. Financial problems and early production flaws haunted the operation, however, and to make things worse, a fire destroyed the plant in April 1968. Later the same year production restarted under the name Grammer Guitar Inc., and Grammers eventually attained some popularity among local performers. They were distributed by Ampeg in 1969-1970 (these guitars have the Ampeg 'a' logo) but the company finally went bankrupt in 1971.

GREENFIELD

In the late 1920s, Edmonton, Alberta, furniture manufacturer William A. Greenfield dabbled in a more sonorous (if not necessarily profitable) enterprise: Hawaiian guitars.

He was granted patents on his designs in both the US and Canada. Greenfield instruments were hollow-necked (like Weissenborn) and asymmetrically shaped from walnut (unlike Weissenborn). Bodies featured a treble horn shaped like a reverse cutaway; on the bass side the hollow neck extended toward the player, increasing the interior volume and giving a support for the bar hand. (The treble side remains unextended in order to allow tilting the bar.) Greenfields, not quite the sonic rival of Weissenborn, Kona, or Brink, have dated paper labels and varying ornamentation.

GRETSCH

For most players today, Gretsch acoustic guitars appear a mere footnote to their more prominent electric brethren. But for a brief spell back when the archtop was king, Gretsch acoustics were right up there with the big names of the genre.

The Fred Gretsch Manufacturing Co was founded in Brooklyn, New York, in 1883 by 27-year-old German immigrant Friedrich Gretsch to build drums, tambourines, and banjos. Upon his death in 1895 the company was passed to the eldest of his seven children, 15-year-old Fred (known as Fred Sr.), who built steadily on its success until the 1920s banjo craze hurled Gretsch to even greater heights. Fred Sr. was followed

Gretsch Synchromatic 400 1945 (left) With its big 18"-wide top, the Synchromatic 400 was designed as a powerful archtop to compete with Gibson's Super 400.

Gretsch Synchromatic Custom 1953 (right) This unusual guitar has the 400's gold-bound soundholes, but the appointments and 17" body of the 6030 model.

Gretsch catalog 1950 (far right) The New York City-based company proudly displays its range of goods and its 19th century foundation.

by sons Bill, and then Fred Jr., who guided the company right into its electrified heyday of the 1950s and '60s.

As the popularity of the banjo slowed toward the late 1920s, the guitar was poised to take its place. Gretsch had already carried a few models from other makers, but in 1933 it launched the first range with its own logo: five archtops in the Gretsch-American Orchestra Series, and a handful of flat-tops. Where its banjos had been austere, all but the starter models of Gretsch archtops were elaborately outfitted, often with multiple bindings, deluxe floral or art deco pearl headstock inlays, fancy tailpieces, and other features. Models 25, 35, 65, and 100 (named for their ascending prices) were all 16" wide with a 24½" scale, and had carved spruce tops with traditional f-holes, arched maple backs and sides, and three-piece maple-rosewood-maple necks with ebony fingerboards. The 100R was similar in construction, but carried a round soundhole.

Both more- and less-deluxe 16" models joined the range in 1935, including the 50, 150, and 250; but the most significant advancement in Gretsch archtops came with the launch of the Synchromatic Series in 1939, at which time most of the Orchestra Series was dropped. The Synchromatic 160, 200, and 300 were bigger and louder.

They had 17" bodies and 26" scales, but are remembered more for their distinctive styling. 'Cat's-eye' soundholes, stairstep bridges and tailpieces, slashed-block fingerboard inlays, and sometimes sparkle or tortoiseshell body and neck bindings made them some of the most eye-catching instruments of their day. Soon after these, Gretsch followed with the 18" Synchromatic 400, which was intended to compete with Gibson's Super 400.

From the start, the archtop guitars did well. Gretsch was a keen competitor with Gibson and Epiphone in the 1930s and into the '40s, and its guitars acquired a top-line reputation. They were rarely as well put together as their rivals, however, and far fewer Gretsches than Gibsons, for example, have survived from 1940 to today in playable condition. Nevertheless, they found their way into the hands of several notable players, including Harry Volpe, and Freddie Green, the great rhythm machine of the Count Basie Orchestra.

Gretsch flat-tops never fared as well, were always a couple rungs down the ladder from their arched siblings in terms of both sound and playability, and are rarely of great interest today (one exception being the western-dress, G-branded Rancher of the 1950s). The early 14½" Broadkaster (mahogany top) and Castilian (spruce) as well

Freddie Green 1968 (*opposite page*) *Green takes a break from covering rhythm duties for Count Basie on his Synchromatic 400.*

Gretsch Rancher 1955 (*right*) *The acoustic version of Gretsch's G-branded 'Western' guitars of the mid 1950s, the Rancher is one of few Gretsch flat-tops to inspire much interest among collectors.*

Gretsch ad 2001 (*center*) *This Japanese ad for contemporary Gretsch flat-tops (themselves built in Japan) shows an emphasis on vintage styling.*

Gretsch White Falcon Rancher 1995 (*left*) *A new-era Gretsch flat-top cousin to sit alongside the elaborate and very collectable White Falcon electric archtop.*

119

as the oddly round-bodied Rhumba lacked the elaborate decoration of the Orchestra Series, but the 18" Synchromatic 400F flat-top introduced in 1947 made up for much of the lost ground in stylistic excess.

Following the enforced reductions of the war years, Gretsch ramped up production once again, and its reputation held fast for a time, but the company had difficulty retaining its foothold in the archtop market.

Gretsch acoustic guitars of the 1950s to 1970s are usually poor examples of the form, and its flat-tops can be especially dire. Inferior materials (often veneered tops instead of solid woods) and construction techniques such as ladder-bracing rather than the tonally superior X-bracing render them no match for Martins or Gibsons, or even many lesser-known brands. Models with triangular soundholes – such as the Synchromatics, Rancher, and Town & Country – spark the most interest today.

Gretsch was sold to Baldwin in 1967 and production eventually ceased in the early 1980s, until Fred Gretsch III (son of Bill) reacquired it in 1985. Through the 1990s the name gradually regained its former cachet – largely on the strength of Japanese-built reissues of its classic 1950s and '60s electrics. In late 2002 Fender Musical Instruments signed a deal to handle all Gretsch manufacturing and distribution.

Current top-of-the-line Gretsch guitars continue to be made in Japan, and although the focus is again on electrics, the catalog includes some of the best-built Gretsch acoustics ever. The line-up relies heavily on reissues based on designs from its early years, and models such as the Roots Style 1 Parlor guitar and a number of Rancher flat-tops are once again hanging in guitar stores.

GRIMES

Luthier Steve Grimes began building archtop guitars in 1972. With clients including George Benson (whose Ibanez signature model Grimes helped to design) and Larry Coryell, Grimes is among the most respected builders of this instrument type. His move to the Hawaiian island of Maui – where he has lived and worked since 1982 – began an interest in building instruments specifically for the islands' slack-key music. His Beamer model (named after slack-key artist Kaola Beamer) is a double-soundhole flat-top design that is optimized for the style's low tunings. In 1991, Grimes collaborated with designer Ned Steinberger in creating a stress-free flat-top guitar, which transferred string tension to a tailpiece rather than the top. Today he continues to concentrate on archtops but also makes flat-tops, ukuleles and mandolins.

Gretsch catalog 2003 (below)
A reissue Hawaiian model graces the cover of the Historic Series catalog.

Guild ad 1998 (far right) *Slash goes unplugged with this endorsement ad for a D-100 flat-top.*

Gretsch 'Custom' c1950s (left)
Gretsch is notorious for having made some guitars which employ features from other, better-defined models – which years later baffle collectors keen to identify particular examples. What's this one? It has no label to offer clues, but includes elements of Synchromatic and Eldorado models from the early 1950s.

Gretsch Rancher 12 1995 (right) *A cutaway 12-string version of the contemporary 6022 model.*

Grimes Jazz Laureate 1996
(*right*) *A custom-ordered blue-finished archtop creation from the Hawaii-based builder.*

G R I M S H A W

Emile Grimshaw, an English banjo virtuoso, founded Grimshaw & Son in 1933, located in Piccadilly, London. At first, Grimshaw mainly sold other makers' products, but in 1940 started his own workshop, meeting an increased demand for guitars. Grimshaw guitars had their heyday in the 1950s. Many of these guitars had distinctive features such as elaborate inlays and a notably deep cutaway.

Grimshaws were generally considered a domestic alternative to the American archtops that could not be imported due to trade restrictions. The last Grimshaw archtops were made in the early 1960s.

G U I L D

Although Guild Guitars, Inc. does not have the 19th Century roots of C.F. Martin or Gibson, it is nevertheless one of the oldest guitar companies in the US. And because Guild grew from the ashes of Epiphone's New York location, the company's origins predate its formation in 1953. For a time, Guild was successfully marketing all three types of acoustic — archtop, flat-top, and classical — from one factory, something no contemporary American guitar company seems able to accomplish. Guild Guitars was

Guild ad 1973 (*above*) *Country-folkster John Denver promotes Guild's take on the 'super jumbo' flat-top.*

Guild F-50R-NT 1975 (*right*) *In the 1960s and '70s Guild was best known for its quality flat-tops, and the F-50R was near the top of the line.*

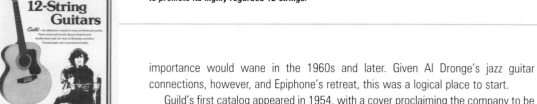

Guild ad *The company uses Tim Buckley to promote its highly regarded 12-strings.*

primarily the vision of one man, Alfred Dronge. Born in Warsaw, Poland, in 1911, Al (given name Avram) and family emigrated to the United States in 1916, where they settled in New York City. By the time he was 25 years old the musical Dronge owned a small music store, and was soon successfully importing Sonola accordions from Italy. He became well connected to both the music industry and to a wide circle of musicians, both proving vital to Guild's growth.

Epiphone's labor difficulties worked in Guild's favor. In October 1952 Dronge and George Mann, who had been Epiphone's vice president a few years earlier, formed Guild Guitars, Inc. and hired several former Epiphone craftsmen, including Enrico Capiello – a 25-year veteran of guitar making in New York – as shop supervisor.

The original Guild factory was a 1,500 square foot second story loft on Pearl Street, near Foley Square.

Rather than pure acoustic instruments, the first Guild guitars were big, hollowbody electric models, made with laminated tops and backs, much like Gibson's ES-5. These electric archtops constituted a major part of Guild's success in the 1950s, but their

importance would wane in the 1960s and later. Given Al Dronge's jazz guitar connections, however, and Epiphone's retreat, this was a logical place to start.

Guild's first catalog appeared in 1954, with a cover proclaiming the company to be "The Stradivari of Guitars." By this time George Mann had left, and Al Dronge was sole owner. Along with about a half dozen electric archtops were three flat-top models, headed by the 17"-wide Navarre F-50, a competitor to Gibson's J-200. The F-40, which would be called a 16" jumbo today, and the F-30, about the size of a Martin 000, rounded out the line.

All had maple backs and sides, with the backs arched and laminated with no back braces, just like on the electric archtops. Less than two years later these models were joined by the smaller F-20, which sold for only $85. Despite the laminated back, the F-50 was considered a deluxe flat-top guitar, and had the fancy mother-of-pearl and abalone neck inlays to prove it. Nobody worried about laminated backs in those days, and a blond F-50 sold for $260, almost 25 percent more than a Martin D-28.

By 1955 Guild's offerings included acoustic archtops, with the Stuart A-550 as the top model. For several years most archtop models were available as electrics (X prefix) or acoustic (A prefix), but only the higher model acoustics had both carved

Guild publicity (*above*) The Savoy A-150, Capri CA-100 and Granada A-50 archtops and Aragon, Valencia, Navarre and Troubadour flat-tops (top). A diverse list of players including The Smothers Brothers, Richie Havens, George Benson, and Eric Clapton endorse Guild guitars, 1968 (above left). The Navarre F-50, Valencia F-40 and Aragon F-30 models (above right).

Guild F-212CR-NT 1979 (*left*) A better-appointed version of the standard F-212 12-string, this model has rosewood back and sides, and ebony fingerboard and bridge.

Tim Buckley 1968 (*opposite page*) Influential singer-songwriter Buckley was a long-time Guild fan.

tops and backs. One distinctive feature of Guild archtops from this date forward was the 'harp' tailpiece – one of the more artistic tailpiece designs of the era – which was made in Germany, along with Guild's headstock and fretboard inlays.

At this point Guild was growing rapidly, having successfully filled the void left by the demise of Epiphone (that trademark had been acquired by Gibson). In 1956 Guild solved both a space problem and its own potential labor troubles by moving across the Hudson River to Hoboken, New Jersey. By late 1956, Guild employed 15 craftsmen and produced an average of 120 guitars each month.

Thanks to Dronge's many contacts in the New York music scene, Guild had impressive endorsements right from the start. Carl Kress, Barry Galbraith, Billy Bauer, and Al Valenti were names well known to guitar players. And in 1955 Dronge landed Johnny Smith, one of the biggest names in jazz guitardom at the time, as an endorser of his archtops. Smith appeared in Guild ads holding a Stuart X-550, and signed an agreement to help develop an acoustic archtop to be called the Johnny Smith model.

In late 1956, the Johnny Smith Award was introduced, a fully carved archtop with a floating DeArmond pickup. Although it was the same size and shape as the A-500, this new model had a larger, more elaborate headstock shape with a huge mother-of-

pearl and abalone inlay nestled between the tuner posts just above the truss-rod cover. At $550 for a blonde version it was one of the most expensive guitars in the country at that time. Although the endorsement deal lasted until 1960, and Smith appeared in Guild ads, there was a basic disagreement about how the top should be carved relative to the cutaway. As a result, Smith never adopted Guild's new flagship guitar as his own. When he signed up with Gibson, the Guild Johnny Smith Award became the Artist Award, and has remained Guild's top archtop model ever since.

In the late 1950s Guild continued to expand both its model offerings and its sales volume. By 1961 Guild was offering its Mark Series classical models, named after Dronge's young son Mark, who worked at the factory part-time. With a full line of six different models, Guild's Mark Series was quite true to the Spanish guitar-building tradition and were far better classical guitars than any of the nylon-string models offered by Gibson or Martin at that time.

Mark Dronge joined his father at Guild in 1960, and can be credited with Guild's expansion to a wider range of guitar types and models in the coming decade. One of the most important changes was the addition of two dreadnought acoustic guitars, the D-40 and D-50, in 1963. They were the first in a long line of D-size Guilds that

became the company's best-selling acoustic flat-tops. The mahogany D-40 was dubbed the Bluegrass Jubilee, while the rosewood D-50 was named the Bluegrass Special. Ironically, Guild dreadnoughts have proved popular in just about every type of American music except bluegrass.

Another important addition to Guild's flat-top line was the pair of 12-string models introduced at the end of 1963. The mahogany F-212 and the rosewood F-312 were both based on model F-47's body, but had blank fretboards. Although these two models were modestly successful, the larger 17" Guild 12-strings introduced a few years later would be acknowledged leaders in the 12-string market for many years.

Guild's flat-top models were soon accounting for an increasing percentage of the company's sales, thanks to the folk music boom that was sweeping the country. Guild guitars were now distinctly different from other American brands, even at first glance. The early Guild headstock, which looked a lot like Gibson's, had been replaced by a somewhat larger design with a raised center portion at the top – a scaled-down version of the headstock shape that first appeared on the Johnny Smith Award model. Beneath the letters spelling out 'Guild' was a pearloid column with a crown shape at the top, a design now commonly known among guitar aficionados as the

Guild D-50 1975 (left) *Guild dreadnought flat-tops, such as this upscale D-50, are highly regarded by a wide range of players.*

Guild catalog 1969 (center) *A dreadnought invites you to turn the page.*

Guild ads c1970s (above left and right) *Promotions for Guild's hand-made classicals.*

Guild Mk1 1963 (right) *Guild's classical guitars are less talked of than their early archtops and mid-period flat-tops, but are quality instruments in their price range.*

'Chesterfield inlay' because of its similarity to the design on Chesterfield-brand cigarette packaging. The new design replaced the large 'G-shield' inlay that had previously adorned headstocks on all but Guild's lowest-priced models. The 'G' inlay would continue to be used on many top-of-the-line Guilds, however, such as the F-50.

Guild flat-tops also had distinctive bridge and pickguard shapes by 1963, replacing earlier designs that were more generic. This move towards a more clearly defined Guild style gave the company its own identity, and among the acoustic flat-top crowd Guild was coming to be recognized as on a par with Martin and Gibson. Fans of the big Gibson J-200, such as Dave Van Ronk, were often swayed to try Guild's F-50 – especially as, beginning in 1965, they could have their jumbo in rosewood (F-50R) instead of the usual maple. Paul Simon, who had previously played Martins, also appeared playing a Guild F-30 Special (a rosewood F-30, introduced in '67). Guild's flat-top sales during the 1960s were also spurred by what was often a two-year wait for many popular Martin models. Some buyers settled for a Guild out of frustration, but were soon won over and never went back.

Avnet, Inc, an electronics company, bought Guild for almost $5million in 1966, and

the factory was soon moved to Westerly, Rhode Island. From late 1967 until almost two years later, Guild built guitars at both the Hoboken and Westerly locations. Alfred Dronge, who had taken up flying as a hobby a few years earlier, flew his twin-engine Beechcraft Baron between New Jersey and Rhode Island to keep a watchful eye on both operations.

Now that the company had more room, Guild began to exploit the popularity of its flat-tops with a spate of new models. The best sellers were the D-25 and D-35, relatively plain mahogany dreadnought models at a lower price than Guild had been able to offer previously. More importantly, Guild's new dreadnoughts were cheaper than the competition. In 1968 its D-35 had a list price a full $90 below that of Martin's $325 D-18, with both guitars having similar features. At the opposite end of the price chart was the D-55 'TV Model,' a new deluxe rosewood dreadnought with the same binding and inlay as the F-50. The highly popular jumbo 12-string, the F-212XL, was also given both maple and rosewood companions, the F-412 and F-512 respectively. Guild 12-strings were highly prized by touring musicians, because with dual truss-rods they could be counted upon to be playable in a wide range of conditions. Singers as

John Renbourn 1978 *The British folk stylist on stage with his Guild at the Cambridge Folk Festival.*

Richie Havens 1969 (*below*)
*Havens has been vociferous about his
preference for Guild's alternative take
on the traditional Martin and Gibson
flat-top format.*

diverse as Howlin' Wolf and Tim Buckley were pictured cradling Guild 12-strings, but John Denver would later be the most visible Guild 12-string artist of all.

Al Dronge took good care of his foremen, and key long-time employees like Carlo Greco, Fred Augusto, and Gilbert Diaz made the move to Westerly. Al's son Mark, however, left Guild in 1968. By late 1969 the manufacturing of all Guild guitars was being done at the new factory, and in December Jim Deurloo was hired as plant manager. Deurloo was a 10-year veteran of Gibson, and brought a thorough knowledge of all stages of guitar production. As Guild rolled into the 1970s, buoyed by the steady demand for acoustic flat-tops fueled by the sounds of folk-rock, it seemed that everything was in order for a great decade. Instead, disaster struck on May 3rd 1972, when Al Dronge flew from New York to Westerly, Rhode Island, only to be turned away from the airport because of bad weather. He missed the runway and crashed while trying to land at an alternative airport under equally bad conditions, and was pronounced dead at the scene. Alfred Dronge was only 61 years old, and Guild Guitars was fatherless at age 20.

Guild continued much as it had before. Leon Tell, who'd served as vice-president for the past decade, now headed the company. Despite continued growth, however,

things were never quite the same without Al Dronge, and two years later Jim Deurloo returned to Gibson.

Virtually all of Guild's acoustic archtops were discontinued in the early 1970s due to slow sales, with the exception of the Artist Award. The company continued to expand its flat-top line with the addition of the G series dreadnoughts. The most popular, and long-lasting, was the G-37, a maple version of the D-40 with arched (laminated) back. The G-41 was a 17"-wide dreadnought with a 26¼" scale length, and the G-75 was a ¾-size D model, but Guild buyers seemed to have little use for either oversized or undersized versions of their favorite guitar shape. Richie Havens, already a long-time Guild fan, was one of the few artists who could handle the jumbo-sized dreadnought.

Sales began to slow for Guild in the late 1970s, as they did for most American guitar companies, and several of Guild's long-time workers such as Carlo Greco drifted back to the New York area. In the early 1980s, as guitar sales continued to slump, a low-priced 'Mahogany Rush Series' of D models was introduced, some of which had satin finishes and no body binding. Guild still had the power to attract popular endorsers, and the Hank Williams Jr. G-45 – a fancy maple dreadnought – was issued

in 1982. Even more elaborate models like the D-70 (1981) and the pearl-bordered D-80 (1983) were offered with wood binding, large 'humptop' fretboard inlays, and the option of decorative carving at the neck heel, making these guitars the most elaborate Guild production models ever. They may have resulted in impressive catalog covers and magazine ads, but did little to lift overall sales.

Like most conglomerates, Guild's corporate parent, Avnet, lost interest in guitar making when profits faltered, and Mark Dronge was given the position of president, plus a contract allowing him the option to buy the company. Under Mark's direction, six new flat-top models, designed by vintage-guitar dealer George Gruhn, debuted in 1984. The most noticeable design element, and one which has survived to Guilds of the present day, came with the move to a headstock that tapered in towards the top, rather than flaring out. The tapered headstock, commonly called a 'snakehead' (after Gibson's similar designs of the mid 1920s), allowed each string to follow a straight line over the nut to the tuning post. Rather than setting new records for price and decoration, the Gruhn models combined elements from Guild's past with both visual and structural modifications – such as lighter top bracing – that made the instruments more competitive in a changing market.

Unhappy with the progress of its exit strategy, however, Avnet sold Guild in August of 1986 to a group of investors that included Gruhn. The result was an ambitious series of changes in the way Guild models were defined. Guild's model designations had always been confusing, but since the early 1970s they had become a nightmare even for those within the company. Gruhn attempted to replace Guild's haphazard model nomenclature with an orderly system consistent throughout the line. Seven style numbers were issued which ran from 15 to 65, with the latter being the familiar deluxe Guild style previously found on the F-50. Model code prefixes were D (dreadnought), GF (16" jumbo, like the original F-40) and JF (17" jumbo). Smaller sizes, such as the F-30, were discontinued.

Despite the new models, and America's renewed interest in the guitar after a fling with synthesizers, Guild floundered. There was renewed competition from Martin, which had reinvented itself with new jumbo models, slimmer necks, and more competitive prices. To make matters worse, Taylor of California and Larrivée of Canada both offered guitar buyers good alternatives to older trademarks. Gruhn left in early 1988, and barely a year later Guild, then in bankruptcy, was sold to the FAAS Corporation. Guild had kept the same plant manager, Willie Fritcher, through the years

Guild A-600B(E) 1968 (far left) The only A-600B(E) ever made, for display at a '68 trade show in Chicago. It has an unusual carved spruce top with oval soundhole, and is fitted with a floating DeArmond pickup.

Back (left) A rear view of the 600 reveals some highly figured maple used in its construction.

Guild ads c1990s (left) An ageing Richie Havens continues to support Guild (far left), while rocker Slash of Guns'N Roses also waves the flag. They should form a duo.

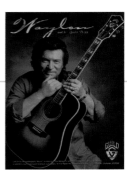

of corporate turmoil, so Guild guitars didn't change dramatically each time new owners took control. But by reverting to some, but not all, of its earlier model designations, and by introducing new models seemingly disconnected to any previous system, the company wound up with a dizzying line-up of flat-top guitars that reads like a tossed salad of letters and numbers.

One of the biggest changes at Guild in the 1990s was the introduction of a wide range of cutaway F-prefix acoustic-electric models, including a series with 3" deep bodies and Guild's typical laminated arched back.

In 1995 Guild was sold again, this time to Fender Musical Instrument Corp. A custom shop was opened in Nashville for special models and prototypes, but production was still based in Westerly, Rhode Island. Although the model offerings were simplified, Guild continued to supply dealers with the cutaway acoustic-electrics and traditional dreadnoughts that had provided most of the company's sales in the 1990s. Some favorites from the past were revived, such as the F-30R, and the D-40, D-50, D-55, and F-50 were eventually reinstated with their original model designations. In 1999 Fender signed an agreement with archtop builder Bob Benedetto, and the first models resulting from this partnership were displayed at a January 2000 trade show. Guild offered a series of Benedetto-brand archtops, with signature models including a Johnny Smith Award, the only Guild acoustic archtop that remained in continuous production through three changes in location and five changes in ownership.

Despite its long history, the Westerly facility had been designed as a furniture factory and was never an ideal location for building acoustic guitars. Along with old equipment and buildings, there was the problem of constantly changing coastal weather. Since Fender already had a modern guitar factory in Corona, California, the decision was made to close the Westerly factory in 2001. The first Guild guitars to be made in Corona were electric archtops, built in the Fender Custom Shop. Production of flat-top models also moved to Corona by the end of the year. Fender sold Guild in 2014 to the Cordoba Music Group, and production of Guild acoustics revived in California. The reinvigorated operation offered a number of acoustic models, including M series and D series guitars, and in 2017 the company promised F models soon.

Ryan Adams c2000 (*above*)
Alt-country songsmith and former Whiskeytown frontman Adams is a Guild devotee.

Johnny Cash (*right*) *The man in black strums a Guild in sunburst.*

Guild GAD-JF30 2013 (*left*)
This guitar dates from just before Fender's sale of Guild to Cordoba, and is a classic Guild-style jumbo.

GURIAN

Michael Gurian started building classical guitars and lutes in Greenwich Village, New York, in the mid 1960s. A year or two later he was making steel-string flat-tops with a distinct classical appearance. In 1971 he moved to New Hampshire where, by the end of the decade, his workforce had grown to more than 20 people – but natural and economic forces conspired against him. In 1979 his factory burned down; then, after his struggle to rebuild it, the popularity of the acoustic guitar plummeted to an all-time low. Gurian closed his guitar business in 1982, but continued to supply parts to the trade. He was one of the first contemporary luthiers to become successful, and many builders today cite the instruments he made in the 1970s as a great inspiration.

HAGSTRÖM
(AND BJÄRTON)

Hagström is best known for electrics – all of which were made in the main factory in Älvdalen, Sweden – but the company also distributed acoustics under its own brand name. A first batch of low to medium-priced nylon and steel string guitars were made in Norway from 1947 to 1955. From 1961 to around 1985, all Hagström acoustics were made by Bjärton in the south of Sweden. Among the most popular were the steel-string B-10 and J-45 (also available in electric and 12-string versions) and the nylon-string Espana, Carina, and Isabella. In the US, Hagströms were distributed by Hershman and Buegeleisen & Jacobson and in the UK by Boosey & Hawkes and Selmer. Bjärton also made guitars sold under its own name, and also supplied them to others, the best known being Fender's 1960s Tarrega series. Most production was of the Spanish and flat-top guitars, but in the 1960s a few archtops were made in collaboration with Jimmy D'Aquisto. Bjärton's endorsers included Abba and jazz guitarist 'Toots' Thielemans. Bjärton was sold to the Italian GEM firm in 1985 and closed in 1989. The Hagström brand was revived in 2008, including a few acoustics.

HARMONY

For many years the world's largest mass-manufacturer of instruments, Harmony was king of the Chicago guitar powerhouses, dominating the beginner-to-intermediate segments of the market. During much of that time it was backed by the economic muscle of its owner, Sears, Roebuck & Company. At its peak, Harmony even attracted endorsements from Roy Smeck and WLS radio stars Bradley Kincaid and Gene Autry.

Harmony-made Supertone Bradley Kincaid Houn' Dog c1929 (left) *This standard-sized flat-top made by Harmony for Sears in honor of the early Western radio star is considered the first 'cowboy' guitar.*

Harmony-made Supertone Gene Autry Roundup 1938 (right) *Note the classic 'decalomania' on this guitar's belly, which depicts a lasso-wielding cowboy on his horse.*

Harmony ad c1930 (second right) *Period promotions.*

Harmony-made Supertone 12D250 America's Greatest Guitar Value Spanish Guitar 1932 (far right) *A mouthful for a budget-priced, standard-sized flat-top, but the mother-of-toiletseat fingerboard and beach-scene 'decolamania' make it all worthwhile.*

Harmony

HAWAIIAN and SPANISH
GUITARS
ELECTRIC GUITARS
and AMPLIFIERS
MANDOLINS · UKULELES
Consult Your Wholesaler for Delivery

THE HARMONY COMPANY
3633 S. RACINE AVE. · CHICAGO 9, ILL

Harmony ad 1940 *Period promotion in an idyllic setting.*

Harmony Cremona No. 1262 1933 (*main guitar*) Grand concert-sized archtop with shaded red mahogany sunburst top.

Harmony Monterey No. 1327 c1948 (*far right*) Grand auditorium-sized archtop.

Harmony catalog 1959 (*top of this page*) An array of archtops in the Harmony acoustic line.

Except for some electric models, all American Harmonys – it may be surprising to learn – featured solid timbers, never laminates.

Harmony was founded in 1892 by Wilhelm J.F. Schultz, a German immigrant from Hamburg. By 1897 it was providing standard and concert-sized guitars for the fledgling Sears, and by 1899 these included guitars with trapeze tails for steel strings. Most had ladder-braced spruce tops with bodies ranging from faux-finished birch to figured oak, mahogany, and magnolia. The first decade of the 20th century saw sizes increase to grand concert and auditorium. In 1914 Harmony introduced perhaps the first adjustable bridge – a metal unit with set screws for adjustments.

It was also in 1914 that the Sears brand name Supertone appeared. Interest in Hawaiian music surged, especially following the popular 1915 Panama Pacific International Exposition in San Francisco. Already selling Harmony ukuleles, Sears purchased the guitar-maker in 1916 and produced a line of Hawaiian instruments, including mahogany and koa guitars. Harmony increasingly used faux finishes and

its WLS radio star and Supertone recording artist Bradley Kincaid.

At that time the Harmony brand began to be identified in jobber catalogs, and it introduced its first 12-strings and a pinless bridge that would also typify Harmonys for years to come.

Harmony thrived during the Depression. In 1932 it debuted stenciled designs, innovative 'crystalline' textured finishes, its popular Vagabond line, a Gene Autry Roundup model, and two other Harmony trademarks: the all-mahogany Patrician flat-top and the Cremona, its first archtop with a 14-fret neck.

Archtops continued to grow with Patricians, and in 1936 Harmony produced its first carved-top guitars for Sears, which matured into the high-end Cremonas of the late 1930s. In 1937 the popular Monterey, Marquise, and Vogue lines appeared, as well as the classic standard-size Harmonys with faux finishes. The following year Harmony bought the Stella and Sovereign brand names from Oscar Schmidt's successor, Fretting Instruments. Stella eventually became the budget standards and Sovereign a line of resonators with National/Dobro parts. Later, Sovereign would

produced a harp guitar with both fretted and unfretted six-string necks. In 1925 Sears' Max Adler installed his nephew, Jay Kraus, as vice president of Harmony. When founder Wilhelm Schultz died soon after, Kraus became president.

By 1925 Harmony was producing guitars trimmed in pearloid and several models had floral 'decalomania' (decorative and often colorful decals) on the bellies, practices that would characterize Harmonys through the Depression.

With Kraus in charge Harmony was on a roll. In 1928 it introduced a novel, fixed airplane-shaped bridge commemorating Charles Lindbergh's 1927 transatlantic solo flight. The bridge featured on a pearl-encrusted Artist and a line of pear-shaped Vita instruments endorsed by Roy Smeck, the 'Wizard of the Strings.' In 1929, in a stroke of brilliant cross-marketing, Sears had Harmony produce the first 'singing cowboy' guitar – a spruce and mahogany Houn' Dog with mountain scene decalomania – for

Harmony Sovereign Model H-1203 1957 (*near right*) *Harmony's long-running Sovereign flat-top in its 'near dreadnought' guise.*

Harmony Sovereign H-55 Dual Purpose 1959 (*second right*) *This Sovereign takes the grand concert size, with built-in pickup.*

Harmony Model H-162 c1960 (*far right*) *Another grand concert-sized flat-top.*

Harmony catalogs 1950s/ 1960s (*top of this page*) *Note the overtly colorful Holiday Colorama and Caribbean series.*

Harmony ad 1963 *British publicity has Harmony clearly fitting the entire bill, from R&B to country'n'western.*

become Harmony's flagship dreadnought. The first ownership change in 25 years came in 1941, when Sears sold Harmony to Jay Kraus and a group of investors. Kraus ran the Harmony operation until his death in 1968, after which the company was governed by a trust.

Following the war, Harmony settled into a groove that would see it through the 1960s guitar boom and beyond. Harmony's 1930s archtops continued, joined by budget models with white striping, and interesting Patricians with contrasting central panels, alternating mahogany and maple. Cutaway archtops debuted in 1952; adjustable reinforced necks waited until 1956. Flat-tops, including an all-mahogany grand concert, initially had a rounded form inherited from Schmidt, but in 1956 began to switch to the square-shouldered shape that would dominate thereafter. That same year saw the introduction of the two-tone, aluminum-trimmed Holiday Colorama guitars. In 1958 the new Western Jumbo Sovereign shape appeared.

Little changed substantially in Harmony acoustics for years. In 1967 mustache bridges with adjustable saddles debuted, and in '68 flat-tops with six-in-line heads. Harmony rolled out a line of Regal dreadnoughts in 1972 and began offering guitars finished in black, but the company soon dwindled in the face of import competition.

In 1975, it made one final push with the Opus series of fancy jumbo flat-tops. Some red, white, and blue Bicentennial dreadnoughts followed, and that was it. In 1976 the name was sold to the Global conglomerate. In 1978 IMC, importers of Hondo guitars, briefly marketed a line of Korean-made Harmonys. Through the intervening years the brand would appear on low-end Asian guitars. In 2000 MBT International attempted to revive the brand, still Asian. Plans for a comprehensive line of historical reissues were laid, but there was not enough equity left in the venerable old name to carry it off. The Harmony name did appear in the early 2000s on some ¾-size flat-tops with a monochrome copy of the old 1960s Singing Cowboys stencil guitars. The Harmony brand was acquired by Westheimer in 2009.

HARPTONE

According to its own accounts, the Harptone Manufacturing Company of Newark, New Jersey, a major instrument-case manufacturer since 1886, 'initiated' production of guitars from 1934-42, but if any were actually made, it may have been by the nearby Oscar Schmidt company.

In 1966 Harptone set up a workshop and hired luthier Sam Koontz to produce a

Harmony Sovereign Model H1260 1965 (left) *A jumbo-sized Sovereign flat-top.*

Harmony Custom Built No. 174 1961 (right) *Top-of-the-line Chicago-built classical guitar.*

Big Joe Williams 1968 (opposite page) *The bluesman plays a modified Harmony Sovereign at the Hammersmith Odeon Jazz Expo, London. Note the extra tuners installed at the headstock to add more strings to Williams's guitar.*

Harmony Patrician No. 1407 1966 *An auditorium-sized archtop with solid spruce top.*

line of Standel guitars – consisting of carved-top, cutaway acoustic-electric archtops, and thinlines – all distinguished by large, cutout headstocks and introduced in 1967. In 1969 Lark, Pioneer, and Eagle flat-tops appeared, and all became Harptones when CMI bought Standel that year. George Harrison and Ringo Starr endorsed these. In 1974, David Sturgill of Nashville's Grammer Guitars purchased the operation for his Diamond S company based in Independence, Virginia, which itself closed in 1976.

H A U S E R

The instruments of the first Hermann Hauser were the first important classical guitars to originate outside Spain. Many would say they are still the greatest.

Hauser was the son of an instrument-maker, and began building zithers at the age of 18 before turning to the guitar, which he also played. His early instruments were in the small, bright European tradition, with shallow bodies and an exaggerated hourglass shape. By 1924, he had built some 250 fine guitars in that mold, even developing and patenting a new system of asymmetrical bracing to enhance their treble notes. Then, in 1925, he was introduced to Segovia, and everything changed. Segovia brought with him his 1912 Manuel Ramírez guitar, usually said to have been built by Santos Hernández in the Torres tradition. Segovia convinced Hauser that his future lay in adopting this Spanish model, which he considered as significant for the guitar as Stradivarius had been for the violin. It took another 12 years before he completed the guitar that Segovia declared the greatest guitar of our epoch.

Hauser would go on to make more than 200 guitars in the Spanish tradition before his death in 1952. Julian Bream was another enthusiastic Hauser owner, noting that the German maker's scientific approach had allowed him to reduce thickness and weight to a minimum while retaining strength. The guitars were also to have a huge influence on other makers, starting with José Ramírez III, who was asked by Segovia to repair the 1937 Hauser I, and took the opportunity to examine the instrument carefully. The experience caused him to reevaluate his own designs.

Later, Bream's 1936 Hauser helped José Romanillos find his way. Bream invited Romanillos to repair the instrument, make drawings of it, and then build six copies. Romanillos made two more. He has since credited the Hauser with launching his own career as a professional guitar-maker. Indeed, the creation of Hauser I copies has become a considerable industry for young makers in Britain and the US.

In due course, Hermann Hauser was joined by his son, known as Hauser II or

Harmony Sovereign 1971
(*left*) *A fat-waisted dreadnought Sovereign in full cowboy dress.*

Harmony Opus XX 1975
(*right*) *This jumbo-sized flat-top was part of the last American-made line before the sale of the company, which triggered the import-only era of Harmony guitars.*

Fred Neil early 1960s (*above*)
Neil spins out his folk-jazz-blues stylings on a Harmony 12-string with add-on soundhole pickup.

Hermann Hauser Jr. While keeping close to his father's tradition, he experimented with different strutting and a larger Ramírez-style guitar. His instruments are elegant and beautifully finished, and were prized by players including Segovia, Bream and the Romeros. He died in 1988, handing on the business to his son Hermann Hauser III, who had trained as an instrument maker before joining the family firm in 1978.

The young man found the legacy hard to manage at first. But he inherited both a strong technical tradition and a formidable quantity of excellent wood, including a supply of spruce said to be more than 80 years old. His own input has come in decorative detail more than design, although he, too, has experimented with strutting and red cedar tops. He offers three models: the Segovia, based on the 1937 instrument; the Bream, based on another Hauser I guitar; and his own Dream, combining features of the two.

He remains essentially a hand-builder, producing a maximum of 17 guitars a year. His guitars have been played by Pepe and Angel Romero, Akinobu Matsudu, and the Argentine player Manuel López Ramos. Hermann Hauser III once said he deplored the tendency among other makers to build ever-louder classical guitars, explaining that loud instruments lack dynamics, clarity, and balance.

HERITAGE

Heritage was founded in Kalamazoo, Michigan, by a handful of former Gibson employees. Although the bulk of the Heritage line consists of electric guitars, it has produced a handful of acoustic instruments over the years, such as the flat-top HTF-445 dreadnought and the H-5 mandolin. By 2017, a couple of archtop guitars — the Sweet 16 and Golden Eagle — were fitted with floating magnetic pickups but at heart were essentially acoustic instruments.

HILO

Thanks to certain similarities at first glance, Hilo Hawaiian guitars are often wrongly attributed to Weissenborn rather than their real manufacturer, the Oscar Schmidt Company. Hilo's distinguishing features include ladder bracing, slotted headstocks, and paper labels with serial numbers. Contrasting with Weissenborn's curved backs and tapered headstock joint, Hilo backs are parallel to the tops and have a pronounced arc where the hollow neck and headstock meet. Hilo models are numbered in the 600s ending in -5 or -0. A 1929 Sherman Clay catalog shows five models: the 625 (western cedar) at $17.50; 640 (rope-bound spruce top with

Harmony Model 167 Folk 1968 (left) *Note the Fender-inspired headstock on this otherwise standard, budget-range flat-top.*

Andrés Segovia (above) *The classical maestro was a noted Hauser player.*

Hauser I 1935 (left) *This example from one of the 20th century's leading classical guitar builders was one of the first to bear his distinctive 'triple-arch' headstock.*

Back (above) *A rear view of this 1935 Hauser reveals the highly prized Brazilian rosewood that complements its European spruce top.*

Hauser II Miguel Llobet Model 1971 (*right*) An elegant example of this model named for noted classical guitarist Llobet.

Pepe Romero album 1996 (*center*) Romero used his Hauser II instrument to record this CD.

Hauser III 1988 (*far right*) In this model, Hauser III introduced some changes to his grandfather's design template, including a top of western red cedar braced by stronger, central fan-pattern bracing.

mahogany) at $25; 650 (mahogany) at $35; 655 (maple with fancy appointments) at $40; and the 670 (black-bound koa) at $50. (Other Hilo model numbers may exist, such as a model 676 with serial number 1 – perhaps a custom order or one-off – that has been documented.)

HODSON

While half of David Hodson's building work is devoted to standard Selmer-style guitars, the remainder of his production efforts are devoted to less 'usual' guitars – such as seven-string Hawaiian models, 12-strings, and tenor guitars – and other fretted instruments like basses, ukeleles, and mandolins. Hodson started making mandolins and dulcimers in 1969 as a hobby and became a full-time instrument-maker in 1993. He was one of a growing number of luthiers who took the Selmer/Maccaferri guitar designs of the 1930s and applied them to other fretted instruments. He died in 2007.

HÖFNER

Höfner was founded in 1887 in Schönbach, Germany by violin-maker Karl Höfner, and by the outbreak of World War I the company was Germany's largest manufacturer of stringed instruments. Sons Josef and Walter joined the company around 1920, and the operation expanded enough to survive the hardships of the second war. In 1950, Höfner opened a new factory in Bubenreuth, where it is still located. The Höfner family had ownership until 1994, when it joined the Boosey & Hawkes Group. In its history so far, Höfner has manufactured over two million stringed instruments.

Although best known for the violin-shaped electric 'Beatle Bass,' Höfner has, since the beginning, been a leading European manufacturer of acoustic guitars, ranging from student models to premium instruments. Höfner's nylon-string (and flat-top steel-string) acoustic guitars have generally been in the lower-to-medium price ranges, but have occasionally offered more distinctive models: the Selmer/Django style 600, for example, made during the second half of the 1970s and also available with a built-in piezo pickup, or the CS-1 thinbody electro-acoustic Spanish guitar, made in the early 1980s.

But Höfner's archtops are generally the most acclaimed of its acoustics, and from the early 1950s onwards it offered several notable archtop models, strictly acoustic as well as fitted with floating pickups. The first archtops (non-cutaway) looked reasonably conventional, but as the 1950s progressed, so did the design efforts.

Inlays – often art déco-ish – literally flourished, as did multiple binding, elaborate headstocks, and f-holes of any shape but an 'f.' A good example is model 461 (made from 1954 to 1964), a cutaway archtop with assymetrical f-holes plus a small oval soundhole at the end of the fretboard, or the 459 (1954-1960) with regular f-holes plus a diamond-shaped soundhole at the end of the fretboard. A collectors' favorite was always the 470 (1961-1994), with a beautiful flamed maple back with black vine-style inlays near the bottom edge. The Committee, President, and Senator archtops were built specially for Selmer UK from 1953, and many fledgling British players had early playing adventures with them, including a teenage George Harrison, whose President had the typical vine-inlay headstock and triple-dot markers of the model.

Archtops gave way to solidbodies during the 1960s, but a couple of noteworthy archtops were introduced in the 1980s: the AZ (a signature model for Hungarian jazz guitarist Attila Zoller) in 1982, and the still-in-catalog Jazzica in 1990. Hofner was sold in 1994 to Boosey & Hawkes, who sold its instrument division in 2003 to The Music Group, and the following year Hofner was sold to Klaus Schöller and Ulrike Schrimpff. They developed Chinese manufacturing in addition to the factory in Hagenau for a line of old and new models, including a couple of flat-tops and several classicals.

Höfner President 1957 (*left*)
This archtop, one of several models built specially for Selmer UK, typifies Höfner's simple elegance of the period.

Höfner ad 1975 (*far left*)
"Höfner … for that good old country music!" declares this ad, though it's hardly associated with the genre.

Höfner late 1950s (*right*) *Note the full-width pearloid block position markers and matching headstock facings on this cutaway archtop model.*

Höfner 491 1966 (*above*) *This big-bodied flat-top has a spruce top and mahogany back and sides.*

H U M P H R E Y

Thomas Humphrey's guitars may not be the most radical ever built, but they are among the most adventurous to have won a following among concert professionals. Humphrey began his career in 1970 in New York City, where he found a job at the guitar workshop of Michael Gurian. He soon realised that this was to be his vocation, and began building his own instruments in a traditional Spanish style, with some Hauser influence. From the beginning he was interested in developing power and speed.

Humphrey insists the idea for his most celebrated innovation, the Millennium guitar, came to him in a dream early in 1985. He quickly sketched its main design idea, setting the neck and strings at an oblique angle to the soundboard rather than running parallel to it. This almost harp-like arrangement provides extra projection as well as improved access to the top frets.

Nonetheless, the guitar is made and finished in traditional materials, Brazilian rosewood for the body and either cedar or spruce for the top. This has, no doubt, eased its acceptance by the concert fraternity. Prominent Humphrey players include Sharon Isbin, Elliot Fisk, David Tanenbaum, and many more. More recently, Humphrey has turned to lattice strutting, rather than the traditional fan arrangement used in his earliest instruments.

In the late 1980s, he designed a Millennium-style guitar for the manufacturer C.F. Martin. Several models were produced, including a Sting model with a pickup. They were not, however, considered a great success.

By 2003 Humphrey was living in Gardiner, New York, where he made about 40 instruments a year, working with his wife Martha. He suggested that one day it might be possible to build a guitar as loud and responsive as a piano – but perhaps not for a thousand years. Humphrey died in 2008 at the age of just 59.

I B A N E Z

Through determination and innovation, Ibanez has built a reputation as one of the world's top producers of electric guitars, but few know that the brand's parent, Hoshino Gakki Ten, began as an acoustic guitar company and actually manufactured its own acoustics longer than it did electrics. Curious copies as well as high-quality

Höfner Model 178 1965 (right)
This German-made classical guitar is an example of the sort of instrument for which Höfner continues to earn respect.

Höfner ads 2003 (top of page)
Classical guitars are the main focus of the contemporary Höfner company.

Humphrey Millennium 1993 (far right) *The most visually evident feature of Thomas Humphrey's distinctive Millennium model is its angled top and 'negative' neck angle, better seen in the side view (center).*

original models are part of the Ibanez heritage. And, yes, their guitars were indeed played by The Grateful Dead.

The Hoshino story began in the 19th century when Matsujiro Hoshino opened a bookstore in Nagoya, Japan, then developed a musical division under his son Yoshitaro in 1908. In 1929, the Hoshino Music Instrument Company was founded to distribute instruments, including guitars sourced from the Salvador Ibanez factory in Valencia, Spain. Salvador Ibanez had begun making guitars in 1875 and became Spain's largest guitar manufacturer. Upon his death in 1920, the company was taken over by two sons.

Hoshino's entry into the guitar market coincided with Andrés Segovia's first tour of Japan – good timing for a company dealing largely in Spanish-built classical guitars. Hoshino's musical success would be primarily the work of Yoshitaro's four sons, Ryohei, Jumpei, Masao, and Yoshihiro.

The Great Depression was good to Hoshino, as hard times encouraged people to create their own entertainment. Hoshino's business soon surpassed the capacity of its Spanish supplier and they began sourcing guitars from small companies in the violin-making region around Matsumoto city. Hoshino began manufacturing its own

flat-top and archtop guitars in Nagoya in 1935, calling them simply Ibanez. Soon Hoshino was exporting regionally and even sent a few guitars to the US. World War II intervened and all of Hoshino's assets were destroyed in bombing raids.

Rebuilding from scratch, Hoshino was manufacturing acoustic guitars again by the mid 1950s. In 1962, a larger factory called Tama Manufacturing Company was built, named for Yoshitaro's recently deceased wife. During the 1960s Hoshino exported beginner-grade acoustic guitars in standard, concert, and auditorium size to the US and other markets. Early Ibanez guitars had solid tops, but shrinkage caused by the severe climate change between Japan and the US led to a switch to laminates, and Hoshino remained wary of solid woods until the early 1990s.

To solidify its position in the American market, in late 1971 Hoshino purchased a share of the Elger Guitar Company of Ardmore, Pennsylvania, a small manufacturer of flat-top and archtop guitars that had been run by Harry Rosenbloom since 1959. In 1974 Rosenbloom sold his shares in Elger, and Yoshitada Hoshino became president. Elger production ceased at this time, and Hoshino put the company's equipment to use primarily for repairs and set-ups rather than for any new guitar-making.

Beginning in the early 1970s Ibanez acoustics entered the 'copy' phase of its

Humphrey Millennium 1987
(*right*) *Another example (see also opposite), this one from six years earlier and displaying a significantly different design. Note in particular the scrolled headstock and the unusual, wide f-holes high on the upper bout.*

Ibanez Model 642 1977 (*far right*) *This Martin-influenced 00-sized flat-top is typical of Japanese-built Ibanez acoustics of the 'copy era.'*

history, alongside most prominent Asian makers of the day. Hoshino named its top-line guitars Tama; they were mainly upscale, solid-topped dreadnoughts (and classicals) inspired initially by Martins, some with three-piece backs and full tree-of-life fingerboard inlays.

At the same time the Ibanez brand emulated popular Gibson and Martin models, but with laminated tops. These included copies of Hummingbirds and Doves, as well as fancy D-41-style dreadnoughts with abalonoid trim. By 1974 original ideas began to creep in, like three-piece jacaranda and maple backs and even perhaps the first maple fingerboard. From 1974-78 Ibanez also made an Artist Series of mahogany, rosewood or flamed maple dreadnoughts and jumbos with what would be the Artist headstock on electric models. Copies of less-imitated Gallagher and Fender dreadnoughts were available from 1975.

In 1976, facing pressure from Gibson, the Ibanez line changed its headstock to the more Guild-like tulip shape – also used on electrics – and these guitars were dubbed the Concord Series. The Tama instruments also took on unique curved headstocks and pickguards, though Martin-style Ibanez guitars made it into the early 1980s.

From 1976 to '79 Hoshino produced a line of Gypsy guitars designed by Mario

Maccaferri in conjunction with Maurice J. Summerfield of Summerfield Brothers in the UK, who was responsible for recruiting many endorsers, including acoustic ace John Pearse.

From around 1978-81 Ibanez acoustics began to diversify, mixing both traditional designs with new ideas, including scalloped braces, a curious series of Arched Back Dreadnoughts, and some models looking like Guilds, but with no back braces, said to improve sound. Also available was an FA-800 cutaway acoustic archtop.

Around the turn of the decade the Tama brand was improved and renamed as Ibanez Artwood, including a few hand-made models. Ibanez produced some inexpensive Champion dreadnoughts in 1979, and also put into production a limited edition Marcel Dadi signature model.

Cutaway flat-tops debuted in 1980 as the Ragtimes, round-bodied models with an oval soundhole. Ragtimes would be periodically reflected in the Ibanez line.

In 1981 the Elger company name was retired in favor of Hoshino (USA). Kimihide (Ken) Hoshino became the new president.

Ibanez returned to all-solid woods for the first time in many years in 1983 with its Naturalwood dreadnoughts, made from cedar, jacaranda, and koa. It also produced its

Ibanez ad 2001 *Paul Gilbert translates his electric shred-metal stylings into some convincing Ibanez acoustic promotion.*

Ibanez catalog 2003 *(center)*
Promo for the jumbo-bodied AE Series.

Ibanez Artwood 2002 *(far left)*
This mid-range dreadnought has a solid spruce top, laminated mahogany back and sides, and rosewood bridge and fingerboard.

Ibanez AEL-20TBS 2003 *(left)*
This maple-bodied cutaway electro has a Fishman Sonicore pickup and Ibanez's own AEQ-SS Shape Shifter on-board equaliser.

Management changes paralleled the continuing evolution of the Ibanez acoustic line through the difficult mid 1980s. In 1985 Ken Hoshino returned to Japan and Mike Shimada was moved from Europe to run Hoshino USA.

Around 1987 Ibanez unveiled the Performance range of laminated-top dreadnoughts. These PFs would anchor the line, but for the latter part of the 1980s Ibanez focused primarily on electric guitars. Also around this time Hoshino began experiencing its perennial problem of unfavorable yen/dollar exchange rates and had to shift production of less expensive guitars to Korea. At this time long-time Hoshino USA associate Tom Tanaka assumed the presidency.

The pace of transfer to Korean production quickened and by about 1992 most Ibanez acoustics were made in Korea, with the lower range having laminated tops and more upscale guitars having solid timbers.

This also coincided with the appearance of the MTV *Unplugged* phenomenon, and Ibanez began to show a renewed interest in acoustics. Hoshino developed a relationship with Fishman pickups, and in 1992 introduced three new Korean-made lines, including Nomad cutaway dreadnoughts, yet more Ragtimes, and a revamped Performance series. A short-lived f-hole flat-top Charleston and Tulsa grand concert

AE (Acoustic Electric) line for a couple years, mainly as Ragtimes with piezo pickups. The AEs came back in 1990 as cutaway dreadnoughts and Ragtimes, staying in production off and on thereafter.

Six-in-line headstocks appeared in 1984 on a line of dreadnoughts and thin-bodies called the Lonestars (which beat Kramer's Ferringtons to the styling), and these were joined by some asymmetrical cutaway models in 1986. From 1986 to '88 the solid-topped Artwood line was revived.

Ibanez AEL-2012THS *(right) A 12-string from the AE Series.*

Ibanez Artwood AW-200CEVV 2003 *(far right) A cutaway dreadnought for the contemporary plugged-in crowd, this Artwood model has a solid spruce top, flamed maple veneer back and sides, and Fishman pickup and EQ.*

Ibanez ad 2012 *(above) An on-stage setting for this promo selling the Artwood (AW) series of flat-tops.*

appeared in 1994. Also at this time the GA series classical guitars debuted, with cool pagoda-shaped heads.

Another long-time Hoshino USA stalwart, Roy Miyahara, assumed the presidency in 1998. A year later Ibanez was innovating again with the MASA series, which featured a magnetic rather than piezo pickup system, a throwback to the early days of acoustic-electrics. In 2000 the Talman mid-bodied, glued-neck acoustic-electrics appeared in the shape of its retro electric brother.

Roy Miyahara retired in 2002 and the helm of Hoshino USA was manned by another long-term employee, this time an American, Bill Reim. Acoustic guitars remain an important part of the current Ibanez offerings.

JONES

The custom-built Dobro-style resonators of Rudy Q. Jones were favored by most of the top Dobro players of the 1980s, including Josh Graves, Jerry Douglas, Mike Auldridge, and Gene Wooten.

Based in Wanette, Oklahoma, Jones made about 500 instruments from 1976-85, introducing such innovative features as solid wood construction (mahogany, maple or seasoned walnut), a wider upper bout, deeper body, wider string spacing, a system of inner baffles, and the absence of a 'soundwell' (a circular piece of wood surrounding the resonator cone). Jones moved later to northern Florida and occasionally built instrument for friends. He died in 2015.

KALAMAZOO

Kalamazoo archtops and flattops were manufactured and marketed by Gibson in the 1930s and early '40s.

These first Kalamazoo guitars were roughly equivalent to the lower-end Gibson models except that they did not have Gibson's patented adjustable truss-rod in the neck. Consequently, Gibson could produce less expensive guitars that were more affordable to Americans recovering from the Great Depression, and the creation of the Kalamazoo brand for these arguably 'inferior' guitars effectively maintained Gibson's status as a premium brand.

Gibson's first venture into budget brands came in 1930 with a pair of inexpensive flat-tops bearing the Kel Kroydon brand. The mahogany bodies were the same as Gibson's L-0 model, but the spruce tops looked quite different as they were decorated

Ibanez GA-5WCE 2003 *(left) A cutaway acoustic-electric classical guitar, made from laminated woods.*

Ibanez PF-60TBL 2003 *(center) This budget-range dreadnought is from Ibanez's Performance Series, a laminated-woods line positioned below the more upscale Artwoods.*

Ibanez SX72TBC 2015 *(right) This SX model has an AP2 magnetic at the neck and a Fishman bridge pickup, which Ibanez said combined punch and definition for the amplified sound.*

with a pair of tropical birds on one model and a Hawaiian volcano scene on the other.

In 1933 Gibson abandoned Kel Kroydon and introduced the Kalamazoo brand. The first model, the KG-11 flat-top, looked cheaper than any Gibson, due to a short, stubby body shape. The models that followed were more Gibson-like in style and overall character: there was the KG-14 of 1936, essentially the Gibson L-0; the ¾-size Sport of 1937; and the KGN-12 of 1940, a natural-top model with a decal of an Oriole bird on the headstock.

The first Kalamazoo archtop, the KG-31, appeared in 1935. It looked like Gibson's 16" midline model, the L-50, but had a mahogany body rather than maple, and the top was pressed into shape rather than carved.

The KG-21, a mahogany version of Gibson's 14¾" L-30, joined the line a year later. The models offered with the Kalamazoo brand eventually included 16"-wide archtops with maple back and sides (KG-32), a true carved-top (KG-22), and natural finish (KGN-32 Oriole).

The prices of Kalamazoos corresponded roughly with their model numbers and sold for around half of comparable Gibsons, but because none of the Kalamazoos produced the volume of the larger-body Gibsons, they were not used by professional musicians, with the possible exception of blues legend Robert Johnson. One of Johnson's contemporaries, Johnny Shines, has said that Johnson preferred Kalamazoos, no doubt due to Kalamazoo's combination of Gibson construction and budget-brand price.

With America's entry into World War II in December 1941, Gibson stopped producing Kalamazoos. After the war, Epiphone (which Gibson acquired in 1957) became in effect Gibson's budget line.

The Kalamazoo brand reappeared only briefly, being seen for about a year from 1968 on the KG-10 model, a lowly flat-top fashioned in the style of Gibson's all-mahogany LG-0.

Gibson now delineates and protects the Gibson brand by geography, making Gibsons in the US and importing Epiphones, although the system was blurred a little by the Nouveau By Gibson brand, used from 1986-87 on guitars assembled in the US from imported parts, and the Orville By Gibson brand, used in the early 1990s on guitars licensed in Japan exclusively for the Japanese market. The concept of a less-expensive guitar made by Gibson, but without the Gibson brand on the instrument, ended with the last Kalamazoo.

Ibanez AW-40NT 2003 *(left)* *Dreadnought-size with solid woods and gloss finish, natural spruce top, mahogany back and sides, and vine inlays on the fingerboard.*

Ibanez EW20ZWE 2007 *(center)* *This member of Ibanez's Exotic Wood series was built from zebrawood, which explains the extravagant figure on show.*

Kalamazoo KG-14 1938 *This budget model resembles the L-style flat-tops of its maker, Gibson, but lacks the L's truss-rod, and was assembled using woods of less good quality.*

KAY

During its heyday, the Kay Musical Instrument Company was usually right behind Harmony as one of the largest of the Chicago guitar powerhouses, providing tons of guitars for the beginner-to-intermediate market and pioneering the use of laminated woods for added durability. Although known mainly as a budget brand after World War II, back when archtops were king it produced some beauties, and some of its early flat-tops were also quite respectable.

Kay was founded in Chicago in 1890 as the Groeshl (or Groeshel) company, producing mandolins and adding guitars around 1918, some with unusual shapes. In 1921 Groeshl became the Stromberg-Voisinet Company (S-V). S-V guitars were said to be of the Stromberg brand (not connected with the Boston maker), although they carried neither labels nor logos. They ranged from typical standard to auditorium flat-tops, with ladder bracing, pin bridges (for gut) or trapeze tails (for steel), spruce or birch tops (some with faux finishes), and solid birch, mahogany, or even koa bodies.

In 1923 Henry Kay Kuhrmeyer joined S-V and became the driving force behind its success. S-V continued to grow, making many of Montgomery Ward's Concertone guitars and Buegeleisen & Jacobson's Serenaders. In the following year S-V began to

Kay K-40 1941 (right) *This big-bodied archtop is a fine example of Kay's better early work.*

Scrapper Blackwell (opposite page) *The bluesman relaxes at home with his strung-up Kay flat-top.*

Kay Kraft Style B c1933 (left) *This unusual asymmetrical-bodied, round-holed archtop was designed by Chicago luthier Joseph Zorzi, who was head of archtop guitar production for Kay from 1927 to 1934.*

Kay catalog 1964 (above) *Promo for the Solo Special flat-top and a pair of midrange archtops.*

use lamination for some tops and bodies, although it continued to use solid timbers as well. Also in 1924 S-V introduced possibly the earliest fake pearl trim. By the mid 1920s S-V was using 'decalomania' (decorative and often colorful body decals).

In 1926 S-V hired former Lyon & Healy luthiers Joseph Zorzi and Philip Gabriel to refresh the line. They infused new ideas, including two-point Venetian guitars (both flat-tops and adjustable bolt-neck archtops) by the following year, plus the telltale Stromberg pointed mustache bridge and half-slotted French curve head with engraved back. Venetian guitars, and a subsequent range of jumbo flat-tops, were called Kay Kraft after Kuhrmeyer. S-V Venetian flat-tops became what were perhaps the first electric guitars, the Stromberg Electros, in 1928, with an early transducer pickup. Probably in late 1931, and certainly before 1934, S-V changed its name to the Kay Musical Instrument Company.

During the Depression Kay continued to thrive and diversify. In 1933 it introduced its first Spanish archtops (with round soundholes) called Arch Kraft. That year Kay also first used f-holes, at the waist on both a flat-top and archtop, and began making National El Trovador resonator guitars, S.S. Maxwell Amplifying Guitars (Targ & Dinner), and some Schireson Bros Hollywood resonator guitars. Its own Kaywood

Amplifying guitars – with ineffective wooden resonators – appeared in 1934. By 1936 Kay was offering genuine carved-top archtops, one almost as expensive as a Gibson, plus a super-jumbo archtop with its first steel-reinforced neck.

Throughout the 1930s Kay was also the primary supplier of Oahu guitars for Harry Stanley's Hawaiian music operation. In 1939 Kay briefly supplied Gretsch with a few of its acoustics. Along with all of these, another brand produced by Kay just before and after the war was Lark.

Use of the Kay brand name itself began around 1937, at the same time that the company produced its strange fiddle-cut Violin Guitars – flat-tops and archtops with lyre-shaped soundholes – and models with new faux-flame finishes. In 1938 Kay introduced its most highly regarded archtop ever, the luxurious Television model.

In 1940-41, as Sears separated from Harmony, some models with Sears' new Silvertone brand were briefly made by Kay.

After the war Kay returned with archtops, including carved spruce Artists and jumbo flat-tops. Kay also produced the budget Kamico brand, the Rex line sold through Gretsch, and some Resonator guitars using National Dobro parts.

In 1952 Kay's first cutaway archtops appeared with fancy carved tops and u-bar

neck reinforcement. A new adjustable Speed Demon neck and cutaway flat-tops debuted in 1955, and Hank Kuhrmeyer retired, succeeded by Sidney M. Katz.

One of the most distinctive Kay designs of all time arrived in 1956 in the form of the plastic 'Kelvinator' headstock facings (so-named for their resemblance to the Sears appliance line of the '50s), and the company introduced its first dreadnought that same year. The following year a bunch of new laminated archtops and flat-tops appeared, with 'Semi-Kelvinator' headstocks, and these defined the line until 1965.

In late 1965, Kay was sold to the Seeburg Corporation, famous for juke-boxes. A number of new flat-tops appeared the following year, with features such as cool bullhorn inlays, bat-shaped bridges, and batwing pickguards.

Seeburg quickly soured on guitar-making and in 1967 Kay was sold to Valco, the post-war evolution of the National Dobro company. Unfortunately debt, plummeting demand, and import competition caused Valco/Kay to close in 1968.

In 1969, the Kay name was sold at auction to Chicago's WMI, owned by Sil Weindling and Barry Hornstein, importers of Teisco del Rey and Checkmate guitars from Japan. WMI began to move its Japanese brands to the Kay name, a process that was complete around 1973. During the rest of the 1970s Kay acoustics were made in Japan and Korea, except for the Kay Force guitars that were produced in the US in 1978-79. These were curious acoustic and acoustic-electric dreadnoughts with molded, round-cornered plastic bodies. Unfortunately a miscalculation in tooling necessitated expensive handwork. In 1980, Tony Blair and A.R. Musical Enterprises near Indianapolis, Indiana, purchase the brand. Blair recently sold A.R. Musical, which continues to import to the US Kay guitars made in various parts of Asia.

K L E I N

California luthier/designer Steve Klein is known for continuously pushing the envelope of traditional guitar design. He built his first instrument in 1967, and has been equally prolific in acoustic and electric guitar designs. His acoustics are heavily influenced by the design concepts of Dr. Michael Kasha, and tend to feature jumbo bodies, flying braces, and asymmetrical bridges. In 1994, Klein entered a partnership with fellow luthier Steve Kauffman, who took on much of the actual construction of Klein guitars. In 1991, Klein co-designed the Taylor AB-1 acoustic bass, and in 2001 he designed a line of acoustics for the Japanese company Kiso Guitars. Players of Klein guitars include Joni Mitchell, Bill Frisell, and Andy Summers.

Kay K-217 1957 (right) This acoustic archtop echoes the styling of the famed Barney Kessel Jazz Special – including 'Kelvinator' headstock – minus the electronics.

Kay K-588 1977 (center) This Korean-made dreadnought is from the final period of WMI's ownership of the Kay brand.

Kay Force 2E 1978 (far right) A plastic-bodied dreadnought made in the USA by Sil Weindling and Barry Hornstein of WMI in an attempt to re-establish American Kay production.

Kay catalog c1970s (above) Folk guitars of the period... with some arguably misguided pickguards.

K O O N T Z

New Jersey native Sam Koontz was famous for mounting devices such as amps and tape recorders into his archtop instruments. He began making guitars around 1959, starting with a classical and graduating to carved-top jazz boxes. His instruments are distinguished by fancy scrolled headstocks and experimental ideas, including an early acoustic six-string/12-string doubleneck.

Koontz designed several lines of guitars for Standel, made from 1967-69 at Harptone in Newark, New Jersey. In 1970 Koontz set up his own shop in Linden, New Jersey, where he supervised production of Harptones during the early 1970s and, before his death early in the following decade, built more than 200 guitars – some for prominent players such as Pat Martino.

K R A M E R / F E R R I N G T O N

If there was an electric-guitar success story of the 1980s it was undoubtedly Kramer, which by 1987 was the largest American guitar company. But Kramer also produced some acoustic and acoustic-electric guitars, most designed by luthier Danny Ferrington, aimed to make acoustic guitars palatable to rockers. This was achieved

Koontz Custom c1977 (near right) *New Jersey-based guitar-maker Sam Koontz was known for his unusual designs. Note the elaborate, even ungainly scrolled upper horn on this imposing cutaway archtop.*

Regent by Kramer KRG1 1985 (right) *This dreadnought, from a range that flopped commercially, was probably made in Korea, and is a predecessor to the Ferrington line.*

Kramer ad 1987 (far right) *The Ferrington thinline electro-acoustics were inspired by Kramer's solidbody models (and before them, without doubt, Fender's two best-known solidbody electrics).*

mainly by building acoustics that looked like electric guitars. The Kramer/Ferrington partnership thus changed the notion of acoustic styling forever.

Kramer decided to try acoustic guitars in 1985 and hooked up with luthier-to-the-stars Danny Ferrington, whose customers include the likes of Jackson Browne, Eric Clapton, and Pete Townshend. Ferrington had already built an acoustic-electric shaped like a Flying V and musicians liked it.

Ferrington designed a series of guitars for Kramer that were made in Korea. The first and most famous was a pair of thin-bodied acoustic-electrics, introduced in 1986: the Strat-shaped KFS-1 and Tele-shaped KFT-1 with plywood bodies in bright colors, bolt-on necks, and pointy heads. Thanks to endorsements by Eddie Van Halen and Dweezil Zappa they quickly took off.

Following fancier versions and changes to electronics, the upscale Kramer Ferrington Signatures included the SB (Stephen Bishop), RT (Richard Thompson), JS (J.D. Souther), and the DS (Danny Steve Ferrington). By 1990 Kramer was entering its death-throws. A few of the Kramer-style models were briefly marketed under the Ferrington brand after Kramer went under, but not for long. Ferrington continued to build custom guitars. The bold idea of acoustic-electric guitars with electric styling – introduced by Ferrington and Kramer – continues to appeal to the rocking crowd, so that periodically, in tribute, their Fender-style shapes reappear.

LAKEWOOD

The German company Lakewood, founded in 1985 by Martin Seeliger, ranks as one of continental Europe's finest medium-level acoustic makers. The six-strong launch range comprised solely dreadnoughts, ranked numerically according to timbers (solid woods throughout) and cosmetics, including the still high-selling spruce/rosewood D-32. M-Series Grand Concerts were added in '94 (and have since become catalog favorites, particularly the M-32), smaller A-Series Auditoriums a couple of years later, then J-Series jumbos in 1997. The late 1990s saw a price breakthrough with the cedar/mahogany D-1, at the time pretty much the cheapest all-solid-wood acoustic on the market, and still in the catalog today.

By 2016, with 12 production staff, Lakewood was celebrating its 30th anniversary, and also was offering models on a custom-menu basis. Pro users included Dave Matthews (two M-32s), Ritchie Blackmore (A-32, Moon Guitar), Radiohead's Thom Yorke (M-14) and The Hooters' Eric Bazilian (D-18).

Lakewood DM 2002 (*left*) An all-solid mahogany dreadnought from the German maker.

Lakewood ad (*above*) The company's promo material here projects the 'rustic workshop' image.

Lakewood M32 2003 (*right*) This spruce-topped grand concert-sized flat-top has become a leading model for Lakewood, and is played by Dave Matthews, among others.

LANDOLA

The company now known as Landola started in 1942 in
Pietarsaari, Finland as Munkers. During its first two
decades Landola aimed only at the domestic market. In
the early 1960s efforts were made to increase exports,
and guitars found their way to the European markets — under Landola's own name —
and to the US by way of wholesale distributors, mostly under España and Val Dez
brand names. Landola also worked as a subcontractor for other European makers,
including Levin. During the 1970s, Landola was owned by Finnish conglomerate Fazer,
and production concentrated on budget models. In 1983 ownership returned to the
Höglund family, involved in the company since the 1950s, and top quality instruments
began to appear. In the 1980s a line of flat-tops, dubbed
Aspen-Landola, was built for IMC in the US. Landola's
ThermoTonewood is artificially 'aged' wood intended to give
new guitars characteristics of those built from wood dried for
decades. Today Landola offers quality Spanish and flat-tops,
and electro-acoustics with Fishman or B-Band pickups.

**Landola-made España 6/12
Double-Neck 1970 (left)** Arguably
*a few years before the height of the
double-neck's popularity, this example
was made in Finland by Landola for sale
in the US through American distributor
Bugeleisen & Jacobson.*

Larrivée C10 1990 (right) *The
spruce-topped C10 is one of this
Canadian maker's longer-running steel-
string flat-tops. It was launched in 1968
just three years after Jean Larrivée
began building guitars.*

Landola ad 1993 (above) *A glass
of homebrew and that rounded cutaway
help our Landola player get to the dusty
end of the fingerboard.*

**Larrivée ad 1979 (far
right)** *One of the more elegant
and understated acoustic guitar
advertisements of the late 1970s.*

L A   P A T R I E

La Patrie classical guitars are made in Canada by Robert Godin's LaSiDo company and share characteristics with the parent Seagull brand. The philosophy is to provide good sound in a lower-priced instrument. They feature solid, old-growth cedar or spruce tops, with alcohol-based satin or high gloss lacquer finishes that allow the top to mature and age gracefully, and either solid or three-ply, cross-grain laminated sides and backs. Fingerboards are Indian rosewood or ebony with typical classical specs.

Originally introduced as Kamouraska guitars in 1982, the name was changed in 1984 to reflect the Quebec town in which they are made. While they appear to be conventional instruments, La Patrie guitars have bolt-on necks like Seagulls. They also have specially designed truss-rods that allow the Honduras mahogany necks to be much thinner than normally unreinforced classical necks.

The most popular model is the Etude, with tri-laminate mahogany/maple/mahogany body. Upscale models such as the Presentation and Collection have laminated Indian rosewood sides and solid backs. The Motif model offers a combination of a parlor-sized body with a full-scale fingerboard. Despite the entry-level price range, La Patrie classicals are played by some professionals, including Sylvain Luc.

Larrivée Cherub 2001 (*main guitar*) *Jean Larrivée's take on the popular 'baby guitar' theme.*

David Mead 2001 (*left*) *The singer-songwriter on-stage with his Larrivée dreadnought.*

Larrivée publicity (*below, left and right*) *These promos emphasize the more elaborate side of this Canadian maker's approach, and the catalog pages featured here show intricate abalone inlays and a highly-figured koa top (right).*

LARRIVÉE

With factories in both the US and Canada, Larrivée is one of the largest manufacturers of mid to high-end steel-string guitars. A student of classical guitar maker Edgar Mönch, Jean Larrivée founded the company in 1968, initially working out of his Toronto home. Following in his mentor's footsteps, Larrivée built classicals exclusively for the first few years of the company's existence. Repeated requests from Toronto's folk-music musicians eventually had him experimenting with the design of a steel-string model, and he eventually began to offer such an instrument beginning in 1971.

By virtue of their wood bindings, classical-style rosettes, and clear pickguards, Larrivée's steel-strings differed drastically from the Gibson or Martin-inspired guitars that dominated the era – and they remain somewhat apart to this day. These differences have always been more than just cosmetic: with a body that essentially used an enlarged classical guitar shape, Larrivée's original steel-strings (now called L-style) had little in common with other maker's steel-string designs. In addition, Larrivée modified the X-bracing typical of steel-string guitars according to his

experience with classical guitars. Featuring a symmetrical pattern, the design uses 90-degree transverse braces, rather than the more common Martin-style angled style.

To this day, the symmetrical bracing pattern remains at the heart of every Larrivée's construction. Although the original L-style body continues to be the company's most popular, Larrivée currently offers guitars also in OM, dreadnought, jumbo, and parlor sizes. In the past, Larrivée has produced 12-fret 00-size guitars, acoustic bass guitars, and a variety of nylon-string models. All of these variations continue to be available as special orders through the company's custom shop. Proving a staunch ability to adjust to the market, Larrivée even built a line of solidbody electric guitars during the 1980s, a period that offered slow sales for all acoustic guitar makers.

Although Larrivée started out making primarily high-end custom guitars, the company greatly expanded its line as it grew in size during the 1990s. The introduction of the satin-finished 03-Series in 1997 (available in all of the company's sizes) resulted in the least expensive all-solid wood guitars made in North America,

Ed Robertson 2000 (*above*) *The guitarist (and sometimes singer) with Canadian quirk-pop group Barenaked Ladies is a long-time Larrivée fan.*

Larrivée L-03 2015 (*left*) *From Larrivée's 03 Recording series, this example has optional micro dot inlays on its ebony fingerbaord.*

and the models continue to be immensely popular. A short time later, Larrivée introduced another affordable favorite in its Parlor model. Featuring a small body, 12-fret neck joint, and a short 24" scale, the guitar is a popular instrument for travel and for smaller players.

While Jean Larrivée's original design ideas are paramount in the company's success, the contribution of his wife Wendy (currently the COO of the company) is important as the force behind the incredible ornamentation found on Larrivée's high-end instruments that turns many of these into works of art by any definition. The Larrivées' sons Matthew and John, as well as daughters Christine and Michelle, are also involved in the family business.

After several moves within Canada over the years, Larrivée settled into its current Vancouver facility in 1998. In 2001 the company opened a second factory, in Oxnard, California. For a while, all satin-finished instruments (including 03 and Parlor series) were manufactured in Canada, with high-end production shifted to Oxnard.

Besides being one of the premier manufacturers of steel-string flat-top guitars, there are other areas of Larrivée that are of interest. For starters, few builders have trained as many luthiers who are highly regarded in their own right as Jean Larrivée.

Linda Manzer, William 'Grit' Laskin, Sergei De Jonge, and David Iannone of Morgan Guitars all started out in the Larrivée shop, and have ended up creating their own visions of guitar design. Additionally, with its own sawmill operation as part of its Vancouver shop, Larrivée is a major wood supplier that counts most other US and Canadian guitar factories among its clients. The company is especially known for providing quality spruce and cedar tops, taking advantage of Canada's vast wood resources. Larrivée has also been at the cutting edge of new manufacturing methods. These include an early adaptation of CNC technology for carving necks and other parts (notably inlay), and being one of the first companies to use UV-cured catalyzed finishes. In 2002, Larrivée began using an exclusive B-Band pickup system for its acoustic-electric models, and in 2003 introduced a line of bluegrass dreadnoughts. The Canadian operation was closed in 2013, with production now entirely in Oxnard.

LEVIN
(AND GOYA)

Herman Carlson Levin (born 1864) was a Swedish carpenter turned luthier who emigrated to the United States around 1880 and opened a shop in New York City. In

Levin Dreadnought 1975
(*right*) *The influences behind this large-bodied flat-top are no surprise, given Martin's ownership of the Swedish Levin company from 1973.*

Levin Goliath 1964 (far right)
This affordable Levin dreadnought of the pre-Martin era was popular in Europe in the 1960s.

1900 he returned to his native Gothenburg, Sweden and founded an instrument factory in his own name. The company made guitars as well as other stringed instruments, and during the peak years in the 1960s Levin had some 130 employees and exported approximately 16,000 guitars annually to the US alone. Levin always took pride in using well-aged wood – including spruce for their tops which could be 300 years old or more (Tyrolean for classicals, Sitka for flat-tops).

The Levin company was family-owned – Herman's son Hartwig took over, and then grandson Göran Levin – until 1973, when C.F. Martin purchased Levin. A large number of Martin D-18s were actually made at the Gothenburg factory – they have a small brand stamp that says "C.F. Martin Sweden." When Martin began applying the Goya brand name (of which more later) on cheap Korean acoustics at the same time, the Levin-made instruments suffered in sales. The Levin craftsmen were also dissatisfied with the way Martin ran the company, and many of them quit. Guitar production in Gothenburg ended in 1979, and as the Levin name was put by Martin on even cheaper guitars, the brand name was diluted until operations finally ceased in 1982.

Most of the 800,000 guitars made by Levin were Spanish guitars, the biggest seller being model LG 17, a 'Hauser' style instrument. In the 1970s, there was also a line of classical guitars designed by Georg Bolin. Larger flat-tops were not launched until the mid 1960s, with the dreadnought-style Goliath being the top seller.

The Levin guitars considered the most collectable today are the archtops from the 1930s to the 1960s. Top of the line models were the De Luxe, the Solist and the Royal. All of these had a very distinctively shaped headstock with massive pearl inlays, the tops were hand-carved from solid spruce, and the sides and backs were made from walnut or flame maple, with alder or mahogany necks and ebony fingerboards. Floating pickups were available as add-ons: first the Swedish-made Wingtone pickups, later units by DeArmond or Kjell, another Swedish brand. (A famous photo of Django Reinhardt shows the guitarist with a Levin archtop that belonged to the Duke Ellington Orchestra.)

In the 1960s a new line of archtops was introduced: models 315, 320, 325, and 330. The top-of-the-line model was the 315, with elaborate pearl inlays and gold-plated metal parts. Archtops were discontinued around 1970.

Goya was a name used by New York distributor Hershman for a number of electric and acoustic guitars offered from around 1953 onwards (the Swedish representatives were told that the name Levin sounded 'too Jewish'!). After Hershman, a number of

Lowden ad 1984 (above)
Fingerstyle virtuoso Pierre Bensusan declares: "This guitar has been a revelation for the music I play." Twenty years later, he continues to play Lowden guitars.

Lowden LSE-II 1998 (left)
A small-bodied jumbo model with Lowden's soft cutaway, built-in Fishman Prefix Pro preamp, and Acoustic Matrix under-saddle pickup.

Lowden O-25 1990s (right)
This example of Lowden's original large-bodied jumbo shaped flat-top displays the maker's frequent preference for cedar tops.

distributors sold Goyas, including Avnet (who also owned Guild briefly) and amp maker Kustom. Most of the Goya acoustics from the 1950s and '60s were made by Levin, who produced a large number of Spanish and flat-top guitars in a wide range of models. The first big seller in the Goya line was the G-10 Spanish guitar. And the most seen Goya guitar is probably the model G-13 strummed by Julie Andrews in the movie *The Sound Of Music*.

All Levin-era Goyas have an interior paper label that carries the words "Made by AB Herman Carlson Levin – Gothenburg, Sweden," plus model and serial number. The last Swedish-made Goyas were produced in 1979. Later Goyas were of lower quality and produced in East Asia. The Goya name was discontinued by Martin in 1996.

LOWDEN

Northern Irish guitar-maker Lowden has developed a reputation as a quality alternative to the medium-sized, upmarket independent US builders of steel-string flat-top guitars – although its instruments are distinctly different from any of the major templates from the other side of the Atlantic. Over the course of its 30-year history, Lowden has grown steadily into a recognized brand in the acoustic world, and

gathered a number of pro endorsements along the way, including players such as Richard Thompson, Pierre Bensusan, Jan Akkerman, Jacques Stotzem, Michael Hedges, David Gray, and others.

George Lowden was born in 1952 in Bangor, Northern Ireland, and made his first guitar at the age of 10. By the the time he was 22 he had completed Lowden guitar No1, and was on the way to establishing himself professionally. By the late 1970s, Lowden was selling guitars in London, Paris, and Geneva, and solidifying an international reputation as a skilled young luthier. By this time he and a small staff of builders were completing some 200 guitars a year in their small Bangor workshop, but it rapidly became clear that demand was outstripping even this respectable supply.

To step up to the market, Lowden established a licensing agreement for a small Japanese factory to produce four models, which rose eventually to as many as 15 models a few years later. As the mid 1980s approached, as many as 1,000 Japanese Lowdens were being built each year. In 1985, however, rather than transfer to a larger Japanese factory – one in which many rival brands were also being manufactured – Lowden decided to bring production back to Northern Ireland, and a second, more prolific era of all-European-built Lowdens began.

Acoustic Alchemy *Nick Webb and Greg Carmichael of the fine guitar-led band with some useful advice for potential Lowden buyers.*

Lowden S-25C 2002 (right)
A small-bodied jumbo model with cedar top and cutaway.

Avalon D-201 2002 (left) *This dreadnought is from the new UK-built Avalon brand, launched by Lowden in 2002 and intended as a more affordable but still professional-grade alternative to the pricey Lowden-branded guitars (see Avalon entry). Built from all-solid woods – this model with a cedar top and rosewood back and sides – Avalons make cost savings through standardization between models and a sparsity of trim.*

Pierre Bensusan 2001 *The maestro digs in on his Lowden.*

Amid a period of continuing growth, the company was sold to new owners in 1989, who established a larger factory in Newtownards, not far from Belfast. George Lowden left to concentrate on his own hand-built guitars, but continued with the new Lowden company in some aspects of design and training. Lowden changed hands once more in 1998, and George has again become more involved in the design and construction side of the business since that time, though he still makes some of his own guitars – now mostly nylon-strung models – under his full name.

From the start, Lowden guitars have been easy to distinguish from the flat-top archetypes established by Martin and Gibson and their followers, by their internal and external features. The 'classic' Lowden body shape tends more toward the rounded

'jumbo' style (though in various sizes) rather than the dreadnought, concert, and orchestra shapes more prominent throughout the traditional flat-top world. Since 1976 Lowden has veered away from the popular X-bracing, too, making most guitars around a modified A-bracing system developed by George himself.

Other design elements help to set Lowden further from the crowd: internal braces (struts) hand-carved to a unique 'tall-thin' design rather than to the scalloped Martin shape; a two-piece bridge saddle to promote more accurate intonation; five-piece necks for greater stability; a unique integral truss-rod design that avoids compressing the wood; all-solid-wood bindings; and a more frequent use of cedar than most steel-string makers. The guitars are generally considered to be tonally apart, too: well rounded, but with prominent, crisp highs and firm, piano-like lows.

Despite Lowden's considerable production rate, the company continues to hand-build all guitars, without the use of CNC technology or any UV finishing. Also, for soundboards and bracings Lowden uses split woods rather than sawn, following George Lowden's theory – and that of many luthiers over the years – that this yields a tonally superior result. The seminal Lowden style continues today in the O Series, also called the 'Original Series Jumbo,' a large-bodied jumbo in a variety of models

Avalon A-100CE 2002 (*left*) *Cutaway auditorium-bodied electro with spruce top and mahogany back and sides.*

Lowden O-328 2003 (*right*) *An 'original' (for Lowden) jumbo-shaped flat-top with Englemann spruce top and Indian rosewood back and sides.*

Avalon D-200E 2003 (*far right*) *A Lowden-built Avalon dreadnought with spruce top, rosewood back and sides, and onboard electronics.*

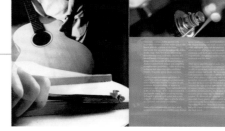

and wood options, cutaway and non, and different degrees of trim. This is followed – in size and approximate popularity – by the F Series 'Midi Jumbo' and S Series 'Small Bodied,' each again with a range of options.

Having traditionally steered its own course in the big-bodied pond, Lowden has also offered a take on the dreadnought for some years – perhaps out of the common necessity for most makers to carry at least an example or two of the ever-popular style. The D Series sticks close to the shape established by Martin some 80 years ago, but employs Lowden's A-bracing as a means of restraining the tendency that many dreadnoughts have toward boominess. The range is rounded out by the thinline electro-acoustic LSE Stage Edition, and the Jazz Series nylon-string cutaway (based on the S body size) with undersaddle pickup and onboard preamp.

In 2002 Lowden launched the more affordable Avalon range (see *Avalon*), and plans were in place for the company to come under the Avalon corporate banner. In fact, Lowden weathered some complicated business moves, and since 2004 it has been a family-owned firm based in Downpatrick, Northern Ireland.

MACCAFERRI

Upon his departure from Selmer in 1933, Mario Maccaferri – after a shortlived attempt to return to the concert stage as a guitarist himself – turned his attention to developing ideas for the design and manufacture of reeds. This eventually led him into the world of plastics and plastic guitars, which would define much of the second half of Maccaferri's career for guitarists. (For Maccaferri's career up to 1933, see the *Selmer* entry.)

Maccaferri opened the French American Reeds Manufacturing Company with his wife Maria in Paris in 1939, just as the war in Europe was beginning. A business trip to New York allowed Mario to visit the World's Fair, where his imagination was captured by the new injection-molded plastics. Maccaferri left his family and returned to Paris where, thanks to a clever ruse and the financial leverage of his life savings, he barely managed to catch the boat for New York – just ahead of the Germans.

During World War II, Maccaferri's new interest in plastics led to the restoration of his fortunes. Diversion of materials had created a shortage of wooden clothespins (clothes pegs). With inspiration, Maccaferri invented the plastic clothespin, leading to the founding of Mastro Industries and a successful plastic-making business. With the

Lowden catalog (*above*) *This Lowden promo gently pushes the pastoral Irish associations.*

Avalon A-200CE 2003 (*far left*) *Jumbo-shaped cutaway electro of the spruce/rosewood format.*

Lowden O35 2015 (*center*) *This example from Lowden's 35 series has a walnut body with cedar top.*

Lowden F32C 2016 (*above*) *Classic spruce and rosewood make up the body of this popular Lowden, with an on-board Baggs pickup system.*

Maccaferri New Romancer 1960 (right) *The New Romancer – clearly aimed at the teen sock-hop crowd, if its colorful scenes are anything to go by – was the most decorated of Maccaferri's plastic guitars. Ads of the time claimed the instrument was "very easy to play, and luxuriously finished – the ideal guitar for any type of music, from classical to popular, folksong to rock'n'roll, etc."*

Maccaferri ad 1955 (center) *"You can really go to town with a Maccaferri..." or so the ad men wanted us to believe.*

Maccaferri Showtime 1962 (far right) *The more spartan Showtime model.*

means now in place, Maccaferri – still a guitarist – focused on the notion of using Dow Styron plastic to make instruments.

In 1949 Mastro introduced the plastic Islander Ukulele and, with a plug from American TV-show host Arthur Godfrey, eventually sold nine million of them. The plastic guitar was next in the pipeline.

Contrary to its appearance, the now-famous Maccaferri plastic guitar was not developed as a toy, but as a real, playable instrument. With help from Dow engineers, Maccaferri developed a smooth spruce-colored formulation for the top and a swirled rosewood plastic for the body and neck. The design proved surprisingly popular. By 1952 Maccaferri had introduced two models, the G-30 flat-top and G-40 archtop. These were rolled out in early '53. They were played by Rey De La Torre, and pop-jazz great Harry Volpe, extensively covered in the press, and endorsed by Andrés Segovia.

Mario had essentially adapted his Selmer cutaway designs to the new plastic guitars, which were roughly equivalent in size to a grand concert model. Internally, much more went into their design and construction than one would first guess: the tops were made with a wood ladder bracing, and the necks were bolted on with a 'heel-less' joint and had a wooden core that extended into the body, where an adjustable bolt allowed the player to alter the pitch of the neck and thus the action.

Many guitarists snigger at these plastic instruments, but an example in good shape will reveal a lovely guitar with a rich, distinctive voice. Unfortunately, too many guitarists *did* snigger and Maccaferri, insulted by the criticism, soon mothballed his serious plastic guitars.

Mastro did continue to make plastic instruments through the 1960s, including Islander, ShowTime and Roco flat-tops, a line of Beatles instruments, even some electric-shaped models. They were most certainly better than 'toy grade' guitars but not up to the standards of the Maccaferri G-30 and G-40.

Throughout all this plasticizing, Maccaferri never abandoned his love of lutherie, and he was constantly tinkering with Mozzani-era harp guitars and building classicals. From 1976 to 1979, with the help of Maurice Summerfield in Britain, the old Selmer-Maccaferris were resurrected as the CSL Gypsy, made in Japan by Hoshino (Ibanez). In the early 1980s Summerfield and Maccaferri tried again with a line produced in Japan by Saga.

Maccaferri struck up a friendship with New York luthier John Monteleone in the late 1980s. Their work together marked the end of the Maccaferri's lutherie career with the production of a number of classical guitars, some even reviving Maccaferri's Selmer-period sound chamber concept.

Mario Maccaferri died in 1993 at the age of 92, concluding a remarkable life and an enormous contribution to the world of the guitar. Despite his death, however, versions of Maccaferri's guitar designs continue to be built, most notably by small makers such as Maurice Dupont, Rob Aylward, John LeVoi, and a few other followers of the Gypsy jazz school.

MAINGARD

Marc Maingard was born in Durban, South Africa, to French immigrant parents, and in his early 20s set up as a repairman and then luthier in the 1970s. He later honed his skills working in the US with Santa Cruz and then Jimmy D'Aquisto before returning to South Africa to establish his own guitar-making business.

Maingard builds both steel and nylon-string guitars, and is known for his finely honed original designs, as well as his use of some lesser-seen tonewoods. Among current models are the 14-fret 'New Shape' Dreadnought, 12-fret Grand Concert, Classic Romantica, and the small slot-head Lucas York model.

Maccaferri G-30 1953 (*right*)
The other half of Maccaferri's original pair of plastic guitars, in the more affordable flat-top style. While the body shapes appear identical, note the distinct difference in bridge designs.

Back (*far right*) *There are plugs in the molded plastic neck-heel that conceal the fixing points for the instrument's bolt-on neck.*

Maccaferri G-40 1955 (*right*)
This archtop guitar – one of Maccaferri's first plastic models – displays similarities to his earlier wood-bodied, Selmer-built instruments, particularly in the bridge, tailpiece, and approximate body shape.

Back (*above*) *A rear view of the Dow Styron-bodied guitar's dark-colored plastic back.*

MANSON

Based in Devon, England, Andy Manson is regarded as one of the UK's finest custom luthiers. He started making guitars in the late 1960s, developing the range through the '70s and '80s to the point where he was offering at least a dozen models, plus mandolins and other folk instruments. Among the guitars, a consistent favorite with Manson's customers has been the medium-size Magpie; another is the cutaway, shallow-body Raven electro-acoustic which appeared in 1991, designed in collaboration with Jethro Tull's Ian Anderson.

For many years, Manson offered his instruments in a choice of three trims – Style 0, I, and II – in ascending order of price, timbers, and cosmetic finery, but Style 0 was eventually dropped (though it did briefly reappear in the mid '90s on a reissue of one of his early guitars, the Nightingale parlor, as well as on his regular Magpie, Heron jumbo, and Dove dreadnought designs).

Multi-neck acoustics have been something of a Manson speciality. Apart from his relatively straightforward Double Neck 6/12, in the late '70s he built a triple neck (6/12 plus mandolin) for John Paul Jones, and then in 1994 a similar but stylistically

different arrangement for Jimmy Page. In 2000, the theme was taken to more esoteric heights when Jones ordered an archtop triple-neck combining mandolin, octave mandola, and bass mandolin. Another Manson owned by John Paul Jones is an eight-string acoustic bass.

By 1993 Manson had taken on two assistant luthiers, Simon Smidmore and Andy Petherick, who three years later took over the Hittisleigh workshop to make Manson flat-tops under license and develop their own Brook line, while Andy moved to nearby premises, the home of his electric guitar-making brother Hugh. Since then, and after a further relocation, to The Ark workshop in Crediton, Devon, Andy has departed from offering a catalog of instruments to become an almost exclusively custom-order maker. Commissions have included The Linley parlor – based on an early French instrument – built for David Linley (the guitar-collecting English Viscount, *not* the LA sessionman David Lindley).

The A.B. Manson & Co headstock brand is pretty much a thing of the past. Manson now dislikes the idea of peghead logoes, preferring his instruments to project their customers' satisfaction, not their maker's promotional message. An absorbing insight into Manson's daily round can be found in his diary-based 1998 book *Talking Wood*.

Manson catalog 1990 *The luthier consults with Ian Anderson of Jethro Tull (seen holding the guitar) for whom he has built six guitars.*

Manson Dove 'Slideslammer' 1987 (right) *This Dove was custom ordered with a Slideslammer device, which raises the nut for slide playing, and has an acoustic B-string bender at the bridge.*

Manson Magpie Custom 1990 (far right) *Having evolved into a purely custom-order builder in recent years, Manson refuses to stick with one 'signature' headstock shape like so many other guitar-makers, and instead has produced numerous variations over the years.*

Manson catalogs early 1990s (above) *Specs for the Magpie and Kingfisher from a time when 'standard' models were still produced.*

MANZER

Canadian guitar-maker Linda Manzer is one of the few luthiers working today who can build archtop, flat-top, and classical guitars with equal facility.

She started building dulcimers as a hobby in 1969, and learned more about building steel-string and nylon-string guitars during her apprenticeship with Jean Larrivée, whom she worked with from 1974 to 1978. She then spent 1983 studying the craft of constructing archtops with premier builder James D'Aquisto.

The most distinctive feature of Manzer's guitars is the wedge shape of the bodies, where the guitar is shallower on the bass side and deeper on the treble side. Manzer developed the wedge design, which she feels makes her guitars more ergonomic to play, while building the Pikasso Guitar, a quadruple-neck custom guitar she made for Pat Metheny. Metheny approached her in 1986 to build a guitar for him that had "as many strings as possible." The result was the 42-string Pikasso. (She later built a second version of Pikasso for guitar collector Scott Chinery.)

Manzer makes around 15 instruments a year, many of them custom instruments, such as an eight-string classical guitar, an acoustic steel-string with a buzzing, sitar-style bridge, a ten-string tiple, and a blue, electric charango.

Manzer Pikasso II 1995 (left)
Canadian maker Linda Manzer's Pikasso model originated from an order by jazz guitarist Pat Metheny for a guitar with "as many strings as possible." This second version was built for guitar collector Scott Chinery.

Back (far left) *A rear view of the instrument emphasizes the truly Picassoesque nature of this guitar.*

161

MARTIN

The C.F. Martin Guitar Company of Nazareth, Pennsylvania, occupies a unique position in the history of American commerce, as well as in the history of the American guitar. Not only has the company been in business since 1833, it has also had the same focus on fretted instruments, specifically guitars, since its inception. Details of this long history are revealed by a remarkably complete set of business and production records, and a large number of surviving examples of even its earliest instruments. It would be difficult to overstate the Martin company's influence on the American guitar, and virtually all acoustic flat-tops made for steel strings incorporate one or more features that Martin either initiated or made popular. In fact, there are now a number of individual luthiers and small guitar companies that build modern versions of old Martins and little else. Anyone playing a dreadnought guitar with an X-braced soundboard, regardless of the name on the headstock, is a strumming tribute to the long influence of the Martin Guitar Company.

Christian Friedrich Martin was born in 1796 in Mark Neukirchen, Saxony, a town in what is now Germany (formerly East Germany). His father, Johann Georg Martin, was

Stauffer (attributed to) c1820 (left, with back far left) *Johann Georg Stauffer (1778-1853) was born in Vienna, Austria. He became one of that country's most notable guitar makers, and in 1824 made a special instrument for the Austrian composer Franz Schubert. Christian Friedrich Martin was a foreman at Stauffer's shop during the 1820s, leaving the business in 1825. Eight years later Martin emigrated to the United States, absorbing much of the style and influence of Stauffer's instruments into the first guitars he built there.*

Ledger 1834 (above) *Company records from the time show that Martin's store sold violins, French horns, bugles – but few guitars.*

a furniture-maker who also made guitars. At age 15, C.F. Martin gained an apprenticeship with Johann Stauffer in Vienna, one of the premier guitar workshops in Europe. Martin rose to the position of foreman before leaving Stauffer 14 years later to work for a harp-maker named Karl Kuhle – a job change inspired probably not out of an interest in harps, but in the harp-maker's daughter, Ottilie, whom he soon married. C.F. Martin Jr. was born the same year, and shortly after that the family moved back to Mark Neukirchen.

C.F. Martin Sr. had learned guitar-making during a long tenure with one of the best-known luthiers of the era, yet building wooden musical instruments in Mark Neukirchen was, at least according to the local Violin Maker's Guild, a trade reserved by law for their members only. Even after several years of squabbling over the right of furniture-makers to build guitars, the dispute still wasn't settled, resulting in an awkward business climate for an ambitious guitar-maker. Like many restless artists who would later play his guitars, C.F. Martin hit the road, taking his family with him, but his roadtrip to self-discovery consisted of sailing across the Atlantic to the USA.

In 1833 C.F. Martin Sr. arrived in New York City and quickly leased a storefront at 196 Hudson Street. There Martin served as a retailer, wholesaler, and importer of all kinds of musical merchandise, and also repaired violins, guitars, and other wooden musical instruments. Soon he was also building guitars with a wide range of prices, the more expensive versions looking much like Stauffer's models with an adjustable neck angle, elaborate bridge, and long, curving headstock with tuners all on one side. Some of these guitars were maple, and a few of other exotic woods, but most had rosewood backs and sides. According to surviving records of the period, Martin had several employees and a thriving business, and built guitars under at least three different partnerships

Financial success was apparently not C.F. Martin's only goal, however, for in 1839 he sold off his entire inventory and moved to Cherry Hill, a hamlet in rural Pennsylvania just a few miles from Nazareth. A sales office was retained in New York, managed by John Coupa, a well-known guitarist and instructor who advertised that his showroom had the largest inventory of guitars in the city. For the next 58 years, Martin guitars would be marked as originating in New York, despite being made in Pennsylvania.

In the 1840s and early '50s Martin guitars shed most of their Austro-German features, and what would soon be recognized as a uniquely American guitar began to emerge. A more slender body with narrow upper bouts replaced the almost figure-8

Stauffer (attributed to) 1820s (left, with back right) *Here is another guitar believed to have been built by Johann Georg Stuaffer. C.F. Martin clearly learned much about the design and construction of guitars during his time with the master German guitar-maker. Compare this guitar to early Martins on the following page – noting especially, for example, the angled fingerboard and, in one case, the delicately ornate bridge.*

'Coffin case' (above) *The severe black-painted wooden cases supplied for Martin's early guitars have since been nicknamed 'coffin' cases, thanks to the look of the angled shape of the body section.*

163

shape of Stauffer's models, and the curves and curls of both headstock and bridge were simplified to rectangular shapes. The soundhole rosette usually featured multiple rings made up of groupings of narrow light and dark lines. On higher models, the three-piece, black-stained neck with cone-shaped heel gave way to a two-piece cedar neck with a natural finish.

Just as important were changes to the inside of Martin's guitars, and the simple ladder bracing of the soundboard was replaced by a more sophisticated fan bracing pattern similar to that used in Spanish guitars of the period. Martin's larger guitars were given X-pattern top bracing, a design whose structural superiority wouldn't be fully realized until almost three-quarters of a century later when the company would finally abandon gut strings and embrace the use of steel strings.

By the early 1850s Martin's body shapes and sizes were standardized, though all would be considered quite small today. The largest was Size 1, which was only 12¾" wide at the lower bout, and sizes 2 through 5 got progressively smaller. In the mid 1850s, and perhaps earlier, the larger Size 0 was introduced, and this would become the company's standard concert model. Martins were produced in a variety of styles, each designated by a 'number of quality,' 17 to 42, which originally indicated the

Martin Stauffer-style 1830s (*right*) *A splendid example of early Martin. The fingerboard is angled at the body join and raised from the body, elements which recall Stauffer's work (as seen on the previous page). The curving bridge design is more typical of this period than that seen on the large guitar pictured opposite.*

Back (*far right*) *The ivory inlaid neck is seen on some early European guitars. Note that Martin has retained the Stauffer-designed key system for adjusting the neck angle, visible at the neck/body join.*

Label (*above*) *The paper label viewed through this guitar's soundhole shows Martin's store address as 196 Hudson Street, New York, and equal emphasis is given to Martin's role then as an "importer of musical instruments" and a "guitar and violin manufacturer."*

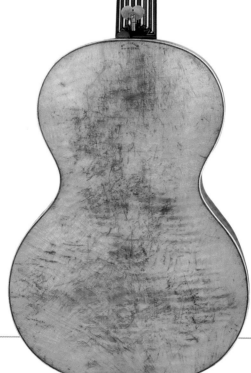

Journal 1836 (above) Among the records of Martin's instrument repairs and sales of violin pegs, sheet music, trombones, pianos, flutes, and the like is an entry (the second on 2nd April 1836) for a trade sale to Messrs Nuns Clark & Co of five guitars and cases. They range in trade price from $7 for one 'with pegs,' to one at $15 with 'patent screws' (Stauffer type) and 'ornament.' Cases add $3 to each sale.

wholesale price. In general, the fancier models numbered 30 and higher were offered only in the smaller sizes, as these were considered more appropriate for women. Although many of Martin's original styles later disappeared, several have survived to the present day. If one looks at the binding and herringbone marquetry on a 0-28 or a 1-21 from the Civil War era, the decorative style is instantly recognizable as that found on the 000-28 and 00-21 models made around World War II. Although these styles were modernized and modified in the mid 1940s, the earlier details have since been revived and are featured in Martin's current Vintage Series. From the 1850s through the next several decades, Martin guitars were further refined, but underwent few structural modifications. The larger size 00 was added in the early 1870s, and Martin's bigger models continued to grow in popularity.

Most of the changes during the latter half of the 19th century were to the Martin

Martin Stauffer-style 1830s (right) This is a highly decorated example from the early days of Martin, with ivory and abalone semi-circles around the edge and a harmonizing circular theme around the soundhole. Note how the use of ivory is also extended to the bridge and the fingerboard, which is also beautifully bound. Such guitars are often referred to now as 'presentation' models, either because they were made to present the best of Martin's handiwork, or because they may have been presented to special customers and/or players.

Back (right) Some splendid rosewood used for the body highlights an early showing of herringbone-pattern trim, for which the Martin company would later become famous.

Martin c1840s (right) Although the neck and especially the headstock still resemble Stauffer's, this guitar shows how C.F. Martin's own style was gradually evolving. Of particular note is the narrower upper body, which gives an overall shape more like a modern guitar.

family and their company. In the late 1850s Martin moved from Cherry Hill to Nazareth proper, building a home with a workshop at the rear of the property. In 1867 the ageing C.F. Sr. took on his son C.F. Martin Jr. and C.F. Hartmann as business partners, changing the stamp on their guitars to read 'C. F. Martin & Co., New York' (distribution was still through New York City).

In 1873, C.F. Sr. died at age 77, and C.F. Martin Jr. died 15 years later in 1888, leaving the company to the third generation, 22-year-old Frank Henry Martin. Although the Martin Guitar Company was highly regarded and its guitars widely copied by the competition, sales were stalled at about the same level as before the Civil War. New manufacturers like Lyon & Healy of Chicago, with well-funded promotion and high-production factories, were selling more guitars in a week than Martin sold in an entire year.

Frank Henry's first significant move was to add Italian-style (bowl-back) mandolins to his company's offerings in 1895. Around the same time he broke away from a tiresome distributor in New York. Martin issued its first guitar catalog in 1898, the same year the labeling stamp was changed to read 'C.F. Martin & Co, Nazareth, Pa.' Another change that would have lasting influence on the company was the birth of

C.F. Martin III, whose steady devotion to both Martin instruments and the people who made them would be felt for over 80 years.

By 1900 Frank Henry had simplified Martin's number of models, building the same style in different sizes rather than having unique model numbers for each guitar. The black neck with cone-shaped heel found on lower models was dropped in favor of cedar, and pearl fret-position markers were added to the fretboard. All Martin guitars at the turn of the century had rosewood backs and sides, an ebony fretboard and 'pyramid' bridge, and a spruce top. Most had slotted headstocks with German or French tuners, but the solid headstock with ivory or ebony friction pegs – a 'peg head' – was also popular with certain players and dealerships.

Martin guitars at the turn of the century were not much different than those built a half-century earlier, but they were larger and the stylistic appointments more refined. The most expensive was the $80 00-42, with gleaming abalone trim around the top's edge and circling the soundhole, genuine ivory binding on the body and neck, and a solid ivory bridge. Yet compared to the top models of any manufacturer today, Martin's Style 42, with its delicate pearl snowflake position markers, is elegant in an almost severe way. At the other end of the price list was Style 18 – and with size 0

Martin & Bruno c1839 (left)
C.F. Martin was involved in many business dealings in the 19th century, but his relationship with Charles Bruno is among the least well documented of them. This guitar's label says Bruno has a shop at "212 Fulton Street, near Broadway, New York" and that Martin & Bruno were "importers and dealers in musical instruments, wholesale and retail." It appears that Bruno was a New York agent similar to Coupa. Interestingly, the guitar also bears a label which says it was repaired by respected Boston-based luthier Elmer Stromberg in the 1950s.

Back (right) *Note the attractive back on the same 1839 Martin & Bruno.*

Martin & Coupa c1840 (right)
C.F. Martin made instruments for sale by New York City guitarist and teacher John Coupa from the 1830s until at least the 1850s, and they usually carried a 'Martin & Coupa' label.

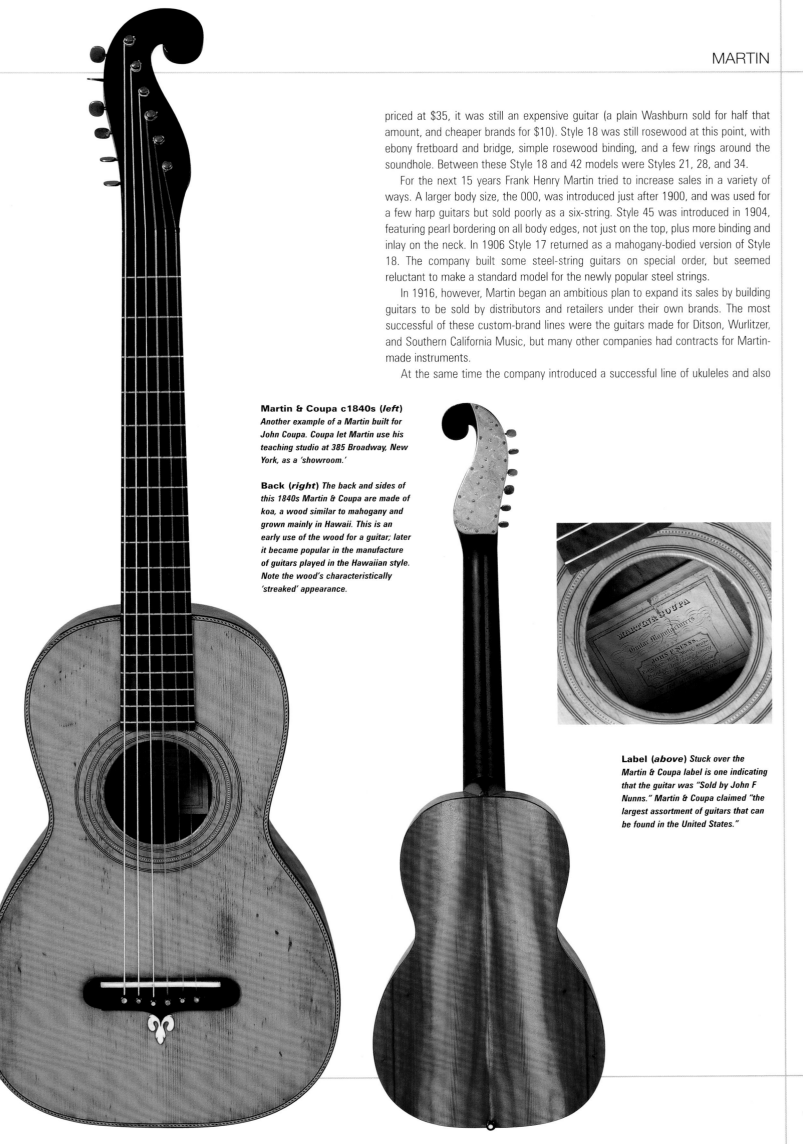

priced at $35, it was still an expensive guitar (a plain Washburn sold for half that amount, and cheaper brands for $10). Style 18 was still rosewood at this point, with ebony fretboard and bridge, simple rosewood binding, and a few rings around the soundhole. Between these Style 18 and 42 models were Styles 21, 28, and 34.

For the next 15 years Frank Henry Martin tried to increase sales in a variety of ways. A larger body size, the 000, was introduced just after 1900, and was used for a few harp guitars but sold poorly as a six-string. Style 45 was introduced in 1904, featuring pearl bordering on all body edges, not just on the top, plus more binding and inlay on the neck. In 1906 Style 17 returned as a mahogany-bodied version of Style 18. The company built some steel-string guitars on special order, but seemed reluctant to make a standard model for the newly popular steel strings.

In 1916, however, Martin began an ambitious plan to expand its sales by building guitars to be sold by distributors and retailers under their own brands. The most successful of these custom-brand lines were the guitars made for Ditson, Wurlitzer, and Southern California Music, but many other companies had contracts for Martin-made instruments.

At the same time the company introduced a successful line of ukuleles and also

Martin & Coupa c1840s (*left*)
Another example of a Martin built for John Coupa. Coupa let Martin use his teaching studio at 385 Broadway, New York, as a 'showroom.'

Back (*right*) *The back and sides of this 1840s Martin & Coupa are made of koa, a wood similar to mahogany and grown mainly in Hawaii. This is an early use of the wood for a guitar; later it became popular in the manufacture of guitars played in the Hawaiian style. Note the wood's characteristically 'streaked' appearance.*

Label (*above*) *Stuck over the Martin & Coupa label is one indicating that the guitar was "Sold by John F Nunns." Martin & Coupa claimed "the largest assortment of guitars that can be found in the United States."*

167

Label *Martin & Schatz's mention of guitars "made in the best Italian style" probably refers to the models which Stauffer made for the famous Italian guitarist Luigi Legnani (1790-1877).*

began to build Martin-brand steel-string guitars for playing in the Hawaiian style, using bodies – including tops – built all of koa. A 'K' suffix was added to the style numbers of the koa models, and the 0-18K and 0-28K were Martin's first official steel-string offerings. Since these early Hawaiian models had raised frets and a standard nut (a nut extender was provided for playing lap-style with a steel), they were widely played as regular guitars. By 1920, Martin was making mahogany-top Style 17 models with steel strings, and in 1922 the small 2-17 was Martin's first non-Hawaiian steel-string model to appear in a catalog. Early photos of America's first guitar-playing superstar, Jimmie Rodgers, show him holding one of these small, all-mahogany Martins.

With inexpensive all-mahogany steel-string guitars, Martin finally achieved the growth that had eluded it for decades. By 1924, Style 18 was offered with steel strings, then Style 21 a year later, until by 1928 Martin's entire guitar line was built for steel strings, with gut strings as an option. Along with steel strings came greater demand for the 000, and Martin's Style 45 became a favorite stage guitar for popular singers. The most famous of these was a special order that would influence the look

of stage guitars forever. Jimmie Rodgers, who had had a slight change of fortune since his days of playing a little 2-17, ordered a custom 000-45 in 1928 with his name inlaid on the fretboard, and the words 'Blue Yodel' on the headstock. That same year, Andres Segovia made a triumphant tour of North America, wowing audiences with his technique and the powerful sound from his Spanish-made classical guitar. Serious classical guitarists had little use for American guitars from then on, so for Martin there was no turning back.

The revolution at Martin brought many changes to the guitars beyond how they were braced and strung. Beginning in 1916, one-piece mahogany necks began to replace the cedar neck with spliced-on headstock, although the carved 'dart' behind the nut would remain on Styles 28 and higher. In 1917, ivory was replaced by ivory-grained celluloid ('ivoroid') for body binding, and ivory bridges were no longer offered. The labor-intensive French polish finish was also abandoned, with shellac and varnish, and later lacquer, taking its place. Expensive European-made tuners were replaced by American examples, and ivory or ebony bridge pins became celluloid. Style 17 guitars now had rosewood fretboards and bridges instead of ebony, and the elegant pyramid

Martin late 1830s (left) *Lavish deployment of ivory (fingerboard, bridge, tuning pegs, body edge and headstock binding) indicates an expensive instrument, this one without the Stauffer-style headstock. Martin's growing ability to impart a subtle beauty to his guitars is evident at the pearl soundhole inlay.*

Martin & Schatz c1830s (right) *This guitar is evidence of a collaboration between C.F. Martin and Heinrich Schatz. It was German guitar-maker Schatz's move to the US that prompted his friend Martin to follow.*

Headstock (far right) *The tuning gears on early Martins' distinctive scrolled headstocks are enclosed by the decorated metal plate on the rear.*

Martin & Coupa c1839 (right) *By 1839 Martin had moved workshop from New York to Pennsylvania, and this relatively plain example of a Martin & Coupa guitar was probably made at the new location. Note also the squared-off headstock with rear-facing tuning pegs rather than the older Stauffer-influenced design.*

bridges on both Style 17 and 18 were made simpler, with flattened tips. Yet Martin guitars still looked much the same, even if they now roared with steel strings rather than oozing the mellower tones of the earlier gut. The body shapes were unchanged, and the wide necks still had but 12 frets clear of the body with a slotted headstock.

The switch to steel strings brought a dramatic rise in the percentage of Martin guitars made with mahogany back and sides. The ukulele boom allowed Martin to expand the North Street factory in 1925 and again in 1927, and along with increased space came new woodworking machinery powered by electricity rather than the

Martin Stauffer-style c1850s (*right*) *Long before Martin's famous Style 45, he was exploiting the decorative potential of abalone inlay on body and fingerboard. Around 1850 Martin also began a significant change inside the guitar: this example is braced in an X-shaped pattern, whereas earlier guitars had fan-shaped bracing. This 'X-bracing', as it's known, proved its true worth on Martin's later steel-string guitars.*

Back (*above*) *This rear view of another Martin from the 1840s reveals the beauty of the 'figured' patterns of the maple back.*

Martin 2-27 c1883 (*right*) *During the 1850s Martin began to standardize body Sizes and decorative Styles, evolving a two-number name. The first number – here 2 – is for the body Size (the lower the number, the bigger the body). Fancy Style 27 was among the first Styles to be established, featuring an abalone soundhole ring and multicolored body-top binding. (The small pickguard on this example is not original.)*

Jethro Tull c1973 (*top right*) *Ian Anderson swaps his flute for a small-bodied Martin model.*

Martin 1-28 c1860s (*right*)
Style 28 with distinctive herringbone body-top binding was officially introduced in 1870. This pre-1867 guitar has the Style's features, but with an unusual pearl soundhole ring.

Martin 1-40 c1874 (*far right*)
Along with Style 42, Style 40 was one of the most ornate of the period, liberally adorned with abalone inlay along the edge of the body top and around the soundhole. The style of bridge here was introduced by Martin during the 1840s, and is known as the 'pyramid' type thanks to the shape of the carvings either side of the saddle.

C. F. Martin & Co.,
MANUFACTURERS OF
GUITARS, ETC.
Size of G.....2. No. of Qual....20.
NOTICE.
When not in use keep the guitar in its case
in a dry room, but not near a fire ; *Avoid the
vicinity of heaters*. With the best of care we
cannot prevent the wood from cracking at
such a place.
C. F. MARTIN & Co., M'n'f'rs.

Case label (*above*) *The Size-and-Style model number was not stamped on guitars until 1930, and during the 1800s it was only marked on the label inside the case. This 2-20 example is from the late 1880s, and has entries for "Size of G(uitar)" and "No. of Qual(ity)".*

complex tangle of drive belts and pulleys driven by a single large gasoline engine. Although rosewood guitars sold well in the 1920s, the bulk of Martin's guitar sales were small Style 17 and 18 models, plain guitars with simple rosewood binding and just three small pearl dots on the fretboard. Demand prompted Martin to build some of these simpler models in batches of two dozen or more, something unheard of a decade earlier.

By 1928 the ukulele craze was fading, and mandolin sales had been dropping for several years. Frank Henry and his son C.F. Martin III (known as Frederick) had been turning down most requests for anything custom or different, other than changing inlays or binding on a stock model, but now their mood had changed. The Martin Company's decade-long fling with small instruments was over, and guitars were once

Flyer 1883 (*left*) This promotional leaflet celebrating Martin's 50th anniversary warns buyers about "inferior and unreliable" copies, demonstrating that the emulation of good designs is not a new trend.

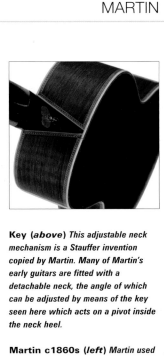

Key (*above*) *This adjustable neck mechanism is a Stauffer invention copied by Martin. Many of Martin's early guitars are fitted with a detachable neck, the angle of which can be adjusted by means of the key seen here which acts on a pivot inside the neck heel.*

Martin c1860s (*left*) *Martin used ivory for binding, nuts, and saddles, as an alternative to wood for bridges, and occasionally for an especially ornate fingerboard (as seen on previous pages). It is sometimes seen on early 'transitional' Martins made without an obvious Style type, like this attractive example. Note especially the pearl and ivory soundhole decoration.*

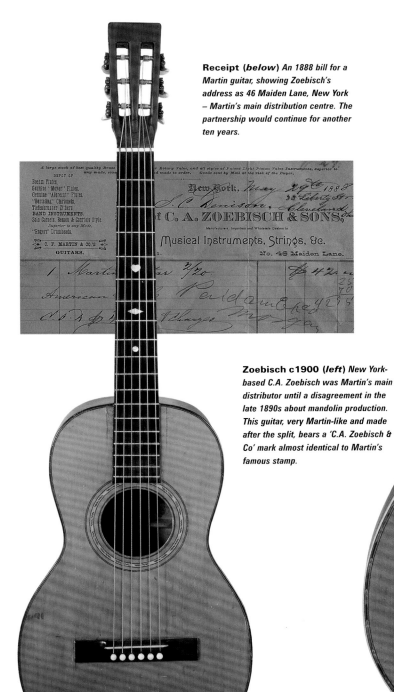

Receipt (*below*) *An 1888 bill for a Martin guitar, showing Zoebisch's address as 46 Maiden Lane, New York – Martin's main distribution centre. The partnership would continue for another ten years.*

Zoebisch c1900 (*left*) *New York-based C.A. Zoebisch was Martin's main distributor until a disagreement in the late 1890s about mandolin production. This guitar, very Martin-like and made after the split, bears a 'C.A. Zoebisch & Co' mark almost identical to Martin's famous stamp.*

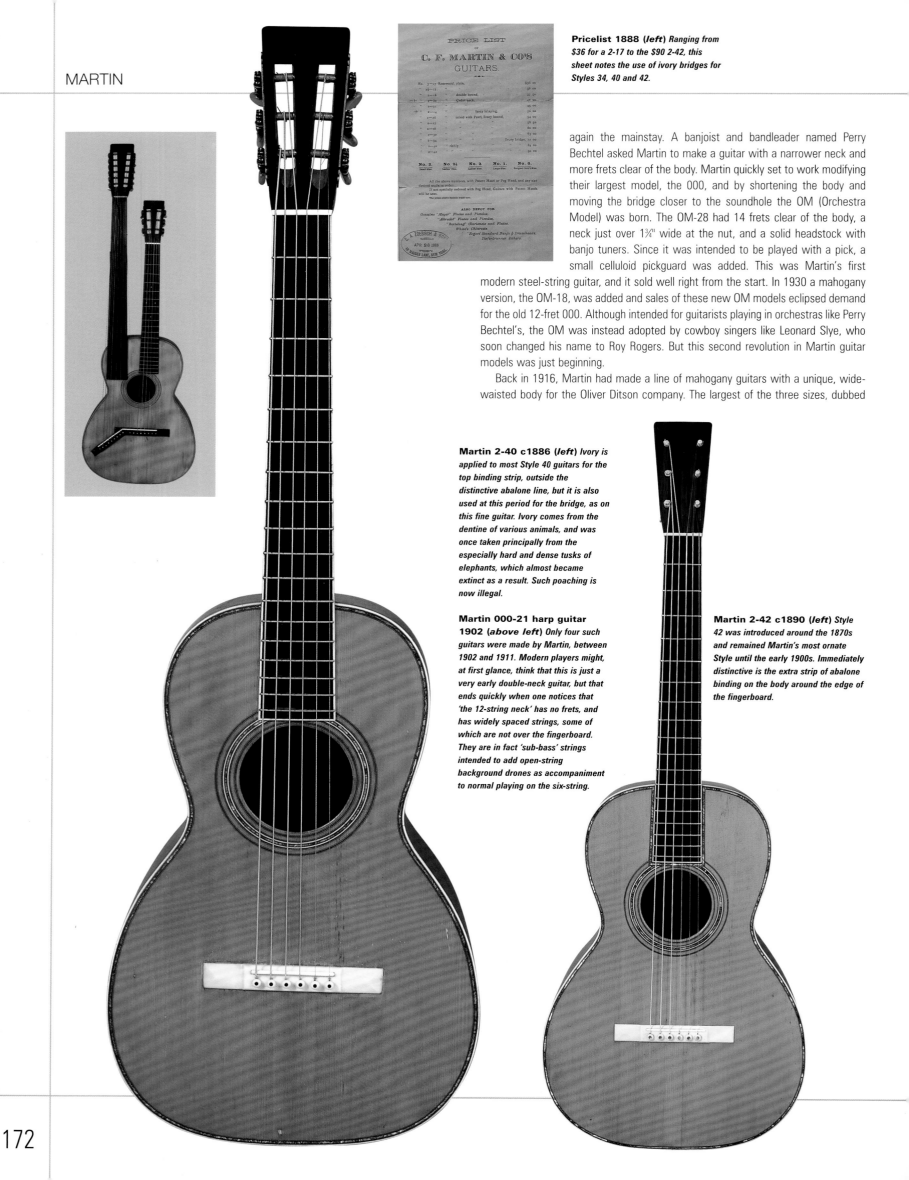

again the mainstay. A banjoist and bandleader named Perry Bechtel asked Martin to make a guitar with a narrower neck and more frets clear of the body. Martin quickly set to work modifying their largest model, the 000, and by shortening the body and moving the bridge closer to the soundhole the OM (Orchestra Model) was born. The OM-28 had 14 frets clear of the body, a neck just over 1¾" wide at the nut, and a solid headstock with banjo tuners. Since it was intended to be played with a pick, a small celluloid pickguard was added. This was Martin's first modern steel-string guitar, and it sold well right from the start. In 1930 a mahogany version, the OM-18, was added and sales of these new OM models eclipsed demand for the old 12-fret 000. Although intended for guitarists playing in orchestras like Perry Bechtel's, the OM was instead adopted by cowboy singers like Leonard Slye, who soon changed his name to Roy Rogers. But this second revolution in Martin guitar models was just beginning.

Back in 1916, Martin had made a line of mahogany guitars with a unique, wide-waisted body for the Oliver Ditson company. The largest of the three sizes, dubbed

Martin 2-40 c1886 (*left*) Ivory is applied to most Style 40 guitars for the top binding strip, outside the distinctive abalone line, but it is also used at this period for the bridge, as on this fine guitar. Ivory comes from the dentine of various animals, and was once taken principally from the especially hard and dense tusks of elephants, which almost became extinct as a result. Such poaching is now illegal.

Martin 000-21 harp guitar 1902 (*above left*) Only four such guitars were made by Martin, between 1902 and 1911. Modern players might, at first glance, think that this is just a very early double-neck guitar, but that ends quickly when one notices that 'the 12-string neck' has no frets, and has widely spaced strings, some of which are not over the fingerboard. They are in fact 'sub-bass' strings intended to add open-string background drones as accompaniment to normal playing on the six-string.

Martin 2-42 c1890 (*left*) Style 42 was introduced around the 1870s and remained Martin's most ornate Style until the early 1900s. Immediately distinctive is the extra strip of abalone binding on the body around the edge of the fingerboard.

Inventory 1900 (*above*) *This record of 'finished goods' lists mainly Sizes 00, 0, and 1, and Styles 18 to 42, noting use of 'pegs' (ie solid head) or 'machines' (slotted head).*

the Dreadnought, was a giant when compared to Martin's 000, as it was over 4¾" deep and nearly 16" wide at the lower bout. Although it didn't sell well initially, orders kept trickling in during the late 1920s when other Ditson models had been abandoned. Martin was reluctant to offer its own 'bass guitar,' as the Dreadnought was often called, but when the Ditson company was sold, Martin relented and adopted the ungainly model as its own. With a large pickguard and the new 'belly' bridge design borrowed from the OM, these were guitars that C.F. Sr. would never have recognized.

The first dreadnoughts with a Martin label were the mahogany D-1 and the rosewood D-2. Two of the first batch made in 1931 were shipped to Chicago, home to the *National Barn Dance*, America's largest live radio show. Stage performers looking for a guitar with more bass response quickly ordered more of the oversized Martins. One of the up-and-coming stars on the Barn Dance was a young singer who already owned two pearl-bordered Martins. He ordered his dreadnought with as

Martin c1890s (*left*) *This unusual guitar was apparently custom made by a Martin employee, and is different from any standard model produced at the factory at that time. Of note are its odd hourglass shape, and high – or 'negative' – neck angle that tilts the neck slightly forward of its usual position (as seen in the side view here, on the far left of this page).*

Martin 0-42 c1898 (*right*) *The fingerboard inlay seen at the fifth fret is a 'snowflake' type, so-called because of its shape, which became closely identified with Martin's understated decorative style. Note also the attractive backstripe inlay on the rear (far right).*

173

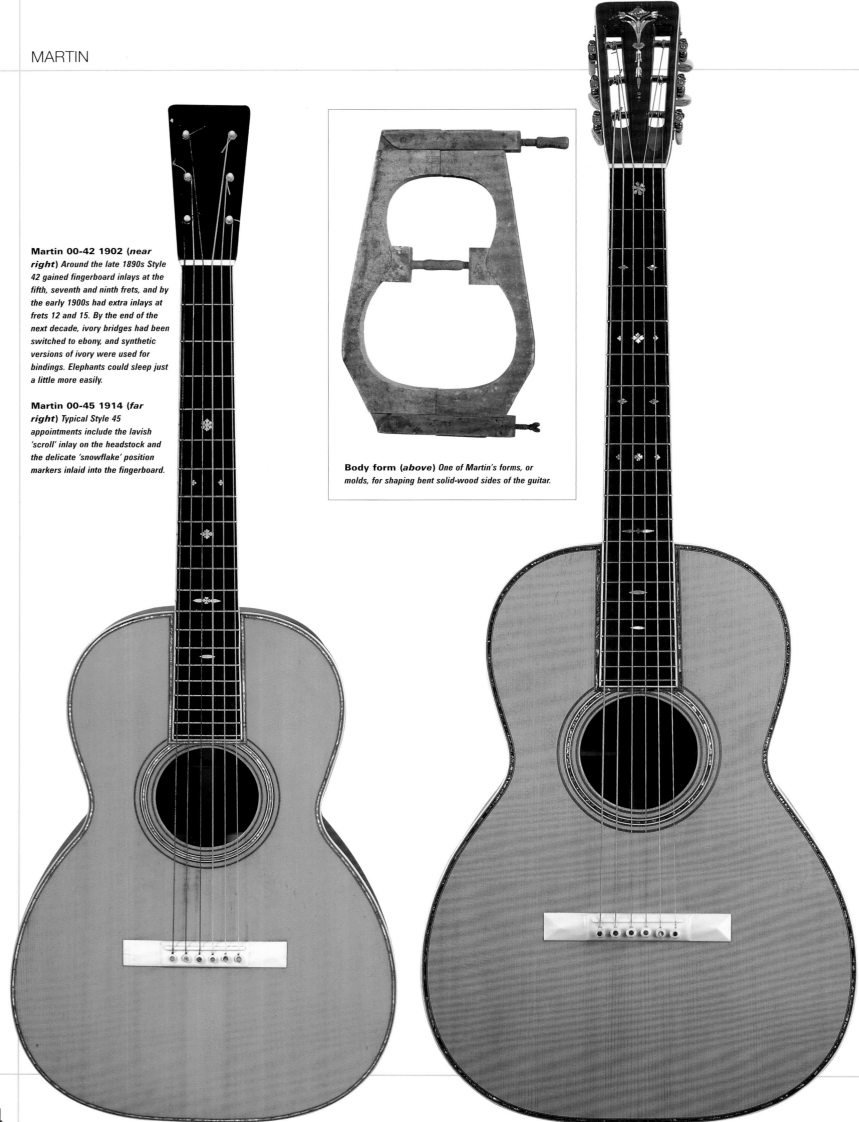

Martin 00-42 1902 (*near right*) Around the late 1890s Style 42 gained fingerboard inlays at the fifth, seventh and ninth frets, and by the early 1900s had extra inlays at frets 12 and 15. By the end of the next decade, ivory bridges had been switched to ebony, and synthetic versions of ivory were used for bindings. Elephants could sleep just a little more easily.

Martin 00-45 1914 (*far right*) Typical Style 45 appointments include the lavish 'scroll' inlay on the headstock and the delicate 'snowflake' position markers inlaid into the fingerboard.

Body form (*above*) One of Martin's forms, or molds, for shaping bent solid-wood sides of the guitar.

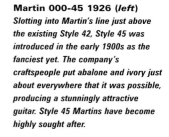

much inlay as possible, including his name on the fretboard to match the Martin played by his recently deceased idol, Jimmie Rodgers. The result was the first D-45, emblazoned with pearl letters on the neck that spelled out 'Gene Autry.' Housed today in the Gene Autry Museum Of Western Heritage near Los Angeles, this 1933 12-fret D-45 is widely regarded as the most valuable American-made guitar in existence.

For reasons unknown, Martin didn't rush its new dreadnought into the catalog as it had the OM, but the company did realize that 14-fret necks were the future. By 1934, Martin had redesigned all its body shapes to allow a longer neck, and a 14-fret version of the dreadnought was also unveiled. Finally, in 1935, the dreadnought appeared in Martin's catalog and sales took off. Within a few years, the D-18 was one of the company's best-selling models. The D-45 didn't appear in the catalog until 1938, and its arrival had the similar effect of boosting sales immediately. Martin's 1930s dreadnought models have been some of the most widely sought-after acoustic instruments ever made, and have come to define the American flat-top steel-string

Martin 000-45 1926 (*left*)
Slotting into Martin's line just above the existing Style 42, Style 45 was introduced in the early 1900s as the fanciest yet. The company's craftspeople put abalone and ivory just about everywhere that it was possible, producing a stunningly attractive guitar. Style 45 Martins have become highly sought after.

Back & side (*far left*) *Instantly distinctive on Style 45 Martins is the superb abalone inlay work on the back and sides.*

Catalog 1904 (*top left*) *The first publicity for Martin's famous Style 45 pictures a 0-45 and lists models 1-45, 0-45, and 00-45. The restrained copywriter says that the "Japan pearl" is "quite narrow and gives a rich effect without being prominent."*

instrument. The 14-fret dreadnought is probably the most copied guitar in the world.

In 1934, Martin's catalog was divided into Orchestra Models – meaning any guitar with a 14-fret neck – and Standard Models, the older 12-fret body shapes. The OM designation thus became a general term, at least to Martin; the OM-28 and 18 were renamed as 000 models, and a few months later were also given the shorter 24⅝" scale length. Also in 1934 Martin finally abandoned the use of bar stock frets in favor of T-shaped fret wire, a change most American companies had made before 1900. Along with the new fret wire came the first use of metal neck-reinforcement, in the shape of a non-adjustable steel bar that was also T-shaped. The next change came in 1938, when all models with the new body shape and longer neck also had the neck width narrowed from 1¾" at the nut to 1¹¹⁄₁₆".

By this time, not many of the older standard model Martins were being sold, with the exception of the 00-21. Other 12-fret models with flush frets and a high nut and saddle were sold to be played with a steel bar in the Hawaiian style ('H' suffix after the model code). Around the same time Martin revived two of its earlier gut-string models, giving them a 'G' suffix. Does all this chatter about model names and numbers seem confusing? Martin dealers certainly thought so at the time, which is

why, beginning in the fall of 1930, the company began stamping the model code on the neck block inside the guitar, just above the serial number. Along with longer necks and pickguards, another change that often appeared on Martins during the 1930s was a shaded 'sunburst' finish, breaking the company's long tradition of offering only a natural, or orange-tinted, finish for the soundboard.

Martin's flat-top models made from 1929 to roughly the end of World War II, in Styles 18 to 45, are the core of what most guitar fanatics consider to be the company's 'Golden Era.' A D-45 from the mid 1930s, if in clean and original condition, has appreciated by almost 200 times its original purchase price. But while the models that garner top dollar in the vintage guitar markets get all the publicity today, at the time Martin paid most of its bills with large numbers of quite inexpensive instruments. Ever mindful of the Great Depression, Martin strove to offer a guitar that retailed as close to $25 as possible, roughly one quarter the price of a Style 28 model. The plain, all-mahogany Style 17 was simplified even further in 1930 by eliminating the binding on the body's edges. In 1934, when the 0-17 got the new 14-fret neck, sales of Style 17 models accounted for almost half of Martin's guitar production. While severely plain, these models brought Martin quality within reach of many aspiring musicians,

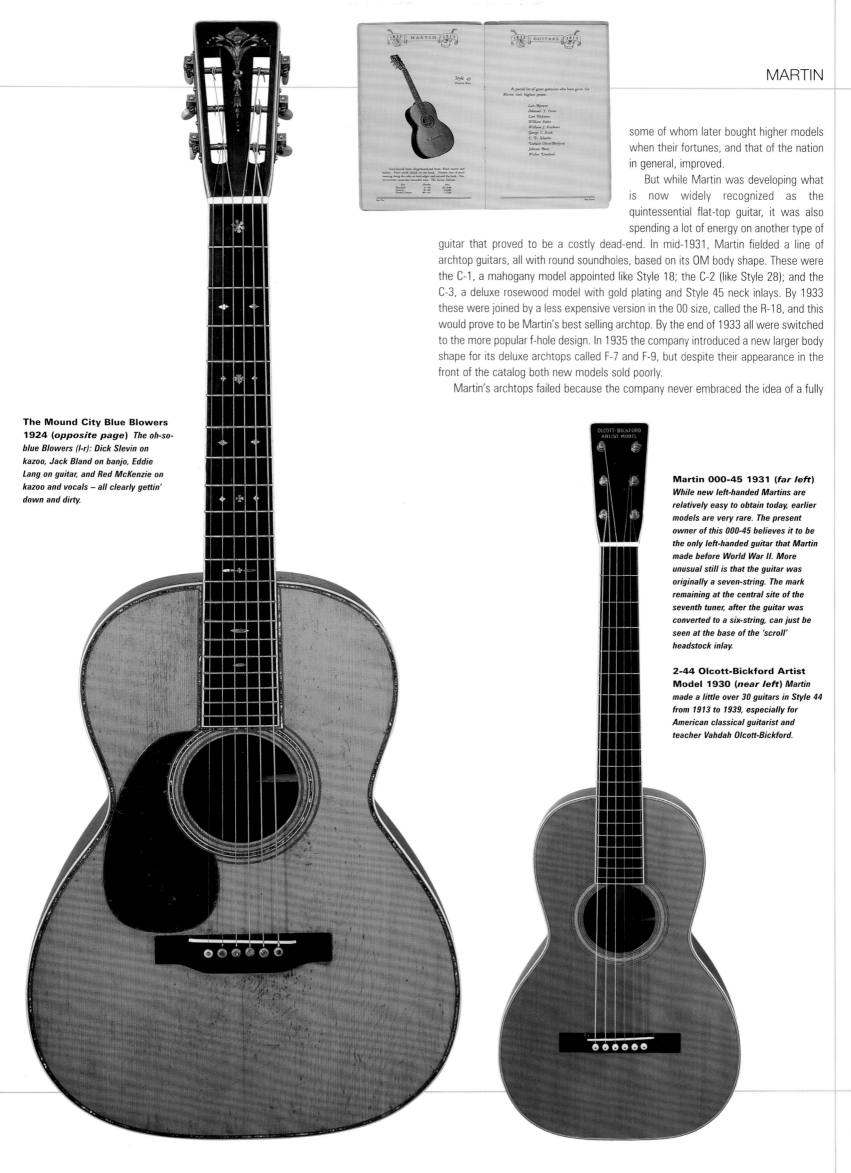

some of whom later bought higher models when their fortunes, and that of the nation in general, improved.

But while Martin was developing what is now widely recognized as the quintessential flat-top guitar, it was also spending a lot of energy on another type of guitar that proved to be a costly dead-end. In mid-1931, Martin fielded a line of archtop guitars, all with round soundholes, based on its OM body shape. These were the C-1, a mahogany model appointed like Style 18; the C-2 (like Style 28); and the C-3, a deluxe rosewood model with gold plating and Style 45 neck inlays. By 1933 these were joined by a less expensive version in the 00 size, called the R-18, and this would prove to be Martin's best selling archtop. By the end of 1933 all were switched to the more popular f-hole design. In 1935 the company introduced a new larger body shape for its deluxe archtops called F-7 and F-9, but despite their appearance in the front of the catalog both new models sold poorly.

Martin's archtops failed because the company never embraced the idea of a fully

The Mound City Blue Blowers 1924 (opposite page) *The oh-so-blue Blowers (l-r): Dick Slevin on kazoo, Jack Bland on banjo, Eddie Lang on guitar, and Red McKenzie on kazoo and vocals – all clearly gettin' down and dirty.*

Martin 000-45 1931 (far left) *While new left-handed Martins are relatively easy to obtain today, earlier models are very rare. The present owner of this 000-45 believes it to be the only left-handed guitar that Martin made before World War II. More unusual still is that the guitar was originally a seven-string. The mark remaining at the central site of the seventh tuner, after the guitar was converted to a six-string, can just be seen at the base of the 'scroll' headstock inlay.*

2-44 Olcott-Bickford Artist Model 1930 (near left) *Martin made a little over 30 guitars in Style 44 from 1913 to 1939, especially for American classical guitarist and teacher Vahdah Olcott-Bickford.*

The Oklahoma Sweethearts
1941 (*left*) *Singer and guitarist Edna Leeper is clearly pleased as punch with her 1940 Martin D-28.*

the more traditional flat-top models. The now-familiar vertical headstock letters and hexagonal fretboard inlays were both initially designed for Martin's archtops, and the black and white top bordering that replaced herringbone trim in 1946 first appeared on the C-2 model 15 years earlier. The body shape of the F series would later become Martin's flat-top M series, which even later became the Martin Jumbo. In summary, Martin's archtops may not have made a lasting impression as guitars, but they helped the company evolve to more contemporary designs.

World War II brought restrictions on materials that put an end to many Martin guitar models, although the company continued to build instruments throughout the war years. Martin was reduced to using the cheapest possible guitar tuners, and went back to ebony neck reinforcement, simply because steel and brass were needed for the war effort. Although it may have been goodbye and good riddance to the archtops, 1942 also saw the last of the pearl-bordered Style 42 and 45 models, and it would be over 25 years before the company would again offer a guitar trimmed in lines of gleaming abalone.

Another goodbye was one few guitarists could see — and probably no one outside the factory noticed — when in 1944 the order was given to no longer scallop the top

carved archtop guitar. Instead, Martin put a carved top on a flat-top body, pitching the neck back to accommodate a high floating bridge and a tailpiece. The result, though pleasant in tone, lacked the power of a Gibson or an Epiphone, both of which offered true archtops with carved tops and backs in the same price range as Martin's models. Although they were discontinued in 1942, Martin's ill-fated archtops left their mark on

Martin 00-21 1904 (*near right*) *It's interesting to compare this 00-21 from 1904 with the late-1930s version at the right of the page. The incarnation seen here, from the model's sixth year of production, was designed for gut strings, and has 19 frets and the typical early 'pyramid'-type bridge.*

Martin 00-21 1938 (*far right*) *Around 1930 Martins began to be braced to take the added strain of steel strings, as players demanded more volume. Note also this guitar's 'belly'-shaped bridge and the new Martin logo on the headstock, both features introduced during the 1930s.*

Jimmie Rodgers 1931 (*left*) *'America's Blue Yodeler' — often credited as the 'Father of Country Music' — was an important Martin endorser of the Depression years, and started the trend for country stars to have their names engraved in the fingerboards of their Martin guitars.*

Catalog 1923 (*above*) *It was around this time that model 000-28, first seen in the early 1900s, began to be produced in greater numbers.*

braces of each Martin guitar. This change was made necessary by the frequent use of heavy-gauge strings intended for big archtop guitars. Although a Gibson L-5 archtop could withstand the extreme tension of .014 to .060 string sets, they wreaked havoc with a lightly braced flat-top. Around the same time, the delicate slotted diamonds and squares fret-position markers on Styles 21 and 28 were replaced with a pattern made of graduated pearl dots. Finally, in late 1946, the herringbone trim that had graced the top of Style 28 for nearly a century was changed to the black and white lines first seen on the C-2 archtop. C.F. Martin III took the helm of the company in 1945 at the age of 50, when his father officially retired. When Frank Henry Martin died in 1948, C.F. III became the Martin company's sole link to its 19th century roots.

Midway through the 20th century, Martin's catalog showed very few instruments that bore any resemblance to what the company had produced 25 years earlier. Ukuleles were still offered, along with two mandolin models, but among several guitar models only the 00-21 looked like Martin guitars made before 1930. Martin was also making 00-18G and 00-28G models, but these wide-neck models built for gut strings (by that time usually nylon) had the same body shape as 14-fret steel-string models but with fan bracing. Despite the odd combination of a 12-fret neck on a 14-fret body, the G models sold quite well, but as folk guitars rather than for true classical playing.

The period from the late 1940s through the end of the 1950s was a quiet one for Martin, as least when it came to new models. The D-21, which combined the looks of a D-18 with the rosewood sound of a D-28, was added in 1955, the same year C.F. III's son, Frank Herbert Martin, joined the company. In terms of Martin's distant future, a more important addition was the birth of C.F. Martin IV, who now heads the company. But if Martin was relatively tranquil in the 1950s, those who played Martin guitars were anything but quiet. Martin's D-18 and D-28 models had long been standard fare for artists in the field now known as country & western, but a young renegade from Memphis who couldn't keep his hips in line with his shoes soon dominated both the pop and country music charts. Elvis Presley was a highly effective

Martin 0-28K 1923 *Martin was one of the first companies to produce guitars especially for playing in the Hawaiian style, and the 0-28K model launched in 1917 was among the earliest. The K-suffix models were made from koa wood. This is chiefly found in Hawaii and is claimed to produce a more suitable tone than the otherwise similar mahogany. Koa guitars were made in a variety of Styles and Sizes, and the 0-28K was produced between 1917 and 1931, using selected figured koa for the top as well as the back (seen right) and sides. This superb example has been subsequently converted to 'regular' low-nut use (and in the process has lost its original bridge).*

Catalogs (*top of page and above*) *Martin literature of the period indicates the popularity of variants on the traditional six-string guitar, such as the tenor guitar (top left), 'plectrum' guitar (top right), and a wide range of stringed instruments promoted on the cover (above).*

rhythm guitar player in his Sun Records period, and the original rock'n'roll power trio was equipped with an acoustic stand-up bass, a hollowbody Gibson electric guitar, and a Martin D-18 or D-28. (Elvis owned both, but the D-28 was encased in a hand-tooled leather cover.)

Around the same time that Elvis was shaking things up with his thumping dreadnought rhythm, far less rebellious fare was being served up by three fresh-faced lads who seemingly never frowned in front of a camera. Two members of The Kingston Trio played Martins, and Bob Shane, who started out on a 000-18 but soon switched to a D-28, inspired so many budding folkies to buy the brand that Martin was quickly swamped with orders. Nick Reynolds played a 0-18T (tenor) model, reviving interest in a type of Martin that had nearly disappeared. By the late 1950s, Martin was heavily backordered, but that didn't keep it from trying to dip its toes into electrified waters by putting ungainly DeArmond pickups into 00-18, D-18, and D-28 models. These E models sold reasonably well, but only for a year or two.

The 1960s were a period of tremendous growth for Martin, and despite being heavily backordered the company released a number of new models. Frank Herbert Martin's influence was seen in two radically different types of Martin guitars. One is

00-40H 1935 (right) *This was the only way to buy a Style 40 Martin in the 1920s and 1930s, the pearl-inlaid Style having been dropped for regular guitars during the 1910s. Martin clearly believed that a fancier Hawaiian instrument would do well, although in retrospect it's not surprising to report that in fact they sold more of the 00-17H, the 00-18H, and especially the Hawaiian version of the small 2-17, the 2-17H. In 1928 a 00-40H retailed at $100, while the 2-17H was priced at just $30.*

Martin D-28H 1936 (far right) *A very rare Hawaiian version of the D-28, still in '12-fret' style at this relatively late stage, originally supplied with high nut and straight bridge. It is one of only two D-28Hs listed in the company's records, the other dating from 1934. This instrument is made even more attractive to seekers of the uncommon by virtue of its shaded top, and its non-28 snowflake fingerboard inlay – presumably specified at the time when the original owner custom-ordered this guitar.*

of little relevance in an encyclopedia of acoustic guitars, but shows something of Martin's waywardness at the time. The F series electrics were shallow-bodied cutaway versions of Martin's earlier F model archtops, only this time with laminated tops and backs, and pickups that would have been just barely acceptable a decade earlier. The F-50 featured a single cutaway and one pickup, while the F-55 had dual pickups. The F-65 sported a double cutaway, twin pickups, and a vibrato tailpiece. Electric guitarists paid little attention, but from 1961 Martin kept the F-Series electrics in the catalog for four years running.

Although he misread what electric players needed, Frank made a better connection with guitarists caught up in the booming folk revival. In 1961 Martin introduced the 0-16NY, its first 'reissue' of one of its older styles. The NY stood for New York, and the model was usually referred to as a '0-16 New Yorker,' simply because it looked a lot like the old 12-fret models made when Martins were still stamped 'C. F. Martin & Co., New York.' With its satin finish, blank fretboard, lack of a pickguard, narrow rectangular bridge, and slotted headstock atop a wide neck, the

Paramount Style L 1930
(*right*) *Martin built some Paramount-branded guitars for William L. Lange in the 1930s, and this rare 'double'-body example shows one of many attempts being made at the time to achieve more volume from the then-unamplified guitar. The close-up photo (above) shows in detail the unusual 'terraced' body sides, with extra soundholes around the edge.*

Martin 2-17 1930 and Catalog 1925 (*left*) *This cheap, plain and spartan guitar was produced from the early 1910s to the late 1930s, and as shown here had a body made entirely from mahogany. In 1922 it had become the first Martin model specifically made to take steel strings (see catalog). Martin describes the $25 "amateur size" 2-17 as being handy "for general knock-about use."*

0-16NY looked like the real thing to folkies of the 1960s, although it would hardly qualify as a historical model by today's standards. The 0-16NY was followed in 1964 by the 00-21NY, which was another folkified Martin model defined by what had been left off the standard 00-21 upon which it was based: no dots on the neck, no pickguard, and no gloss to the finish. The 0-16NY remained a popular model well into the 1970s, but the 00-21NY only lasted a few years.

Martin was clearly the darling of the folk revival, and the list of folk artists who played a Martin guitar reads like a Who's Who of the era. Whether it was button-down ivy leaguers or scruffy hobo wannabes, a Martin was part of almost any acoustic guitarist's uniform. As a result, Martin was too backordered for its own health, and Frank Herbert pushed to get the company out of the old North Street factory. In early 1964 Martin purchased a large plot of land on Sycamore Street on the outskirts of Nazareth, and in the fall of that year the company left its over-100-year-old home and moved to a spacious, one-story building. Tom Paxton and Judy Collins sang from the loading dock as Martin celebrated the long-overdue move to larger and more modern quarters.

The mid to late 1960s were a lively time at Martin. Thanks to the greater capacity

OM-28 1930 (far left) *OM stands for Orchestra Model. It was introduced by Martin in 1929 after banjo player Perry Bechtel came to the company asking for a guitar that was audible in orchestras (in the big-band sense). He also wanted access to more frets, and a narrower neck to which banjo players could adapt. The request resulted in the steel-string OMs, Martin's first guitars with a longer '14-fret neck' that provided 14 frets clear of the body, rather than the company's customary 12.*

Catalog 1930 (center) *OM models were first shown in this catalog's entry, listed as being "designed especially for plectrum playing in orchestra work. Made only for steel strings, in Auditorium size." After 1933 the OM prefix was lost and the design features were incorporated into the regular 000 Size models.*

OM-18 1932 (near left) *Martin occasionally finished guitars with a sunburst top, referred to at the time as 'shaded.' Compare the Style 18's minimal decoration with the famous herringbone trim of the OM-28 pictured to the left on this page. A total of 765 OM-18s and 487 OM-28s were made between 1929 and 1933.*

OM-45 1933 (*right*) Only 40 OM-45 guitars were made between 1930 and 1933, making this a very desirable instrument indeed. It has all the playability of the OM models, plus the top-of-the-line appointments of Style 45. Of particular note is the (for Martin) lavish use of abalone inlay on the front, back (far right) and side. (An abalone is a shellfish, but the name is used interchangeably with 'pearl' for the lustrous mother-of-pearl inside its shell, the small 'green heart' of which is especially valued for inlay work.)

Label (*above*) More than 60 years after the model's introduction, Perry Bechtel's widow signed Martin's special limited-edition OM-28 guitars that were "handcrafted in honor of Mr Perry Bechtel."

allowed by the new factory, Martin was selling more guitars but was also less backordered, thus leaving energy for new models. (Some of these ideas were not at all successful, such as yet another stab at making electric archtops. In 1965, the F series electrics were replaced by the GT series, which had long pointy ends on the headstock but still sported the same outdated pickups. By 1967 they were gone, and now have the distinction of being one of the few electric guitars from the 1960s that is not collectible.)

But when it came to flat-top models it seemed Martin could do no wrong, and the company continued to expand what had become a rather meager catalog of choices just a few years earlier. By the mid 1960s the original 12-fret dreadnought shape was revived, but in two radically different versions. In 1964 Martin finally succumbed to popular pressure and offered a 12-string model, the D12-20 (Style 20 was like Style 18, but with a Style 28 backstrip and an extra line of binding on the back). This was a mahogany 12-fret dreadnought with an elongated slotted headstock, and despite the frustration of fishing 12 string-ends through the narrow slots, the model sold extremely well. The six-string version of the old 12-fret dreadnought had been made in limited numbers, on special order, since the mid 1950s. By 1962, Wurlitzer of Boston was ordering enough D-28S models to have them stamped D-28SW. One of these new old-style dreadnoughts wound up in the hands of Peter Yarrow, of Peter Paul & Mary, and soon the 12-fret dreadnought was back in fashion. Both the D-28S and D-18S were again in the catalog by 1968.

One of the most popular new Martin models introduced in the mid 1960s was dictated by necessity, rather than being inspired by popular requests or an earlier model. Demand for big dreadnoughts increased just as it became more difficult to find Brazilian rosewood logs of sufficient size, leaving Martin with lots of rosewood too narrow to make a two-piece dreadnought guitar back. One of the company's less-traditional new employees suggested a three-piece back, and the D-35 was born. Along with extra binding on the fretboard and sides of the guitar, Martin gave the model lighter braces for both the top and back, yielding a different sound than the D-28, and also gave it a slightly higher price tag. Within just a few years Martin was selling as many D-35s as D-28s. A 12-string version, the D12-35, also debuted in

Ditson Dreadnought-style 1924 (right) *The long-popular dreadnought first appeared in 1916 as a special model made by Martin for the Ditson music stores in Boston and New York. The general design was suggested to Martin by Harry L. Hunt, manager of Ditson's New York branch.*

Back (left) *Martin made guitars in a variety of different sizes and styles for Ditson between 1916 and 1930. This mid-period Ditson does not conform to the set Ditson dreadnought Styles (111, 222 and 333), and is stamped "Oliver Ditson & Co, Boston, New York" inside the body.*

Catalog 1937 (far left) *This catalog page notes the virtues of the Martin neck of the late 1930s, including the reinforcing steel T-bar.*

GUITAR NECKS

ALL Martin Arched Model and Orchestra Model guitars have mahogany necks, re-enforced with a steel T-bar, hand-shaped and fitted. This picture shows some of the notable features of these necks:

A. Solid mahogany, air-dried, quarter-sawn, hand shaped, 1¾ inches wide at the nut.

B. Deep dove-tail joint, hand fitted.

C. Steel T-bar inlaid from first to fifteenth frets.

D. Oval fingerboard, hand fretted after gluing to neck.

E. Wide frets made of hard nickel-silver T-wire, low and smooth.

18

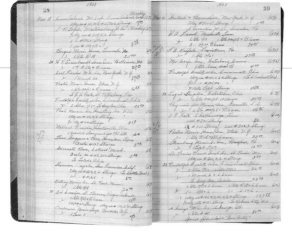

1965, and by 1968 a 12-fret six-string, the D-35S, was added to the catalog. Models with three-piece backs weren't the only concession to modern times as the '60s wound down. In 1967, the tortoiseshell-pattern celluloid pickguard on all models was replaced by black acetate, and the celluloid binding – tortoiseshell pattern for Styles 16, 18, and 21, ivory-colored for Styles 28 and higher – was replaced by black or white Boltaron.

The most impressive new model of the '60s was the 1968 reissue of the legendary D-45. The company had ceased production of all pearl-bordered models in 1942, and only 91 original examples of the D-45 had been produced. To head the project, Martin hired Mike Longworth, a young Tennessean who had already discovered that country stars would pay big money to have their D-28s converted to look like D-45s. Although the D-45 wasn't a strict reissue in the current sense, it did have all the requisite pearl bordering, hexagonal fretboard inlays, and vertical C.F. Martin letters on the headstock. Despite a list price of $1,200 – three times that of a D-28 – the orders poured in, and in a few months Martin had sold

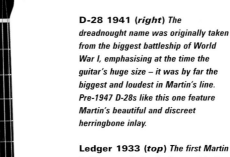

D-28 1941 (right) *The dreadnought name was originally taken from the biggest battleship of World War I, emphasising at the time the guitar's huge size – it was by far the biggest and loudest in Martin's line. Pre-1947 D-28s like this one feature Martin's beautiful and discreet herringbone inlay.*

Ledger 1933 (top) *The first Martin D-45 was made for the famous 'singing cowboy' Gene Autry in 1933. An entry (bottom right) records this historic order, made through the Chicago Musical Instrument Co.*

D-18 1937 (above) *Originally called the D-1, the D-18 was launched in 1931 and, as the base model of the dreadnought line, has been a popular guitar ever since. The restrained level of decoration on Style 18 Martins makes for a rather austere appearance, so the visual distinction and relative rarity of the shaded top make this late-1930s instrument especially attractive to collectors as well as players.*

D-18 1939 (right) *Another classic – and more typical example – of the plain pre-war dreadnought.*

Hank Snow c1952 (*main photo*) Another country & western artist for whom the Martin dreadnought was standard-issue.

more D-45s than in the entire eight years of the model's original production. The following year the D-41 debuted. Longworth had accurately gauged demand for a less expensive pearly Martin. With pearl bordering only around the soundhole and top edge, and two fewer fretboard inlays, the D-41 looked like a D-45 from the audience, but was only two-thirds the price. In its second year of production, the D-41 outsold the D-45 five to one.

In less than a decade, the Martin catalog had gone from Spartan listings of historical survivors to a colorful selection of a wide range of models. But not all the additions were winners. Despite strong sales of its steel-string models, Martin couldn't seem to resist attempting to win back the classical guitar crowd, and in 1968 two new N models were introduced with fan bracing and the shape of a typical Spanish classical guitar. Fortunately one of the early rosewood versions, an N-20, wound up in the hands of Willie Nelson, who added a Baldwin bridge pickup to get his signature sound. The N series nevertheless sold poorly, but Martin kept them in the catalog until 1995.

In terms of Martin's rosewood models, 1970 marked more than just the end of the 1960s. The shortage of Brazilian rosewood had prompted the three-piece-back Style

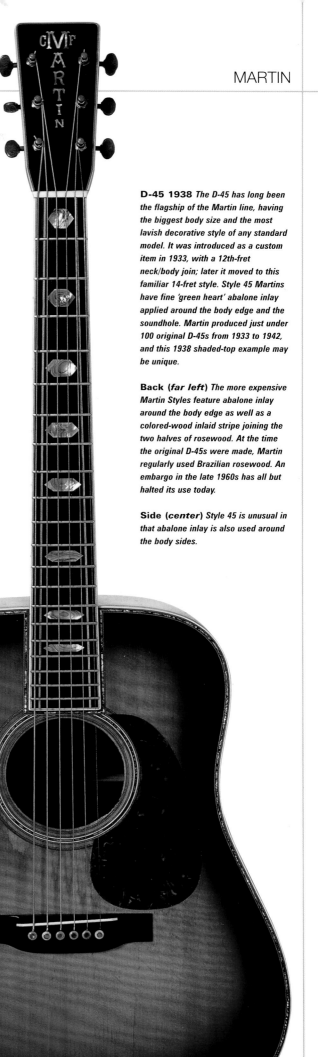

D-45 1938 *The D-45 has long been the flagship of the Martin line, having the biggest body size and the most lavish decorative style of any standard model. It was introduced as a custom item in 1933, with a 12th-fret neck/body join; later it moved to this familiar 14-fret style. Style 45 Martins have fine 'green heart' abalone inlay applied around the body edge and the soundhole. Martin produced just under 100 original D-45s from 1933 to 1942, and this 1938 shaded-top example may be unique.*

Back (far left) *The more expensive Martin Styles feature abalone inlay around the body edge as well as a colored-wood inlaid stripe joining the two halves of rosewood. At the time the original D-45s were made, Martin regularly used Brazilian rosewood. An embargo in the late 1960s has all but halted its use today.*

Side (center) *Style 45 is unusual in that abalone inlay is also used around the body sides.*

35, but there was no such solution to Brazil's 1969 embargo on the export of whole logs of the sought-after wood. Martin switched to Indian rosewood, and by 1970 only a few models would trickle through production with Brazilian rosewood backs and sides. At the time, only a few guitar nuts noticed the difference. What many long-time Martin owners did notice, however, was that regardless of what rosewood the newish Martins were made of, they seemed to lack the sparkle and warmth of earlier

D-45 1940 (*left, back far left***)** *Martin's original D-45 guitars, made in small numbers between 1933 and 1942, are among the rarest and most collectible of all American guitars. The rarity of the D-45s derives in part from the fact that these models did not prove to be popular instruments when they were first introduced. By the time country and bluegrass music were at the forefront of American popular music, however, there was a D Size Martin on practically every bandstand.*

Lonnie Johnson 1940s (*above left***)** *The jazz and blues pioneer with his 12-fret 00.*

Bill Monroe 1940s (*opposite page***)** *Monroe, the 'Father of Bluegrass,' set the standard for country rhythm guitar on a Martin D-28.*

generations. This wasn't just because they were newer, for Martin had added a large rosewood bridge plate under the bridge and left the top braces heavier at the ends than in previous years. It may have kept the tops flatter and reduced warranty claims over high string action, but the added stability also took a chunk out of that legendary Martin tone.

As the company entered the 1970s it seemed poised for a blockbuster decade, and Frank Martin began an aggressive campaign to acquire other music industry companies and build a Martin conglomerate, titled the C.F. Martin Organisation, with the telltale corporate cuteness of substituting a British spelling using 's' instead of the usual American 'z.' One of the first acquisitions was Darco Strings in 1970, a move that proved profitable right from the start. Martin also began importing guitars from Japan under the Sigma label (the Greek letter of that name looks like an M turned on its side). After seeing other importers such as Takamine adopting Martin designs, Martin figured 'if you can't beat 'em, join 'em,' and Sigma guitars were another profitable expansion. Other purchases were the Vega banjo company, Fibes Drums, and a couple of years later the Herman Carlson Levin company of Sweden. These, and several other purchases, proved to be dismal failures, but more on that later.

Martin C-3 1931 (right) Today we associate Martin almost entirely with flat-tops, but the company was among the first American guitar-makers to try to capitalize upon the trend toward archtop guitars in the early 1930s. This first-year example of the unpopular C-series archtops demonstrates Martin's early combination of a round-soundhole 000-size body with an arched top and back. The C-3, with its bound ebony fingerboard (the inlays here are not entirely original), was the top model of a line that also included the C-1 and C-2, all with shaded tops. The vertical 'C F MARTIN' headstock logo first appeared in 1931 on these models.

F-7 1938 (right) An attractive and workmanlike archtop, the F-7 appeared as part of a new two-model line in 1935. The main visual distinction when compared to the company's earlier C series archtops was the inclusion of f-holes. These gave the Martin F series guitars a similar look, at least, to the pattern that had been established by Gibson and Lloyd Loar in the 1920s.

F-1S 12-string 1941 (far right) This instrument is the only example of a 12-string F-series guitar that Martin made, and according to the company's records is one of only six documented pre-war Martin 12-string guitars.

F-5 1940 (*right*) *This rare guitar is one of only two trial F-5 models made at the Martin factory during 1940. One can assume that the company at first intended this spruce-top, maple-back-and-sides guitar to sit in the middle of their F series – two humbler models, the F-1 and F-2, were added to the bottom of the line in the same year. But the F-5 never went into production. Certainly maple was an unusual material for Martin to use: they had traditionally employed rosewood for guitar backs and sides. But maple was the premier wood used for backs and sides by Gibson for its respected archtop guitars, so perhaps Martin decided to back off from such direct competition with Gibson?*

Martin's production continued to climb each year, but the 22,637 Martin guitars that left Nazareth in 1971 would represent a long-standing record. When the folk music revival was morphing into the folk-rock sound of groups like Crosby Stills & Nash, Martin sales continued to be strong and the company saw little reason to do anything different. Instead of bothering with new models, Martin focused on corporate expansion fueled by profits from all those dreadnoughts. But the more acoustic side of folk-rock was soon less than hip, and by the mid 1970s sales had fallen enough to get Martin's management worried. As in the past, the company responded to slower sales with a flurry of new models.

The first new dreadnought was met with 'what took them so long?' approval, as the old herringbone-trimmed D-28s were already hot items in the fast-growing vintage guitar market. In 1976 Martin finally responded to rising demand for a 'pre-war' D-28 and issued the HD-28 (H for herringbone). With herringbone marquetry around the top edge, an old Style 28 zigzag or 'zipper' backstrip, and scalloped top bracing with a small maple bridgeplate, the HD-28 was an instant success, despite a price that was 25 per cent higher than the standard D-28. Martin joined America's bicentennial in a big way, offering a total of 1,976 special D-76 models. Styled like a

Back & side (*right*) *Note the beautiful figured maple used on this trial F-5. As on Martin's other archtop guitars, this instrument has a carved top, while the arched back is formed by internal bracing rather than carving.*

Elvis Presley's Martin D-18 1942 (right) *The King of Rock'n'Roll was no mean rhythm guitarist in his early years, and in the days when the drums were still well back in the mix – if they existed at all – Elvis was banging out the beat on one of his Martin dreadnoughts. He applied his name to the top of his D-18 with stick-on letters, but the 'S' was later lost, in effect changing the instrument's name to the mysterious 'ELVI.'*

Elvis Presley 1956 (main photo) *This photo taken during a break at Victor recording studios in New York City shows record label A&R supervisor Steve Sholes conferring with a young Presley – purportedly during the session for 'Hound Dog' – with B.J. Fontana (second from left) and Scotty Moore (seated). Note the tan leather cover concealing the mahogany back of Elvis's D-18*

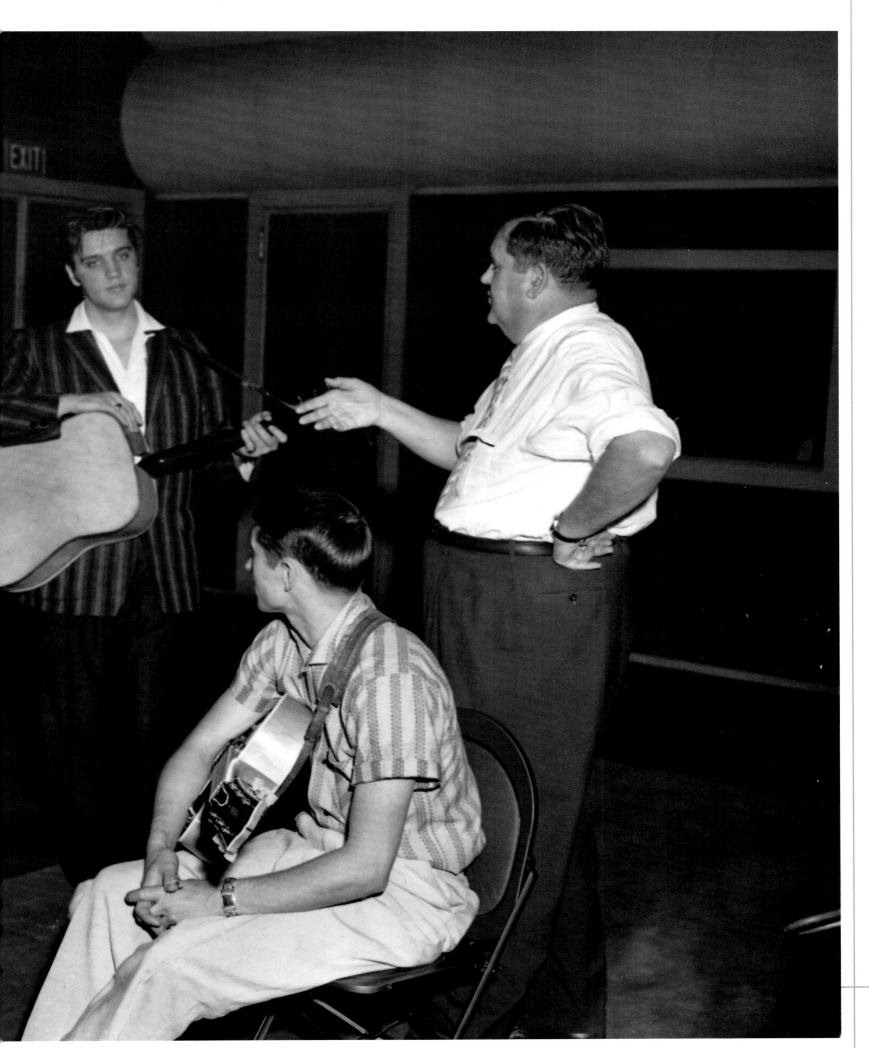

D-35 with extra herringbone and a pearl eagle on the headstock, the D-76 was nevertheless priced above the D-41. Although billed as collectibles, most collected dust on dealers' shelves despite lots of advertising, souring the company on limited editions. A more low-key addition was the D-19, which was basically a D-18 with some extra binding and soundhole rings, and a brown stain on the spruce top.

But new dreadnoughts took a back seat to other news coming from Nazareth in mid 1976. Frank Herbert's sometimes abrasive style of handling the company's employees had gone from bad to worse as sales slowed, and the workers became bitter when a tough new personnel manager was hired. The mood turned even more acrimonious when Martin workers tried to join a local union, and in September of 1977 almost 200 went on strike. Managers and front-office people, many of whom hadn't worked at building a guitar in years, pitched in to keep a few new Martins flowing out to dealers with empty display cases. The strike lasted eight and a half months, with the company hanging tough and waiting out the strikers, most of whom had no better prospects elsewhere. When it was over, Martin had a lot of catching up to do.

To the surprise of many, in 1977 Martin finally introduced its first truly new flat-top

model in more than 40 years. It was the result of combining the earlier F series archtop body shape with a standard Martin soundboard, something that more than one repairman had already done when faced with an F-7 or F-9, which were practically unsaleable in the 1970s. David Bromberg, who played a converted F-7, was at least partly responsible for prodding Martin to make its own version. As with the D-35 a decade earlier, Martin wisely chose to make the new model more deluxe than most Martin guitars, adding a pearl rosette, bound neck and headstock, tinted top, a tortoiseshell acetate pickguard, and the colorful backstrip usually found on the D-41 and D-45.

Although it qualified as a 0000 in size, the new model was called the M-38. A less expensive version, the M-36, was unveiled in 1978, with the stylistic features of Martin's D-35. Both M models shared the highly arched rosewood back of the old F series, and both had scalloped top braces. The result was a more balanced response than the typical Martin rosewood D, for although the M was a bit wider than the dreadnought it had shallow sides like the 000. The M-38 and M-36 were not runaway best sellers like the HD-28, but these models quickly gained favor among many players, including some who had previously shunned Martin guitars.

Martin D-28 1951 (right)
Economic pressures and materials shortages after the war made Martin abandon herringbone trim in 1947 for a much simpler black-and-white top binding. Herringbone stayed off the menu until 1976 and the arrival of the HD-28, a herringbone-equipped and scallop-braced alternative to the contemporary D-28.

Big Bill Broonzy c1940s (above, and opposite page)
Delta blues fingerstylist Broonzy typifies the blues player's long-standing preference for the smaller-bodied Martins over the dreadnought models. Note the herringbone trim on Broonzy's 14-fret 000-28, the guitar seen in both pictures.

Martin 5-16 1962 (right)
Something of a remnant from Martin's past, this undecorated small-bodied Size 5 model, in Style 16, was made for just two years in the early 1960s.

With the strike over and new models getting favorable reviews, the late 1970s should have been good for Martin, but instead two headaches plagued the company. The first was a dramatically reduced demand for acoustic guitars: in 1978, the first full year of production after the strike, Martin barely sold 8,000 instruments. And while cashflow was slowed, the debt from Frank's numerous ill-advised purchases of companies like Levin and Fibes put Martin in a precarious fiscal condition.

One reaction to this plight was to try building electric guitars again, this time solidbody models. Although better conceived than earlier Martin electrics, it quickly became clear that 'electric guitar' and 'Martin guitar' was not a connection consumers could make.

In 1979 Martin made one of its smartest moves of the decade, perhaps second only to bringing back the herringbone D-28. Instead of dealing with special orders erratically as it had in the past, Martin opened its Custom Shop to allow dealers and consumers the option of ordering a unique, or at least unusual, guitar. Although built by the same workers that made standard models, the Custom Shop gave Martin fanatics a chance to participate in the design of a guitar

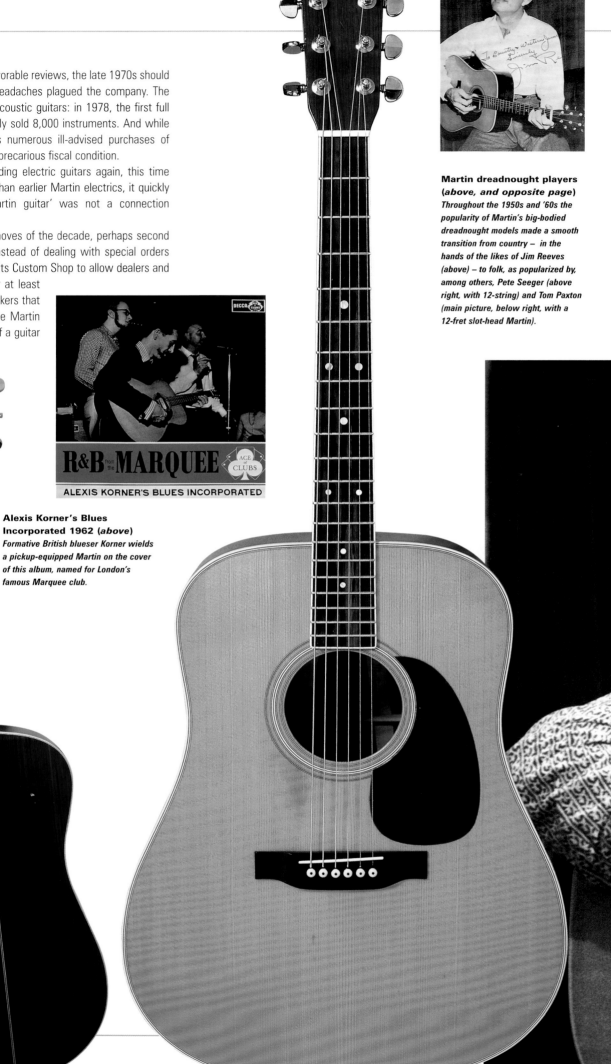

Martin dreadnought players
(*above, and opposite page*)
Throughout the 1950s and '60s the popularity of Martin's big-bodied dreadnought models made a smooth transition from country – in the hands of the likes of Jim Reeves (above) – to folk, as popularized by, among others, Pete Seeger (above right, with 12-string) and Tom Paxton (main picture, below right, with a 12-fret slot-head Martin).

Martin D-35 1968 (*far right*)
The innovative feature of this model, introduced in 1965, was its new back (see near right). Still in production, the D-35 has proved a successful addition to the dreadnoughts.

Back (*near right*) *In the early 1960s Martin found it difficult to obtain large enough pieces of Brazilian rosewood to make all their guitars with the company's traditional two-piece back. The solution appeared on the D-35 in 1965, with this new three-piece rosewood construction.*

R&B from the **MARQUEE** ACE of CLUBS
ALEXIS KORNER'S BLUES INCORPORATED

Alexis Korner's Blues Incorporated 1962 (*above*)
Formative British blueser Korner wields a pickup-equipped Martin on the cover of this album, named for London's famous Marquee club.

made just for them. An unexpected bonus from this concept was that the company got to see just what kinds of Martin guitars the public really wanted – and most requests seemed to be for reissues that recaptured older models, or for special instruments incorporating features that were no longer found on current Martin guitars.

The eighth and fifteenth custom orders received, both versions of the HD-28 more closely resembling a 1930s model, were often repeated and soon became stock models, although they didn't appear in the catalog. Both dreadnoughts had diamonds and squares fretboard inlays, a V-shaped neck with more squared-off headstock, and the X-brace moved closer to the soundhole (sometimes called 'high X' or 'forward shifted' bracing). Custom 8 featured ivoroid binding, while the Custom 15 had standard Boltaron (white) binding. Martin also used 'aging toner' in the top finish, giving the instruments the yellowed look of an older guitar. These Custom Shop models were the seeds that years later grew into the Vintage Series Martins. In 1990,

Neiman-Marcus offered a pearl-encrusted D-45 in its Christmas catalog with a price tag three times that of a standard D-45. Such over-the-top custom models soon became part of the Martin mystique.

By 1980 C.F. Martin IV, known as Chris, was working at the factory, and despite a flurry of new models the company continued to flounder in a market obsessed with synthesizers and electronic gadgetry. A line of guitars made from Hawaiian koa was introduced that year, including the D-25K, which was similar to a Style 18 (dark binding, rosewood fretboard and bridge, but with Style 28 backstrip and rosette), and the D-37K, which had more highly figured koa bordered in white bindings as on the D-35, along with a pearl rosette. Koa-top versions of both were also offered, with these being given a 2 suffix after the K in the model code. A 00 size version of Style 25K was also offered. Martin must have had high hopes for these koa models, for over 1,300 D-25K models were made in 1980 alone. Style 37K was fortunately produced in much smaller numbers and sold

reasonably well, but Martin was still selling the first batch of D-25K guitars two years later. The 125 00-25K models made in 1980 lasted even longer, and were one of the reasons Martin was later reluctant to offer new 00 and 000 models. Another less than successful introduction in 1980 was the Size 7, which was a ⅞-scale dreadnought, made in Style 28 and 37. Both models lasted only two years.

In 1981 Martin tried to catch up with the times by offering two cutaway models, the MC-28 and the DC-28. Both had oval soundholes instead of the usual round soundhole, which limited their appeal, but at least the company was finally taking the new playing styles, and new competitors, seriously. The following year sales hit their lowest level since WWII, with Martin barely shipping 3,000 guitars. Both Martin's creditors and the Board of Directors had had enough, and Frank Herbert Martin was asked to retire at age 49. Brighter notes were sounded that

Martin Carthy (*right*)
Fingerstylist Carthy was one of an elite band of gifted guitarists at the center of the British folk boom of the 1960s. Martin has recently issued a 000-18MC signature model in recognition of Carthy's long-time favorite guitar.

Joan Baez c1969 (*below*) *With her famous pre-war 0-45 in tow, Baez headed the protest-singer movement in the US during the Vietnam War years. More recently, a Martin 0-45JB signature model has been offered.*

Martin ads 1971 & '67 (*above left*) *Martin's advertising campaign sought to appeal to the 'ordinary player' rather than merely boasting about star endorsers. These featured Martin employee Mike Longworth (left, from 1971) and 'folky' Bobby Joe Fenster (right, from 1967).*

Joni Mitchell c1970s (*opposite page*) *Jazz-folkster Mitchell puts her Martin dreadnought to work.*

Martin D12-45 1969 (*left*) *Other than a few rare early guitars, Martin did not start to make 12-strings until the 1960s folk boom defined the market. The luxurious Style 45 appeared in 12-string form late in the decade: this first-year example was one of only three made in 1969. The 12-fret neck, as seen here, had been reintroduced as an 'unofficial' option in 1954, and became popular with many folk players.*

MARTIN

year when Martin was able to purchase some Brazilian rosewood, and in '83 the first new D-28 models with Brazilian backs and sides (stamped D-28V, and with Custom 8 appointments) were eagerly snapped up by savvy buyers.

Chris Martin had been voted in as a vice president after his father's resignation, and his aging grandfather was still chairman of the board, but the Martin company's financial position was no better than before. One of the brightest moves in 1984 was the Guitars Of The Month program, despite the fact that the project was scaled back so that only three guitars were issued, and all at the same time during the annual NAMM trade show. These were limited editions with Custom Shop features not found on standard Martin models, and with paper labels signed by Chris and C.F. III. Martin had learned its lesson when it came to limited editions, and the size of the edition was determined by the number of orders placed. Although the first year's

Jimmy Page 1975 (*right*)
Page is pictured on tour with his Martin dreadnought. The Led Zeppelin guitarist is perhaps best known for his electric work, but he is a skilled acoustic fingerstylist as well, blending English folk and Eastern influences, and often delivered using 'open' tunings.

Martin D-76 1976 (*left*) *The D-76 limited edition guitar was built to celebrate the American Bicentennial. Martin gave it special star-shaped fingerboard inlays and an eagle on the headstock, and built 1,976 guitars, along with 98 D-76E models for employees, and this single prototype, which is serial-numbered 000000.*

Martin ads c1970s (*above left*) *These magazine ads focus on the build quality of Martin guitars, reminding us that they are "still handmade" and, therefore, sometimes expensive – like the 00-45 shown.*

Neil Young 1970s (*above*) *Like his sometime colleagues in CSN&Y, Young often favored a Martin D-45 for the folkier side of his rock.*

Catalog c1970 (*above*) *Sigma, launched in 1970, was Martin's own imported guitar brand.*

M-38
GRAND AUDITORIUM

The M-38 is a flat-top version of the Martin "F" style carved-top guitar manufactured between 1935 and 1942. An important characteristic of the M style Grand Auditorium body is the acoustic properties that make it ideal for sound system and recording studio use.

The sides and matboned two-piece back are made of solid rosewood. A light stain adds character to the solid spruce top which is supported by braces scalloped in the pre-war style. The soundhole rosette is hand inlaid with abalone pearl and the body finish is polished lacquer.

Body bindings are white with black and white inlay around the top, sides and back. An unusual feature is a connecting link of binding and inlay adjacent to the heel of the neck. (See detail, page 29).

The slim mahogany neck joins the body at the 14th fret and features chrome plated, enclosed gear tuning machines. The headstock and fingerboard are bound in white with black and white trim. Unique to this model is the combination of an ebony fingerboard and rosewood bridge.

A very special guitar.

Martin M-36 1993 (*right*)
Launched in 1978, the M-36 features the unusual pairing of rosewood bridge with ebony fingerboard. This member of the Martin M series – another is promoted in the catalog page above – is designed to produce a bassier tone, which is probably helped by its distinctive three-piece rosewood back (left), which recalls that of the earlier D-35 model. The M Size is less deep than a D, and slightly larger in outline.

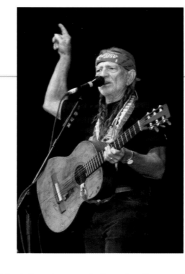

Martin N-20 1972 (*right*) Martin had made guitars designed for classical players, with wide fingerboards, slotted headstocks, and tied bridges, since the 1930s, but had never fared particularly well in this specialist market. The N-10 and N-20 classicals, with characteristic wide-waisted classical body shapes, were launched in the 1960s. They were produced through the 1970s, with the better-appointed N-20 surviving into the 1990s.

Crosby Stills & Nash 1976 (*opposite page*) David Crosby and Graham Nash show off a matching pair of top-of-the-line Martin dreadnoughts, and Stephen Stills often played one too. How many other bands could afford three D-45s – and four when Neil Young was onboard? Guess that's why they called them a 'supergroup.'

Willie Nelson 1990s (*above*) One of few major artists known to use a Martin classical, Nelson has played his N-20 – nicknamed 'Trigger' – for 35 years. His persistent use of a pick on a nylon strung guitar with no pickguard has worn a hole through the body.

sales only totaled 68 guitars for the three models, it was the beginning of Martin's later Limited Edition and Signature Edition series that have proved to be extremely successful. Many of the popular Vintage Series models got their start as Guitars of the Month, including the D-18V, OM-28V, and the HD-28LSV (large soundhole).

Martin's marketing plan was to offer its dealers instruments at all price points, from inexpensive to over-the-top extravagant. The Sigmas started at quite a low price range, and Martin even had a line of Goya guitars which were below the Sigmas. But the leap in price from Sigmas to a D-18 was too great, and Martin couldn't afford to retool so it could make cheaper guitars in Nazareth. The solution was to import unfinished guitar bodies and necks from Japan, finish and assemble them in Nazareth, then add an under-the-saddle pickup and hardshell case. At that point, more than 50 per cent of the guitar's value had been added in the US, so technically it qualified for 'Made in USA' on the label. Martin even gave these new models the usual decal on the headstock, but with 'Shenandoah' replacing the 'Est.

Brownie McGhee 1967 (*above*) Seminal folk-blueser McGhee was fond of his D-18, as seen above (with harp-playing partner Sonny Terry, left). What appears to be the same guitar has taken on a DeArmond soundhole pickup in this cover photo for the October 1973 issue of Guitar Player magazine (right).

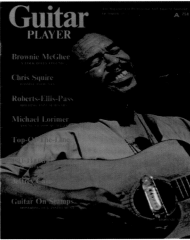

MARTIN

Country Joe McDonald mid 1970s (below) *The country-tinged protest singer with Martin D-45.*

1833.' They were given regular Martin serial numbers, and the model designations were the same as standard Martins, but with '32' added, because all Shenandoah models had Martin's Thinline 332 pickup. Was it Martin's finest moment? Hardly, since all Shenandoah models were made with laminated backs and sides, but in 1984 over 4,000 Shenandoahs were sold (over 2,100 D-2832 models alone) in a year when the company sold barely 7,200 instruments in all. Do the math, and it's clear that Martin probably wouldn't have survived without the Shenandoah Series.

The big turning point for Martin was 1985, for this was the year it made sweeping changes in several directions at once. The company introduced new models, modified old ones, and achieved several years' worth of updates in a short period of time. The most important new model was the J-40M (called simply J-40 after 1989), Martin's first jumbo and Chris Martin's first successful design. By using the M body shape but making the sides as deep as a dreadnought, Martin got the bass response of its D models but in a sexy new package that had more style and better balance between bass and treble. With small hexagon inlays on the bound fretboard, eight-ply top binding, and gold tuners, the J-40M may not have had quite enough abalone to live up to its Style 40 moniker, but it was a flashy new Martin unlike any before it. For those who wanted the sound of a rosewood Martin Jumbo but at a lower price, there was the J-21. The mahogany J-18 was added in 1987. In 1996, Martin gave the J-40 a pearl rosette and a bound headstock with the vertical C.F. Martin lettering.

Not only did the J-40M look unlike any earlier Martin, it also played unlike earlier Martins as well. This was thanks to a new adjustable truss-rod in the neck that allowed a new 'Low Profile' neck shape. The rod, mounted in a stiff aluminum U channel, was adjusted from within the soundhole so traditionalists were not alarmed.

Martin 00-18 1983 (right) This particular guitar has an internal factory-mounted pickup, the controls for which are on the upper body side. Martin has offered various pickup options since the mid 1970s.

Catalog 1986 (top of opposite page) Mid-1980s economics caused Martin to import the laminated-body Shenandoah models in kit form from Japan and assemble them into finished instruments at their Pennsylvania factory. For a time this allowed the company to market a lower-priced Martin-branded guitar.

The playability of Martins as they came from the factory had always been a distant second to its competitors like Taylor, but with the new neck shape and closer tolerances at the factory Martin was back in the game. For a brief while, any of the old standard Martin models were given a 'P' suffix to the model code if they were given the new Low Profile neck, but by 1989 that designation was dropped as virtually all Martins had the truss-rod neck.

Martin also added the new Series 60 guitars in 1985, using figured maple for the back and sides. These were the J-65M Jumbo and a matching 12-string, plus the shallow-bodied M-64 and the MC-68, a cutaway model. The 65 and 64 were given tortoiseshell binding and pickguard, and a Style 45 backstrip. The MC-68 had an oval soundhole and white bindings. Although sales were promising for the first few years, and other maple models like the D-62 were added, most were discontinued by the mid 1990s. In 1985, however, they were a much-needed breath of fresh air for a company that was trying to shed its stodgy reputation. Many more cutaway models were sold now that Martin had a slimmer neck, and the company also sold lots of guitars with Fishman piezo pickups and onboard controls.

Along with other minor tweaking of model offerings, 1986 brought two major

Martin OM-45 Custom 1983 (right) Through its custom service, Martin offers made-to-order guitars to players who want their own particular combination of features. High on the list of requested details is extra inlay, as on this ornately finished custom OM-45 model, made in the early 1980s.

Martin ad 1987 (above) This magazine ad announces the new J-40M 'Jumbo.'

Martin D-45 Neiman Marcus Custom 1980 (*left*) *The high-end department store Neiman Marcus ordered this one-off D-45 to include in its 1980 Christmas mail-order catalog (cover and featured page far left). The Custom Shop model has Brazilian rosewood back and sides, hand-inlaid abalone 'tree-of-life' fingerboard decoration, and solid gold bridge pins – all for a price back then of $9,500. The 'standard' D-45 of that time listed for $2,820.*

Martin D-45 Custom 1983 (*right*) *This is another example of a one-off special-order D-45 built to a customer's specifications. Martin's Custom Shop – publicized in the ad seen to the right of this guitar – has welcomed special orders like this one since its inception in 1979.*

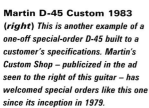

**Martin 7-45 Custom 1981
(right)** Martin has maintained a
tradition that after a certain length of
service with the company, employees
can make a personal instrument for
themselves. To celebrate five years
with Martin, Dick Boak built this
exquisitely crafted dreadnought-
shaped guitar to smaller Size 7
proportions, with Style 45 decoration
and his signature inlaid at the 19th fret.

Sigma ad c1970s (top right)
By the late 1970s the Sigma budget
line contained an impressive range of
models in its own right.

**Martin D-42LE 1988 (far
right)** The 1980s saw Martin launch
clever marketing schemes with LE
(Limited Edition) and 'Guitar Of The
Month' instruments.

changes at Martin. The first was the D-16K, a trade-show special not shown in the
catalog, with Martin taking orders from dealers for only a limited time. With no back
binding and the simplest appointments, it was priced well below the D-18 despite the
koa body, making it the least expensive Martin dreadnought. But the company gave
the D-16K the scalloped top braces and small maple bridge plate that it had been
using for all the new models introduced at higher prices. With a low-profile neck and
adjustable truss-rod, lower string action, and booming sound, here at last was a
model that could compete with some of Martin's newer competitors — namely Taylor
— and thus lure buyers who wouldn't settle for a Shenandoah. The next year Martin
offered the D-16M, a mahogany version, and the following year the D-16A, made with
ash back and sides. By 1989 the D-16 was joined by a 000-16, both in mahogany.
These 16 models were soon offered year round, and formed the basis of a second-

Martin ad 1980 (above) This
magazine ad for the newly offered all-
koa D-37K2 marks a return to a wood
popular more than 50 years before
during the Hawaiian music craze.

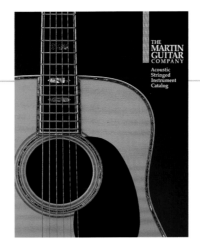

tier guitar line, greatly widening Martin's appeal. It's important to point out that '16' became a series of Martin guitars, quite unlike a distinct style number with set features.

The second major change at Martin in 1986 was the loss of its patriarch, C.F. Martin III, who died on June 21. In settlement of his estate, auditors recommended the company be liquidated and sold to settle the outstanding debts resulting from all those disastrous acquisitions made during the 1970s. Chris and company were able to stave off such a drastic move, but it was clear Martin wasn't out of the woods yet.

In 1986 Martin had offered the J-45M Deluxe, its first beyond-45 Martin (the maple Style 60 series isn't fancy, so doesn't count). With almost twice the amount of pearl bordering found on regular Style 45 models, including the neck, backstrip, and pickguard, it was the most expensive Martin ever shown that wasn't a Custom Shop one-off. Offered as a Guitar Of The Month Limited Edition, 17 were sold. The following year, however, a similar concept was applied to the D-45, but using Brazilian rosewood, and the stated edition of 50 D-45LE examples sold out immediately.

Specially inlaid limited editions of the D-45 soon became a staple in the Guitar Of The Month offerings each year.

Martin's adaptation to the needs of modern guitar players and its increased model line-up was key to the company's return to stability in the late 1980s, but renewed popularity in acoustic guitars in general played an equal role. An added bonus was new interest in travel guitars. The Martin Backpacker, made in Mexico and introduced in 1991, sold far better than the company had expected. Yet new manufacturing trends, specifically the CNC (computer numeric control) milling machines pioneered at Taylor, kept Martin on the defensive in the early 1990s. Martin's competitors were not only building better guitars than they had in the past, improved efficiency was also allowing new models to be introduced at prices Martin couldn't match. The 16 Series, which included a cutaway 000 in 1990, seemed about as low on the price scale as the company could go, with the sticking point being Martin's time-honored, and hand-fitted, dovetail neck joint and the equally old-fashioned nitrocellulose lacquer finish.

In 1993 Martin introduced the D-1, its first break with many of the company's

Martin catalogs (*left and opposite page*) Martin continues to adorn its catalog covers with Style 45-appointed guitars.

Martin J-40BK 1994 (*left*) This black version of the J-40 was introduced by Martin in 1988. Incredibly, it's the first color option that the company offered, other than the 'shaded-top' (or sunburst) finish.

Martin JC-40 1994 (*left*) The new J series body design was first produced with a cutaway on the JC-40 model, introduced in 1987. The J models are some three-quarters of an inch deeper than the M series, the same depth as a dreadnought.

Martin HD-28P 1990 (*left*) After making guitars for 157 years, Martin finally produced their 500,000th instrument in 1990. The building of half a million guitars could not go unmarked, and so the instrument concerned, an HD-28P (which translated as a herringbone-trim D-28 with low profile neck), was signed on the top by Martin's entire workforce, including company boss Chris Martin IV. (Clue: it's somewhere between autographs 65 and 67 in the first column.) Thanks to heavy production throughout the 1990s, by the new millennium Martin was already closing in on its 800,000th instrument – with the millionth not too far off.

Martin Guitars Fretted Instrument Catalog 1993

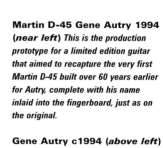

long-standing traditions, and a giant step toward closing the gap between those traditions and state-of-the-art manufacturing. The D-1 used a new mortise-and-tenon neck joint, and had laminated sides but a solid mahogany back. Thanks to a simpler but stronger X bracing pattern with an A-frame around the soundhole, and a low-gloss catalyzed finish called cross-link lacquer, the D-1 was far cheaper than the plainest D-16. A 000-1 soon followed, along with rosewood versions of both the 000 and D, made with laminated sides and back. Also new was a gold-foil logo on the headstock replacing the old decal. Martin had finally reclaimed its 'made in Nazareth' heritage with competitively priced guitars, and Shenandoah models, which had been dying off anyway, were soon forgotten.

Meanwhile, in 1994, at the other end of the price scale, Martin offered its first 'Signature Edition' model, a replica of Gene Autry's famous D-45 — complete with paper label signed by Autry. An impressive 66 were sold, despite the list price of $22,000. The following year the signature edition was a 000-42 EC, for Eric Clapton,

Martin D-45 Gene Autry 1994 (*near left*) *This is the production prototype for a limited edition guitar that aimed to recapture the very first Martin D-45 built over 60 years earlier for Autry, complete with his name inlaid into the fingerboard, just as on the original.*

Gene Autry c1994 (*above left*) *The most famous 'singing cowboy,' Autry owned the first Martin D-45, custom built for him in 1933, and is pictured here cradling the special signature edition made in the 1990s.*

Martin D-45 Deluxe Limited Edition 1993 (*left*) *Number 50 of a limited run of 50 guitars, this extraordinarily elaborate D-45 features an overflowing 'tree-of-life' decoration on the fingerboard. It is owned by the current head of the company, Chris Martin IV.*

Martin 1833 Shop catalog
The 1833 Shop at the Martin factory sells memorabilia, clothing, and kits, but no guitars.

which gathered 461 orders in just a few hours after its introduction at the annual trade show (the number was to honor his comeback album, *461 Ocean Boulevard*). More signature-edition models have followed, including guitars with unique decorations (HD-40MS for Marty Stuart, HD-18JB for Jimmy Buffet, and several others) and models that are highly accurate facsimiles of the original Martin guitars the artist played (000-45JR for Jimmie Rodgers, 0-45JB for Joan Baez, 000-18MC for Martin Carthy, and many others). Today, Martin's Signature Series has largely replaced the Guitars Of The Month program. The company unveils several new editions twice a year, at the Winter NAMM show in southern California and the Summer NAMM show in Nashville. Artists represented in this series are too numerous to mention, but include Paul Simon, David Crosby, Keb Mo, and Shawn Colvin, to name just a few. A portion of the profits from most of these models are donated to charitable causes selected by the artists, with Eric Clapton models being notable for raising money for his Charitable Trust for Children.

Another winner introduced in 1995 was the D-18 Golden Era, styled more exactly like a 1930s original than any previous Martin reissue. More than 300 were sold that year, including about 50 with the unusual dark sunburst that Martin had used in the

mid 1930s. With that success as a mandate, the following year Martin finally collected all its various vintage reissue models under one banner, called the Vintage Series, and gave them consistent features. This included the HD-28V, HD-28VS (12-fret), D-18V, OM-28V, and 000-28EC (Eric Clapton again), which was a short-scale 000-28. These all got aging toner on the top, modified V-shape necks, and open-back vintage-style tuners with 'butter bean' knobs (similar to old Grover G-98 gears). Since then more models have been added, such as the 000-28VS 12-fret, the OM-18V, and 00-18V.

The mid 1990s were another high-energy period at Martin, with the company expanding both the high-end Vintage Series and lower-priced lines made possible by the new D-1 technology. In 1996 the 16 Series was switched to the new mortise-and-tenon neck joint and the D-16 became the D-16T (for technology). Unlike the 1

Martin CHD-28 1994 (*left*) *As guitar-makers became increasingly aware of possible shortages of traditional tonewoods, Martin began to experiment with timbers unfamiliar to*

the company. This new optional version of the HD-28, using cedar in place of the conventional spruce top, is one such example.

Odetta c1990s (*above*) *The gospel and blues-tinged folk singer uses a powerful dreadnought to accompany her equally powerful voice.*

213

Series, the 16T models used all solid woods and had a new hybrid X pattern that combined Martin's traditional scalloped X top bracing with the A-frame soundhole reinforcement of the D-1. The following year the SP (Special) 16 Series guitars were introduced – deluxe models with snowflake inlays on the fretboard, a pearl rosette, gloss finish, and gold tuners. Both D and 000 models were offered in the SP Series, along with cutaway versions, in both rosewood as well as mahogany. Models with built-in pickups and onboard electronics were also included. A new 'Women in Music' 16 Series model, the 00-16DBM, was also introduced, designed by Martin's female employees. This was a deep-bodied 00 with a narrow 14-fret neck and slotted headstock. Several variants of this concept have followed.

In 1998 several different woods were also added to the SP 16 Series, primarily in D models, including walnut, maple, and koa. At this point Martin's 16 Series guitars alone were offered in greater variety than the company's entire catalog of less than a decade earlier. But the model codes became baffling: what was an SP000C-16TREP, for instance? The answer: a Special 000 Cutaway 16 Technology model, with Rosewood body and Electric pickup with Prefix onboard electronics. The plethora of prefixes and suffixes could leave a Martin fan pining for a simple D-18 and a shady

Martin 000-42ECB 2000
(*right*) *Martin's first Clapton signature model of 1995 (as advertised above) sold out its run of 461 guitars within days. A stock model still available today has notched up more than 4,000 sales. For the backs and sides of this later hand-signed edition of 200 guitars for 2000-'01, Martin dipped carefully into its stocks of rare Brazilian rosewood.*

Martin HD-28VS 2002 (*right*)
This Vintage Series dreadnought returns to the herringbone trim, slotted headstock, and 12-fret neck of its predecessor from the early 1930s – all features that have seen renewed interest from players in recent years. In this case, the 'S' suffix on the model name indicates 'short neck.'

park bench. Martin took the D-1 concept even further in 1997, introducing the Road Series. These guitars were given the letter M after the body code (DM, 000M, JM, etc). Made with laminated mahogany sides and backs but a solid spruce top, the thinner finish, black binding, and single ring of herringbone for a soundhole rosette is about all that makes them distinguishable from the 1 Series guitars.

At the same time, the all-mahogany 15 Series was introduced. With solid mahogany for the sides, back, and top, the company came close to its all-mahogany 'chocolate' Martins of years past. These models have no body binding, a thin low-gloss finish like on the Road (M) Series, and a herringbone decal rosette.

The 15 Series was soon followed by a more deluxe all-mahogany line, called the 17 Series, with gloss finish, body binding, and top bracing like the 16 Series. At one trade show during the late 1990s, Martin introduced no fewer than 32 new models, with at least half that many more at the summer show barely six months later.

As the Martin Guitar Company faced yet another turn of the century, it found itself in quite a different position in relation to its competitors, and the world in general. That year, a new addition to the Sycamore Street factory was completed, one that nearly doubled the instrument plant's size. Although the company had been in a

precarious financial position barely a decade earlier, it had now managed to find a stable footing and was matching its competitors as new technologies swept through the guitar-making industry.

In 1990, Martin had celebrated its completion of an HD-28 with serial number 500,000. At the end of 1999, the company completed number 780,500, meaning that Martin had built the same number of guitars in the last decade as it had built in its first 137 years! (Ukuleles, mandolins, and custom brand guitars without Martin serial numbers would trim that gap by a few years, but production totals for the 1990s are impressive any way you look at them.) And entering its third century, Martin continued the double-barreled approach to a wider market share that had proven so successful since introduction of the D-1.

At the upper end of the pricing scale, Martin dug even deeper into exact reissues of its legendary 1930s guitars by seeking out sources of Adirondack spruce for the soundboards, the same species it had used before the mid 1940s. For Style 28 and higher models in this new GE Series (for Golden Era) Martin also used Brazilian rosewood for the backs and sides.

The first models introduced were the D-18GE, D-28GE, and D-45GE, with others

Mini-Martin Limited Edition 2000 (left) *After the success of its backpacker, Martin offered this downsized model patterned on its old Style 5. The 'baby' guitar concept has been successful for other makers such as Taylor and Tacoma.*

Martin HD-35JC Judy Collins (right) *Another limited-issue signature model patterned after an artist's long-time favorite Martin – in this case Judy Collins's D-35. This example is number 23 out of 50 built.*

Martin Backpacker 2000 *Martin's popular travel guitar has been built in the company's Mexican factory since 1994.*

Bill Frisell *The jazz ace proves a surprising proponent of Martin's take-it-anywhere traveling Backpacker.*

such as the OM-18GE following close behind. These models quickly put Martin on a more equal footing with some of its smaller guitar-making rivals that specialize in building near-replicas of Martin instruments from the pre-Word War II era. Martin has also adopted Golden Era Series woods and styling for some of the models in the company's Signature Series, notably an OM-18 cutaway built for fingerstyle guru Laurence Juber.

Beyond the vintage angle, Chris Martin has sponsored a number of highly decorated art model D-45s by inlay artist Larry Robinson, although they were for display purposes only and not offered for sale. One of these models became the D-50 Deluxe Edition in 2001, setting a new price record when offered to Martin dealers at a list price of $50,000.

In quite the opposite direction, Martin introduced its least expensive models to date, the X Series, made with high-pressure composites of wood fiber finished with a photo-film of mahogany or spruce. These models were given a whole new bracing pattern, plus a neck of multiple laminates that needs no finishing.

Although the X Series sales increased dramatically when a version was introduced with a solid spruce top, other alternative-materials versions have also been popular.

Martin HD-28LSV 1999 (far left) *This relatively recent addition to the D-28 family has an enlarged soundhole patterned after a Martin famously used by bluegrass ace Clarence White, as well as the popular herringbone trim and scalloped braces (which in this case accounts for the 'S' in the suffix of this 14-fret model).*

Martin OM-42 2000 (left) *This is Martin's first Style 42 model in the OM Size since the original appeared in 1930. The OM was the company's first 14-fret model.*

Martin ad 2011 (left) *James Valentine of Maroon 5 works out on his GPCPA1 with Fishman pickup system.*

MARTIN

One was the Alternative X, with a thin aluminum soundboard, while the Cowboy X was a new take on the old 'cowboy stencil' guitars, but this time with a full-color print of Western scenes from original art by cartoonist and illustrator Robert Armstrong. And, just to be safe, Martin expanded its popular 16 Series guitars with the 16GT (for gloss top) models, lowering the price from what the earlier 16T versions had sold for. These solid-wood guitars have proved highly popular, and the line now includes old-style 12-fret models as well as cutaway versions with onboard electronics in four different body shapes. Despite the flurry of new models, Martin still sells a lot of HD-28s and D-35s, along with most all of the other Martin models that fueled its growth in the 1960s and preserved the company's stature in the tough years that followed. Even with all the expansion, the Martin Guitar Company has retained a remarkably cohesive workforce, with many employees making Martin a lifetime career – just like in the old days.

In 2005 Martin further secured its relationship with Martin owners by inaugurating an official Martin Owners Club. For Martin fans, the former home and factory in downtown Nazareth has been turned into a museum and visitor center, opened at the end of 2005, and an unmissable Buy From Factory program so that the visitor could go home with a souvenir instrument.

Martin 000-1 2001 (far left) *Following the introduction of the D-1 in 1993, Martin offered the similarly 'budget priced' 000-1. Both save on construction costs by using laminated sides with solid top and back, and satin rather than gloss top finish.*

Martin HPD-41 2001 (left) *This elaborate new take on the dreadnought features abalone inlaid inside its herringbone trim, with a slightly restrained take on the Style 45's abalone position markers.*

Coldplay 2002 (far left) *Martin's appeal shows little sign of waning as yet another generation of musicians takes up the instrument. Here, vocalist Chris Martin of British alt-rock band Coldplay covers rhythm duties on a mahogany-topped cutaway model.*

Martin OM-45GE '1933' 2001
(*right*) This deluxe OM model is part
of the 'Golden Era' series, and was
built to the specifications of the 1933
OM-45. Brazilian rosewood back and
sides, Adirondack spruce top, and gold
hardware are among its many lavish
appointments.

**Bob Dylan and The Rolling
Stones late 1970s** (*above
right*) Dylan (center) makes like a
Rolling Stone in this heavy-hitting trio
of Martin maulers – with Ron Wood
(left) and Keith Richards (right).

**Martin 000-28LD Lonnie
Donegan 2002 (far *right*)** The
signature model of British 'skiffle' king
Lonnie Donegan was limited to an
edition of 72. The guitar features the
lesser-seen sunburst top, and special
position markers.

Mama did the drivin' for the family
And frank made a livin' with a song
Home was just a camp along the highway
The pickup bed is where we bedded down

219

Martin ad 2012 (*left*) *Marcus Mumford of Mumford & Sons is noted here as playing a D-28, a D-18VS, an OM-21 and an LX1 Little Martin.*

Martin 000-16RGT 2002 (*right*) *Another of Martin's more affordable models, this 16 Series guitar was a little better appointed than its laminated sisters, with solid Indian rosewood back and sides, and a gloss top finish.*

Martin 000X1 2006 (*centre*) *The X1 series offered a sensible combination of fine Martin quality and a reasonable price.*

Martin SPD-16K Special Edition 2002 (*far right*) *Like other recent koa-based models before it, this special edition was built with solid koa back and sides, and a spruce top (the SPD-16K2 had a koa top).*

In 2002 Martin brought in a new president, Keith Lombardi, who came from a background in investment equity, and he in turn was replaced in 2014 with the company's first woman president, Jacqueline M. Renner. An important change came when longtime Martin historian Mike Longworth retired in 1995. Early in his career with Martin he was featured in an advertisement under the headline "Meet Mike." Longworth died in 2003 and was remembered with a signature model. In addition to Chris Martin's increasing public appearances, Dick Boak emerged as the employee who best represented the new Martin company.

In 2004, Martin unveiled its one millionth guitar – a dreadnought of Brazilian rosewood with most surfaces covered in pearl inlay. By contrast, a new theme model – with a body and top of a plastic material called HPL, or high pressure laminate – commemorated the cartoon character Felix the Cat with colorful graphics. And in a new direction, Martin debuted a new line of shortlived archtop guitars designed in conjunction with Dale Unger of American Archtop Guitars, the first it had produced

since the years before World War II. By 2017, Martin offered a typically large range of models, divided into various series, including Authentic & Vintage, Limited & Special Editions, Custom Signature Editions, Retro, Standard, Performing Artist, 15, 17, and 17 series, Road, X, Little Martin, Junior, and Backpacker. Martin also offered several ukulele models for the trend that showed no signs of dying.

The guitar models ranged in list price from a $429 Little Martin, with its minimal proportions and 23" scale length, up to a $150,000 new-for-2017 D-200 Deluxe, produced in celebration of the guitar company's two millionth intrument and with a very elaborate theme that was based, appropriately, on the passage of time. It was created in collaboration with the high-end watchmaker Roland G. Murphy of RGM.

Martin took the opportunity to promote this extremely limited edition by declaring: "Since 1833, we've made two million guitars and not one compromise." CEO Chris Martin added that his company's commitment remained "to make guitars that people will fall in love with over and over again."

It isn't the small company it once was, but it's still in Nazareth, headed by a fifth generation Martin named Chris, and still focused on building guitars. Not many old-world companies can make such a claim to consistency, and none of them make a product that can sing or roar when brushed with the human hand.

Martin Felix II 2006 (*left*)
Martin's development of HPL (high pressure laminate) offers a canvas for varied graphics, as on this second version of a model dedicated to the cartoon character Felix The Cat.

Martin M-36 2016 (*far right*)
This reintroduced member of the M series has that line's typical slim body depth and three-piece back.

Martin D-28 Authentic 1941 2014 (*center*) *This nitpicking re-creation of the treasured pre-war D-28 was made with all the historical accuracy Martin could muster, based on a prized instrument from the company's own collection.*

M A T O N

Probably the best-known guitar-maker 'down under,' Maton has been around since 1946, founded by Melbourne musician and luthier Bill May (hence the name 'May-Tone'). Maton's catalog has been extensive over the years, counting over 300 models, basses and electrics included. Acoustic guitars include the Messiah, which comes in a number of versions: six or 12-string, acoustic and electro-acoustic, with or without a cutaway. Maton has always had a reputation for high quality, and distinguishes itself further in the guitar world through its use of Australian timber. The company is still run by May's daughter and son-in-law, Linda and Neville Kitchen.

M A U R E R

Maurer was the principal brand name used on guitars made by the Larson brothers of Chicago, Illinois, from 1900 until 1935 or '36, when the Euphonon brand replaced it. Like Bohmann guitars before them and unlike most other guitars of the time, Maurer guitars were designed to handle steel strings, eliminating the need for a tailpiece. Most Maurers were produced in the small workshop of the Larsons and feature the innovations typical of their early work. The Maurer story begins even before that of

Maton ad *Promo material for the Southern Star six-string and 12-string dreadnoughts.*

Maton ad *Man gets intimate with Maton – and who could blame him after spying the figured timber on the sides of this EA-80 dreadnought?*

Maurer Style 590 c1930 (left) *The auditorium-sized model is the largest Maurer the Larson Brothers produced, and was made in the most ornate style, with intricate inlays on body, fingerboard, and headstock.*

Harty Taylor 1930s (below left) *This rugged mountaineer who sang sweet and sentimental songs in the old style – shown here with his Maurer flat-top – was the other half of the unforgettable Karl & Harty team.*

Neil Finn 1995 (*below*) **The**
Crowded House frontman performs live
with his concert-bodied Maton flat-top.

MAURER

the Larsons, however, with Robert Maurer, a Chicago music teacher and publisher who also imported instruments and manufactured Champion guitars and mandolins, as well as providing instruments for other distributors carrying their brands, beginning in the 1880s. In 1897 Maurer stopped making guitars for others and concentrated on his own Maurer parlor guitars. In 1900 Maurer sold his instrument factory to August Larson, Edward P. Longworthy, and Joshua H. Lewis, who formed Maurer & Company.

Carl Johan Ferdinand Larson (born 1867) emigrated from Sweden to Chicago in the 1880s. A trained woodworker, he got a job making parts for Edwin J. Cubley, a manufacturer of guitars, mandolins and banjos, until Cubley's factory burned down in 1893. When he'd saved enough money, Carl brought his brother, Peter August Larson (born 1873), and sisters to join him. Shortly after the purchase of Maurer, August began working with Carl, and the other partners dropped from sight, leaving Maurer & Co as the Larson brothers, and Maurer their core brand.

Larson's Maurer line consisted of a variety of slot-headed standard (12¾"), concert (13½"), grand concert (14") and auditorium (15") models made of quartersawn oak, mahogany or rosewood, though some maple guitars were made on special order. All had spruce tops. Necks were mahogany with ebony fingerboards. Maurer decoration ranged from simple colored purfling to marquetry and pearl trim on the best guitars. Inlays ran from pearl dots up to full tree-of-life inlays.

All Larson guitars were built with 'stressed' tops and backs that were bent over arched braces when glued. In 1904 the Larsons received a patent for laminated braces. Lower grade Maurer guitars were ladder braced, while middle and higher-grade Maurers featured X-bracing, augmented by lots of smaller braces. The laminated braces were reserved for the better models. Upscale Maurers also had laminated necks. Some Maurers also had extra reinforcement on the sides.

Also patented in 1904 was a new harp-guitar design that was sold as Maurer. This had two necks, one fretted, the other unfretted. The lower half was like a regular guitar, with a much larger, 'giant guitar' on the top half, yielding a kind of cutaway effect, picked up later when the Larsons reworked the Knutsen Dyer design in 1912.

Probably during the 1920s the Larsons received another patent for a neck-tilt adjustment that was available as an option on Maurer guitars, although it's rarely seen. Essentially this was a bolt-on neck with two adjustment screws, one through the heel into the heel block, the other into a block of wood under the top at the end of the fingerboard. To lower the action, you backed off the fingerboard screw a bit to

tilt the angle back. To raise it, you backed off the heel screw to tilt the neck forward.

In the late 1920s the Larsons applied for yet another patent that was offered as an option on Maurers. This was billed as a device to help students obtain a lower action to make practicing easier, and consisted of a metal bridge and saddle cover that was screwed on through the top (it had holes to accommodate bridge pins). Action was adjusted by loosening the strings and slipping in a lower saddle beneath the metal cover. It would seem the device was unnecessary, given that it was just as easy – or easier – to simply change saddles in the first place, which is probably why these are also almost never encountered.

In 1927 the Larsons filed more patents for a pair of internal metal stabilizing rods. These were the basis of Maurer & Co.'s Prairie State line (see entry), but some also appeared on Maurer guitars. Around 1935 or so the Larson brothers changed their necks from 12 to 14 frets clear of the body, and changed their brand name to Euphonon. A few of these new models were sold to Wack Sales Co in Milwaukee stamped as Maurer rather than Euphonon. Carl Larson retired in 1940, but some Maurer & Co guitars were built as late as 1942. August Larson died in 1944, Carl in 1946. The Larson Bros name was revived as a brandname in France in 2007.

Monteleone Radio Flyer 1995
This spruce-topped jazzer is signed inside by its respected maker, John Monteleone, with the legend "Islip, New York, No. 168."

Back (left) *This rear view reveals the Radio Flyer's beautifully flamed maple back and neck.*

M C P H E R S O N

Wisconsin maker McPherson's guitars are set apart from most others by their small, oval soundhole, located near the upper bout, which – according to the luthier – increases the flexible surface area on the central part of the guitar. Other, less-visible features are a proprietary bracing system and a fingerboard that is raised off the top (which can be cedar, sitka spruce or redwood, with sides and bottom made from rosewood). There are also versions made with carbon fibre, "a new material for a new age" the company says. All McPhersons are intonated with the Buzz Feiten system.

M O N T E L E O N E

Long Island-based luthier John Monteleone is a prime example of a guitar maker who merges unusual design ideas with great sound. Monteleone started out by building mandolins and doing repair work for New York's renowned Mandolin Brothers guitar shop, and is now considered to be one of the world's premier builders of archtop guitars. Drawing inspiration from classic archtop builders such as Gibson and D'Angelico, he inserts an almost metropolitan sense of aesthetics into his one-of-a-kind creations. In 1996, Monteleone was given the distinguished honor of completing

construction on the last guitar started by the late Jimmy D'Aquisto. He is constantly striving to advance his instruments' sound, and recently developed what he calls the Side Sound system, which consists of a series of soundholes in the side of the guitar (sometimes featuring shutters that open and close) intended to improve the player's perception of the guitar's sound. Although archtop guitars have become his primary focus, Monteleone continues to build his highly-acclaimed mandolins, and he also offers steel-string flat-tops.

M O R G A N

Representing fine craftsmanship from Vancouver, Canada, Morgan is named for the eldest son of company boss David Iannone, who was apprenticed to Larrivée Guitars in 1981, later becoming acoustic production manager. Beginning to establish Morgan part-time in 1986, Iannone went solo a couple of years later, and today runs a five-strong workshop producing around 200 instruments a year. Some models are sprayed up by and utilize various components supplied by Larrivée, an indication of the close personal ties Iannone maintains with Jean and Wendy Larrivée.

The bulk of sales – embracing dreadnought, jumbo, OM, and concert designs, plus

Monteleone Dreadnought 1975 (*left*) *Monteleone is best known for his fine archtop guitars, but his flat-tops are also highly acclaimed. Note the intricate vine inlay on this example's fingerboard and headstock.*

Monteleone Rocket Convertible 1995 (*right*) *This stunning blue 18"-wide archtop was custom-ordered with two 'convertible' Side Sound ports on its upper side (see side-view photo, far right). A special lever – positioned near the neck – opens and closes the guitar's oval front soundhole.*

an extensive menu of custom options including fancy inlay-work – have been available within North America, but recent years have seen growing representation overseas, including Germany, Japan, Italy, and the UK. Morgan pro users span a diverse musical spectrum – from Grammy-nominated Canadian singer-songwriter Sarah McLachan (who has three Concerts), through twice US fingerpicking champion Don Ross, to rockers Nickelback, who own no fewer than six Morgans.

M O S S M A N

Before the proliferation of high-end 'boutique' guitar companies there was Mossman, which arose from a profound reaction to mass-marketed guitars. Founded in 1965 by Stuart L. Mossman in Winfield, Kansas, Mossman instruments had proprietary bracing, a unique glued/bolt-on neck joint, and, on the Golden Era, abalone tree-of-life inlays.

In 1970 Mossman expanded and began to grow. After a disastrous 1975 fire, the company recovered with a 1976 distribution agreement with C.G. Conn, but poor guitar storage ended in a fiasco. In 1986 Scott Baxendale bought Mossman and moved to Dallas, Texas. John Kinsey and Bob Casey of Sulphur Springs, Texas, took over in 1989 and continue to build to a long waiting list. Pros who have played

Mossmans range from Dan Crary to Emmylou Harris, Hank Snow, Cat Stevens, Merle Travis, Red Steegal, and Clay Walker.

M O Z Z A N I

As well as being a skilled guitarist and composer, Luigi Mozzani was one of the most innovative luthiers in the early part of the 20th century. His most famous instruments were his flamboyant harp guitars, which he dubbed chitarra-lyras. He also built standard classical guitars, all members of the violin family, and a variety of mandolins in different sizes. In 1907 he opened a luthierie and music school in Cento, Italy, where he trained a generation of Italian instrument-makers. His most famous pupil was Mario Maccaferri, who went on to design the Selmer-Maccaferri guitar. In 1927 he moved his school to Bologna. His new school was shut down in 1934 by Mussolini's fascist government, after which Mozzani returned to Cento where he continued to build instruments on his own. Mozzani reopened his school in 1942, but he died the following year. His wife kept the school going until 1947. During the 1950s Farfisa offered a line of guitars bearing the Mozzani label, but they were not based on Mozzani's own designs.

National Style O Round Neck c1931 (left) *The Style 0 is National's best-known single-cone resonator guitar.*

Back (right) *The Hawaiian scene sandblasted onto this guitar's back is even more elaborate than its front decoration. This view also shows the round neck profile of this instrument, intended to be played like a traditional 'Spanish' guitar.*

Resonator (above) *A view beneath the cover of this National Style 0 reveals a spun aluminum resonator cone and the 'biscuit bridge' at its center.*

NATIONAL

National's innovative metalbody guitar, with its three resonator cones, was welcomed as a savior by Hawaiian and blues guitarists in the late 1920s, but by the mid 1930s, when the electric guitar gained a foothold, the revolutionary National had become an evolutionary dead-end. However, the unique sound produced by a thin aluminum cone functioning as an audio speaker never lost its appeal, and a new National company revived the original style in 1989. Nationals were successful, first and foremost, because they were louder than conventional acoustic guitars, which were not able to compete with the horns in the jazz bands of the 1920s. It wasn't only standard-style guitarists who wanted more volume; Hawaiian players, who held their instruments in their laps, were also in need of a louder guitar.

One of these Hawaiian players, a Texas-born vaudeville performer named George Beauchamp, had an idea to increase the volume of a guitar by incorporating an amplifying horn like those used in early phonographs. He sought out Los Angeles inventor John Dopyera to help him turn the concept into an instrument. Dopyera had formed the National company in 1926 to exploit his patents for banjo improvements. He made a guitar for Beauchamp and then began experimenting with another type of

National Style O Square Neck 1935 *This square-necked version of the brass-bodied Style O was intended to be played 'Hawaiian' or 'lap-style' with a slide.*

Back (below) *Another evocative Hawaiian scene sandblasted onto the back of a National Style O.*

National catalog 1929/30 (above) *The cover of the leading reso company's early promotional catalog depicts an art deco fantasy scene of close-encounters proportions.*

amplifying device that was being used in the new electrified phonograph systems: the cone of an audio speaker. Using cones made of thin, spun aluminum, he experimented with various numbers of cones and configurations. On April 9th 1927, he filed a patent application for a guitar with the three-cone configuration that would become the National 'tri-cone' guitar. The cones were contained inside the guitar and they opened toward the back of the instrument. The bridge was mounted on a three-armed piece of cast aluminum that rested directly on the peaks of the cones. The area directly above the cones had a coverplate with large screened openings to allow the sound to project from the body, and the upper bouts had additional lattice-like openings.

The individual cones were very lightweight – almost flimsy – but they supported the weight of the string tension, and they increased the volume of the guitar considerably. The body of the new National 'tri-cone' was made of 'German silver,' a nickel alloy, and its sweet tone, coupled with the increased volume, made it the perfect instrument for Hawaiian players. In 1927 Beauchamp enlisted Sol Hoopii, the most popular and influential Hawaiian guitarist of the time, as National's first big-name endorser. Hoopii became the first person to record with a National, and the new resonator guitars were immediately embraced by Hawaiian players.

National's original tri-cone or Silver Hawaiian line included four models. Style 1 had a plain, unengraved body and sold for $125. Style 2 was engraved with a relatively simple rose pattern and carried a price of $145. Style 3 was more heavily engraved with a lily of the valley motif and was priced at $165. Style 4 was the most expensive, with elaborate chrysanthemum engraving and a price of $195. All models were offered with a standard guitar neck or a square neck (of metal) for Hawaiian play. The squarenecks were by far the best sellers.

Even in the flush times before the stock market crash of 1929, these were expensive instruments, and almost from the beginning there was stiff competition. John Dopyera had left National in a dispute with his partners in 1928 and invented a new type of resonator guitar called the Dobro – short for Dopyera Brothers. (See *Dobro* entry.) National responded with a similar woodbody model called the Triolian. The name came from the original design, which used three cones, and when it was re-designed with only a single cone, it retained the Triolian name. It featured a large, backwards-opening cone. The bridge was fitted into a circular piece of wood, about the size of a biscuit, that rested on the peak of the cone, resulting in the nickname 'biscuit resonator' for the National-style cone configuration. The Dobro system, by

National Model 35 Tri-cone c1937 (*far left*) *The first National resonator guitars – introduced in 1927, though this example is from a decade later – followed the 'Tri-cone' design, with three separate resonator cones and a large T-shaped cover.*

Triple resonators (*near left*) *A view beneath this Model 35's triangular cover reveals its three pressed resonators, and the T-shaped bar that connects their centers. The strings' vibration across the bridge moves the T-bar, which in turn vibrates the cones, which resonate and amplify the guitar's sound.*

National catalog (*right*) *The resonator guitar takes a much-needed beach vacation.*

Book cover (*right*) *The cover of this biography, 'The Story Of Peetie Wheatstraw And His Songs' by Paul Caron, shows blues singer Wheatstraw (born William Bunch) cradling a National Tri-cone from around 1930.*

229

contrast, had an eight-armed bridge unit that rested on the lip of the inverted cone, and that system is generally referred to as the 'spider' system.

The original National Triolian of 1928 had a wood body, painted yellow with blue and red highlights, and decorated further with a decal of a Hawaiian hula girl on the back. The wood body didn't last long. It was replaced in 1929 with a steel body that sported a painted finish ranging from yellow on some examples to green on others. Like the Triolian name, the Polychrome finish name stayed with the model after it had adopted the monochromatic green/yellow style. The hula girl decal was replaced by a Hawaiian scene with palm trees and an orange sun. On the Triolian and other single-cone models, the upperbody soundholes were a pair of small, violin-style f-holes rather than the large latticework openings of the tri-cones. The coverplate over the single-cone resonator had groupings of small holes, like a sieve or a colander.

Around 1930, the Triolian was fitted with a Bakelite neck, but this was unreliable and didn't last. The Triolian sold for $45, undercutting the Dobro by $10, and its success, along with the onset of the Depression, prompted National to introduce an even less expensive steelbody model in 1930 called the Duolian. Like the Triolian, the Duolian had only a single resonator cone (there was never a Monolian). Its finish,

The Hands of Bukka White 1963 (above) *Mississippi bluesman White chose a National to partner his lonesome freight-train of a voice.*

National Style 4 Tri-cone c1931 (near right) *The Style 4 was National's top model of the time, and this one is a square-neck guitar for Hawaiian-style playing. Note the ornate floral engravings (best seen on the back photo, far right), which are somewhat more elegant than the Hawaiian and western scenes of many other models.*

called 'frosted Duco,' was dark green or gray with a swirling, crystallized textured, as if it had been placed in a too-hot oven and then in a freezer. It sold for $32.50 and, not surprisingly, was more popular than the Triolian.

A third single-cone model, the Style O, was also introduced in 1930. With a price of $85 initially, then $62.50, it was a bit more expensive than the Triolian, but it looked as if it belonged in the upper echelons of the line, with the German silver tri-cones. The first Style Os had a nickel-plated steel body, but a brass body – 'bell brass' according to literature – was quickly substituted. The gleaming nickel plating of the body was etched by sandblasting, rather than engraved, with images of Hawaiian palm trees. A plain version, without the etching, known as Style N, was also available for a short time.

Like the tri-cones, the single-cone models were available with either a round neck for standard play or a square neck for Hawaiian style, although the squareneck models had a wood neck rather than the metal neck of the tri-cones. Ironically, despite the obvious target market indicated by the Hawaiian imagery on the Triolian and the Style O, few Hawaiian-style players bought single-cone models. The vast majority were sold with the standard round neck.

After Hawaiian players, the next group of guitarists to embrace the metalbody Nationals were blues players. Not long after Sol Hoopii made the first recordings with a National, Tampa Red became the first blues artist to record with one. Contrary to the accepted image of the blues artist as an itinerant, always-broke musician who played whatever guitar he could get out of pawn, Tampa Red played an ultra-fancy Style 4 that had been gold-plated – at least it appeared to be gold-plated. He was nicknamed 'The man with the gold guitar.'

Many other bluesmen followed Tampa Red's example, although none went as far as the gold tri-cone. The price range of the single-cone models – from $32.50 to $62.50 – was much closer to a bluesman's budgetary requirements than the $125 minimum for a tri-cone. The single-cones produced a crisper, harsher tone than the tri-cones, but that cutting tone worked well for performers who might be found on streetcorners, at house parties, in juke joints, or in other situations where the guitar needed to be heard above a crowd having a good time. The resonator guitar had been conceived as an instrument for a slide guitar style – albeit Hawaiian – so Nationals worked well for blues bottleneck stylists.

So many influential blues performers of the 1930s used Nationals that the

Taj Mahal 1970 *Mahal often turns to a National to produce his powerful blend of blues, jazz, and world music.*

presence of a National metalbody guitar in a photograph is now a badge of identification for a bluesman. Their need for volume is evident in the forceful style of Bukka White, and White got the most volume out of a National single-cone. Son House played his quintessential Delta blues licks on a single-cone model, and in his case, the National may have been the only guitar that could equal the volume of his powerful voice. Blind Boy Fuller, primarily a street musician, played an original-style single-cone with 12 frets clear of the body, and 'upgraded' in the late 1930s to one of the new 14-fret models. Scrapper Blackwell used a Triolian to keep up in volume with the piano played by his partner Leroy Carr. Although legendary blues artist Robert Johnson was never photographed with a National, the distinctive sound of a National single-cone metalbody guitar is a vital part of his seminal recordings.

National also introduced single-cone guitars with wood bodies, but it seems that the company's heart was never in a woodbody guitar. (This would be true in the post-World War II years as well.) The Rosita of 1933 had a laminated body of maple or birch that National probably bought from the Harmony company, a Chicago-based maker of inexpensive instruments. Instead of the f-holes in the upper bouts, the Rosita had holes shaped like a lyre or a trident.

The Rosita was not only National's first woodbody model (the original Triolian notwithstanding), it was also National's first model of any kind with 14 frets clear of the body. All of the earlier roundneck models had 12 frets clear, and National lagged behind other guitar makers in this area. Martin had started moving from 12 to 14 frets clear of the body in 1929, and Gibson had implemented 14-fret necks across the entire line in 1932. National's single-cone metalbodies wouldn't be redesigned with 14 frets clear until late 1934 or 1935. The company offered a second woodbody model in 1933 called the El Trovador.

National introduced two additional woodbody models in 1934. Although the expansion of the line might be an indication of growing confidence in woodbody models, it was more likely a result of John Dopyera and the Dobro company having settled their differences with National in late 1933, although it would take almost two years before their merger into the National-Dobro company was official. It was a period when conventional woodbody archtop guitars were growing in popularity, in no small part because they had become larger and louder. They were approaching Nationals in volume, and when strummed hard, as they were in big-band settings, they retained more of the inherent resonance of their wood bodies, which is to say a

Memphis Minnie 1940 *The singer and her Chicago-built, wood-bodied National archtop.*

National/Valco-made Supro Resophonic Folk Star 1964 (*left*) *A striking but not overly toneful hollowbody made from red 'resoglas.'*

National N-720 1968 (*right*) *A wood-bodied dreadnought made just before the close of Valco/Kay in early 1968. Did anyone say ugly?*

National catalog 1940 (*right*)
By this time the company's promotional emphasis has switched to electric steel guitars, archtops, and amplifiers.

Mark Knopfler 1982 (*below*) *The Dire Straits guitarist sparked a major revival of Nationals, especially when his gleaming chrome model appeared on the cover of the band's multi-platinum album Brothers In Arms.*

NATIONAL

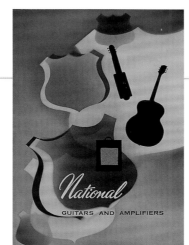

'warmer' sound, than the National metalbodies did.

National's two new woodbodies of 1934 were probably designed with the idea of competing against the new archtops. The Trojan was specified with a laminated maple body (all of Gibson's archtops had maple back and sides), made by Harmony. The Estralita had a laminated mahogany body, which gave it a warmer tone than maple. (Not coincidentally, the midline model in the basic Dobro line had a mahogany body.) And the Estralita also had fancier trim, with multi-ply binding and a varied pattern to its pearl fingerboard inlay. Previously, only the Styles 3 and 4 tri-cones had had anything fancier than dot inlay. The upper model of the basic three Dobros had a spruce top – and not surprisingly, a spruce-topped National, the Havana model, appeared in 1938.

National's last single-cone woodbody model showed the influence of conventional guitar design – particularly the ever-increasing body size of archtop guitars in the

1930s. The Aragon had an 18" archtop body – the same size as Gibson's Super 400, which was a full four inches wider than the typical National – made by Harmony or Kay. The combination of a vibrating top, large body, and National resonator produced enormous volume, but the day of the resonator guitar was virtually over, and the Aragon remains the rarest of National's woodbody models.

Except for the Aragon, the woodbody Nationals had neither the power nor the tonal 'personality' of the metalbodies, and National continued to enhance the metalbody models. Two less expensive tri-cones appeared with nickel-plated brass bodies – rather than the nickel alloy of the original four tri-cones – and etched images on the body, rather than engraved. The squareneck versions of these models had a wood neck, like the single-cone models, rather than the metal neck that had been the style of the tri-cone. Style 35, introduced in 1936, featured an image of a Renaissance musician under a willow tree, etched into the back of the body. Style 97, introduced a year later, had an etched Hawaiian scene on the back, showing a girl on a surfboard (inexplicably holding a tow-rope, like a water skier). On both models, the images were enhanced with enamel paint. One last brass-body tri-cone, the M-3, appeared around the same time, and over the next few years it was catalogued with a plain nickel-

National Model D 2003 *A current example of one of the wood-bodied, single-resonator models from the re-established National Reso-Phonic Guitars company.*

plated body, then a wood-grain paint finish, and finally a uniform yellow paint finish.

National also upgraded the single-cone metalbody models, starting with the move to 14-fret necks by 1935. The Triolian and Duolian received new finishes that simulated walnut wood grain in 1937. Upgrades to the Style O included block inlay on the fingerboard in 1936 (replacing the original dot inlay) and then parallelograms in 1937. The 14-fret neck was an arguable improvement – while it provided greater access to the upper frets, it also necessitated a shorter, smaller body, which to some ears equated with sacrificing some of the instrument's tone. The other improvements were merely cosmetic, and none of them slowed the plunging market for the acoustic resonator guitar.

The man responsible for the demise of the resonator guitar in the 1930s was, ironically, the same man who was responsible for its birth – George Beauchamp. The dispute that had caused John Dopyera to leave the company had intensified over Beauchamp's claim of inventing National's single-cone 'biscuit' resonator system. After a series of lawsuits between National and Dobro, Beauchamp was forced out of the company in 1931. By that time he was involved in a new project with one of National's vendors, Adolph Rickenbacker, to develop an electric guitar, which they

Eurythmics 1999 (below) *Dave Stewart takes the National message to the masses as he performs alongside musical partner Annie Lennox during the UK's Brit Awards ceremony.*

NATIONAL

introduced in 1932. Again, the first musicians to embrace a new guitar with increased volume were Hawaiian players, among them National's biggest endorser, Sol Hoopii. When Hoopii's photograph appeared in a Rickenbacker catalog showing him with an electric Hawaiian in late 1935, Beauchamp had his revenge, and the resonator guitar's days were numbered.

National continued offering acoustic resonator guitars through 1941, but the company had recognized the coming electric age and started making electric guitars in 1935. After World War II, Valco focused almost entirely on electrics. A line of conventional flat-tops and archtops appeared in 1947, apparently as a matter of convenience. National had moved its offices to Chicago in 1936 and reorganized in 1943 as Valco, a combination of the first names of owners Victor Smith, Al Frost, and Louis Dopyera (John's brother). Valco entered into a distribution agreement with Chicago Musical Instrument Co., which acquired Gibson in 1944. The new National acoustics reflected this new family affiliation with Gibson. They looked very much like Gibsons because they were in fact made by Gibson.

The two National archtop guitars of 1947 were essentially Gibson's 17" L-7 and 16" L-50. (There were also two non-Gibson archtops, with bodies probably made by Kay, that appeared only in 1947.) The flat-tops were Gibson's 17" super jumbo J-200, 16" dreadnought J-45, and 14¼" LG-1 models. The inlay patterns, headstock overlays, and headstock shapes may have been National's, but the bodies and necks were Gibson's. Consequently, these postwar National acoustics were good-quality instruments, but only for two years. In 1949, National began fitting them with its newly developed Stylist neck, a heel-less design that was relatively unstable and resulted in decidedly inferior instruments. Some of the acoustics stayed in the catalogs as late as 1961, but few were sold after the neck change.

National did revive the acoustic resonator guitar in the postwar years, but the Reso-phonic of 1956 was more of a funky toy than a musical instrument. The next, and final, National acoustic resonator guitar, was equally toylike in appearance. In 1961 National had started making bodies for its electric guitars out of fiberglas, using an injection-mold process, and in 1963 an acoustic resonator guitar was designed of the same material. Under the National brand, it had a white body and was called the Bluegrass 35. It also appeared in red as the Supro Folk Star and in black with Montgomery Ward's house brand, Airline. Although these fiberglass models were full-size guitars that sounded considerably better than the Reso-phonic, they were

nevertheless a laughable attempt at recapturing the sound of the 1930s models. Valco acquired Kay, but after a line of low-quality imported National-brand flat-tops, they went bankrupt in 1968.

Although professional quality Nationals hadn't been produced since the 1930s, the sound as well as the instruments themselves endured in blues music. Early bluesmen were rediscovered – along with their Nationals – and by the 1970s modern day bluesmen such as Taj Mahal and John Hammond Jr. were introducing the single-cone Nationals to an ever-widening audience. When Dire Straits put a Style O on the cover of their 1985 album *Brothers In Arms*, the resonator guitar was introduced to millions of pop fans worldwide.

In Hawaiian music, the National sound did not fare so well. Electric guitars took over, and the only element of the Hawaiian music played on Nationals that survived was the technique of playing an acoustic guitar held flat in the lap – but this survived only in the world of bluegrass and played exclusively on the Dobro-style woodbody resonator guitars.

One of the strongest forces in the revival of interest in Hawaiian-style Nationals in the 1990s was Bob Brozman, who featured tri-cone Nationals in his eclectic repertoire of blues and Hawaiian music. Brozman 'rediscovered' and recorded with Hawaiian guitarist Tau Moe, reintroducing the traditional acoustic Hawaiian style that had seldom been heard since the introduction of the electric guitar into Hawaiian music. Brozman also recorded with slack-key guitarist Ledward Kaapana, bringing the National tri-cone into contemporary Hawaiian music.

The steady rise of interest in the old Nationals inspired two former employees of the Original Musical Instrument company (makers of Dobro resonator guitars since 1970) to try their hands at making National-style resonator guitars. Don Young and McGregor Gaines formed the National Reso-phonic company in 1989 in San Luis Obispo, California, and started building single-cone woodbody models, all of them with a round neck and 12 frets clear of the body. In 1992 the new company made its first metalbody models, the brass-body Style O and the steel-body Delphi (called Duolian for a short period). Two years later its first tri-cone appeared, based on the old Style 1. Other models have ornamentation and other features not found on the originals, such as a cutaway body shape. With more consistent quality and improved intonation, these new National resonator guitars are better suited to the demands of modern guitarists than many of the originals.

National Polychrome Tri-Cone 2001 (*near right*) *This new entry-level metal-bodied model is structurally similar to the Style 1, but has a baked-on 'wrinkle' finish.*

National Style EN 2002 (*left*) *The etched version of the mirror-finished, brass-bodied Style N.*

Corey Harris 2001 (*opposite page, left*) *The roots-influenced musician is seen here picking on a National for his blend of blues, gospel, world music, and R&B.*

Norman B-50 1990 (*opposite page, right*) *The top-of-the-line flat-top from Norman's B series of the time.*

NORMAN

Norman guitars get their name from their original maker, the late Norman Boucher, who started building guitars in 1968, setting up production in the Canadian village of La Patrie in 1972.

During the 1970s, Robert Godin helped Boucher to develop the business, and when the company went bankrupt in 1988 Godin bought the Norman facilities and absorbed the brand into his burgeoning LaSiDo empire – which was also predominantly based in La Patrie.

Though there have been model changes over the years, the range has remained remarkably constant, the nucleus being variants of the solid spruce/wild cherry B-20 dreadnought and the smaller-bodied B-20 folk.

Normans share construction features with other Godin-made acoustics (see *La Patrie*, *Seagull*, and *Simon & Patrick*) such as bolt-on necks, maple dowel-reinforced heels, and lightly applied alcohol lacquer.

The spruce and cedar tops are claimed to come from trees at least 600 years old. Though not cosmetically exciting, Normans enjoy a deserved reputation for consistently good sound-quality and value.

OAHU

The Oahu Publishing Company, described by Hawaiian string wizard Bob Brozman as "the Amway of Hawaiian musical instruction," was the vision of the charismatic Harry G. Stanley, Hollywood publicity agent turned steel-guitar mogul. Starting in Flint, Michigan, in 1926, then opening branches in Detroit and Toledo, Ohio, before settling in Cleveland, Oahu not only supplied instruction and sheet music, but a broad variety of related supplies: strings, picks, bars – even grass skirts and leis. It has been estimated that in its six decades in business, Oahu published 38 million pieces of sheet music.

Oahu was a prolific seller of instruments, with its acoustic guitars manufactured by Kay and Regal. Oahu marketed squareneck and roundneck acoustics, including archtop f-hole and tenor models. Perhaps the most familiar is the small-body sunburst student steel ($22.50 in 1936) with a pyramid-style aluminum bridge, and a gold-and-black-and-white Oahu decal on the headstock. In the middle of the line was a larger-body mahogany model with the black and white checkerboard binding also found on various Regal guitars of the 1930s and '40s.

Oahu managed to exploit World War II to its advantage thanks to the US

237

government's Limitation Order L-37A suspending production of all musical instruments except guitars (the thinking behind which was never fully explained). In 1943 Oahu ran an ad that beckoned: "Come On Over ... Where The Pasture Isn't Drying Up!" encouraging retailers to expand their guitar business. Just as Oahu designed instruction courses for aspiring professionals, it also marketed guitars commensurate with top-flight technique and showmanship. The Jumbo Deluxe ($158.00) boasted a spruce top, African rosewood body, and pearl trim. Though its great days were in the past, Oahu still published catalogs, now with Japanese-made guitars, into the 1960s.

OLD KRAFTSMAN

Old Kraftsman was a 'house brand' of the Spiegel company, the third leg of the powerhouse Chicago mail-order catalog retailers (with Montgomery Ward and Sears) that supplied the largely rural population of America with limited access to consumer goods prior to World War II. Joseph Spiegel founded a furniture store in 1865 and

Oahu c1927 (left) *This roughly 000-sized Oahu flat-top's label reads "F.W. Konkua, Hilo, Hawaii," but the guitar was built by Kay in Chicago.*

Oahu Deluxe Jumbo 68 c1936 (right) *An elaborately-decorated square-neck Hawaiian flat-top guitar, also made in Chicago by Kay.*

Norman ads (top of page) *On display are dreadnoughts and a folk-bodied guitar from Canadian maker Norman, now part of the large Godin stable of brands.*

entered the general merchandise catalog trade in 1905. Precisely when Spiegel began selling guitars is unknown, but by the 1930s it sold Old Kraftsman instruments (as well as those with a Del Oro brand), mainly decorated 'decalomania' flat-tops, archtops (some carved), even a resonator, mostly made of the least expensive materials (hardwoods, laminates) by Stromberg-Voisinet/Kay.

In 1936-37 a few carved-top acoustics were supplied by Gibson. Otherwise these were poor-men's copies of Kays that survived into the 1960s.

OLSON

Self-taught US luthier Jim Olson has been building guitars since 1977. Based in Minnesota, he has become one of the most successful individual flat-top builders on the scene. During the 1990s, Olson became known for his clever tooling, willingness to use power-tools, and pioneering efforts in using CNC technology for manufacturing his own parts. Although he works almost exclusively by himself, these measures have allowed him to work in large batches, producing upwards of 70 instruments per year.

While Olson also offers parlor and dreadnought models, his SJ (small jumbo) model is by far the most popular. The word was spread by players like Phil Keaggy,

Leo Kottke, and especially James Taylor, and the SJ may be responsible for creating a trend toward this body style as a preference for fingerstyle players. In 2002, Olson offered a limited edition James Taylor signature model, as well as a 25th anniversary model. Even though prices for his guitars have skyrocketed, Olson has built up a several-year-long waiting list, and today he is taking only a limited number of orders.

Old Kraftsman 'Crown' c1941 (*left*) *Ye olde worlde jazz box? Kay made this unusual model – with its odd crown-shaped soundhole and knights-in-armor fingerboard inlays – for the Spiegel catalog company of Chicago.*

Ovation Custom Legend 1976 (*near left*) *A classic example of the wooden-topped, 'lyrachord' fiberglas bowl-backed guitar from Ovation.*

Ovation ads 1970s (*above and center*) *"Glen Campbell plays Ovation," and so – it seemed – did everyone else at the time, including the members of Bread.*

Paul and Linda McCartney
1976 *The former Beatle thrums an*
Ovation 12-string.

OVATION

Guitars with round backs made of fiberglas seemed like a crazy idea when they were invented back in the 1960s, but today, after single-handedly creating the modern acoustic-electric guitar category, Ovation is a mainstay of the guitar world. In the hands of musicians as diverse as fingerstylist Adrian Legg, jazz guitarists Larry Coryell and Al DiMeola, and rocker Nancy Wilson of Heart, Ovation has forged the way in putting acoustic-electric guitars in the studio and on the concert stage.

Ovation guitars were the brainchild of jazz guitarist and aeronautical engineer Charles H. Kaman (born 1917). While a student in Washington, DC, Kaman made extra money performing with a small jazz combo. One night the great Tommy Dorsey Orchestra came to town and Kaman was offered the guitar chair, which had just opened up. He decided to stay with engineering and went on to build a successful helicopter company, though a guitar was always near at hand in his office.

In the early 1960s he decided to diversify. While visiting Martin to have a cracked guitar-back repaired, Kaman realized that he had experience working with the fine tolerances needed to make guitars. He inquired about buying Martin, but it wasn't for sale. He also looked into buying Harmony, but that didn't work out either. Kaman

decided to go his own way. Working with an employee who built violins, John Ringso, Kaman applied the composite fiberglass technology, as used for his helicopter blades, to designing a guitar that would solve some of the inherent problems associated with wood, such as cracking and warping.

The first prototypes had square backs, but the bowl-back shape emerged on the sixth try in early 1965 as a self-reinforcing solution, eliminating the need for braces and improving transmission of vibrations to the top.

Ringso was soon joined by Jim Rickard, fresh out of college, who'd once built a solidbody electric and had worked on guitars. Rickard would be in charge of engineering Ovation's tops. He owned a pre-war Martin D-45 and that guitar became the standard that all tops were supposed to meet.

The first artist to try one was jazz guitarist Charlie Byrd, who liked the sound and said it deserved an ovation. The brand was named. Byrd, who played a classical guitar, eventually got his own Ovation, though he had trouble with it sliding off his leg. Ovation fixed that by gluing ground walnut shells to the waist, though Byrd soon discovered he had a closet full of trousers with holes in one leg.

The guitar that Byrd sampled was a steel-string and he recommended that Kaman

Ovation Adamas 1978 (right) *This model joined Ovation's high-end models in 1975. Its top was made from a sandwich of carbon fibers and birch veneers, with 22 small soundholes replacing the usual central hole.*

Ovation ad 1973 (above) *Kenny Loggins was an early supporter of the revolutionary Ovation approach.*

Ovation Applause 1976 (near right) *A deep-bowled flat-top with bolt-on neck, at an entry-level price.*

Back (above) *The Applause's foam urethane back.*

Ovation Country Artist 1972
The groundbreaking model 1624-4, which was a shallow-bowl, nylon-string electro-acoustic.

Back (*far right*) *A rear view of the shallow-bowled fiberglas back. Note the input jack positioned on the lower left bout.*

show it to folksinger Josh White, who was performing in town that night. Kaman intercepted White in a hotel lobby and the guitarist fell in love with the new guitar. White agreed to have a signature model made – and brought his entire family to Connecticut to receive the first guitar.

Ovation guitar production began in 1966 with the deep-bowl Standard Balladeer model made in North Hartford, Connecticut. A year later the factory was relocated to New Hartford, Connecticut, and the line expanded to include the Deluxe Balladeer, Classic, and Josh White models.

In 1968 Ovation introduced its first 12-string. Early models had smooth bodies that, recalling Byrd's experience, caused problems, and the design was changed to a rough-textured finish. Josh White died in 1970 and his signature guitar was retired, though it reappeared as the Folklore model in 1972. Also in that year the original Deluxe Balladeer was renamed the Legend, and the 12-string became the Pacemaker.

Despite the enthusiastic reception by a few professionals, Ovation's real breakthrough came in 1968 when Kaman let Glen Campbell try the first Balladeer guitar. Campbell liked it and Kaman ended up building one with a shallower bowl that became the Glen Campbell Artist Balladeer, which he played on his weekly network

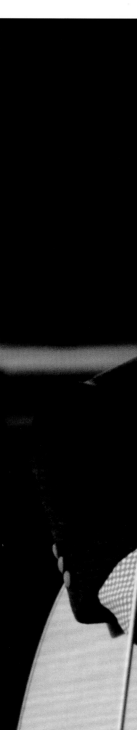

Glen Campbell c1970
(***opposite page***) *Country picker and TV star Campbell was one of Ovation's most important endorsers of the 1970s.*

TV show *Goodtime Hour* that began in January, 1969. Campbell felt constrained by having to stand in front of a microphone while playing, and wanted to move around. He asked Ovation to solve that problem and the result was the first Ovation piezoelectric pickup, introduced in 1970, an option on Ovations thereafter.

Campbell's shallow-bowl was put on the Country Artist nylon-string model that went into production in 1971. Other models followed, including the abalone-inlaid deep-bowl Custom Legend in 1974, which also came in a limited-edition of 1,776 as the Patriot Bicentennial model in 1976. Additional guitarists who switched to Ovations early on were Jim Croce and Jerry Reed.

In an effort to make its own less expensive 'copies' during a period when most American guitar designs were being copied in Asia, in 1973 Ovation developed the Applause line. Applauses featured innovations such as new bowl materials, a laminated top, an aluminum neck backed with urethane foam plastic to make if feel like wood, and an aluminum fingerboard.

Applause was intended to be the brand name sold only through Kaman's distribution arms and was rolled out in 1975. In order to provide Ovation's own sales reps with something comparable, the headstock was redesigned and a shortlived model was called the Ovation Medallion. In 1976 the Applause was redesigned to look like the Medallions, and Medallions were renamed to become the Matrix line. Applause production shifted to Korea around 1983.

In 1974, Charles' son C. William Kaman II, who'd been working summers and part time for his father, joined Ovation full time, preparing to eventually assume control.

Another research effort of the early 1970s yielded the first really high-end Ovation guitar, the revolutionary deep-bowl acoustic-electric Adamas, which was introduced in 1976 and entered production the following year. The Adamas was available as both an acoustic and acoustic-electric guitar. They featured thin carbon-graphite/birch laminate tops with 22 small soundholes dressed with colored-wood epaulets and a walnut neck and fingerboard with patented 'Kaman Bar' (u-shaped aluminum) reinforcement. Each guitar has a suffix number that indicates its natural resonant frequency. Later epaulets would become simulated wood mylar. The first Adamas

guitars were non-cutaway, and the first 600 had labels signed by Charles H. Kaman; after this – until 1998 – they were signed by his son Bill. A 12-string model debuted in 1978.

One of the early artists to play the Adamas was Larry Coryell, who'd switched from a LoPrinzi guitar to an Ovation Custom Legend after hearing John Abercrombie playing one with Billy Cobham. When the Adamas appeared, Coryell snagged both six-string and 12-string versions. The Adamas guitars were successful, and were joined by somewhat less fancy Adamas II acoustic-electric guitars in 1981.

Ovation also continued to work on the electronics for its pickup systems. In 1979 it introduced its FET-3 Preamp system with a three-band EQ. Around this time cutaways began to appear on selected models, including the Adamas. By 1982 cutaways were showing up on other Ovation models, including the Legend, Custom Legend, Classic, Country Artist, and Adamas II.

The Adamas sound was not to everyone's taste and some players found it cold. In 1982 Ovation introduced the Elite guitar, an attempt to adapt Adamas technology to a warmer sound. Elites had solid spruce tops but otherwise looked like the multi-soundhole Adamas.

When guitar sales nosedived universally in the early 1980s, and Ovation suffered a number of setbacks, Bill Kaman came up with the successful Collectors Series in 1982 to give the company a boost. This has since become the place in the line for Ovation to experiment. The following year saw Bill Kaman promoting a new cutaway model with Nancy Wilson of Heart. It was a good 3" shallower than a typical Ovation and marked the debut of the super-shallow bowl guitar. By 1984 the new super-shallow bowl – always with a cutaway – had supplanted the earlier shallow-bowls, which were discontinued.

In 1983 the Ultra series was developed, offering deep-bowl acoustic or acoustic-electric guitars very similar to the highly synthetic Applause/Matrix guitars, with laminated tops and the aluminum-and-urethane necks, but with real wood fingerboards. These were joined by the Ultra Deluxe models in 1984, with multi-hole solid wood tops like the Elite. In 1985 the Ultra acquired a regular wooden neck and cutaways began to appear on the Ultra Deluxe. Ultra Deluxes with super-shallow bowls and 12-string versions appeared in 1989.

Ovation introduced the Celebrity range in 1984, made in Korea like the Applause and including acoustic and acoustic-electric deep-bowl steel-strings and classicals with laminated spruce tops and varying degrees of decoration. Despite the slow period for guitar sales, from 1982 to 1985 Bill Kaman supervised construction of a new factory in North Carolina. Upon completion of the new plant, Charles Kaman retired and Bill became Kaman Music Corporation's new president.

One of the first guitars to debut under the new leadership was the Thunderbolt, targeted at the rock market which was increasingly drawn to acoustic-electrics at the time. It's probably stretching things to consider any Ovation guitars as being particularly 'traditional,' but the Thunderbolts were among the more progressive-looking of the Kaman designs.

From 1987 to 1994 Ovation again expanded its international repertoire with the deluxe Pinnacle series, built primarily in Japan (at a time when most manufacturers could not afford Japanese prices). The old shallow-bowl bodies were revived in 1993, originally developed for Glen Campbell way back in '68, although they were now called mid-depth. The following year saw the Viper series of steel and nylon-stringed guitars, including a 12-string, shaped like a super-shallow-bowl cutaway but with a

1987 Ovation Collectors' Series Guitar
"This is the finest Collectors' Series model we have made."
C. William Kaman, II

Collectors of unique guitars will find the 1987 Ovation Collectors' most desirable. It is beautiful as well as functional. The deep cutaway bowl brings out the rich acoustic sound of the luxury stained sitka spruce top. The bound walnut headstock and rare woods surrounding the soundholes are unique to this guitar, as is the combination of abalone purfling around the fingerboard and soundboard. Only 100 of the 1987 Collectors' Series will be produced. Become one of the select few to experience the sensation of owning one of the world's finest instruments. See the 1987 Collectors' Series guitar at your Ovation dealer or write to us for more information.

Ovation Thunderbolt 1989
(*near left*) *A super-shallow-bowl acoustic-electric model that was clearly aimed at the rockers.*

Back (*far left*) *This rear view reveals the Thunderbolt's back as far flatter than the kind of thing found on other Ovation roundbacks.*

Ovation ad 1987 (*above*)
C. William Kaman II, heir to the fiberglas throne, displays the year's Collectors' Series.

Julian Cope (*main photo*) *The eclectic, eccentric British musician Cope – former mainman of Teardrop Explodes – does his thing with a green Ovation Adamas 12-string.*

245

solid mahogany body with routed sound chambers, a fiberglass back covering, and Adamas-style soundholes.

The 1995 Collectors Edition debuted another Ovation innovation, the OptiMax Preamp system, which combines a conventional under-saddle piezo pickup with a small microphone sticking out of the front of the bridge under the strings. Unlike other combinations, making the small Telex microphone part of the bridge helped the new design avoid capturing too much 'boom' inside the body. Output was stereo or mono, and both pickup and mike could be blended for the player's ideal sound. In tribute to several decades of support, in 1998 Ovation introduced its first real signature guitar since the Josh White, a special black-finished Custom Legend named for Al DiMeola.

Many players have used Ovations through the years, including Kenny Loggins, Paul Simon, Eddie Van Halen, Robert Fripp, Seal, Brian May, Richie Sambora, Greg Lake, Neil Diamond, Mick Jagger, Joan Armatrading, Steve Morse, and Paul McCartney.

Kaman was bought by Fender in 2007, and later, in 2014, Fender closed the New Hartford plant. In 2015, Drum Workshop bought the Ovation brand.

No one could have predicted the success of Ovation's odd fiberglas roundbacked guitars when Charles Kaman dreamed up the idea. But the instruments came to stay,

and they have been among the most respected and influential acoustic and acoustic-electric guitars in the world.

PARAMOUNT
(AND ORPHEUM)

Paramount and Orpheum guitars arrived on the heels of the better-known banjos bearing the same brand names that had their heyday in the 1910s and '20s. The first guitars bearing the Paramount brand appear to have been introduced during 1934 by the William L. Lange company of New York, and it seems he sold some Orpheums after that time, too, but the history is sketchy at best.

By the late 1930s the Paramount range – built in part by Martin, along with other makers – is known to have included at least six archtops, headed by the elaborate and unusual $300 Free Tone Artist Supreme. Other guitars in the Orpheum line included the Artist Leader model, as well as Models B, C, D and E.

Lange sold to Maurice Lipsky in 1944. The majority of Orpheum guitars date from that period into the early 1960s, and comprise instruments built by Kay and others, including some later imports. Neither brand is of major interest to collectors.

Ovation Collectors Edition 1990 (right) *Some beautiful figured maple was used for this limited-edition model, and there is a "1990" inlay at the 12th fret.*

Ovation Model 1621 2003 (far right) *A contemporary example of the company's distinctive fiberglas bowlback (rear view, above).*

Ovation ads (above) *Promos featuring Al Di Meola (2008, above left) and Lacuna Coil (2007, above right).*

PARK

Shelley Park started building guitars in the Selmer style in 1991 under the tutelage of Michael Dunn. Like many Canadian builders, she also worked for Jean Larrivée for a couple of years. Park is a fine guitarist who played in the Hot Club-style band Pearl Django for a number of years – a performance career which has given her a special insight into what Gypsy jazz musicians want from a guitar. Today, she offers the Encore, a 14-fret oval hole model; Montmartre, an oval-hole 13.5-fret; Elan, a 12-fret D-soundhole; and Avance, a hybrid wedding a 14-fret neck to a D-soundhole body.

PEAVEY

Despite Peavey's giant musical equipment portfolio, the company's acoustic presence has thus far been modest, and halting in its progress. Its debut instrument, in 1991, was the US-made, mid-price, Tele-influenced Ecoustic thinline electro, joined a couple of years later by the vaguely wacky ATS version that had a patented vibrato unit incorporated into its folk-style bridge. Steve Morse was an Ecoustic user, and both instruments remained in the catalog until 2002.

The first mainstream acoustics, made for Peavey by Landola, were launched in '94, but the combination did not work out to the satisfaction of both parties, and it turned out to be a short-lived project. A handful of Korean dreadnoughts appeared in 1997 along with pricier, solid-timbered, Japanese-made electros – the latter influenced by previous Landola body styles – but these proved still-born and few, if any, were seen beyond prototypes at a US trade show during that year.

Peavey's efforts finally began to bear fruit in 1999 when the company turned its attentions to the budget market with the Delta Series, initially a concise, Korean-sourced line-up of dreadnoughts named after the Mississippi birthplaces of famous artists – Tupelo (Elvis Presley), Indianola (B.B. King), and so on. Further models and electro variants were subsequently added. By 2017, Peavey offered its carbon fiber Composite series, the small-body Composer models with offset soundhole, and the relatively conventional DW series.

PRAIRIE STATE

Prairie State guitars were built in Chicago by Carl and August Larson and their Maurer & Co (later Euphonon), and they carry many of the brothers' most famous design features. Some later Euphonon-era Prairie States were played by WLS radio stars

Paramount Style M c1934
(**right**) *This round-hole archtop with unusual neck-tilt adjustment was built for the William L. Lange company by big Chicago maker Regal, and was among the first guitars to be sold with Lange's Paramount brand.*

Joe Strummer 1998 *The former Clash singer and guitarist struts it with a thoroughly un-punk archtop by Orpheum (see Paramount).*

PRAIRIE STATE

such as Bob Atcher, Prairie Sweethearts, Hoosier Sod Busters, and Mac and Bob. Prairie State guitars debuted around 1927 or so and were essentially the more upscale rosewood, 12-fret Maurer models featuring August Larson's latest ideas, including a central adjustable hollow metal bar between the neck heel and tail block to relieve top stress.

A second solid steel bar ran from inside the body and encircled the lower neck heel, helping to keep the neck tight to the body. Sizes were concert to auditorium. Some of these Prairie States were provided to William C. Stahl for his Milwaukee-based retail business. Around 1935 or '36, the Larsons introduced their 14-fret Euphonon line and began to build jumbo 16" and 17" bodies, with a new square-shouldered shape and flat headstock. Euphonons with the metal rod systems continued to provide the Prairie State line – some with giant 19" or even 21" bodies. Prairie States also included the Larsons' only f-hole guitars – which were more or less the same as the rod-equipped flat-tops, except for the soundholes and flamed maple bodies. By the late 1930s a few of these appeared with a single cutaway.

The brand ceased in the early 1940s, but it was revived in 2013 with the launch of a new Larson Bros company at a workshop near Cognac in France.

RAINSONG

The first Rainsong all-graphite acoustics were introduced in 1995 after a number of years' research and development involving a team of hi-tech and composite-materials specialists headed by guitarist and former aeronautical engineer Dr John Decker and including classical master-luthier Lorenzo Pimentel. To avoid pure graphite's tendency to produce tinny top-end sounds, small amounts of the wood-like fiber Kevlar were added to the build formula.

The first models from the Hawaii-based company, initially produced on a custom-order basis, were a dreadnought and nylon-strung classic, but the line-up rapidly expanded to other designs, including a hybrid piezo/humbucker model; an f-holed jazz guitar; a cutaway, thinline Stagesong electro with no soundhole; and an electro-

Larson Custom 1939 (*near right*) *This extraordinary cutaway flat-top was built for country performer Jay Rich by August Larson, who was also responsible for Prairie State-brand guitars. It has an enormous 19"-wide body, and elaborate abalone inlays.*

Back (*center*) *Note the beautiful walnut-stained flamed maple back on this guitar.*

Prairie State c1939 (*near left*) *This large-bodied flat-top is similar in dimensions to some of the Larsons' Euphonon models. But note the steel supporting rod inside its body, found on most known examples of Prairie States, though not on Euphonons.*

Jessie Fuller 1960 *The bluesman in repose at the south-London home of writer-photographer Val Wilmer. That battered guitar looks like one of the Larson brothers' big-bodied creations, possibly a Prairie State model.*

WAVENEY

Rainsong catalog 2003 *Pages promoting this newer maker's graphite-fiber-and-wood Flamenco and Dreadnought models.*

acoustic bass. Early Rainsongs tended to use uni-directional graphite tops that had a rather rough-cast appearance, but 1998 saw a second generation of instruments, led by the WS1000 grand auditorium cutaway electro. This employed a more attractive cross-weave and heralded 'Projection Tuned Layering', or PTL, essentially a means of achieving uniform stiffness across the top, obviating the need for strutting and improving sound quality. Rainsong's president Ashvin Coomar claimed that these guitars with PTL were dramatically louder and had a more balanced sound.

With the line rationalized to DR dreadnoughts, JM jumbos, WS grand auditoriums, and OM orchestral models, the company relocated to Woodinville, Washington, in 2001, and towards the end of 2002 announced the addition of the Projection Series. Made in Korea and roughly half the price of the All-Graphites, these carry PTL graphite tops (supplied from Woodinville) but the back, sides and necks are traditional mahogany.

Despite Rainsong's claims for its instruments — "clear, rich and resonant, similar to a piano" — plus the All-Graphites' imperviousness to climate changes, most players won't be persuaded to venture far from familiar and traditional wood acoustics; nevertheless, it's clear that the brand is gaining ground. By 2017, Rainsong offered its guitars in seven series and in five different shapes, ranging from dreadnought to parlor. The company no longer operates an endorser policy, but artists known to have toted Rainsongs at one time or another include ex-Velvet Undergrounder John Cale, The Doors' Robby Krieger, David Hidalgo of Los Lobos, and Jon Anderson of Yes.

RAMÍREZ

No name has greater importance in the history of the classical guitar than that of Ramírez. The Ramírez guitar established the standard form of the concert instrument, to the satisfaction of players and composers alike.

The story begins with the brothers José and Manuel Ramírez. José was an apprentice with the Madrid guitar-maker Francisco González. Once qualified, he took

Prairie State Style 235 c1932 (*near right*) *This concert-sized guitar was offered as the middle version of three decorative options.*

Prairie State 'F-hole Guitar' c1930 (*second right*) *This model was one of the few f-hole guitars made by the Larson brothers. It was built with the Larsons' internal strengthening rod, but uses ladder-shaped top bracing rather than the X-bracing of most Larson flat-tops.*

Ramirez label 1897 (*above*) *The label of the guitar (right) gives an address of "Concepción Jerónima No. 2" in Madrid, Spain. After nearly a century there, the company has only recently moved to a new showroom.*

J. Ramírez I c1897 (*above*) *The catalog refers to this model as "small size, suitable for senoritas." Made with cypress back and sides and a spruce top, it was probably not an expensive guitar in its day, though the elaborate rosette might have raised its price.*

on his younger brother Manuel as his apprentice, and the two began building guitars in their own name. It was not to last. In 1891, after planning a move to Paris, Manuel instead set up in competition elsewhere in Madrid. The result was a bitter feud.

José Ramírez had followed González in creating broad, shallow guitars with arched tops and a loud, hard sound for nightclub use. Manuel soon took a new direction, probably after repairing a couple of historic Torres instruments. These guitars had lighter and more flexible soundboards and a more delicate strutting pattern. His craftsmen included such masters as Domingo Esteso and Santos Hernández.

Manuel Ramírez seems to have quickly won over the flamenco community, but he owes his immortality to a different player. In 1916, an eccentric-looking youth came into the shop and asked to borrow a guitar for a concert. Having heard him play, Ramírez gave him the instrument. The man was Andrés Segovia.

Segovia not only used the guitar for many years, he encouraged other makers, notably Hermann Hauser, to copy it, spreading Ramírez's reputation around the world. But Manuel Ramírez died the same year, and his firm did not long survive him. The instruments are today highly prized, and the guitar given to Segovia is now in the Metropolitan Museum Of Art in New York.

José Ramírez, meanwhile, clung to his old-fashioned model. He never produced such important instruments as Manuel, but he built a stronger business, employing an impressive string of apprentices, including Enrique García, Julián Gómez Ramírez, Francisco Simplicio, and his own son, José Ramírez II. He also began to supply cheaper, student instruments, not built in his own workshop.

José Ramírez II joined his father as an apprentice in the early years of the 20th century, but in 1904 went off to tour South America with a folk group. He stayed for 20 years, only returning to take charge two years after his fathers death. He made his mark as a luthier by quality of craftsmanship. His guitars moved away from the arched-top formula developed by his father and closer to the classical pattern developed by his uncle Manuel. José Ramírez II also created the plain, elegant headstock synonymous with Ramírez guitars.

When José Ramírez III, known as Pepé, came into the business, he experimented endlessly, to the dismay of his father. When he took over, in 1957, he was able to carry his experiments through. The most important of these, for the whole industry, was the use of western red cedar, a North American conifer, for the guitar's soundboard. Ramírez found that it could be made to perform as well as spruce, the

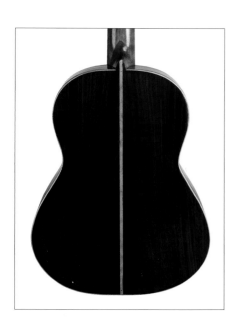

M. Ramírez 1912 (*near right*)
This instrument is similar in appearance to the M. Ramírez guitar that was given to a young Andrés Segovia in the same year.

Back (*above*) *The guitar's original Brazilian rosewood back was at some time replaced with a different wood, and the guitar has received extensive repairs to its bridge and braces.*

Label (*above right*) *This label from 1912 makes reference to Ramírez's recent promotion to the post of luthier to the National Conservatoire in Madrid. It also gives the address of the Ramírez workshops as "Arlabán No. 10" in Madrid.*

Julián Gómez Ramírez 1936 (*far right*) *Another Ramírez – no relation to the famous family – built this simple and solidly-made concert guitar in the tradition of Manuel Ramírez and Santos Hernández.*

wood preferred by instrument makers for centuries. He also made design changes intended to improve the instrument's performance in the concert hall. In 1960, he produced a guitar that Andrés Segovia liked, beginning an important association for the firm.

Ramírez III's real forte was balancing quantity and quality. In the Spanish guitar-making tradition, the master craftsman lays down the plan and determines the standards for instruments built by journeymen: they are, however, considered the master's instruments. Ramírez III took this system to its limits, specifying procedures so tightly that he could run a large workshop while maintaining control.

Without resorting to mass production, Ramírez III produced 20,000 hand-built instruments in his lifetime, at least 20 times as many as most makers manage. They bear the initials of the masters who supervised their construction, including Paulino Bernabé and Manuel Contreras.

The system enabled Ramírez to dominate the professional market, attracting

Agustin Barrios *The Paraguayan virtuoso and composer sent this postcard to Ramírez II.*

Ramírez II 1956 (*near left*) *Some experts consider guitars of this era from the workshop of José Ramírez II to be the finest of all guitars produced by Ramírez during its long history. This attractive nylon-string concert guitar was made only a year before Ramírez II's death.*

Back (*center*) *This rear view shows the rich color and subtle but distinctive graining of the Ramírez II's Brazilian rosewood back.*

Ramírez III 1965 (*far left*) *This flamenco guitar comes from the workshop of José Ramírez III in Madrid, and was made by employee Antonio Martinez, whose initials are stamped on the foot of the neck. It has the typical cypress back and sides of the flamenco instrument.*

players including Segovia, Christopher Parkening, Liona Boyd, Oscar Ghiglia, José Tomas, Alexandre Lagoya, and Narciso Yepes. George Harrison even strummed a Ramírez in the film of *A Hard Day's Night*.

When José Ramírez III died, in 1995, his son José Ramírez IV and daughter Amalia were running the family business. In the late 1980s, Ramírez IV was worried about the the rich, slightly mellow character of his father's instrument, and created a new, brighter, lighter guitar. The 1a or primera that had always been Ramírez's top hand-built model now came in two versions, Tradicionel and the new Especial.

Ramírez IV also invigorated the company's factory line. Since the 1990s, the company has offered two ranges, the E (for Estudio) and the R, built by different Spanish companies to Ramírez's designs.

In 1993, the company scaled down its workshop. After the death of José Ramírez IV in 2000, Amalia Ramírez carried on the family business, later adding her niece Cristina and nephew José Enrique to the team, who build versions of the 1a, as well as built-to-order guitars.

The Ramírez shop now also sells electro-acoustic guitars, flamenco instruments, and even some solidbody electrics.

REGAL

Regal – traditionally the 'catch-all' manufacturer to which people attributed any unknown older guitar – is probably the least documented and most under-appreciated major American maker. This is undoubtedly due to the many relatively humble birch guitars it produced for both itself and others. However, Regal also turned out many better flat-tops and archtops that compare very favorably with those of its chief competitors, Harmony and Kay. Regal was founded around 1896 in Indianapolis, Indiana, by a local businessman named Emil Wulschner. Almost no information about its early guitars and mandolins is available, but the few examples that turn up are workmanlike for the time, and better models employ genuine rosewood. Wulschner died in 1900, the company passed into other hands, and instrument manufacturing had ended by 1904. The entire Regal operation, including the name and remaining stock, was purchased by Lyon & Healy and moved up to Chicago in 1904; it's not known if any Regal-brand instruments were produced for the next few years.

The classic Regal Musical Instrument Company re-emerged around 1908 and is reported to have provided instruments carrying other brand names – including possibly Washburn – through the 1920s. Whether this included any guitars cannot be

George Harrison 1964 (*above*)
The Beatle plays his Ramírez classical guitar on the song 'And I Love Her' from the movie A Hard Day's Night. At one point in the movie the camera zooms in so close that the viewer can almost read the label through the guitar's soundhole.

Regal 16M Artist 1935 (*left*)
In the 1930s Regal of Chicago made Dobro-designed resonator guitars under license from Dobro, using bodies, resonators, and coverplates manufactured in Los Angeles by Dobro. Regal made the necks, completed the assembly, and plated the guitars.

Back (*above*) *Regal's elegant engraving here is more subtle than that on many Dobro and National guitars.*

verified. In 1914 Regal made its mark with an asymmetrical scrolled mandolin that was marketed by others carrying the Regal name, and by the late 1920s was known for its tenor guitars and banjos.

In early 1929 Regal unveiled its new lines of Custom Built mandolins and guitars, the latter with spruce tops and mahogany or rosewood bodies, with varying amounts of trim, though none was luxurious. Throughout most of its run, Regal employed solid timbers, not laminates. Regal's Custom Builts were an official line until the war, but the name remained as a designation of better models well into the 1950s.

Regal guitars from the early 1930s were all flat-tops, in sizes ranging from standard to grand concert. Some models featured slotted heads with a tell-tale French curve on the top, and some had pearlette fingerboards. Others had a distinctive Regal shape, with narrow upper shoulders and a much wider lower bout, possibly inherited from Washburn. As a sign of the incestuous state of the Chicago guitar-making scene, a few early '30s Regals were actually made by rival Stromberg-Voisinet (in other words Kay).

In 1930 Regal purchased from owner Tonk the equipment and brand names of Le Domino and J.R. Stewart when J.R. Stewart (also a maker of Washburns) went

bankrupt. From 1931 onwards, these brands were Regal-made. In 1932 Regal introduced its first carved-top archtop (roundhole) with 14 frets clear of the body, produced through the decade. The same year, Regal struck a licensing deal to produce Dobro and Regal-brand resonator guitars. It also made many Slingerland flat-tops at this time, and began to employ stencil and decorated 'decalomania' designs. In 1934 Regal began to screw pickguards onto its Custom Builts.

In 1935 Regal increased its relationship with Tonk Bros, taking on production of virtually the entire Tonk line. This included guitars with flat headstocks, various auditorium and jumbo sizes, and modern f-hole archtops. In addition, Tonk, which had purchased Lyon & Healy's distribution business in 1928, re-introduced the Washburn name with a range of downscale flat-tops and archtops with stenciled logos, all Regal-made, though quality improved as the decade progressed (some Tonk Washburns were made by Gibson from 1938-40).

While most Depression-era Regals were fairly conventional, there were also some unique instruments. In 1934 Regal introduced the Contra Bass or Harp Guitar, a doubleneck, Regal-shaped guitar with a regular six-string neck plus a fretless six-string bass neck. In 1937 Regal debuted the Bassoguitar, a gigantic doghouse bass-

Regal Esquire 1185 c1939
(*near right*) This Chicago-made archtop 'Orchestra Guitar' was second from the top of a four-model Regal line.

Regal Prince 1170 c1939
(*center*) The Prince, one rung below the Esquire in Regal's archtop line, has a carved spruce top with mahogany back and sides.

Regal Harp Guitar c1930
(*right*) This 19"-wide harp guitar does not appear in Regal catalogs of the time, and may have been a one-off custom order.

size guitar, and also began producing 12-strings. Regal was also producing upscale Bacon & Day flat-tops and archtops, including the very deluxe Sultana, and making fancy archtops for Montgomery Ward (including some Recording Kings) and Continental. It's also possible that Regal had begun sourcing some instruments – or at least parts – from Kay.

By 1939 Regal was offering an enormous array of guitars, ranging from beginner hardwood guitars with faux graining to dreadnoughts, wood and metal-body Dobros, and some luxurious 18" to 18½" carved archtops such as the Prince, Esquire, and Crown ($250).

Regal doesn't seem to have recovered after World War II. It appears to have introduced its first cutaway guitars in the late 1940s, typically with a fairly radical angle. Probably also from this time were some flat-tops with Gretsch-like, harp-shaped pin bridges, including an integrated unit with adjustable bridge, and a cutaway with the harp tail separated from the adjustable bridge. While the company still offered a few better-grade spruce and mahogany guitars, most were lower-end models smacking of Kay, with hardwood and laminate construction, stenciled cowboy scenes, and white-line trim. Among the more interesting guitars was the Hawaiian

Type Guitar, a squareneck with no waist, looking something like a potato, and the Radio-tone Amplifying Guitar, with the Regal shape, a small metal resonator device, and screened 'Cyclops' soundhole sitting between stenciled radio towers.

In 1954 Regal threw in the towel and sold everything to Harmony. From 1959-62 Harmony produced some basic Regal folk and dreadnought flat-tops and an archtop exclusively for Fender. Harmony revived the brand in 1972 on some grand concerts and dreadnoughts, selling some through US wholesaler Targ & Dinner, the high point being some red, white, and blue models branded Bicentennial for 1976.

After Harmony folded in 1976, the Regal brand disappeared until it was revived again in 1987, now applied to a line of resonator guitars, reviving the historical association with Dobros and carrying on the Regal tradition of serving buyers of more moderately priced instruments.

RIBBECKE

Northern California luthier Tom Ribbecke began building guitars in 1972. Already well established for his innovative steel-string flat-tops, archtops, and electrics, he was forced to temporarily cease operation in 1983 due to severe allergies to lacquer and

Regal Oak Leaf Hawaiian c1938 (left) *A small-bodied Hawaiian guitar.*

Regal Concert-Size c1951 (right) *An all-mahogany bodied flat-top 'Spanish' guitar. Note the unusual bridge design.*

Regal ad 1960 (above) *Harmony-era promotion for Regal flat-top guitars.*

Regal Model 312C 1952 (right) *This model was a cutaway archtop with laminated maple top.*

other material used in his shop. Ribbecke returned to building guitars in the 1990s, quickly establishing himself as one of the world's premier archtop makers. In 2003, Ribbecke developed the Halfling design, which aims to blend a steel-string or classical type body with an archtop. By 2017, Ribbecke was no longer accepting regular commissions, instead accepting orders only for his Masterpiece series of unique instruments that, he said, would be "individual and uncomporised."

RICKENBACKER

While the Rickenbacker company's reputation mainly stems from its pioneering role as a developer of the electric guitar, this California maker has also produced some memorable flat-top and archtop acoustics – or 'non-electrics,' as the archtops were billed in the catalogs. In 1958, newly owned by Francis C. Hall and supervised by German expatriate designer Roger Rossmeisl, Rickenbacker proposed a series of startling, art deco-ish electric and acoustic guitars, including flat-top Model 385 and

Rick Nelson c1957 *A guitar-toting star on TV's Ozzie & Harriet show, Nelson here promotes a rare Rickenbacker archtop acoustic.*

ACCORDION *and* GUITAR
WORLD

prototype-only archtops 380 and 390, which had a distinctive 'German carve' and scimitar-shaped soundholes. Their colors were the typical Rickenbacker Hi Lustre Blonde (natural maple finish), Autumnglo (two-tone brown sunburst), and Fireglo (the company's well-known reddish sunburst finish). In the late 1990s, Rickenbacker reintroduced a line of acoustic guitars that lasted to 2006 and included the flat-top jumbo models Shasta and Comstock, the dreadnoughts Shiloh and Laramie – also available as 12-strings – and the archtop model Jazz-Bo, which externally owed a lot to the 1958 model 390. All had a distinctive light and dark wood-laminate headstock.

ROGER

German jazz guitarist Wenzel Rossmeisl, born in 1902, began building archtop guitars in the mid 1930s, and named them after his son, Roger – who would also become a famous designer for Rickenbacker and Fender. Wenzel may also have been the first to produce electric guitars in Germany.

After the war, Rossmeisl restarted his shop, and during the 1950s and into the '60s, Roger archtop guitars were highly esteemed. The most distinct feature of these instruments is their tops, laminated with light-dark-light wood, that gives a shaded

Regal-made Le Domino 4010 c1932 (*left*) *Regal acquired J.R. Stewart's Le Domino brand name in 1930, and produced this appropriately decorated small-bodied flat-top two years later.*

Regal R-75 2003 (*center*) *A contemporary Korean-built Dobro-style resonator guitar.*

Rickenbacker Model 385 c1960 (*right*) *Natural-finished flat-top from a company far better known for its electric guitars.*

Roger catalog 1960 (*right*) A
selection of the German archtop guitars
in a British brochure.

edge to the so-called 'German carve' (achieved
when a top is carved with a distinct bevel around
the edge), and a skill his son would take with him
to Rickenbacker. Wenzel died in 1975, and Roger
passed away just four years later.

ROMANILLOS

The classical guitars of José Romanillos, though built in England, bring together
elements of both the Torres and Hauser traditions. Romanillos was born in Madrid in
1932, and moved to England in 1956. In 1969, he met Julian Bream, who was
sufficiently impressed with these early guitars to give Romanillos some cheap
workshop space and a commission for two new instruments. His breakthrough came
when Bream brought Romanillos his 1936 Hauser for repair, which involved removal
of the back. It was the first time he had worked on a top-class instrument.

From then, Romanillos's guitars were based on the light, precise Hauser and Torres
instruments, on which he became an authority. In 1991 the firm officially became
Romanillos & Son, recognising the contribution of Liam Romanillos. Today, Liam builds

**Rickenbacker Model 390
1957 (*right*)** This prototype for a
proposed Rickenbacker archtop was
designed by Roger Rossmeisl, and
carries his distinctive 'German carve'
around the edge of its top.

Romanillos 1996 *An elegant and
well-crafted classical guitar, one of
José and Liam Romanillos's smaller,
Torres-inspired instruments. The
spruce-topped guitar is complemented
by a back and sides of Indian
rosewood (inset photos).*

Julian Bream (*below*) *Virtuoso
Bream is pictured holding a Romanillos
classical guitar on the cover of this
album recorded at Wardour Chapel in
Wiltshire, England.*

guitars in England, while José divides his time between Britain and Spain, where the pair teach an annual course in guitar-making. José Romanillos has many disciples among young makers, and has attracted many players since Bream, including the Assad brothers, Eleftheria Kotzia, Marco de Santi, Tadeu do Amaral, and Antigoni Goni.

RUCK

Robert Ruck is amongst the most acclaimed of American guitar-makers, with a waiting list of at least eight years. Ruck started as a classical guitar student, and picked up the basics of guitar-making by watching a maker in his native Florida build an instrument for him. By the time he was 20, in 1965, he had become a full-time guitar-maker. His early instruments stuck close to the Spanish pattern, and he sold them cheaply, considering them part of the learning process.

During the 1990s, he preferred to work with Indian rather than the Brazilian rosewood that, as an endangered species, was in short supply. Throughout his career, Ruck has continued to study classical and flamenco guitar, and has developed an unusually intuitive approach to guitar-making, trying to 'visualise' the eventual sound at every step in the building process. This intensity of craftsmanship has secured his place on a short list alongside the most accomplished contemporary builders. His first guitars were championed by Juan Mercadal, the brilliant Cuban guitarist, whose student Manuel Barrueco built his early career with a favorite Ruck.

Recently, Ruck has made a radical departure from traditional design, cutting two small holes in the body, either side of the heel of the neck, which he calls 'acoustic ports.' He believes they give the player more intimate contact with the sound, which benefits the performance. Ruck has relocated twice since his beginnings in Florida, and since 1990 has lived in Washington state to be closer to wood supplies and other fellow luthiers. He builds up to 30 guitars a year. Unusually, he also makes related stringed instruments, including vihuelas, violas de gamba, and lutes.

SAMICK

Chances are that you have played a guitar made by the Samick Musical Instruments Co. even if you don't know it, since it makes more guitars than anyone else in the world, both under its own name and the brands of many other companies. And while the guitar is likely to have come at a budget price, it's very possible it will have had a solid top, a sweet tone, and some fancy pearl and abalone appointments associated

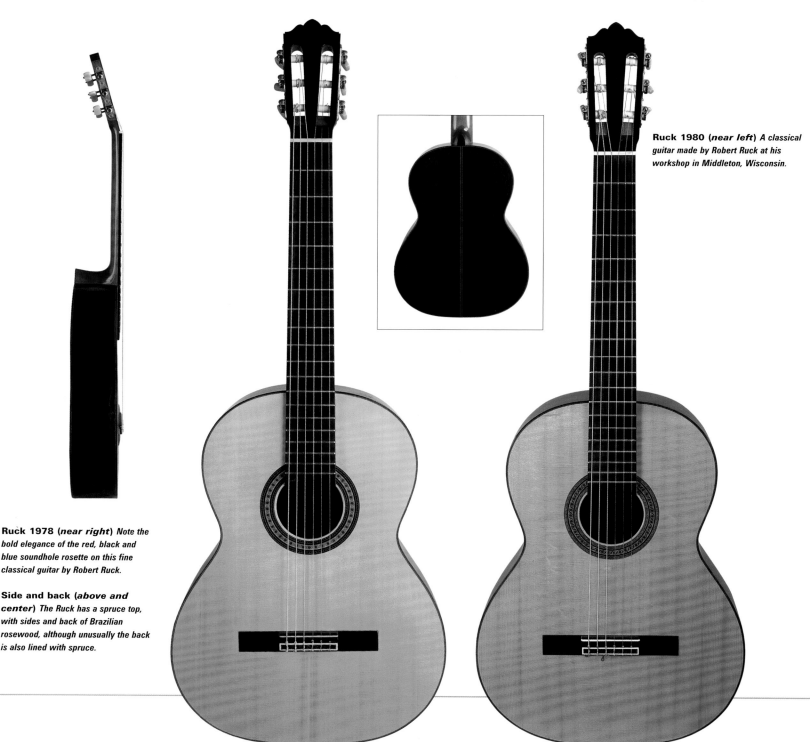

Ruck 1980 (*near left*) A classical guitar made by Robert Ruck at his workshop in Middleton, Wisconsin.

Ruck 1978 (*near right*) Note the bold elegance of the red, black and blue soundhole rosette on this fine classical guitar by Robert Ruck.

Side and back (*above and center*) The Ruck has a spruce top, with sides and back of Brazilian rosewood, although unusually the back is also lined with spruce.

with more expensive instruments. Samick has come a long way from its beginnings.

Samick was founded as a piano company in Inchon, Korea, in 1958, and expanded into guitar-making in 1965. Its big break came in 1969 when Tommy Moore and Jerry Fried of the International Music Co (IMC) of Fort Worth, Texas, joined with Samick to manufacture IMC's Hondo line of acoustic guitars. Initially pretty basic, low-end beginner guitars, the quality of Samick-made instruments steadily improved throughout the 1970s. Samick built a new, highly automated guitar factory in Korea in 1979, and quality and quantity continued to grow through the 1980s as more companies sourced their budget lines from the facility.

In 1991 Samick finally introduced its own line of guitars, carrying the Samick brand name. This included a full range of acoustic and acoustic-electric dreadnought, jumbo, folk, 12-string, and classical models in a variety of laminated timbers. Also sold at that time was a line of solid-top 'handcrafted' guitars made by Hiroshi Yairi. By 1992 the Yairi name had departed, but handcrafted guitars continued.

Samick began to produce its 'value' line at a new guitar factory in Indonesia during 1993, still making its better guitars in Korea. The line expanded into thin-bodied acoustic-electrics, some of which had figured maple tops and abalone trim. The

following year Samick introduced guitars with pearl tree-of-life inlays, and by 1995 was featuring all-solid woods, fancy paint jobs, and unusual decoration. The exotic-shaped Twango – endorsed by Blues Saraceno – joined the line in 1996, and resonator guitars were added in 1998. Around 2001 Samick decided to give its guitars a new look and hired Nashville designer Greg Bennett to redo both its electric and acoustic lines, the results of which were unveiled in 2002. In addition to a redesigned headstock, acoustic guitars acquired features such as rounded fingerboard ends that follow the soundhole curve, and scalloped braces. Samick today owns the Bennett brand, as well as Silvertone.

SANTA CRUZ

Luthier Richard Hoover and repairmen Bruce Ross and William Davis started the Santa Cruz Guitar Company in 1976 to hand-build custom instruments for guitarists who weren't finding what they wanted from large companies like Martin, Gibson, and Guild. Santa Cruz wasn't the first to do this, but their attention to cosmetic detail, use of high-grade materials, and the rich tone of the guitars quickly earned the new company an excellent reputation among discerning musicians. Tony Rice, Eric

Samick Cheyenne OM-8CE 2002 (near right) *An elaborately-decorated flat-top designed for Samick by Greg Bennett.*

Samick ad 1992 (center) *An idealized sylvan setting for this promo for Samick's latest acoustics (and electrics) of the early 1990s.*

Santa Cruz D 1999 (far right) *Richard Hoover avoided Martin-style designs in the early years of Santa Cruz, but as with most steel-string makers the company has found 'classic' models – such as this big dreadnought – consistently popular.*

SANTA CRUZ

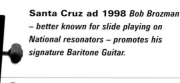

Santa Cruz ad 1998 *Bob Brozman – better known for slide playing on National resonators – promotes his signature Baritone Guitar.*

Clapton, Jerry Garcia, Janis Ian, Elvis Costello, Bob Brozman, and David Crosby are just a few of the artists who have played Santa Cruz guitars.

The first Santa Cruz model was a dreadnought with koa back and sides and a headstock with a distinctive shape that came to be known as the 'paddle-head.' The company's logo was a stylized SCGC cut from pearl and inlaid into the headstock. The D, as they dubbed it, was voiced to have a more balanced, less bass-heavy tone than the standard dreadnought of the time. The fretboard of the new guitar measured 1¹³⁄₁₆" at the nut, instead of 1¹¹⁄₁₆", which was the industry standard. The balanced tone and wider fretboard made it popular with the local fingerpicking community, who were looking for a less boomy sounding guitar than the rosewood dreadnoughts that were common at the time.

In 1978 Santa Cruz introduced its second model, which was based in part on the Gibson Nick Lucas as built between 1931 and 1933. The new guitar was dubbed the H in honor of Paul Hostetter, a local musician, luthier, and artist who designed the first version of the instrument. Hostetter's H had a small 00 body that was as deep as a

Santa Cruz Tony Rice Model 1998 (*near left*) *This guitar is based on the Martin D-28 with enlarged soundhole made famous by flatpicker Rice.*

Santa Cruz PJ 2003 (*center*) *Santa Cruz's version of the increasingly popular parlor-size guitar, with 12 frets to the body.*

Santa Cruz OM/E 2000 (*far left*) *For its E Series, Santa Cruz toned down the trim and finish details slightly to offer a more affordable but still high-quality guitar.*

dreadnought. It also had a long 25⅞" scale length, which meant that when the bridge was properly placed on the top's sweet spot, the neck had thirteen frets clear of the body. The H had the bright, clear tone of a smaller bodied guitar, but the extra body depth gave it the power of a much larger instrument.

The 13-fret H sold poorly and was redesigned with a shallower body depth and a 12-fret neck, extended to 14-frets a few years later. The first version of the H gained a reputation for a remarkable sound, and in 2002 Santa Cruz reissued a limited run of 13-fret H models built to the original specifications.

Also in 1978, Santa Cruz introduced the FTC, which had a flat top and a carved, arched back. Santa Cruz based the body shape of the FTC on Gibson's J-185, a smaller, plainer version of the venerable J-200. The concept of building a flat-top with an arched back was inspired by an old Epiphone Deluxe Cutaway Flat-Top that Bruce Ross owned. (Epiphone introduced a series of guitars with flat tops and arched, plywood 'tone backs' in 1949.) The first Santa Cruz FTC (the initials stood for Flat Top Carved back) had a cutaway, a feature that Hoover, Ross, and Davis felt was musically useful but visually overpowering. The asymmetrical headstock and art deco fretboard inlays they came up with to balance the cutaway recalled the art-deco designs of

archtop guitars built in the 1930s by Gibson, Epiphone, and D'Angelico.

Santa Cruz hoped its new guitar, which blended the clarity and presence of an archtop with the warmth and sustain of a flat-top, would appeal to fingerstyle jazz guitarists, but like the H, the FTC was sonically but not financially successful. The FTC may have been a disappointment in terms of sales, but the instrument became the company's most visible model when it was used on the cover of the first Santa Cruz catalog and in the early print ads. Santa Cruz later simplified the FTC by making it with a flat back. The F, as the new version was called, has remained in the company's catalog ever since.

In the late 1970s William Davis grew tired of working long hours for very little money, so he sold out his interest in the Santa Cruz Guitar Company to Richard Hoover and Bruce Ross. In 1979 guitarist Tony Rice, who played a jazzy brand of bluegrass known as spacegrass, stopped by the Santa Cruz workshop to order a guitar. He wanted a replica of his main instrument, a 1935 Martin D-28 that had formerly belonged to the legendary flatpicker Clarence White, and a guitar that was in rough shape when Rice got it, with many scuffs and cracks, including a bullet hole in the top. The soundhole had also been enlarged, probably in a clumsy attempt to deal with

Tom Paxton (*above*) *Folk great Paxton swaps his Martin for a Santa Cruz dreadnought.*

pick wear at the hole's edges, and the original Martin fretboard had been replaced with a bound one made by Gretsch. Because of the guitar's delicate condition, Rice was reluctant to take it on the road, so he asked Hoover and Ross if they would make him a replica of the instrument.

Rice played his Santa Cruz almost exclusively over the next few years at his many concerts and bluegrass festival appearances. After that, Hoover and Ross got so many requests for replicas of Rice's guitar that in 1981 they began to offer the Tony Rice Model as part of the standard line. The new version replicated the large soundhole and bound fretboard of Rice's original 1935 Martin. It also sparked a debate among luthiers and musicians about what effect the size of the soundhole has on tone, with the consensus emerging over time that the larger soundhole slightly increases the treble and midrange frequencies. The commercial and sonic success of the Tony Rice Model eventually led other builders such as Martin and Collings to offer their own large-soundhole models. Santa Cruz currently makes two versions: the standard Tony Rice has a Sitka spruce top and Indian rosewood back and sides; the Tony Rice Professional is closest to the guitar that Rice himself plays, and has a German spruce top and Brazilian rosewood back and sides.

Tuners

Pegheads

Other Options

Santa Cruz catalog 2003 *An impressive array of tuner, peghead, and finish options offered by the company.*

Joan Baez c2001 *Formerly a famous Martin user, Baez now performs with a Santa Cruz.*

Santa Cruz OM 2002 *The popular vintage-styled OM model from the upscale line, with spruce top and rosewood back and sides. Note subtle herringbone trim along both body edge and soundhole.*

Santa Cruz catalog 2003 *The striking cover shot emphasizes the elegant 'Scgc' logo inlaid at the 14th fret of many models.*

From the beginning, Hoover and Ross had resisted the urge to base their guitars on Martin's designs, but the constantly increasing sales of the Tony Rice Model made them rethink their stand. In 1984 they introduced the OM, which was a modern version of an early 1930s Martin OM-28. The smaller body made it an immediate hit with a wide range of players, including fingerpickers and female guitarists, while the clear, balanced tone found favor with recording engineers who were weary of trying to get boomy dreadnoughts to sound good on tape. Like the Tony Rice Model, the OM had the Santa Cruz logo inlaid in the fretboard.

In 1987 sales had increased so much that Hoover and Ross took on their first employees. The first two workers hired were Michael Hornick and Jeff Traugott. Both men later left the Santa Cruz Guitar Company to start building guitars themselves; Hornick as Shanti Guitars and Traugott under his own name. (Bill Hardin, an employee who was hired a few years later, also set out on his own and started Bear Creek Guitars in Hawaii.) Around the same time, Santa Cruz came out with a cedar-top, rosewood-back-and-sides variation on the F that it called the FS, which stood for Finger Style. The new guitar was designed for new fingerstyle players who followed

in the wake of Michael Hedges, Alex de Grassi, and Will Ackermann.

By 1989 the Santa Cruz Guitar Company was on a firm financial footing – its instruments were desired by musicians and frequently emulated by other builders. Now that their venture was successful, Hoover and Ross began to disagree about which direction to take the company. Each made the other a buy-out offer, and Ross accepted Hoover's. The Santa Cruz Guitar Company was now the sole property of Richard Hoover.

In 1992 Hoover redesigned some of the guitars. The D, F, and H had their nuts narrowed from 1¹³⁄₁₆″ to 1¹⁄₁₆″, and the 'paddle-head' headstock was switched on the D and H to a simpler, squared-off Martin-style headstock.

Santa Cruz continued to introduce new models throughout the 1990's, but rather than build good sounding but marginally commercial guitars like the FTC and the 13-fret H, it opted to capitalize on the success on the Tony Rice and the OM and build guitars that more closely replicated the classic Martins and Gibsons of the 1930s.

Over the next few years Santa Cruz brought out a 12-fret 000, a 12-fret 00, and 12-fret dreadnought. It also introduced the Vintage D, an elegant updating of a mid 1930s Martin dreadnought, and the AJ, which was inspired by Gibson's Advanced

Santa Cruz 12 Fret Dreadnought 2003 (*left*) *Flat-pick artist and studio great Norman Blake inspired this dreadnought which has a mahogany back and sides.*

Santa Cruz D-Law 2015 (*center*) *Developed with Scott Law and designed to be a responsive, playable dreadnought.*

Santa Cruz 1929-00 2016 (*far right*) *This small-body model pays homage to the simple, elegant guitars made during the depression years.*

Jumbo. The new guitars Santa Cruz built were more refined versions of the instruments that inspired them, rather than just straight copies. But not everything it made was a reworking of a vintage design. The Janis Ian Model was a small bodied, short-scale guitar with a striking black finish and a Lloyd Baggs pickup, designed to be played plugged in. The Bob Brozman Baritone was a 12-fret dreadnought with a 27" scale length that was designed to be tuned down to C with extra heavy strings.

By the early 2000s, the Santa Cruz Guitar Company employed around a dozen full-time luthiers. Over the years Richard Hoover automated the production of sonically neutral parts like the bridges and the inlays. (Hoover estimates that before automating the pearl cutting, he spent between eight and ten hours a week hand cutting more than 2,000 pearl SCGC logos himself.) By letting CNC machines cut the fret slots and rough-carve the necks, his builders have more time to spend on important tasks such as voicing the tops and hand-carving the braces. And because so much of a Santa Cruz guitar is still made by hand, the company is able to take on almost any custom order. Today at least half of the guitars Santa Cruz makes are specially ordered with custom features, ranging from different neck shapes and personalized inlays to unusual wood choices and fancier ornamentation.

SCHEERHORN

Tim Scheerhorn is the leading individual maker of Dobro-style resonator guitars. Although he uses a traditional spun-aluminum resonator cone and 'spider' bridge, his instruments are fundamentally different in materials and internal organisation.

A Dobro player himself, Scheerhorn was living in Kentwood, Michigan, when his dissatisfaction with traditional instruments led him to make his first resonator guitar in 1989. "I knew what I didn't want: plywood and soundwell," he said.

Instead of a three-ply laminated body, Scheerhorn used solid wood (mostly maple), and he eliminated the 'soundwell' – a ring of laminated wood that surrounds the resonator cone and, in Scheerhorn's view, acts as a tone compressor. His soundposts and baffles used the entire body as a speaker cabinet. The result was a fuller, richer tone that suited the eclectic, beyond-bluegrass repertoires of modern resonator guitarists like Mike Auldridge, Jerry Douglas, Rob Ickes, and Sally VanMeter.

He moved in 2001 to Dickson, Tennessee, near Nashville (mainly to escape the snows of Michigan, not to be near a music center), and was making some 40 instruments a year. In 2013 he went into partnership with National Reso-Phonic, which today produces a Scheerhorn line.

Santa Cruz OM/PW Redwood 2016 (left) *Santa Cruz's Pre-War Orchestra model features an advanced X and scalloped top bracing, and this example has a fine redwood top.*

Seagull Grand 2001 (near right) *From Seagull's S Series, this instrument is based on the 'grand concert' shape that was popular early in the 19th century – named because it was at least slightly 'grander' than many other petite-bodied guitars.*

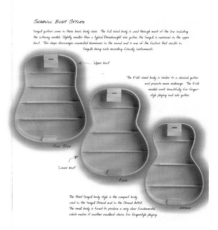

Seagull catalog 2003 (above) *Pages from the current promo publication show the Seagull body sizes, plus an S Series S-6 dreadnought with solid cedar top.*

SCHOENBERG

The brainchild of fingerpicker Eric Schoenberg, Schoenberg was established in 1986 to build accurate reproductions of vintage OM models in collaboration with C.F. Martin – a project often credited with getting Martin to reintroduce vintage-style OMs. After severing direct ties with the Martin factory in 1993, Schoenbergs have been built by a succession of luthiers, including Dana Bourgeois, Julius Borges, and Bruce Sexauer. While the original OM-style Soloist model remains the heart of the line, Schoenberg also offers a number of other designs. Some are virtually exact repros of golden-era Martins; others depart in things like woods, scale-lengths, and cutaways.

SEAGULL

The Seagull guitar began with the fairly radical notion that entry-level guitars should focus more on sound than cosmetics, and has evolved into one of the most respected brands produced in Canada.

Seagull was the brainchild of Robert Godin, who established a custom guitar shop called Harmony Lab in Montreal in 1968. Godin hooked up with Norman Boucher, who had founded Norman Guitars in La Patrie, Quebec, in 1972, and in the late 1970s they worked together. Anxious to pursue his own ideas, Godin left Norman to work on the Seagull concept in 1980.

The first Seagull had some unusual features for the time: it was slightly smaller than a typical dreadnought and had a neck that was bolted on (a method designed to provide better consistency of neck pitch on a production guitar, but which also proved to provide excellent sound transfer). Two dowels were inserted into the neck heel to improve strength and stability. The head's sides were tapered inward to keep the strings straight and in tune. Godin also found that plentiful Canadian wild cherry, laminated cross-grain in three layers, made an excellent tonewood for sides and backs. Tops were either solid, old-growth cedar, or spruce. And the guitars featured a satin lacquer finish at a time when entry-level guitars deadened their tops with shiny, thick polyurethane. Initially finding a cool reception in the lucrative US market, Godin hit the road himself, selling guitars to music shops and building his business.

Godin incorporated as LaSiDo in 1982 and the Seagull entered regular production in La Patrie. Around 1986 Seagull began to offer L.R. Baggs pickups as an option. In 1991 the Seagull line added a second style – often referred to as the 'compact' or folk guitar – a grand concert. Cutaways joined the line a few years later. Godin and

Seagull ad 2007 (*above*) *A promo featuring James Blunt, whose first guitar was a Seagull S6 Original.*

David Poe 2001 (*right*) *The Ohio-born singer-songwriter on stage with a Seagull folk-size guitar.*

his staff continually refined his designs over the years. In 2001 he began a research effort to revisit his original ideas, resulting in the Artist and GT series that debuted in early 2003. The main new feature of these was the 'compound curve top,' a design that uses the added strength of an arch above the soundhole to allow for a thinner, more resonant top, combined with a flat surface on the lower bout that does not inhibit vibration.

Even though Seagull guitars were aimed more at the beginning guitarist, their sound and playability have earned professional allegiance from such as Peppino D'Agostino. They can also be heard on Fareed Haque's Blue Note recording, *Déjà Vu*.

SELMER

In 1933 Selmer, the French saxophone manufacturer, teamed up with Italian guitarist and luthier Mario Maccaferri to build some of the most innovative guitars of the 1930s. Selmer's Maccaferri-designed instruments were among the first guitars to include now common features such as cutaways and sealed tuning machines, along with more unusual innovations such as the internal resonating chamber that was fitted into certain models. Today, Selmers are best known as the guitar of choice of

the legendary Gypsy guitarist Django Reinhardt. Mario Maccaferri was born on May 20, 1900 in the Italian village of Cento. At the age of 11 he apprenticed with Luigi Mozanni, who ran a school for instrument building and guitar playing. Maccaferri proved to be an able student and by his early 20s he had a dual career as a concert guitarist and luthier. He opened his first workshop in Cento in 1923, where he made guitars, mandolins, and violins.

By 1927 Maccaferri was living in Paris, where he concentrated on his performing career, although he did manage to make a violin now and then. In 1928 he moved to London, where he gave guitar lessons and began to work seriously on developing the ideas he had about improving the guitar.

In 1931 Maccaferri applied for a British patent for what he described as an "auxiliary sounding-box attached under or to the harmonic table." Maccaferri showed his design to Ben Davis, who ran Selmer's London branch.

Davis was looking for a line of guitars for his shop, so he and Maccaferri presented the idea to Henri Selmer in Paris, who agreed to devote a small corner of his factory to the manufacture of guitars. The first Selmers were shipped to Ben Davis's shop in 1932, and the early models included both gut-string and steel-string guitars. Since

Maccaferri was a classical guitarist himself, he took particular care with the four gut-strung models in the new Selmer line: the Concert, the Concert Harpe, the Espagnol, and the Classique models.

With its cutaway and large D-shaped soundhole, the Concert was a radical departure from the standard classical guitar as developed in Spain by Torres. The Concert Harpe was a harp-guitar version of the Concert with three sub-bass strings. Maccaferri himself was partial to this model and often played it in his concerts. The Espagnol looked like a standard non-cutaway, round-soundhole classical guitar, but it actually had a resonator fitted inside the sound box. The Classique was a standard classical guitar with a fan-braced top.

The steel-string models included the Orchestre, the Hawaien, and three different styles of tenor guitar. With its D-shaped soundhole and cutaway, the Orchestre was the steel-string equivalent to the gut-strung Concert. The Hawaien was available with six or seven strings and had a D-shaped soundhole and resonator but no cutaway.

The three tenor models were the Grand Modèle, basically a 4-string version of the Orchestre; the Eddie Freeman Special, which was named for a now-obscure English tenor guitarist of the early 1930s; and the Ténor, which had a slightly smaller body

Django Reinhardt c1937 (*left*)
The legendary Gypsy jazz guitarist is by far the most famous user of Selmer's Maccaferri-designed guitar – although fellow members of The Quintet of the Hot Club of France clearly did their bit to help keep the guitar-maker in business … and popularize a particular style of mustache. Violinist Stéphane Grappelli is seen on the far right here.

Selmer-Maccaferri Orchestre 1932 (*left*) *It has been estimated that no more than 100 of this early D-hole model were built. The instrument was Django Reinhardt's guitar of choice early in his career, though he later moved on to oval-hole models.*

Record sleeve 1951 (*above*)
Man and guitar on an LP of late-1940s radio broadcasts … on which Reinhardt actually played electric guitar.

than the Grand Modèle. Half of Selmer's production in 1932 and 1933 was devoted to making tenor guitars, but it is now rare to find them with their original four-string necks as many were fitted with new six-string necks in the 1950s and 1960s.

All the Selmer-Maccaferri guitars were built using similar construction techniques. The backs and sides were laminated, usually with an Indian rosewood veneer over a mahogany core, although three-ply models – rosewood on the outside, poplar in the middle, and mahogany on the inside – occasionally turn up. This was not a cost-cutting measure, but rather an attempt to build a guitar that wasn't prone to cracking and splitting. Maccaferri also felt the laminated back and sides added clarity and definition to the tone. The only all-solid-wood guitars Selmer made were the handful of maple models produced in the late 1930s and the harp-guitars, which had solid mahogany back and sides.

The necks were made of walnut and the Selmer logo was engraved in the ebony headstock overlay by the same worker who engraved the logo into the clarinets. The sealed tuning machines and brass tailpiece were made by the same Selmer craftsmen who made the saxophones. The custom fitted cases were also made at the Selmer factory. The Concert, Espagnol, Hawaien, and Orchestre were fitted with

The Rosenberg Trio 2000
(*above*) *The Rosenbergs pictured with their Selmer guitars. Lead guitarist Stochelo (center) plays No.504, the very next instrument built after Reinhardt's own oval-hole No.503, while cousin Nous'che plays a D-hole, which bears serial No.423.*

Selmer Modèle Jazz 1951
(*left*) *Selmer continued to make guitars in a design similar to Maccaferri's even after the designer departed the company, but later employed this smaller oval soundhole. A total of around 500 guitars were made in this style.*

Diz Disley 1992 (*below*) *The*
Canadian jazz guitarist – here with
Selmer oval-hole – was instrumental in
reviving violinist Stéphane Grappelli's
career during the 1970s.

SELMER

Maccaferri's patented internal resonator, which was described in an early Selmer ad as an "exponential tone-chamber which amplifies and impels the sound in complete balance throughout the registers." Unfortunately, it didn't perform as advertised. Instead of acting like an amplifier and making the guitar louder and more focused, the resonator worked like a compressor and smoothed out the guitar's dynamic range. The resonator boxes also had a tendency to work loose and rattle and buzz and guitarists began to specially order guitars without them, while musicians who had guitars that came with resonators began to pull them out.

In 1933 Mario Maccaferri got into a dispute with Henri Selmer over the terms of their contract. Maccaferri left the company and returned to his concert career. That summer he got a small part in a movie, but while cooling off in the studio swimming-pool during a break in filming, he collided with another swimmer and fractured his wrist, which ended his performing days. (For more information on Maccaferri's guitar-making career in the US, see the *Maccaferri* entry.)

Not long after Maccaferri and Selmer parted company, Django Reinhardt began playing an Orchestre model. Because the soundhole was so large, it's easy to tell from old photos that he played a model without a resonator. Selmer set up an endorsement deal with the rising young jazz guitarist. In exchange for appearing in their ads, Reinhardt was given a guitar or two a year, which in turn he promptly gave away to friends or his numerous relatives.

With Maccaferri gone, Selmer management took a hard look at the entire guitar line. The first thing they did was to remove Maccaferri's name from the headstock and interior label. The second was to phase out all of the models except the Orchestre, which they renamed the Modèle Jazz. Over the next few months a now forgotten craftsman began to alter Maccaferri's original design. The first thing to go was the resonator. The D-shaped soundhole was dropped in 1934 in favor of a round one, and then a small oval soundhole. In 1935, the neck was switched from 12 to 14 frets clear of the body; legend has it that Reinhardt himself suggested the change. By 1936 the Selmer Modèle Jazz had achieved its final form, and it remained essentially unchanged until the company shut down the guitar business in 1952.

In the 20 years that Selmer was making guitars the company produced approximately 900 instruments. The bulk of them, perhaps 500, were in the 14-fret Modèle Jazz style. Most of the rest were the 12-fret Orchestre and the four-string tenor guitars. Selmer only made a small handful of gut-strung and Hawaien guitars.

SILVERTONE
(AND SUPERTONE)

Legions of guitarists started on a budget-priced, mail-order Silvertone guitar from the Sears, Roebuck and Co catalog, whether it was a Gene Autry cowboy guitar or one of the brand's jumbo flat-tops or fancy archtops.

The Silvertone brand debuted in 1940, when Sears divested itself of its Harmony subsidiary, which had made most of its Supertone line since it appeared in 1914. Except for a few initial Kays and some EKOs in the early 1960s, Silvertone acoustics were also made by Harmony, always slightly lower-grade versions of comparable Harmonys. Gone by the 1970s, Silvertone was revived more recently on Korean guitars by Samick, including a reissue of the 604 parlor model.

SIMON & PATRICK

Simon & Patrick Luthier is a further line of Canadian-made guitars created by Robert Godin's LaSiDo company and produced in La Patrie, Quebec.

Originally developed in response to dealer requests for more traditional dreadnought guitars with square-topped headstocks, Simon & Patrick Luthier (named

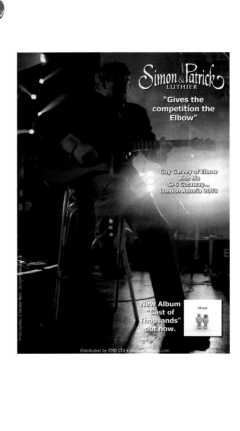

Simon & Patrick P-6 2002 (*right*) *A spruce-topped dreadnought with onboard electronics.*

Simon & Patrick ad 2004 (*far right*) *Elbow main man Guy Garvey is pictured in this promo with his SP6 Cutaway.*

Silvertone Crest 1941 (*left*) *This archtop was built by Kay during the transition from Sears-owned Harmony to employee-owned Harmony, and marks the first appearance of the Sears brand name Silvertone.*

Simon & Patrick catalog 2003
*An invitation through the soundhole of
one of the Canadian brand's guitars.*

for Godin's two sons) debuted around 1986, and share features common to its predecessor, Seagull guitars. With solid, old-growth cedar or spruce tops, laminated wild cherry bodies, satin or high-gloss lacquer finishes, and bolt-on necks, Simon & Patrick soon became LaSiDo's premier line. L.R. Baggs pickup systems and left-handed models were available options. Cutaway and 12-string models were added in the early 1990s.

By the mid 1990s the Pro Series had debuted, featuring bodies of tri-laminate mahogany, flamed maple, rosewood, or quilted maple. The Pro Folk followed in 1999, available with spruce top and solid rosewood back.

Recent additions include a small-bodied, laminated wild cherry Parlor model with either a natural spruce or a sunburst finished cedar top. In 2003 Simon & Patrick guitars were built using Godin's new compound curve top technology, which employs an arched upper bout combined with a flat lower bout.

SLINGERLAND

The classic name in drums (now owned by Gibson), Slingerland marketed both upscale archtops and lower grade flat-tops during the 1930s. The company was founded during a card game in 1912 when H.H. Slingerland won a Chicago ukulele-music publishing house. Ukulele manufacturing (1916) was followed by banjos (around 1919) and drums (1928).

Slingerland's May-Bell brand was used on standard and concert size flat-tops, some with cherub decals, others with fake resonators (covers, no cones), including the Cathedranola model, all made by Regal. By 1936 Slingerland was selling a Marvel line of archtops. By around 1937 its May-Bell Violin Craft line had debuted with Harmony bodies and probably Slingerland's own metal-reinforced necks, the premier Nite Hawk sporting fancy pearl, gold, and silver inlays.

SMALLMAN

Although Greg Smallman's instruments are largely traditional in appearance, they represent the most important and influential new direction in classical guitar design since Torres. Smallman had until 2002 lived and worked in Glen Innes, in the

Smallman 1992 (*right*) *This fine classical guitar employs Greg Smallman's light balsa-and-carbon-fiber 'lattice' strutting beneath an exceptionally thin solid cedar top, with heavy laminated Brazilian rosewood back and sides to support the configuration (back pictured far right).*

Slingerland May Bell Cathedranola c1933 (*above*) *This 'Amplifying Guitar' deceptively carries the coverplate of a resonator guitar, but has a secondary wooden soundboard inside rather than the aluminum cone one would expect.*

Slingerland May Bell No. 7 c1932 (*near right*) *A Regal-made flat-top 'Spanish' guitar.*

Australian bush, 200 miles south of Brisbane. Working with his sons Damon and Kym, whose names now feature on his labels, he produces only a handful of guitars each year. They have always been in great demand, thanks to the endorsement of John Williams and a string of concert players, and to their inherent qualities.

Smallman began building guitars in 1972, producing traditional models based on the Fleta design. Later, he began working with another Australian luthier, Peter Biffin, producing more experimental models, some of them steel-strung. These experiments led, in 1980, to the development of Smallman's celebrated lattice strutting system. As a boy, Smallman had built model aircraft, stretching a fine paper skin over wooden struts to form light but strong wings and fuselages. He reasoned now that the soundboard of a guitar requires a maximum of stiffness and a minimum of weight, and he achieved this by using a thin, light, and necessarily flexible cedar top and bracing it with a criss-cross lattice.

The lattice is made of carbon-fiber, an immensely strong and light material, backed with balsa-wood to make it easier to fit to the soundboard. The stiffness is concentrated at the center, near the bridge, leaving the soundboard flexible where it meets the body of the guitar. Prior to the completion of his guitars, individual

soundboards are fitted to a dummy body and tuned. The analogy Smallman uses is with a drum. The soundboard of a guitar is the light, fast-moving diaphragm. By extension, the body must be rigid so as not to absorb vibrations from the soundboard. To achieve this end, Smallman uses laminated rosewood sides and slightly arches the back, which has no internal bracing.

More recently, Smallman has added a truss-rod to the neck and introduced padauk bridges in place of more traditional woods.

The result is a loud guitar designed for the concert-hall, responsive to the player and evenly balanced across the frequency range.

John Williams took up Smallman's guitars in 1981, putting aside his Fletas, and has wasted few opportunities to promote his fellow Australian's work. Other important Smallman players include Julian Byzantine, Stephan Rak, Benjamin Verdery, David Tannenbaum, and Carlos Bonell.

Furthermore, Smallman's influence in the world of guitar-making has been immense, both in Australia and around the world. While traditionalists continue to scorn them, enthusiasts for lattice-strutted guitars argue that their responsiveness and reach suits the modern concert repertoire.

Stahl 1910 (*right*) A student-grade, non-X-braced model built by Larson Brothers of Chicago.

Stahl 1930 (*left*) Another Larsons-built Stahl, this one a far more elaborate, high quality guitar. Note the internal metal support rod, usually found in Prairie State guitars.

Somogyi 1992 (*above*) An elaborate cutaway steel-string guitar of dreadnought proportions built by Ervin Somogyi.

SOBELL

Northumberland luthier Stefan Sobell began making guitars in the 1980s after having built a cittern (a mandola-type instrument of his own design) followed by bouzoukis and mandolins. Today he offers a number of flat-top and roundhole archtop models all individually built by hand, and with numerous custom order options. His production amounts to about three instruments per month. For the 'flat'-tops, Sobell has designed a new bracing system on a heavily curved soundboard.

SOMOGYI

Ervin Somogyi started building guitars in 1971, but he sprang to prominence in the mid 1980s when his guitars were favored by Windham Hill artists Will Ackermann, Alex de Grassi, and Daniel Hecht. Somogyi builds guitars in Oakland, California, in a variety of sizes, but his dreadnought is perhaps his best known model.

He is a fearless builder who will tackle just about any custom order, including harp guitars, seven-string flat-tops, and fanned-fret guitars. Although he is best known for his steel-string guitars, Somogyi is a fine flamenco guitarist and has built a number of highly regarded nylon-string instruments.

STAHL

Few people would be likely to remember Stahl guitars today if not for the name's connection with Chicago's illustrious guitar-making siblings, Carl and August Larson.

An accomplished violinist, banjoist, and mandolinist, William C. Stahl (born 1869, Westin, Missouri) was a prominent music retailer and publisher in Milwaukee, Wisconsin, where he'd set up shop in the late 1890s. Perhaps as early as 1904 Stahl was selling his own-brand guitars, some, if not all, made by the Larsons' Maurer & Co. Despite what the guitars' labels say, Stahl is not known to have been a builder.

Except for the label, most Stahls were typical Larson guitars: they employed stressed tops and backs, were braced for steel strings, and came in various grades of decoration. The Larson brothers made Stahl guitars until around 1935, when the Maurer brand ended. Washburn and later Regal also built some guitars and other instruments for Stahl. William Stahl's death in 1941 closed the business.

Another Milwaukee music store that also distributed instruments was the Wack Sales Co., run by Adolph Waech and his son Waldemar. Wack was introduced to Larson guitars by Stahl, and it sold Maurer and Prairie State brands from 1932 until the 1940s. It's not known if any Wack-brand guitars were produced.

Stella 12-String c1930 (left)
An Oscar Schmidt-made Stella similar to the slightly later guitar played by legendary folk-bluesman Ledbelly.

Stella Concert-Size c1932 (near right) *A six-string Stella flat-top, also made by Oscar Schmidt of Jersey City, New Jersey.*

Sleepy John Estes 1966 *The great blues singer takes his Harmony-made Stella to work.*

S T E L L A
(A N D   S O V E R E I G N)

If not for their use by a who's-who of blues players – including Huddie 'Leadbelly' Ledbetter, Charlie Patton, Barbecue Bob Hicks, Blind Blake, Blind Willie McTell, Willie Brown, and many others – Stella guitars might be just a dim memory rather than the revered relics they are today. Stella guitars – including the legendary 12-string – were produced by the Oscar Schmidt Company of Jersey City, New Jersey, and were part of a range that spanned inexpensive all-birch parlor guitars to some fairly elaborately appointed and impressive-sounding behemoths.

Oscar Schmidt emigrated to the US from Saxony and went into music publishing, expanding into music schools. In 1879 he began manufacturing stringed instruments to provide to his students, and among the best known was his autoharp. By the turn of the century, Schmidt had managed to join Harmony as a supplier to Sears and other mail-order retailers, providing some of the better-grade gut and steel-string parlor guitars, either of birch – with faux finishes – or genuine oak, mahogany, or rosewood, some with quite fancy inlays and trim. Other brands occasionally produced by Schmidt included La Scala and Galiano.

Schmidt also developed a sales force that sold guitars in more remote areas without music stores. The two plusses of being both inexpensive and readily available probably accounts for the guitars' popularity among bluesmen. Even though most were ladder braced, Schmidt guitars had an early reputation for volume.

When the Stella brand name appeared is uncertain, but it was probably prior to the 1920s. Stella was used on Schmidt's humbler guitars, with the brand appearing sometimes on the headstock and always on a paper label inside. Many were all-birch models, often featuring early decalomania decoration, typically around the soundhole with floral designs under the strings, although marquetry trim was also employed. Other models still used the faux finishes with spruce tops. Stella models could be had in standard, grand concert, and auditorium sizes.

Also available by the early 1920s was the Stella 12-string guitar, favored by Leadbelly and others, making Schmidt (along with Harmony) one of the few guitar-makers to produce a 12-string model before World War II. Another Stella instrument of note was the Contra Bass, or Harp Guitar, a doubleneck with a regular guitar neck on the bottom (with slotted six-tuners-in-line headstock) and a fretless neck on top with six strings (with three-tuners-a-side slothead).

Stella Sundale 1955 *This concert-sized flat-top with stenciled white art deco face over a blue finish was made by Harmony.*

The Band c1968 (*main picture*) Robbie Robertson picks a stencil-topped Stella down in the basement with the boys.

Schmidt's deluxe guitar line was branded Sovereign, again with the name on the head and a paper label inside. These appeared quite early, and some examples had mustache pin bridges. By the 1920s many had huge jumbo bodies by contemporary standards. Many subtly varying shapes were employed, but by the 1930s the Sovereign model had a graceful, big, round form.

By the 1920s many of Schmidt's grand concert and auditorium Stella and Sovereign guitars also sported long scales, often 26" or even 26½", making them almost baritone guitars. These were intended to be tuned a step down, and they produce a wonderful voice.

In 1929 founder Oscar Schmidt died in an airplane crash. The company continued on but was hit hard by the Depression.

By the early 1930s both Stella and Sovereign guitars had begun to appear with pearloid fingerboards, headstock face plates, and trim, and many models started to feature pickguards. Indeed, even though Schmidt had catalog models, there is a confusing amount of variation in its guitars from this era.

The Oscar Schmidt Company sold its Jersey City guitar-making operation to John Carver in 1935, and the new owner continued at the same location. Reportedly Leadbelly's 12-string dates from this period. A few models of the time were produced with X-bracing and flat headstocks.

Carver did not thrive, and in 1938 he sold the Stella and Sovereign brand names to Harmony in Chicago. The old Schmidt factory was sold to a company that would become United Guitar Manufacturing. Following the war, United would produce Premier and Orpheum guitars, among others.

In 1939 Harmony continued the Schmidt tradition by promptly applying the Stella name to a budget range of guitars and the Sovereign name to more upscale models. These included a birch grand concert Stella in the round Sovereign shape, plus a variety of standard-sized birch models, some with faux finishes, most with stamped tailpieces. These had white striping paint instead of real bindings and stenciled markers. Such standard Stellas would reappear following the war and would typify Harmony-made Stellas until 1975.

Harmony's pre-war Sovereigns were amplifying guitars outfitted with genuine National-Dobro resonators. After the war they picked up the full, rounded Schmidt/Stella shape, which lasted until 1956, after which the guitar became a typical Harmony square-shouldered auditorium in spruce and mahogany (a single-coil-

pickup-equipped acoustic-electric was also available in later years). In 1958 a Jumbo version debuted – a kind of frumpy dreadnought with wide, square shoulders and thick waist that would become Harmony's flagship acoustic (later versions with mustache bridges) until 1975. The line also included some black-finished versions.

Both Stella and Sovereign went into hiatus until around 2000, when the owners of the Harmony brand reintroduced versions made in Asia.

STROMBERG

In the quest to make bigger and louder archtop guitars, Elmer Stromberg topped them all. After legendary makers Gibson, Epiphone, and D'Angelico established 18" as the accepted maximum body width for a guitar, Stromberg went an extra inch, and as a result his 19" archtops are among the loudest acoustic guitars ever made.

Although the Stromberg name appeared on the headstock, the name on the label (which was typically a business card) was Chas. Stromberg and Son. Charles Stromberg was born in Sweden and came to the US as a cabinetmaker. After supervising guitar production for a Boston maker, he opened his own instrument-making business around 1905. Son Elmer joined him in 1910 at the age of 15. Until

the 1930s, the Stromberg shop mostly turned out banjos, and when the guitar began to rise in popularity, Elmer took over all of the guitar work.

Stromberg's first archtops were 16" wide, the same width as the first version of Gibson's L-5, but with early-Epiphone style three-segment f-holes and a bracing pattern that combined lateral braces with an X brace. His G-3 and Deluxe models took the body width to 17⅜". These were high quality guitars, with pearl slashed-block fingerboard inlays, bound f-holes, and gold-plated metal parts.

Gibson had pushed its archtops to 18" wide with the Super 400 in 1934. Epiphone followed in 1935 with the Emperor, and D'Angelico in 1936 with his New Yorker. By the end of the decade, Stromberg had overtaken and surpassed them all with two 19" models: the Master 300 and the fancier Master 400. The top bracing on these behemoths was reduced to a single diagonal bar. Eventually all the Stromberg models were available with cutaway bodies.

Aesthetically, the Master 400 fit right in with its contemporaries, with large pearl block fingerboard inlays and a heavy metal tailpiece similar to Gibson's, and a stairstep pickguard design that was so close to D'Angelico's that the two makers reportedly argued – good-naturedly – about who had copied whom. The Stromberg

B&J Serenader 1924 (*left*) *The trio of instruments on this page illustrate 'the other Stromberg,' definitely not to be confused with the revered archtop guitars made by Elmer Stromberg in Boston, shown opposite. This student model was made in Chicago by the Stromberg-Voisinet company, the precursor to Kay. (See also the Kay entry.)*

Stromberg D-800 1929 (*right*) *A Spanish flat-top, also made by Stromberg-Voisinet.*

Stromberg No. 49 (*right*) *A low-priced flat-top from Stromberg-Voisinet of Chicago – an instrument a world away from the big Stromberg archtops of Elmer and Charles.*

headstock was also fancy in the style of the day, but instead of pearl inlay, the inlay effect was achieved by carving through a celluloid veneer to reveal a lighter-colored layer of celluloid underneath. Multiple layers of 'binding' around the peghead were simulated by beveling the edge of the veneers.

Strombergs were made to be played hard. (In fact, the relatively thick top of the Master 400 produces very little sound until the guitar is strummed hard.) At a volume level where other guitars of the day would begin to 'break up,' Strombergs maintained a clear tone. This combination of volume and tone made them the preferred guitar for holding down the rhythm in big band jazz settings, where acoustic guitarists struggled to be heard through the trumpets, trombones, and saxophones.

Among the best known Stromberg players in jazz bands were Freddie Green, longtime guitarist in the Count Basie band, and Irving Ashby of the Lionel Hampton and Nat King Cole groups. Ashby was so strongly identified with the Stromberg that he released a single entitled 'Big Guitar.' Guitarists in other genres also embraced the Stromberg's big sound, among them Henry 'Homer' Haynes of the country comedy duo Homer & Jethro, Brazilian guitarist Laurindo Almeida, and Douglas 'Ranger Doug' Green of the Western cowboy group Riders In The Sky. Charles and Elmer Stromberg

Stromberg Deluxe Cutaway 1945 (*left*) *Only a very small number of this top-of-the-line model by Elmer Stromberg of Boston were produced with a blonde (natural) spruce top.*

Stromberg G-1 c1945 (*center*) *Stromberg archtops came in six models, though each instrument was built to order. The G-1 (sometimes called the G-100) was second-from-bottom of the line.*

Stromberg c1931 (*far left*) *This example of the Boston-based Stromberg's early style is distinctive for its relatively spartan trim and three-piece, 'segmented' f-holes.*

worked together virtually all of their lives. They both died in 1955, Charles the father first, and then Elmer just a few months later. Their total archtop guitar production is estimated to have been around 640 instruments.

TACOMA

Named after its factory location near Seattle, Washington, Tacoma might sound an all-American affair, but this mid-to-pro-market brand, which in the space of just seven years claimed to be the third largest US acoustic manufacturer (after Taylor and Martin), owed its origins to the Korean piano industry.

In 1991, Young Chang set up the Sound Mill in Tacoma to process local hardwoods for piano soundboards, and also opened an acoustic guitar plant nearby, building on a contract basis, mainly for Washburn. Subsequently, the mill's management, headed by J.C. Kim, decided it would be preferable to develop their own line of instruments, and in 1996 Tacoma Guitars was founded as a wholly owned subsidiary of Young Chang. A change of ownership occurred in the late '99 when, due to the Asian economic downturn, Young Chang pulled out, selling the plants and the Tacoma name to Kim. He remains a key director of the firm.

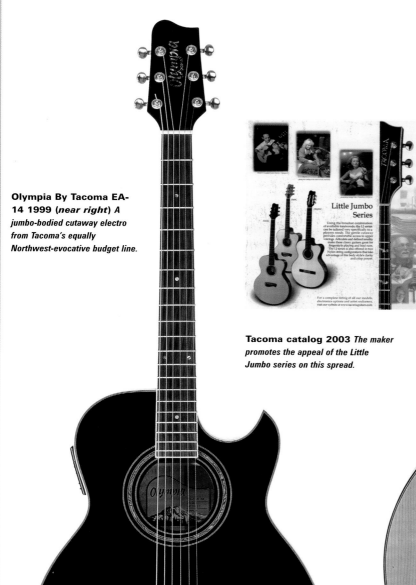

Olympia By Tacoma EA-14 1999 (near right) *A jumbo-bodied cutaway electro from Tacoma's equally Northwest-evocative budget line.*

Tacoma catalog 2003 *The maker promotes the appeal of the Little Jumbo series on this spread.*

Tacoma EM-9CE7 2001 *This guitar is a round-soundhole cutaway 'mini-jumbo' electro.*

Tacoma ad 1998 (above) *"Pros play Tacoma," we're told, and on this evidence Phil Keaggy, Vince Gill, and Chris Duarte certainly do.*

Tacoma ad 1997 (above left) *A good showing of the various models – along with a plug for Tacoma's "voiced support bracing."*

Oliver Mtukudzi 1999 (*far right*) The African guitarist on stage with a Tacoma C-1C Chief. The model's distinctive offset soundhole helped to establish the brand's identity.

TACOMA

Tacoma's debut at a 1997 US trade show made a big impact – not so much for the handful of traditionally-based designs but for the little A-pitch P1 Papoose, co-designed by vintage dealer George Gruhn, and its medium-bodied, cutaway cousin, the C1C Chief. Distinctive for their minimalist cosmetics (no body binding), top-bout 'paisley' soundhole, and eager sound and tone, both used simple, mandolin-derived A-style bracing, made possible by the absence of a central soundhole.

Other design aspects claimed to enhance tone and volume include an asymmetric maple bridge plate and similarly asymmetrical bridge profile, features that are applicable to most other Tacomas.

Helped by Gruhn's artist contacts, the Papoose in particular quickly found favor on the country circuit, and users include Ricky Skaggs, Vince Gill, Travis Tritt, and The Dixie Chicks. Bonnie Raitt and Jackson Browne are Papoose owners too. Subsequent years have seen further, more elaborately-specified Papooses and Chiefs (plus the Thunderchief bass), and the paisley soundhole concept has since been applied to the Roadking dreadnoughts, AJF archtop jazzers, and Tacoma's mandolin series.

Building on a launch line that already included dreadnoughts, jumbos, and parlors, the company introduced the Thinline Series in '99 – a couple of Florentine-cutaway

instruments, the EM-10 and 16, in profile somewhat reminiscent of Washburn's Festival Series. That year also saw an upgrade to solid woods throughout, where previously a few of the cheaper models, like the DM-10 dreadnought and PM-20 parlor, had laminated sides.

Another series launched around this time was the LJ, the 'Little Jumbos,' co-designed by guitarist Laurence Juber and, confusingly, carrying 'E' model prefixes. Starting with the spruce/mahogany EM-9, the LJs have been a central part of a burgeoning catalog, with around ten models plus four new debuts for 2003, including the Brazilian rosewood EBZ-24 and all-koa EKK-19C.

A limited edition in 2000, the EK-36C was especially handsome, featuring a 600-year-old cedar front and flamed koa back and sides. In 2002, two LJ-sized cutaway nylon-string classicals – models ECR-15NC and ER-64NC – were introduced under the Europa Series banner.

Some rationalization of the line took place in 2003, but the Tacoma catalog still numbers over 70 instruments, and there are five pickup-system options that can be requested on most models. Current production is around 40 instruments a day, from a 90-strong workforce. Another string to the company's bow is the offshore-sourced

TAKAMINE

Olympia By Tacoma line, a budget line introduced in 1998. Originally, these instruments bore little design resemblance to the US product beyond headstock and bridge shapes, but the line-up, aside from traditional body styles, did include the Chief-type OMC-1CE and the OB-3CE bass. Fender bought Tacoma in 2004, but the revised operation ceased business four years later.

TAKAMINE

The idea of acoustic-electric guitars goes back to the late 1920s, but no other guitar company did more to pioneer the form in otherwise traditional acoustic guitars than Takamine. Embraced by artists as diverse as Nils Lofgren, John Jorgenson, producer Steve Wariner, Glenn Frey, Darius Rucker, Mark Chesnutt, John Scofield, Toby Keith, Jennifer Turner, Bruce Springsteen, Garth Brooks, and bands such as Linkin Park and India.Arie, Takamine is almost synonymous with quality 'plugged-in unplugged' guitars that deliver a natural sound.

Named for the mountain where it's located, Takamine was founded in 1962 in Sakashita, Japan. Under other names the make established a good reputation for its

acoustic guitars in Japan during the early 1960s, and at some point established a relationship with Coast Wholesale Music in San Francisco, California.

Coast distributed Martin guitars and lobbied Martin to develop a line of less expensive Japanese imports, recommending that they talk to Takamine. Martin asked Coast to handle the project and it began working on prototypes. In the meantime, Coast began distributing Ovation guitars made by the Kaman Corporation.

Kaman decided to acquire some distribution channels and purchased Coast in 1968. Since Martin considered Ovation to be a competitor, the deal with Takamine was off, and Martin went elsewhere for what became its Sigma line. Kaman/Coast continued to encourage Takamine to establish itself as a brand, and provided help with financing. Several years later Takamine reciprocated by giving Kaman/Coast a minority share of the company and exclusive rights to distribute in the US.

Also in 1968, Takamine was joined by Mass Hirade, a talented luthier who would direct the company's development into the future. Hirade worked to improve product designs and quality.

Takamine F-150 Bruno 1984 (left) Remarkably for a company founded in 1962, this is a 150th anniversary model. This 'antiqued' parlor-size guitar in fact celebrates the 150th anniversary of the C. Bruno company, which Takamine's partner Kaman purchased in the 1960s.

Takamine LTD 90 (right) The cutaway dreadnought LTD model for 1990, with solid bookmatched Koa top, back and sides.

Takamine Santa Fe Ltd Edition 1997 (above) The annual Santa Fe Series introduced artfully modern, western-themed trim and high-end electronics. Note the 'circling lizard' inlay on the soundhole of this cutaway jumbo electro instrument.

Takamine ad 1988 (above) Promo for this year's LTD model, of which only 500 were built.

'copy era,' and – as usual for the type – early models were 'copies' of Martin dreadnought and OM guitars, as well as of other brands.

Even the script logos on the square-headed guitars looked like 'Martin' from across the room. By the end of the decade there were even some copies of the popular Gallagher guitars.

The same year also saw the debut of guitars with Takamine's first bridge-mounted pickup system, the Palathetic pickup. In a way, these more conventional acoustic-electric classicals and steel-strings were a perfect complement to the more revolutionary acoustic-electrics Ovation sold, and helped build demand for that sector.

By 1978, if not earlier, Takamine was selling the H series Hirade Concert classicals with solid tops. By 1982 these had been joined by acoustic-electric versions (E series) and models with a right-angle cutaway reminiscent of the old Selmer/Maccaferri designs. Some of these featured laminated tops. By 1989 the cutaway Hirades also had a Selmer-style oval soundhole.

By 1979 Takamine had introduced the original features that inform the line till this day, including the distinctive tapered, center-peaked head. Cheaper guitars had laminated tops; better models had solid spruce or cedar and were signified by an S

Hirade's strength was classical guitars, and Takamine's premier classicals would bear his name. However, the first Takamine steel-string instruments that appeared – this was around 1969 – were largely based on Martin guitars, with which the company was familiar.

How many early Takamines were exported is unknown, but in 1975 Takamine began to trade internationally. The guitars hit the market at the height of the 1970s

Takamine Santa Fe Ltd Edition 1998 (*near right*) *An evocative celestial inlay decorates this limited-run model for 1998.*

Takamine GB-Seven-C 1997 (*right*) *The Garth Brooks model electro, with cutaway-dreadnought-shaped soundhole.*

Takamine ad 1993 (*above*) *The Santa Fe goes south of the border.*

TAKAMINE

suffix; the F series included dreadnoughts and 'folk' (OM) models; an EF prefix indicated that it was an acoustic-electric version; the C series models were classicals, with electronics on the ECs. Cutaways (C suffix) were also added around 1982.

During the mid 1980s, Takamine produced what many might well consider to be its strangest beast. The guitar in question was effectively an acoustic-electric version of Gibson's oddball Flying V, later called the Flying A. Whichever way you looked at this most curious concoction, it had to be a rocker's dream turned into reality.

By 1988 Takamine had introduced a parametric equalizer to its acoustic-electrics and debuted the Natural series acoustic (N) and acoustic-electric (EN) models, including dreadnoughts and cutaway jumbos. Also new was a low-end G series. More new releases for 1988 were Takamine's first Korean instruments, known as Jasmine By Takamine, essentially budget copies of the core line. These continue to be made in various Asian factories.

Around the same time, Takamine picked up on the success of Ovation's Collector's Series and began to offer its Limited Edition LTD series. The first was the 500-unit

Takamine EG-5609 2002 (*left*) Here's a cutaway dreadnought with onboard electronics.

Takamine EF-108K 1999 (*far left*) An all-koa-bodied cutaway jumbo acoustic-electric.

Takamine AN-15 2001 (*near left*) One of the maker's more straightforward models – a spruce-topped all-acoustic dreadnought.

LTD-88, one of the new EN jumbos finished in black with abalone trim and a split, compensated saddle that would be featured on upscale models of the future. The LTDs continue to be represented in the Takamine catalog to this day. The same idea was tried briefly on Hirade classical instruments in 1990, with an all-koa model, but these did not last.

In 1990 Takamine continued the expansion of its various guitar lines. The Artist series appeared with a flamed maple dreadnought, and the company's first thinbody, the ST-26, which had a downsized, rounded, jumbo shape with cutaway. It was built with a white solid spruce top and synthetic sonatex body. A 12-string version was also offered.

Takamine's first Signature model debuted in 1991 with the SW-341S built for Steve Wariner, finished in black to match his taste in wardrobe. In 1999 a second Signature appeared, the GB-7C, a groovy cutaway dreadnought designed by and for Garth Brooks – its most distinctive feature a soundhole shaped like the cutaway body. In 2002 a John Jorgenson dreadnought debuted.

In 1993 the downsized Artist body was adapted to further lines, including the G series, and called the NEX shape. Takamine also introduced its limited-edition Santa

Fe models – especially novel because they featured exotic trim such as turquoise and were inspired by Native American motifs. Most were NEX or cutaway dreadnought style, though in 1995 a small-bodied version with a 'New Yorker' body was produced. A plainer series of these, called Nouveau, appeared in 2002, and included the first NEX body shape/size without a cutaway. The smaller body that debuted on the Santa Fe was applied to the Small Body series in 1996.

Until 1998 all Takamines had been manufactyred in Japan, but at that time production of the budget-price G series was shifted to Korea. The company's better models continue to be Japanese-made.

Takamine debuted the Advanced Natural and Supernatural series in 2001, both with NEX and dreadnought shapes and a new CT4B preamp system. Two new signature models appeared in later years: the Glenn Frey EF360GF (2009); and the Toby Keith #6 (2012).

It's almost certainly the case that guitairsts would have been offered acoustic-electric guitars even if there had been no Takamine. But no one company has carved out a place in the general marketplace with quite the verve and style of Takamine guitars, built at the foot of a mountain in Japan.

Takamine EAN-10C 2001 (*left*) *Red cedar-topped dreadnought.*

Takamine AN-45 Super Natural 2001 (*center*) This non-cutaway jumbo sports subtle yet elegant styling.

Takamine ad 2014 (*right*) Simon Neil of Biffy Clyro and his evidently played-in Takamine P7DC.

Takamine GN93CE 2014 (*far right*) This guitar features the sleek NEX-style body and Takamine's own pre-amp system with built-in tuner.

Takamine EAN-10C 2001 (*above*) Red cedar-topped dreadnought.

THE HARDEST WORKING GUITAR

SIMON NEIL AND HIS PRO SERIES P7DC

TAYLOR

Taylor emerged from the thriving Southern California luthier's scene of the early 1970s to become one of the most significant American guitar-makers of the new millennium. At the time of writing, the company is still owned by Bob Taylor and Kurt Listug, two of the three original partners.

With an output of about 270 guitars a day, Taylor is one of the largest producers of acoustic guitars in the US. It was one of the first guitar companies to use high-tech building methods such as computer numeric control (CNC) to fabricate parts, which in turn allowed it to build high-quality acoustic guitars more quickly and efficiently, and its successful use of the bolt-on neck legitimized this formerly controversial neck-joint.

Bob Taylor was born in 1955 in Oakland, California, and his family moved to San Diego when he was in the third grade. Taylor was the sort of boy who would rather take a toy train apart to see how it worked than watch it run in circles. When he was nine years old he bought his first guitar, an instrument with a red and black sunburst finish and painted-on white binding. The binding was scuffed, so he attempted to 'repair' it by repainting it with model airplane paint, which only made a bigger mess. Young Taylor had to sand the paint off and repaint the binding a couple of times before

Taylor LKSM-6 Leo Kottke 1997 *Taylor first offered a 12-string signature model for Kottke – who is more often associated with that format – but followed it with this six-string model in 1996.*

Taylor 814CE 1998 (near right) *A cutaway electro version of one of Taylor's most popular models.*

Taylor ad 1983 (center) *Here is the Guild-inspired, pre-Kottke-endorsed Taylor 12-string. The copywriter declares: "Actually easier to play than most six-strings!"*

Leo Kottke 1994 *This Taylor catalog features Kottke with his 12-string signature model.*

he was satisfied with the result. A year or so later he sawed off that guitar's neck in an attempt to convert it to a solid body electric ... but that project proved beyond his abilities at the time.

A few years later, when he was in high school, Taylor decided to build an acoustic guitar from scratch, using an EKO 12-string from a local music store as his model. His woodshop teacher gave him a copy of Irving Sloane's 1966 book *Classic Guitar Construction*, which taught him the basics of guitar building. After this instrument was completed, he immediately returned to the workbench to build a six-string, followed by another 12-string, which he finished before graduating from high school. During the time he was building his first guitars, Taylor began hanging out at American Dream Musical Instrument Manufacturing, a local company that built guitars and sold luthier's supplies such as binding material and fret wire.

Kurt Listug was born in San Diego in 1952, and he became obsessed with guitars after hearing The Beatles in 1964. He got a guitar for Christmas that year and played in a series of garage bands over the next few years. During class he would draw

guitars and amplifiers rather than pay attention to the teacher. When he was in high school he built a speaker cabinet, which he later sold to a friend. After graduating high school he attended San Diego State University, where he took classes in German and Philosophy. In 1973 Listug got a job finishing guitars at the American Dream and dropped out of school. A few weeks later, on September 15th, Bob Taylor also started working at the American Dream.

The American Dream was a number of musical instrument-related businesses rolled up into one handy package. Brothers Sam and Gene Radding started the firm in 1970 to sell the guitars and dulcimers that Sam had been building for the last few years. In its first incarnation the Dream, as many people came to call it, was a small store in San Diego with a retail section in the front half of the building and workshop in the back half. Sam soon discovered that he needed more room for his instrument building and so he, along with two friends named Lee Folmer and Bob Morrisey, moved the workshop to the nearby town of Lemon Grove.

Sam Radding ran his workshop as a co-operative, and the luthiers who worked there acted as independent contractors. Each builder had his own workbench where he made guitars based on Radding's designs, and passed along a percentage of the

Taylor 712C 1997 (*near left*) *This smaller-bodied model with pointed cutaway has a solid cedar top.*

Taylor Baby 2001 (*far left*) *Taylor helped to introduce the idea of a quality 'child sized' guitar, and many pro players have since found a use for the diminutive darling. The model now comes in a variety of timber options for back-and-sides woods, including rosewood, mahogany, koa, maple, and the gorgeous figured bubinga of this example (see back view, center).*

Taylor ad 1990 (*above*) *A promo emphasizing the electric-like playability of Taylor necks.*

money made. Along with building guitars, the Dream workshop also sold supplies such as tuning machines, binding, fret wire, and tonewoods. The Dream also had a repair shop that was run by Greg Deering, who would go on to found his own banjo-building company.

The Dream was at the center of San Diego's lutherie community by 1973, the year Bob Taylor and Kurt Listug started working there. Aspiring guitar-makers would stop by to pick up supplies and learn a few building or finishing techniques from Radding, who was always happy to pass on his knowledge. Guitar-makers James Goodall and Larry Breedlove, ukulele builder Tony Graziano, and banjo-maker Geoff Stelling are just a few of the luthiers who used to hang around the Dream, even though they never got benches at the shop.

Bob Taylor didn't really fit in socially at the Dream; he was a straight-laced, awkward teenager, while a lot of the crew were a few years older and seemed to be more interested in getting stoned than they were in making guitars. But Taylor impressed everyone with his abilities and his drive to learn more about building guitars. Within a few months Taylor was making more guitars than anyone else and was the major source of income for the shop. Sometime in early 1974 Taylor was

repairing a Guild G-37 for a friend, and after removing the neck decided that refitting the dovetail neck-joint would be too much bother. He cut the dovetail off the neck, glued the block of wood into the body, put some bolts in the heel, and bolted the neck to the body. Taylor had just made his first bolt-on neck.

In the autumn of 1974 Sam Radding decided to close the American Dream when he realized that although he loved to build guitars, he hated running a business. Most of the workers wanted to keep the company going, so Radding said that he would go camping for a week and when he came back he would entertain any and all offers to buy the business. Bob Taylor and his friend Jerry Pike put together an offer, as did Kurt Listug and his friend Steve Schemmer, who was working in the finishing department.

Listug spent a great deal of time researching his offer, and when it came time to present it to Radding, everyone agreed that it was the best of the bunch. Listug went to his father to borrow the money for the buyout, who spotted a major flaw in Kurt's business plan. Listug's father pointed out that his son and Schemmer didn't actually know how to build guitars – but he said that if they added a partner who *did* know how, he would loan Kurt the money. To that end, Listug approached Bob Taylor about joining them, and the young guitar-maker agreed.

chemmer each put up $3,500, and Taylor put up $3,000. They gave
ing to cover the cost of the tools and the outstanding debts. During
Taylor, Listug, and Schemmer discovered that, although they were
rican Dream guitar-making company, Gene Radding was keeping the
ail shop. So the three new partners called their new partnership the
Company, and on October 15th 1974 opened for business.

to build on Sam Radding's original concept and offer a wide range of
musicians and luthiers, so they continued to do repairs and sell parts
guitars. Listug discovered that Radding's 'independent contractor'
was of dubious legality, so he made salaried employees of the luthiers
The original crew consisted of Taylor, Listug, and Schemmer along
, Bob Huff, Tony Louscher, and Bob 'Moze' Mossay.

cial day at Westland was not an auspicious one. When the crew
, they discovered that during the night a major rainstorm had caused
f and the shop floor was under two or three inches of water. Instead
s everyone spent the day mopping up and trying to get their precious
p off the floor. But after the near-disaster was averted, they settled

in to their real work. The first order of business was to complete the outstanding
orders for American Dream guitars. The second was for the Westland crew to come
up with a name to put on the headstock of their guitars, since they couldn't use the
American Dream name anymore. After a number of meetings they settled on Taylor.
The new partners felt it sounded good, was relatively easy to inlay on a headstock,
and Bob Taylor was the only one of the three who could actually build a guitar.

The first Taylor guitars were built using Sam Radding's designs. There were three
basic styles: a jumbo, a dreadnought, and a shallow-bodied dreadnought that was
popular with local fingerpickers. Each guitar was made to order for the customer, so
there were no model numbers as such. But the jumbos were usually made of maple,
the dreadnoughts were made of Brazilian rosewood, and the shallow dreadnoughts
were usually made of walnut. The guitars were often very fancy, with lots of abalone
trim and intricate fretboard inlays.

The jumbos had an ornate 'mustache' shaped bridge that was designed by a local
musician named David Randle. The necks were attached with a complex T-shaped
joint that Radding had designed to be cut out on a table saw, and the headstock had
a distinctive three-scoop shape that later evolved into the modern Taylor shape.

**Taylor 25th Anniversary 1999
(*left*)** *This was a model offered in a
limited run of 500 to celebrate the
company's 25th birthday. Note the
elegant celebratory abalone inlay
between the 12th and 18th frets.*

**Taylor Pallet Guitar 2000 (*far
left*)** *In 1995, Bob Taylor made his
first Pallet guitar to prove that a guitar-
maker's skill plays a bigger part than
his materials in producing a toneful
instrument. Players and collectors
liked the idea, and a limited run of 25
guitars followed in 2000, again made
from rough 'pallet-grade' oak – but this
time with a fingerboard inlay of a
forklift truck.*

Taylor ad 1992 (*center*) *Promo
for an especially decorative trio of
Taylors.*

Over the next year Bob Taylor started working on refining Radding's designs, and developing methods for building guitars more efficiently. After hand cutting a number of Radding's T-block neck joints, Taylor switched to a bolt-on mortise and tenon joint. Up until then all of the guitars were built to order using a wide variety of cosmetic features, but now the company also began to standardize the line.

Once they'd produced some prototypes, the crew decided that the dreadnought with Brazilian rosewood back and sides, spruce top, white binding, abalone soundhole rosette, and diamond-shaped fretboard inlays had the best combination of features. They dubbed the new model the 815, but after developing a more comprehensive naming system a few weeks later, they changed the model designation to 810.

Under the new system the first digit of the three-digit model number would indicate the wood and level of ornamentation, the second digit would designate whether the guitar was a six-string (1) or a 12-string (5), and the third digit would designate the size. So the model number 855, for example, would be a rosewood back and sides (8), 12-string (5), jumbo (5), while the 810 was a rosewood back and sides (8), six-string (1), dreadnought (0). Guitars with cutaways were designated with a C suffix (815-C). During this time Taylor also worked out its first serial number

Taylor 514CE 1999 *Displayed for your pleasure, a cutaway grand auditorium-sized Taylor with onboard electronics and a solid cedar top.*

Taylor 310 1998 (near right) *This 300 series dreadnought model is made with solid spruce top and solid sapele back and sides, and has simple black plastic binding.*

Blur mid 1990s (*below*) *Singer
Damon Albarn struts the Glastonbury
Festival stage with his Taylor electro-
acoustic dreadnought.*

TAYLOR

system. Under the first system, the first digit of the five-digit serial number recorded the year in which the guitar was made, while the final four digits indicated where it fell in the total production.

Taylor started its serial numbers sequence with guitar number 10109 because the partners wanted their customers to think they had built more guitars than they really had. They also figured that when they were successful, their early guitars would be more valuable, and that they could just build their first guitars at a later date. In 1977 they dropped the first digit and started using a straightforward sequential system.

Taylor switched to a new nine-digit sequence in 1993 . The new number encoded the year, month, day, and where in that day's sequence the guitar stood. So a guitar with serial number 951016022 was made in 1995 (95) on October (10) 16th (16). The 0 after the 16 indicates the guitar is a 400 Series or lower, while a 1 in that position would indicate a guitar in the 500 series or above. The 22 shows that this particular instrument was the 22nd guitar started on that day. In 2000 Taylor changed the system again and started using an eleven-digit number, which added the complete year rather than just the last two digits.

In 1975 the Westland Music Company made 36 guitars, which brought in hardly enough money to support the three owners, let alone the rest of the workforce, so at the end of the year Taylor, Listug, and Schemmer laid everyone off. The partners realized that they would have to change the way they did business. Listug and Taylor felt that they had saturated the local market for custom-built guitars; if they wanted to grow, they would need to start selling wholesale to stores. Schemmer wasn't entirely convinced that was the direction in which they should go, but he went along with the majority opinion.

At the beginning of 1976 the company changed its name to Taylor Guitars, dropped the retail business, and Listug hit the road in an attempt to sign up dealers.

The traveling-salesman routine showed some early promise. Listug secured a few new accounts in the Los Angeles area, and the checks he brought back kept the struggling company going for a few more months. The new dealers liked the guitars that Taylor was building, but they wanted a broader line of instruments to sell. To fit the bill, Taylor introduced two new series in early 1977: the 900s, with birdseye maple back and sides, and the 700s, a cosmetically plainer version of the 800 series.

That same year they stopped using Brazilian rosewood and switched to East Indian Rosewood. Bob Taylor also redesigned his mortise and tenon bolt-on neck joint. On

Nanci Griffith c1995 (*below*)
Country-folkster Griffith – seen here on
stage with a sunburst-finished cutaway
jumbo – is a long-time Taylor player.

the new version, the heel of the guitar butts up against the body and is held in place by two bolts that extend through the neck block.

At about this time Taylor Guitars caught the eye of Paul Rothchild, a successful record producer who wanted to start a distribution company for high-end musical instruments. Rothchild had worked at Elektra Records in the 1960s, where he produced records for artists like Judy Collins, Phil Ochs, Fred Neil, Tom Paxton, and a host of other prominent folk acts. Rothchild had signed Paul Butterfield to the label, which is how he wound up running the mixing board at the 1965 Newport Folk Festival, when Bob Dylan famously played electric guitar for the first time in public. Rothchild also worked with The Doors, and pretty much knew everyone.

A reputation such as his attracted a wide range of makers, and when Rothchild Musical Instruments opened for business it was representing guitar-builders Alembic, Larrivée, Travis Bean, and Augustino LoPrinzi, as well as the pickup-maker Bartolini. Rothchild encouraged Taylor to make more new models; in 1978 it introduced the 500 series – with mahogany back and sides, rosewood fretboard, and black binding – and the 600 series – with dark-stained mahogany back and sides, ebony fretboard, and white binding. Taylor expanded its workforce to 11 in anticipation of the increased

sales promised by Rothchild, and in 1978 the company built 449 guitars, almost twice as many as it had made the year before. That same year Neil Young purchased an 855 at a shop in Northern California, making him the highest profile musician to play a Taylor up to that point.

Unfortunately, Rothchild wasn't able to translate his ability to sell music into an ability to sell guitars, and in 1979 Taylor terminated the deal. Once again Taylor had to lay off its entire workforce, leaving just the three partners to run the company and build all the guitars. It dropped the mahogany 600 series from the line at this time. As disappointing as the Rothchild experience was, it did yield a few benefits. Bob Taylor became friends with luthiers Jean Larrivée, Augustino LoPrinzi, and Rick Turner of Alembic, who would offer valuable advice and support during the company's difficult early years; and Kurt Listug learned the importance of keeping the company free of outside entanglements, along with the valuable lesson that knowing how to sell guitars was as important as knowing how to build them.

Over the next few years, Listug would load guitars into the trunk of his car and head out across America looking for new dealers, while Taylor and Schemmer stayed behind and built the instruments. Because there were only two full-time builders

making guitars, Bob Taylor began to devise new tools, jigs, and fixtures to make the construction process as efficient as possible. In 1981 Taylor took out a $30,000 bank loan to buy new equipment to put Bob's ideas into action. The new set-up reaped immediate rewards, as the production of the tiny shop more than doubled, from 100 guitars built in 1980 to 269 in 1981. That year Taylor reintroduced the 600 series, but this time it was made of maple instead of stained mahogany.

By 1982 Listug stopped working on guitars altogether and began to concentrate all his energies on selling them. To take his place in the workshop, the company hired a builder named Bob Miller. Although Listug was selling a number of guitars, he wasn't selling enough to pay the bills. To generate some cash, they arranged to sell 100 guitars to a large dealer in Texas at an extra discount, and used the money to finance one major cross-country selling trip for Listug.

From early October to late December '82 Listug lived out of his car and hotel rooms, opening accounts with dealers all over America. When he returned just before Christmas he had enough orders to keep the company going for a few more months.

In 1983 Bob Taylor and Kurt Listug bought out Steve Schemmer and renamed the new partnership Taylor-Listug, Inc. That year they also bought more machinery and

Taylor 455CE-12 2000 *Here's an electrified cutaway 12-string, with solid ovangkol back and sides.*

hired a few more workers. One of the workers was Tim Luranc, who had worked at Taylor on their first day of business, and was let go during their first lay-off. Following all of these changes, the company finally began to show a profit. At this time, Taylor also introduced a line of guitars made of koa. In a departure from standard naming, the spruce-top dreadnought was the K-10 and the koa top version the K-20.

In the early 1980s the airwaves were ruled by synth-pop bands like Duran Duran, heavy metal 'hair' bands like Quiet Riot and Ratt, and smooth singers like Lionel Richie and Billy Ocean, none of whom had any use for acoustic guitars. Consequently, 1984 was a terrible year for the acoustic business. It was Martin's worst year since the Great Depression, and smaller guitar companies could barely sell enough guitars to stay in business. Taylor, conversely, had been struggling their entire ten-year history, so it barely noticed the bad times of the electro-pop years.

In fact, 1984 turned out to be a very important year for them. In January, Taylor introduced the small-bodied Grand Concert to the line. The new model, which was given the '2' body size designation, was the first model designed by Bob Taylor from the ground up. (Taylor had inherited the dreadnought and jumbo body shapes from Sam Radding.) Taylor showed two versions of the new guitar at a trade show in

Taylor NS32-CE 2002 *This cutaway-body nylon-string electro has a solid spruce top and solid sapele back and sides. It features a slightly narrower neck than the traditional classical guitar to help its appeal to players more familiar with the neck widths of steel-string instruments .*

Taylor Big Baby 2000 (*left*) *If a little Baby is good, then a Big Baby has got to be better, right? In fact the ¹⁵/₁₆ths sized dreadnought has proved popular – if not quite so much as its little sister.*

Taylor catalog 2003 (*above*) *Babies strum the Baby. Its shorter scale "makes it ideal for high-strung tunings and mandolin-like effects."*

California – a 512 in mahogany and an 812 in rosewood – but also offered the new size in the 600, 700, 900, and Koa series as well.

At that same trade show, Taylor exhibited a maple 610 that was stained bright blue, the result of an order by McCabe's Guitar Shop in Santa Monica for a guitar that was visually exciting but that wasn't loaded down with abalone trim. Larry Breedlove, who had joined the Taylor crew in early 1983, developed the method for finishing the guitar with a translucent stain that let the figure of the maple show through. The blue guitar caught the eye of Glenn Wetterlund, who worked at Podium Music, a Taylor dealer in Minneapolis. Wetterlund had just rented a Taylor 555 12-string to Prince, who was working on his follow-up to the hugely popular *Purple Rain*.

Listug and Wetterlund decided to make a purple jumbo 12-string on spec, just to see if Prince would like it. Since Prince refused to play an instrument with a visible logo, Taylor had to leave their logo off the headstock; but when the artist bought the guitar and used it in the video for 'Raspberry Beret,' that small indignity was forgotten.

Prince's purple Taylor sparked a mini-fad for colored-finish guitars. Over the next couple of years the company received orders for a number of custom guitars from celebrities, including one for a green dreadnought for Jeff Cook of the band Alabama,

and another for a pair of guitars for Billy Idol and his guitarist Steve Stevens. Taylor added the color-finished guitars to the line as the Artist Series. The guitars had maple back and sides, maple necks and spruce tops, and came in red, blue, green, and black. The soundhole decoration was a multicolored flame pattern that was hand painted by Larry Breedlove. The novelty of the brightly colored guitars soon wore off and the Artist Series ended in 1989, but it had helped Taylor broaden their reputation.

In 1986 Taylor introduced the Dan Crary Signature Model, its first artist designed guitar. Crary was an influential bluegrass flatpicker who wanted an instrument with a bright, clear tone that was easy to record in the studio and sounded good in front of a microphone on stage. That same year it also started offering the 900 series in rosewood as well as maple. Sales of the new version quickly outpaced the older one, and a few years later the maple 900s were dropped.

Taylor sales increased so much that in 1987 it moved out of the 1,500-square-foot building in Lemon Grove that Listug and Taylor had occupied since 1974. There were now a dozen workers building more than 800 guitars a year, and the old shop was just too small to accommodate everyone. In July it moved to a new 4,700-square-foot factory in Santee, California. The last guitar built in Lemon Grove was a 510-C (serial

Taylor catalog 2003 *The promo spread for the spruce or cedar and mahogany 500 series.*

Taylor Baby 305GB 2002 (*left*) *A recent example of the ever popular short-scale Baby guitar.*

Taylor 512 1998 (*right*) *Formerly available in this purely acoustic, non-cutaway model, Taylor's grand concert-sized guitar with spruce top and mahogany back and sides is now made only in a cutaway electro format, following overwhelming demand for that type of instrument.*

number 5300), which was transferred to the new facility and strung up there. Kurt Listug relinquished his role as salesman in 1988 when he hired T.J. Baden to become the company's first sales rep. From then on Listug devoted his efforts to running the business end of the company, which allowed Bob Taylor the time and the freedom to design and build the new tools he needed to make guitars – which demanded most of his efforts after the move.

In 1989 Bob bought his first Fadal, a computer numeric control (CNC) machine. At first he used it to shape and contour fretboards, but he soon figured out how to use it to make bridges, cut fret slots, and carve necks. Other luthiers sniffed at the process at the time, saying that Taylor guitars were made by robots instead of humans. But when they saw how quickly and precisely the CNC machine fabricated parts, they stopped griping and made the trek to Santee, where Bob Taylor was happy to show them how it all worked. Today, nearly every guitar-maker who builds more than a handful of instruments a year either has a CNC machine of their own, or contracts to have parts made on someone else's.

The Taylor crew had grown to 38 workers, who were making more than 2,000 guitars a year, and they soon found that they were turning out instruments faster than

their case suppliers could get cases to them. The shipping department had a perennial backlog of caseless guitars, so in 1989 Bob Taylor designed and started building his own cases. The first version had a brown exterior with maroon velvet lining, which guitarists quickly dubbed the 'pink-poodle plush lining.' A few years later, when the supply of the velvet lining dried up, Taylor had to switch to a black plush lining, which was soon called the 'monkey-fur lining.'

By 1990 the new Taylor factory was running smoothly. After two years of development, the company introduced the Leo Kottke Signature Model 12-string. The mahogany jumbo featured a Selmer-style cutaway and, in a throwback to the Stella 12-string of the 1930s, was designed to be tuned down in pitch to C-sharp. The style proved to be so popular that in 1996 Taylor introduced a six-string version. The 400 series – the only sub-$1,000 all-solid-wood guitar built in America at the time of its debut – was offered in 1991, available in mahogany (410, 412) and rosewood (420, 422). To keep costs down, the 400s had a satin finish and a pinless bridge.

The new series helped boost Taylor's sales to over 4,800 instruments a year, and the company had to add a late shift of workers to fulfill the demand. Although it had just moved in, Taylor was already outgrowing its new factory. In August 1992 the

Taylor 610CE-LTD 2002 (right) *A spruce-topped, maple-bodied dreadnought in the popular cutaway electro format.*

Taylor 315CE 2002 *A super-jumbo cutaway electro built using Taylor's 'first rung' woods.*

Taylor 310 2003 (left) *The entry-level spruce and sapele dread continues to be a popular model.*

operation moved into a new 25,000-square-foot facility in El Cajon. The new building was completely designed by Bob Taylor, down to the placement of the electrical outlets, the size of the offices, and the width of the doors. Just as they did when they moved from Lemon Grove to Santee, Taylor completed a guitar in the old factory, in this case a 712 (serial number 16250), and restrung it in the new factory.

The Taylor crew quickly settled into the new facility, and Bob Taylor began to renew his efforts on some projects that he had been unable to complete while overseeing the building of the new factory. These included collaboration with the innovative luthier Steve Klein on an acoustic bass; work on a new guitar model that would become the Grand Auditorium; and the invention of a new method of curing the finishes on guitars, using ultra-violet light.

Meanwhile, Listug worked with an advertising firm to create a series of ads called 'Trees,' a major departure from the usual way acoustic guitars were promoted in print. Instead of showing photos of guitars, or people posing with them, the ads pictured forests and trees – and became a notable Taylor image. In 1993, declining sales of the 12-string models prompted Taylor to drop all of the dreadnought models from the line, along with the maple 655 and the fancy 955. It also dropped the koa guitars from

the line because of the scarcity of the Hawaiian hardwood. Over the next few years it could only get enough koa to make an occasional limited-production series.

Taylor released the Grand Auditorium in 1994 as a limited edition to commemorate the company's 20th anniversary. Two models were offered, the XX-RS, which had rosewood back and sides with a spruce top, and the XX-GA, with mahogany back and sides and a cedar top. The 20th anniversary guitars sold out so quickly that the following year Taylor offered six limited-edition variations of the grand auditorium body shape; the GA-BE (Brazilian rosewood topped with Englemann spruce), the GA-WS (walnut and spruce), the GA-KC (koa and cedar), the GA-KS (koa and spruce), the GA-RS (Indian rosewood and spruce), and the GA-MC (mahogany and cedar).

The variety of styles not only allowed the company to introduce the grand auditorium body shape in a number of price ranges, it gave it a chance to experiment with different wood combinations to see which might appeal to guitarists. In 1996 Taylor added the grand auditorium to the standard line. Unlike the limited editions, which were all non-cutaways, most of the new versions of the standard grand auditoriums came with cutaways. The only exception was the PS-14, part of the new Presentation Series, which, along with the grand auditorium, included the PS-10, the

Dixie Chicks 2001 (above)
Emily Robison of the outspoken new-country trio hits the stage with her Taylor 714C.

Taylor ad 2003 (left) *From the popular 'Maniac singing through screen door' advertising campaign, here is a set of promo pages for the maple-bodied 600 Series.*

Taylor 614CE 2002 (right)
Here's a maple-bodied jumbo with striking cherry red sunburst finish, gold-plated hardware, and abalone soundhole inlay.

PS-12, and the PS-15. All four models featured Brazilian rosewood back and sides, abalone trim, and a tree-of-life fretboard inlay.

The long-mooted acoustic bass – based in part on designs of the innovative luthier Steve Klein – was introduced in 1995. It was the largest instrument in the Taylor line, but its designers were able to use some of the structural ideas on their smallest guitar, which arrived the following year. The Baby was an inexpensive ¾-size guitar with laminated back and sides and solid spruce top. Bob Taylor initially designed it as a children's guitar. To everyone's surprise, adults embraced it as the ideal travel guitar. The Baby was so popular that it was soon offered with a wide variety of veneer choices for the back and sides, include bubinga, koa, maple, and Indian rosewood.

By the end of 1996, Taylor had 167 employees on the payroll who built just over 15,000 guitars, securing the company as one of the most successful US makers.

Over the next couple of years, Bob Taylor devoted his time to refining the line of guitars. All the headstock shapes were redesigned to have slightly curved sides, while the dreadnoughts were given a slightly rounder, less boxy look. In 1997 the company released the Cujo model, a limited-edition guitar made from the wood of a walnut tree that appeared in a scene from the movie based on Stephen King's book of the same

name. Also in '97, Taylor started to install Fishman pickups with side-mounted controls in every guitar made with a cutaway.

1998 was a particularly busy year. At a US trade show in January Taylor introduced the 300 series, made from sapele, an African wood that was similar in tone and appearance to mahogany; reintroduced a series of Koa guitars; and – in a nod to their earliest days – started making guitars out of walnut again. Many instruments in the standard line were also reworked. The 400 series now featured a gloss top with satin-finish back and sides (the wood in the back and sides was also switched from mahogany to ovangkol). The 700 series had the tops changed from spruce to cedar, and the company reintroduced colored finishes such as red, purple, and blue on the 600 series. At the end of the year the Taylor catalog carried 61 different models, and the company employed 250 workers who produced 21,000 instruments.

Following his changes to headstocks and body shapes, Bob Taylor also spent a great of deal of time completely redesigning the necks and neck-joints on his guitars. The new neck system, dubbed New-Tech (NT), featured a stacked heel and headstock that are grafted on using a complex finger joint. In addition, the fretboard extension is actually inlaid into the top, rather than glued to the top in the traditional

Taylor catalog 2003 (above) A promo for the full 300 Series (top), and a further spread from the same catalog (above) where Taylor sums up the aim of guitar-makers from Torres to today: "It's man in concert with machine."

Taylor 914CE 2003 (right) The lavish 900 Series features 'master grade' spruce tops, deluxe rosewood back and sides, abalone inlays and colored purfling at the body edges.

Taylor custom double-neck 2003 (far right) Built for Richie Sambora and designed to match his regular koa-body signature model.

style. This new method allows for minute neck adjustments and quick neck resets. Bob Taylor was granted a patent on the NT neck in 2000, and it's the method of neck join still in use by Taylor at the time of writing.

Taylor Guitars celebrated its 25th anniversary in 1999 with the introduction of two limited-edition models. The XXV-DR dreadnought and the XXV-GA grand auditorium both featured figured sapele sides and back, a spruce top, and custom fretboard inlays. Taylor also came up with a series of commemorative editions based on some standard-line models, including small runs of mahogany-top 300s, Indian rosewood 400s, abalone-trimmed 500s and 600s, and Brazilian rosewood 700s and 800s.

Taylor Guitars entered the new millennium in excellent shape. It now had more than 375 employees and was producing almost 50,000 guitars a year. The Baby model was selling so well the company had to open a new facility devoted to building just that one instrument. It also introduced a larger version of the guitar, a 15/16-size dreadnought it dubbed the Big Baby, and released a number of limited edition signature models, featuring guitars built with the input of artists Clint Black, Jewel, Kenny Loggins, Richie Sambora (who also had a custom-order Taylor double-neck acoustic), blues legend John Cephas, and fingerpickers Doyle Dykes and Chris Proctor.

The Doyle Dykes model, a maple-bodied cutaway grand auditorium, was the only model to be added to the permanent line.

The Gallery Series was also introduced in 2000. The batch for that year featured an underwater theme and included the GSST, a grand auditorium with sea-turtle inlays in the fretboard and jellyfish inlaid on the back; the GSGW, which had gray whale fretboard inlays; and the GSLJ, a blue dreadnought with multicolored koi inlaid in the fretboard and top. In 2001 Taylor introduced a sunburst finish as an option.

Resolutely a steel-string builder up to this point, Taylor introduced a series of nylon-string guitars in 2002. They were based on the grand concert body, but were as deep as a dreadnought. The new guitars, which had radiused fretboards like a steel-string, a cutaway, and onboard electronics, were designed to appeal to players who wanted the mellow nylon-string tone, but didn't want to adjust to the feel of a traditional classical guitar.

The models included the sapele and spruce NS-32ce, ovangkol and spruce NS-42ce, mahogany and cedar NS-52ce, maple and Englemann spruce NS-62ce, and the Indian rosewood and cedar NS-72ce. Later in '02 came the NS-64 and the NS-74, limited-edition non-cutaway grand auditorium nylon-string guitars.

Taylor catalog 2005 (*right*) *A page featuring several examples from the 2005 Fall Limiteds, one of Taylor's seasonal limited-edition collections.*

Taylor W65ce 2005 (*left*) *Some occasionally spectacular timber was used for the bodies of the Walnut series that ran from 1998 to 2006.*

Taylor XXX-MC 2004 (*center*) *This special 30th anniversary model had a cedar top and mahogany body.*

Taylor 816ce 2008 (*far right*) *Taylor's model system identifies this as a series 800 (8), six-string (1), Grand Symphony body size (6), with cutaway body (c) and onboard electronics (e).*

Limited to an edition of 400, the Liberty Tree guitar of 2000 was made from the wood of a tulip poplar tree related to the Revolutionary War. There were enough smaller pieces left over for Taylor also to build a few limited-edition Baby models.

One of Taylor's biggest innovations for 2003 was the introduction of the Expression System pickup, which was designed in-house over a three year period by long-time employees Bob Hosler, Matt Guzetta, and David Judd, and featured a preamp that was designed by the audio pioneer Rupert Neve. It combined two body sensors that were affixed under the top in carefully chosen spots, and a string sensor set underneath the fretboard. Around the same time, Taylor introduced a few models that kickstarted the inexpensive 100 and 200 Series.

Taylor's 30th anniversary guitars of 2004 introduced a new shorter scale option, 24⅞" rather than Taylor's regular 25½, and two years later the new Grand Symphony (GS) body shape appeared, designed by Taylor, Larry Breedlove, and Ed Granero and sitting between the existing Grand Auditorium and Dreadnought shapes. There was a shortlived sub-brand, R.Taylor, intended to produce high-end boutique-style guitars within the Taylor factory, running from 2006 to 2011.

A new take on Taylor's successful Baby models appeared in 2010, the GS Mini, a three-quarter size guitar, the first model designed from the ground up to be manufactured in Taylor's Tecate plant in Mexico. Around this time, Bob Taylor began to wonder about his place in the future of his company, and as a result he hired Andy Powers. Taylor was looking not only for someone who could take over guitar design duties from longterm Taylor people such as Larry Breedlove (who was due to retire), but also for someone who could lead the firm into its future development. Powers was a musician and a respected small-shop guitar builder with a strong pro clientele. He set to work redesigning the Taylor lines and introduced new ideas. Powers said in Taylor's *Wood & Steel* magazine: "I still want to build guitars that are going to allow musicians, whether they know three chords or are reinventing the repertoire, to contribute to their artistic vision. Only it's on a far broader platform now."

Bob Taylor and Kurt Listug started with a tiny custom guitar shop in 1974, and over the course of several decades turned it into one of the largest and most successful guitar factories in America. They did it by combining Bob Taylor's desire to build guitars with Kurt Listug's drive to sell them. Taylor has sold many tens of thousands of guitars over the years, so it has certainly proved its value to the guitar-playing public. But Bob Taylor's real legacy might be in the way he introduced late 20th century building techniques to an industry still doing things in a way that would have been more or less familiar to 19th century luthiers.

Taylor magazine 2010 (*left*) The cover of the firm's promo magazine features Steven Curtis Chapman's 714-based signature model.

Taylor 522 12-fret 2015 (*left*) This 12-fret version of the Grand Concert style was introduced in 2009.

Taylor BTO Jumbo 2014 (*center*) Taylor called its custom shop the Build To Order (BTO) program, and this highly customized model is a good example of its work.

Taylor 914ce 2015 (*right*) Andy Powers's redesign of the 900 series included an ebony armrest-bevel.

Smashing Pumpkins 2000 (*opposite*) Noise merchant Billy Corgan reaches for the dusty end of a Taylor fingerboard.

Andy Powers (*right*) *At the same time as Taylor's 40th anniversary in 2014, Andy Powers began redesigning the company's entire line.*

TORRES

Every classical guitar in use today owes something to the work of Antonio de Torres, a Spanish guitar-maker who lived in poverty all his life and never achieved more than local renown.

Torres did not invent anything: he merely brought together all the best ideas and practices of his day to create an instrument with unprecedented musical qualities. The fundamentals of the Torres design have not altered in 150 years, making him a figure of comparable importance to Stradivarius in the world of the violin.

Born in Almería, in the south of Spain, in 1817, Antonio de Torres worked first as a carpenter, taking up guitar-making professionally only in the 1850s. He was lucky to attract a number of celebrated clients, including Julián Arcas and Francisco Tárrega, the first great name of the classical instrument, who played a Torres guitar constantly for 20 years.

In 1870, Torres abandoned guitar-making for five years, then started again in what is called his second epoch, continuing until his death in 1892. According to José Romanillos, author of the standard biography of Torres, he built 320 guitars in his lifetime, of which 88 are known to exist.

The most fundamental change Torres made to the guitar was to establish a larger body size. Torres guitars have soundboards up to 20 per cent bigger than those of earlier instruments. He distributed the extra area across the soundboard, establishing the harmonious figure-of-eight shape always associated with the classical instrument. He also kept decoration to a minimum, establishing an austere style for an instrument that had sometimes been wildly decorated in the past.

Underneath the soundboard, usually slightly arched, he used a system of fan-strutting for support. The strings, meanwhile, were anchored to a bridge with a separate adjustable bone saddle. Again, not a new idea, but the best available practice at the time. Only one of his design decisions has not carried through to the present: he often used a tornavoz, a brass cylinder of the same diameter as the sound hole, mounted inside it and intended to funnel vibrations out from the guitar's body. They have not been used since the 1930s.

Torres's recipe was successful in his own time, with both classical and flamenco

players, and close study of the guitars has enriched the designs and techniques of many subsequent guitar-makers, including Manuel Ramírez, Santos Hernández, Enrique García, Francisco Simplicio, Hermann Hauser I, Ignacio Fleta, and José Romanillos. But the instruments have also been the subject of blatant counterfeiting as their value has grown.

T R A U G O T T

Working alone in his shop in Santa Cruz, California, Jeff Traugott has become one of the star luthiers of our time. Traugott started building guitars in the early 1980s, and went to work for the Santa Cruz Guitar Co. in 1986. After establishing his own independent shop in 1991, Traugott designed a line of steel-string flat-tops that is based on grand concert to grand auditorium sizes. He is known for using some of the highest-quality woods available, often including rare Brazilian rosewood. As such, he has been at the forefront of a trend that has focused on ultra-clean designs with almost austere appointments, which beg comparison with some of the finest classical guitars. Traugott has also been known for a willingness to experiment with new ideas. He has built several seven and even eight-string guitars featuring fanned

Torres 1860 (*near right*) An early example from the father of the modern classical guitar, this one with a spruce top, four-piece cypress back, and cypress sides.

Torres 1882 (*far right*) This spruce-topped instrument was built at Torres's second workshop during what is called his 'second epoch' of guitar-making. The shop was at 23 Calle Real in Almeria, Spain.

Novax frets, and has offered a thin-bodied acoustic-electric model. Players of Traugott guitars include Alex de Grassi, Martin Simpson, and Lyle Workman. Traugott's enormous success and his dedication to a small production (about 20 annually) has kept his instruments very exclusive. With a waiting list growing to be several years long, in 2017 Traugott explained that his work would not speed up to meet demand.

T U R N E R

Luthier Rick Turner can easily claim one of the more colorful resumés in the guitar business. He played guitar with folk-duo Ian & Sylvia during the 1960s, then went on to co-found Alembic Guitars in 1970. After leaving Alembic in 1978, Turner began custom-building guitars under his own name, most significantly designing an electric guitar (now called the Model 1) for Fleetwood Mac frontman Lindsey Buckingham, who continues to be one of Turner's most visible players.

After several years of running a Los Angeles guitar repair shop, Turner came up with his semi-hollow, acoustic-electric Renaissance design, which is now available in many configurations, including steel-string, nylon-string, 12-string, and bass versions. During this time, Turner also co-founded Highlander Pickups, a company he left in

1995. In addition to manufacturing Renaissance guitars in his current shop in Santa Cruz, California, Turner began building custom acoustic guitars in the mid 1990s. These feature radical design ideas such as floating neck joints, flying buttress braces, and graphite reinforcements, and are available in very limited quantities. One of Turner's acoustics was used by guitarist Henry Kaiser to record an album of guitar music in Antarctica in 2001. In 2003, Turner began a partnership with Seymour Duncan pickups, designing acoustic amplification products under the D-TAR name.

V A N D E N

Scottish luthier Mike Vanden builds high-class archtop guitars with superb timber and elaborate inlays. His prime model is the one originally built for British jazz guitarist Martin Taylor, fitted with Vanden's own Mimesis floating pickup system.

Distinctive among his other models is the Cadenza, which comes with or without a cutaway and is intended even more specifically as an acoustic instrument. Tops are hand-carved from sitka spruce and the maple necks are graphite-reinforced. Vanden's process of hand-building his guitars allows for the player's personal requirements and specifications to be incoporated.

Vega Cremona 1932 (*right*)
This unusual archtop – with a flat-top-styled pin bridge – was the top model in Vega's line at the time. At $220 it cost just $55 less than Gibson's L-5, but it used a pressed rather than carved arched top. The strange twin pickguards seen here appear to be later additions.

Vanden c1995 *This large-bodied archtop is in Vanden's earlier, more traditional style. Noteworthy are the floating Mimesis pickup (mounted on the pickguard), the distinctive bronze-to-gold sunburst finish, and the highly figured flamed maple of the guitar's back (smaller picture, above).*

V E G A

With a reputation based on its banjos, Boston's Vega company nevertheless had its roots in guitars – and during the early days of the company, at least, it produced some impressive instruments.

The original company was founded in 1881 by Swedish cabinetmaker Julius Nelson and two former employees of luthier Pehr Anderberg named Sunderberg and Swenson. (Anderberg was ex-C. Bruno, and later at Haynes). Guitar production began in 1889. Julius and brother Carl took over control and created the Vega company in 1903, keeping the original partners as employees.

Vega is a bright star, first photographed by astronomers in 1850. This heavenly body may be the origin of the brand's star logo, although it was common on other guitars, too. Whatever the reasons for its logo, Vega produced standard, concert, and grand concert flat-tops, some with stunning, pearl-encrusted, presentation-grade decoration and scalloped bracing. These appear to be mainly intended for gut strings.

In 1903 or '04 Vega added banjo manufacturing with the purchase of A.C. Fairbanks & Company. Vega's general manager David L. Day joined Frederick J. Bacon to form Bacon & Day banjos and guitars in 1921. During the banjo boom of the 1920s

Vega's focus was more on banjos and mandolins, and guitars became considerably plainer, made of mahogany, rosewood or flamed maple and available in an extra-large grand concert size. Engraved diamonds were about as fancy as it got. By now, the guitars were designed for steel strings. In 1925 the company's flat-top guitars (and banjos) began to be called Vegaphone.

The founder's son, William W. Nelson, joined Vega in 1923 and became president in 1932. With the Depression, guitars resumed a more prominent role and Vega expanded into distributing guitars by other makers, including Harmony. Its instruments were still relatively unadorned, and by the early 1930s Vega was offering an all-mahogany flat-top and three archtops, including an auditorium-sized roundhole and a model with f-holes on the waist, and all now with pickguards.

Vega also produced a line of budget flat-tops called Odell (after a Boston music publisher). In 1933 Vega introduced a new Vegaphone line of professional-grade 16⅛" carved spruce and maple archtops with f-holes on the lower bout, steel reinforced necks, fancy pearl inlays (some engraved), and gold hardware on the better models. At this time a few upscale carved-top guitars were even built with bodies obtained from Epiphone. These guitars were of very high quality in terms of both sound and

Vega c1930s (*near right*) This flat-top with a black finish has approximately the same body shape as 'L'-size Gibson flat-tops of the same time. A label inside says it was made by Vega in Boston, Massachusetts.

Vega Custom c1936 (*left*) This ornately decorated flat-top might have been a custom-order instrument, as it does not appear in any Vega catalogs of the time. The inlays are similar to those applied to high-end Vega banjos of the 1930s.

Vega ad 1976 (*above*) Highlighted here are dreadnoughts made during the time that Martin owned the brand.

workmanship. In the mid 1930s Vega began to market some guitars made for them by other manufacturers, including Regal archtops and, conversely, began to provide guitars to other manufacturers, including Weymann & Son in Philadelphia. Vega introduced its first electrified archtops in 1936.

Following World War II, Vega picked up where it left off, with both flat-tops and archtops, although much of its early-1950s focus was on electrics. Some Vegas were made using bodies sourced from Harmony. With the folk revival of the late 1950s Vega found renewed success and returned to its acoustic roots, although during the mid 1960s the company emphasized its banjo line.

Guitars made during this period were made in natural-finished spruce and either mahogany or rosewood grand concerts ('folk') or dreadnoughts, and had clearly been conceived in a Martin mode.

Vega continued on through the 1960s, but with a small and ageing staff, and with some acoustics sourced from Harmony. In 1968 Vega introduced its Artist Grand dreadnought, heavily influenced by Guild, and was still advertising it in early 1970, but was clearly defensive about competition from abroad.

With an eye on the banjo operation, Martin purchased Vega on May 15th 1970

and closed down the guitar division. Some Vega guitars were produced for Martin at its Swedish Levin factory in the early 1970s before that operation closed due to labor problems, after which limited production was shifted to The Netherlands. In 1980 Martin sold the Vega name to Sun Pyo Hong of the Galaxie Trading Corporation in Korea, which used the Vega brand on instruments made in that country.

WASHBURN
(AND LYON & HEALY)

Of all the guitar brands in the long story of the American guitar, none has a more varied and puzzling history than that of Washburn and its parent company, Lyon & Healy. George Washburn Lyon, born in 1820, was already a long-time employee of the Oliver Ditson Company of Boston when he was teamed with Patrick Healy, an energetic Irishman 20 years his junior, and sent to Chicago in 1864 to open a Ditson branch out west. Ditson was primarily a music publisher and retailer, but also sold a wide range of musical instruments. Lyon & Healy followed the proven business model.

The combination of Lyon's experience, Healy's drive, and Chicago's rapid growth at the hub of the Midwestern US resulted in Lyon & Healy soon surpassing the Ditson

Washburn Style A c1928 (left) *This guitar is from the end of the Lyon & Healy era, which ran from the 1880s until the end of the 1920s. The model was usually referred to as the Deluxe Style 5238, but this is stamped "Style A" on the back of the headstock.*

Washburn Style 108 c1892 (far left) *A beautiful Chicago-built Lyon & Healy Washburn from the end of the 19th century.*

Washburn 'Bell' Style 5271 c1929 (above) *The Lyon & Healy catalog described the expensive $195 Bell designed for the player "who feels that he must have the very best guitar that money can buy." The instrument was made only for about four years.*

company, partly by buying out other music firms in Chicago. By the 1890s Lyon & Healy had become one of the largest music houses in the world, selling everything from tin whistles to grand pianos and an equally wide range of sheet music. The company certainly lived up to its motto: "Everything in Music."

By the early 1880s the firm had opened a factory. A line of guitars was the first priority, soon to be followed by mandolins, zithers, and banjos. Lyon was an accomplished musician with a penchant for working on musical instruments, so the trademark chosen for these new instruments was a guitar encircled by a belt bearing the name George Washburn.

Lyon was in his sixties by the time the first Washburn guitars were marketed, and there's no doubt that they were factory instruments from the beginning. Back then people weren't wary of factory-made instruments, and believed that mass-production by machinery was superior to some lowly craftsman building a guitar by hand.

The first Washburn guitars were made of rosewood and spruce in shapes much like Martin's, with a narrow waist and small upper bout. The headstock and bridge were simple rectangular shapes, again probably owing to Martin's influence. While Washburn's catalog showed many pages of highly decorated guitars, its success

depended upon creating demand for plain, inexpensive instruments bearing a brand associated with expensive models endorsed by well-known artists. Most of the Washburns sold were moderately-priced guitars with simple top bracing barely evolved beyond rudimentary ladder bracing, and construction quality far below that of Martin. Lyon & Healy sold quite a high percentage of its lower Washburn models through mail-order catalogs, as well as later budget brands such as Lakewood and American Conservatory.

By 1889 Washburn had an impressive catalog, complete with photos of artists giving lavish praise for the guitars. Five sizes were offered, ¾ and 1 through 4, with size 4 both wider and deeper than Martin's 00. The grade number followed the size, with model 308 the top of the line at $100, roughly equivalent to Martin's Style 42, although the Washburn sported more inlays, especially on the neck. The catalog from 1892 offered an even fancier style 9, with the price for the Grand Concert Model 309 at $155. Unlike the small squiggles of pearl on the fretboard of Model 308, style 9 had a continuous pattern of engraved pearl and silver wire running from the soundhole to the nut. Later top Washburn models had fingerboards completely covered in mother-of-pearl, with either engraved designs or inlays of colorful abalone inset as position

Washburn ad 1978 *A happy customer of the revitalized Washburn operation cradles his vintage-styled dreadnought with its solid spruce top and herringbone binding.*

Washburn Deluxe Style 5238 c1930 (left) *An elaborately decorated 000-sized flat-top.*

Washburn Style 5244 c1930 (right) *A sunburst-finish jumbo from the brand's Tonk Bros era, with 14 frets clear of the body. A label inside reveals that the guitar was originally sold by a "band and orchestra instruments" store in Los Angeles.*

markers. Washburn mandolins and banjos of the period had similar decoration. There were other fretted instrument manufacturers in the US at the time, all larger than Martin, but when it came to lavish decoration Washburn made its competitors look downright frumpy. The George Washburn brand continued for decades, but the man behind the name retired in 1889 and died five years later.

Lyon & Healy rarely kept its styles of decoration or Washburn model nomenclature the same from one catalog to the next, and the numbering system is confusing to say the least. But the guitars remained largely the same structurally until around World War I, when the line was simplified and X-bracing of the tops became more common. And despite all the company's wild advertising claims and inlaid finery, Washburn guitars offered few innovations beyond the abundance of glitter.

An exception was the Washburn Contra Bass guitar that appeared in the 1889 catalog, indicating that Lyon & Healy saw the eventual need for a large guitar as the bass voice in groups of mandolins, banjos, or even other guitars. At 15" wide, 5" deep, and with steel strings tuned down to C over a 27½" scale, this model sounded

a lot like a modern-day baritone guitar. Washburn made a number of attempts to market an oversized steel-string model as a 'bass guitar' for accompaniment, including the bizarre College Line Monster Bass that measured over 22" across the lower bout. It shows Lyon & Healy ahead of the steel-string jumbo guitar craze that followed in the 1930s – even if none of these early models sold well.

During World War I, Lyon & Healy resorted to price reductions to bolster sales, and Washburn's model line-up was severely curtailed after the war, with the fancy models dropped from the catalog. Thanks to X-braced tops, however, these later Washburns are superior-sounding guitars to the earlier versions, and the top-of-the-line Model 2175 Grand Concert could hold its own with most guitars of the era. With multiple rows of herringbone marquetry, lots of binding, and inlays on the headstock, fretboard, and bridge tips, it was hardly a plain guitar.

In the 1920s, Washburns were simplified even further and styles were assigned letters A to G, with lower models only available in mahogany. The design of the bridge was altered with a slight upward curve on the lower edge of the tips, and is now

Washburn Style 5257 c1930s
(**left**) *This natural-topped jumbo produced during the Tonk Bros years carries a Washburn label that reads: "Made of choicest materials by workmen of exceptional skill, knowledge & experience."*

John Hiatt 1987 (above) *The rootsy singer-songwriter pictured here with his Washburn EA-40.*

Washburn EA40 1990 (right) *A contemporary styled acoustic-electric from the revived Washburn brand.*

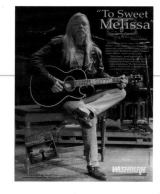

known as the 'smile bridge.' The most expensive A (later called the Deluxe) models had gold-leaf stenciling on the face, a curious mix of an old-world design on what was otherwise a modern and rather plain instrument. Among all the 12-fret Washburns, however, these 1920s examples are generally considered to sound better than the models that preceded them, partly because most of the newer versions were intended for steel strings.

Washburn wasn't finished taking odd ideas to market, and a series of bell-shaped guitars were offered in the mid 1920s, with appointments identical to the Deluxe. Since they were not only odd but also more expensive than the standard model, few were sold. Meanwhile, Patrick Healy had died in 1905, and since then the firm had been managed by a succession of his sons and captains who had learned the business from him. In the mid 1920s, however, Raymond Durham took the helm and Lyon & Healy went through a series of dramatic changes that ended with Chicago wholesaling powerhouse Tonk Bros owning Lyon & Healy, including rights to the Washburn trademark. Tonk continued to market Washburns, but the instruments

were made by Regal (see separate entry), another big Chicago manufacturer formerly owned by Lyon & Healy. Judging by how few Washburns from the 1920s are seen today, Lyon & Healy probably had good reason to sell the factory in 1928. As it turned out, many changes converged in the next few years to bring the once-mighty Washburn trademark to its knees. The most devastating was the Great Depression, which reduced Gibson to a wooden-toy maker for a while in the early 1930s.

Another change was the new fashion in larger flat-top guitars with 14 frets clear of the body. Tonk Bros responded with some poorly-selling models, including 1937's Solo Deluxe with art deco headstock inlays, but Tonk's attempts at marketing Washburn archtop models were feeble at best. Washburns were little more than standard Regal models with a different logo on the headstock and a 'Washburn by Tonk Bros' label. The once-proud Washburn trademark was allowed to fade away when World War II put an end to production.

Decades later, the Washburn trademark was revived in 1974 by Beckman Musical Instruments of Los Angeles, who published a catalog depicting acoustic guitars,

Lucinda Williams 2000
(*below*) *The alt-country artist backs her evocative smokey drawl with a contemporary Washburn.*

Washburn D-31S 1980 (*left*)
The Japanese-made 'Southern Jumbo Dreadnought.'

Washburn ad 1990 *Washburn evokes its past ("since 1876") to support the guitars it makes today.*

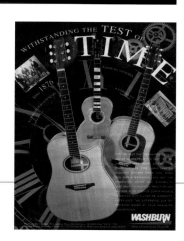

mandolins, and banjos with the still-familiar Washburn logo from the 1930s. Any resemblance to original Washburns stopped at the headstock, however, for all models were made in Japan and were similar to other imports of the period.

Beckman soon found more compelling music business, and the Washburn trademark and all inventory was sold to a small Chicago company called Fretted Industries. The new owners of Washburn, Rick Johnstone and Rudy Schlacher, wasted no time in expanding the line of imports to include classical guitars, as well as upgrading the banjo and mandolin lines. Innovative solidbody electric guitars were especially important to the new Washburn.

In 1980 the most influential guitar design of Washburn's new era was unveiled: the Festival Series cutaway flat-tops. With thin bodies, piezo bridge pickups, and onboard preamp and controls, these models quickly set the style for plugged-in acoustic guitars for stage use. In 1987, a new full-bodied flat-top with extra-deep cutaway was introduced featuring a neck with virtually no heel, allowing full access to the upper frets. Around this time Johnstone left the business and the name was changed to Washburn International, with Schlacher as sole owner. Washburn had the most ambitious artist endorsement program in the industry and imported every style

of guitar for the American and world markets. Although Washburn often imported acoustic guitars with solid spruce tops, some models were offered with solid woods for the back and sides as well.

In 1994 some acoustic prototypes were made for Wasburn by small US companies, including dreadnoughts by Dana Bourgeois of Maine and a fancy 12-fret model by Santa Cruz. In 1995 a new line of dreadnoughts was made for Washburn by the newly formed Tacoma guitar company of Tacoma, Washington. Called the Native American Series, these featured the new crown-shaped headstock and butterfly bridge. By 2017, Washburn acoustics were divided into no fewer than 13 series, from the scaled-down Travel models, to the classic stylings of the Woodcraft, Woodline, Heritage and Parlor series, and on to cutaway performance instruments that included Comfort and Festival models. Many Washburns were offered with on-board pickup and EQ systems and came in a variety of materials and finish options.

Just as it was over a century ago, Washburn is a dynamic company that changes both quickly and often. With constant innovation, and the proven value of keen advertising and visible endorsements, the firm has grown to be one of the largest in the music industry … yet again.

Washburn SBT-21 1990 (left)
Washburn's contribution to the craze for feedback-proof acoustic-electric stage guitars.

Washburn HD10S 2016 (center) *From Washburn's Heritage 10 series, this basic dreadnought flat-top has a solid spruce top and mahogany body.*

Washburn WCG 20SCE 2015 (far right) *This is one of the Comfort series, with belly and top carves designed to hug the player's body, and a Fishman pickup system.*

Washburn ad 2008 (right) *A promo for Washburn's small-body Baby Jumbo, later redesigned to become the Mini Jumbo.*

WECHTER

Abe Wechter began designing and building guitars in the early 1970s. He worked with the late Richard Schneider, making the radically designed Kasha guitars. He also served as a designer for Gibson. He quickly earned a reputation for his custom-made instruments built for the likes of Al DiMeola, Earl Klugh, and John McLaughlin. The guitars for McLaughlin in particular are famous for their extra resonator strings, which the fusion guitarist used in his group Shakti. Wechter ran his own shop from 1984, offering both US-made as well as import versions of his innovative designs, such as the Pathmaker. In 2013 he moved his shop to Guangzhou in China.

WEISSENBORN

The koa hollowneck Hawaiian guitars of Hermann C. Weissenborn enjoyed a dramatic resurgence in popularity two generations after resonator and electric instruments had consigned them to attics and pawnshops. Players like David Lindley, Steve Fishell (with Emmylou Harris), Ben Harper, Ry Cooder, and John Fahey turned heads with Weissenborn's sweet, haunting tones. Their somewhat odd shape comes from the body cavity that extends all the way up their square necks, an early attempt

(pioneered by Chris Knutsen) to achieve greater volume and tone. Weissenborn was born in Hanover, Germany in 1863, and emigrated to the US around 1900, moving to Los Angeles about nine years later. By the 1920s the Weissenborn Guitar Company Limited had moved and expanded its facilities, and this seems to coincide with changes to and standardization of his Hawaiian guitars.

Most Weissenborns found today show the later appointments: wood-burned brand inside the soundhole, 3" body depth, available in four styles. Priced at $39, Style 1 had no binding; Style 2 ($56) featured black trim, while Style 3 ($67.50) and Style 4 ($79) displayed different amounts of contrasting wood 'rope' binding. Fingerboard inlays progressed from single dots on Style 1 to multiple shapes on Style 4. Weissenborn instruments enjoyed wide distribution through wholesalers like Tonk Bros in Chicago and the Henry L. Stadlmair company of New York.

Many of Weissenborn's early instruments were branded for outside concerns. One prolific and long-running association was the manufacture of Kona Hawaiians for Los Angeles teacher and publisher C.S. DeLano. Konas look similar to Weissenborns, but in fact are narrower and deeper, with seven-fret solid necks joined to the body at an acute angle. Weissenborn also made Martin 0-size 12-fret Spanish guitars, designated

Weissenborn Style C 1925 *A koa-bodied, round-neck Spanish guitar built by Hermann C. Weissenborn, who is better known for his hollow-neck Hawaiian models made for lap-style slide playing.*

Wechter ad 2012 (*above***)** *Guitar stylist Carl Verheyen is shown with his Pathmaker model.*

Wilkanowski Airway W2 1939 (*left***)** *The Boston and New York-based violin-maker built very few guitars, around 30, but most – like this one – bore a striking resemblance to the smaller instruments he made.*

Back (*above left***)** *This gorgeous, highly figured back is from another, similar Wilkanowski Airway guitar.*

John McLaughlin 1976 (*above***)** *This famous 'drone-string' guitar was made by Abe Wechter in 1976 while he was still working as a designer for Gibson, and in fact says "The Gibson" on the headstock.*

Models A, B, C and D, similar to Hawaiians 1 through 4. He built plain and rope-bound tenor and plectrum guitars, and the operation was small enough to make some uncatalogued instruments. The brand was revived in 2005 by a Spanish firm.

WILKANOWSKI

Willi Wilkanowski was a Polish immigrant and violin-maker who arrived in the United States around 1920. First active in Boston working for the Ditson Co., he relocated to New York in 1938, where he built violins for the Gretsch Co. The bulk of Wilkanowski's work includes bowed string instruments, but some time between 1939 and 1941 he built around 30 archtop, f-hole guitars that in many respects reflected his violin making background. These are distinctive in a number of ways: the points on the upper bouts owe much to traditional violin shapes, and the equally hand-carved pickguards follow the shape of the upper bout, while the headstock has a finish not unlike that on later Ovation guitars. Within the overall design, features differ. Some have metal tailpieces, others are wooden; some have drop-shaped soundholes, others have traditional f-holes. Some of Wilkanowski's guitars bear the model name Airway, occasionally with mother-of-pearl inlays in a typical art deco style.

YAMAHA

Most Japanese guitar-makers started by providing guitars for export through trading companies, often making 'copies' of famous Western models before establishing their own identities. One of the few exceptions is Yamaha, which more or less charted its own course from the beginning – and never looked back. It was a good approach that earned the company an excellent reputation among players almost from the start, and was fundamental in improving the way Japanese guitars were perceived abroad.

Today Yamaha is a huge conglomerate that makes everything from tennis rackets to motorcycles, consumer electronics, and industrial robots, but it began when Torakusu Yamaha invented a pedal-driven reed organ in 1887. Ten years later Yamaha founded the Nippon Gakki Co, Ltd, and in 1900 began making pianos. Yamaha turned to building guitars in 1946, constructing its original factory in Hamamatsu, Japan.

Little is known of these early guitars, but they were probably classicals – which makes sense from a company that built pianos – and at some point became identified as Dynamic guitars. Examples from the early 1960s have a distinctive squarish shape with a fairly thick waist. Rather than work through importers, Yamaha established a subsidiary in the US, Yamaha International Corporation (later called Yamaha

Yamaha Model 85 c1965 (near left) A well-built and popular classical model from Yamaha.

Yamaha Model 150c 1966 (center) Cedar-topped classical.

Wilkanowski 1940 (far left) The violin theme is further echoed in the pickguard and headstock of this rare guitar from Willi Wilkanowski.

Yamaha ad 1969 (above) "Do your own thing," declares this groovy but – retrospectively – rather unhip ad. Cowboy faces off with hippie, yet each plays a Yamaha.

Yamaha ad 1974 *This Yamaha campaign emphasizes the care that the company puts into its wood selection.*

Corporation of America) which opened in Los Angeles in 1960, and began to market pianos. The first promotion of Dynamic classical guitars in the US began around 1964. These had solid spruce tops, laminated bodies (birch on lesser models, better woods on the upper range), and a 'patented' bracing system. By 1966 the line was doing well and expanding.

Yamaha Dynamics were identified by number, with a higher number indicating a better grade (Model 130, for example, was better than a Model 65). When a model was improved, it acquired an A suffix.

Precisely when Yamaha expanded into steel-string guitars is uncertain, but it was possibly as early as 1967. The first models were two orchestra-style folk guitars (spruce tops, in maple or mahogany) and six and 12-string dreadnoughts (spruce and mahogany) that Yamaha called 'jumbos.' These came with Yamaha's characteristic headstock design with a gentle V-dip in the top, distinctly non-Martin pickguard, and orange labels. At this time model designations added an alphabetical prefix, which identified the line. These first steel-strings were the FG or Folk Guitar models, a prefix that would continue – along with G for classicals – as Yamaha's core line.

By 1970 Yamaha had established a new climate-controlled manufacturing facility,

with input provided by an established Spanish craftsman. Yamaha's line had grown considerably to include classicals in rosewood, mahogany or maple, with a new head with a pointed crown shape on top. More steel-strings were offered, including the rosewood FG-300 Deluxe Jumbo with a bound fingerboard, fancy inlays, and a batwing plastic pickguard with floral colored designs. It had a metal adjustable bridge that did not, like most, detract from the excellent sound. Late in 1970 Yamaha redesigned its classical heads with more of a pagoda shape, and gave them the tuning-fork logo that would typify later models. To mark the change, the Model G-130 became the G-130A, and so on through the line.

While other Japanese guitar companies were producing copies of American models during the early 1970s, Yamaha stayed its course and continued to expand and improve its core line. By 1974 better FG dreadnoughts had jacaranda bodies, while lower-end folk guitars came with katsura bodies and bubinga fingerboards. Yamaha was now enjoying its first flirtations with acoustic electrics, but with a magnetic pickup at the end of the fingerboard. By this time, if not even earlier,

Bert Jansch 1990 *The influential British fingerstylist played Yamahas for most of his long career.*

Yamaha's lower range had laminated spruce tops, whereas the better models had solid spruce. By 1976 Yamaha folk guitars had acquired a crisp, modern look, with better guitars sporting bound headstocks. The old tuning fork logo was replaced by a new block-letter device. In Japan, at least, several more upscale dreadnought lines were introduced. The spectacular N series had a new tulip-shaped head similar to a Guild style (with a large stylized N inlay made to look like a fleur de lis), with bound ebony fingerboards, fancy pearl inlays, and cool mottled-tortoise batwing pickguards. The top-of-the-line had large inlays and an elegant pearl-inlaid mustache bridge.

Also new was an L range of handmade guitars, with scalloped braces and a new, unique L-block design that had a heel block with an L extension under the fingerboard to increase soundboard response. These had bound heads and ebony 'boards, and various special inlays, including an L-31 with split wing inlays and pearl around the top, the soundhole, and even around the fingerboard extension onto the top.

These may have been primarily for domestic consumption, but by 1978 some less luxuriously appointed L-series dreadnoughts were being exported as 'handcrafted folk guitars,' with pearl oval inlays. Yamaha's venerable FG series reached the 700 level by this time. Three-piece rosewood backs and two-tone red/yellow sunbursts were used

on better FG dreadnoughts. Yamaha's first proper jumbos also debuted in 1979 with the CJ Jumbo series. In addition to the true jumbo body, these also had the tulip-shaped heads that had appeared in Japan a few years before.

As with the L and N series, the models available in Japan were far fancier than the export versions (the L-53 Custom even offered an abalone head faceplate). In addition to the tulip-headed CJs, there were a group of spectacular CJs with block, cloud or split-wing inlays, and a new headstock with a flat top and gentle notches on the corners that would show up on later Yamahas, including the APX series.

Top of the line was the CJ-52 Custom, a black beauty with double white pickguards (giving almost a Gibson Everly Brothers look) set off with abalone trim and punctuated with mother-of-pearl inlays on a large mustache bridge. Yamaha also debuted an S series, which were dreadnought shaped but had just slightly smaller dimensions. Again, the line leader S-51 Custom was dressed up in abalone.

As the 1970s drew to a close Yamaha redesigned its classical 'pagoda' headstock to have more of a distinct, double-notched peak, and was using jacaranda on its top models, while lesser guitars were using woods such as ovankol and nato. By 1979 Yamaha had adopted the convention of adding an S suffix to models with solid tops.

Yamaha FG-300 c1971 (far left) Like most Japanese makers of the time, Yamaha felt obliged to give this big dreadnought more than a passing resemblance to a major American make – in this case Gibson.

Yamaha FG-336SB 1981 (near left) A sunburst dreadnought from the early years of Taiwanese production.

Yamaha ads 1978 and 1986 (above and center) Promos for the long-running Handcrafted Series (above) and for Yamaha's entry level Eterna range (above left).

Despite their successes, Japanese guitar-makers were having a hard time in the 1970s, primarily because of growing labor costs and unfavorable exchange rates with overseas customers, combined with some markets that would not yet support premium prices for their products. Yamaha was no exception.

In order to continue supplying quality guitars at an acceptable price, Yamaha traveled to Taiwan, which offered much cheaper labor. There were guitar factories on the island, but Yamaha chose to build its own plant at Kaoshiung, Taiwan, making it fully climate controlled and equipping it with the same level of advanced equipment as it had in its Japanese facility. As a result, Yamaha avoided the 'learning curve' experienced by most manufacturers beginning to obtain guitars from less expensive, and less developed, countries. Beginning around 1981 Yamaha began making its production-grade acoustics in Taiwan, with no noticeable diminution in quality. Its prototypes, upscale, and handmade models continued to be made in Japan.

Yamaha marked yet more milestones in 1981 with the introduction of its first modern acoustic-electric equipped with a piezo-electric pickup system, the FG-335E. (As you might guess, the suffix E stood for electric.) Also introduced were more true jumbos with the SJ series. Another significant model was the FG-340T, the T

representing the use of tinted finishes. Initially the tint was an amber but as the decade progressed one could choose from black or a number of sunbursts, including a blue. A new line of upscale handcrafted classical guitars with solid spruce or cedar tops, the GC series, debuted. It featured laminated and solid bodies, including solid jacaranda on the top models. The top models were special-order instruments, the GC-71 sporting solid German spruce top and genuine Honduran mahogany body. It would remain as Yamaha's top classical line into the future. Reminiscent of early Japanese classicals, by the late 1980s these featured several new headstock shapes, including several new carved versions of the classic pagoda.

The early 1980s saw a recession in demand for guitars, and Yamaha's offerings pretty much marked time during this period. By 1985 things began to shake loose and Yamaha exploded with new ideas, many developed years before in Japan.

Yamaha revived the 1970s L-series handmades (using the L-block design) with some high-class dreadnoughts. The LLs features solid spruce tops and a variety of solid timbers, including jacaranda, plus bound ebony fingerboards. Top models featured fancy pearl inlays and abalone trim. Yamaha's first cutaway acoustics appeared in the LL range, with a pair in rosewood or mahogany, either straight

Yamaha FG-612S 1983 (*near right*) *A Taiwan-made folk-jumbo dreadnought 12-string.*

Yamaha LL-11E 1997 (*far right*) *A jumbo/dreadnought-shaped model from the upscale, Japanese-made LL Series.*

Yamaha ad 1999 *Producer and singer/songwriter David Pack promotes the Handcrafted range.*

Bruce Springsteen c1993
(*below*) *The Boss here chooses a*
black-finished Yamaha on stage.

YAMAHA

acoustic or with a piezo pickup system. This handmade line also included some new LS guitars, in effect the previous Japanese S series 'semi-jumbos' with a body size larger than a folk but smaller than a dreadnought. Also appearing were some LA guitars, dreadnoughts with downsized body and tulip head. A downscale but still handmade LD series debuted in 1990. These were all professional-grade instruments.

Production guitars also went through some changes. At this time Yamaha changed the designation for its production classicals to a CG prefix. The FG line also got its first cutaway models, in acoustic or acoustic-electric versions. Yamaha started to use flamed sycamore for some tops. Its first thin-body cutaways also debuted with the FN and CN guitars. The FNs were cool models that came in all-sycamore or spruce-and-birch, with split wing inlays, a bound fingerboard that extended over the soundhole, and a new head with notches on both top corners. The CN was similar in spruce and rosewood for nylon strings (C=cutaway, N=nylon). These new guitars dominated Yamaha's late-1980s acoustic line.

Until now, Yamaha had established a solid reputation among players for the quality of its acoustics but, despite producing some killer guitars, it was still ignored by some. The breakout occurred in 1987 with the introduction of the APX series of cutaway

thin-body acoustic-electric guitars. Essentially, the APX line was the previous thin-bodied FN/CN range enhanced with a new piezo-electric pickup system coupled to an FET+IC preamp system.

By 1989 the APX line was impressive, with eight models, all with spruce tops in a variety of body materials ranging from agathis and ovnankol to sycamore and Indian rosewood. They included a 12-string plus two classicals, one with and one without a cutaway. These came in a variety of color options similar to the tinteds. The top-of-the-line APX-20 was decked out in abalone trim.

By 1990 refinements appeared such as the ability to lock control knobs once set. Some SPL models were produced with backs and sides made of a single piece of molded composite material. By 1994 the APX line was joined by a Deep Body series with full-depth bodies and solid spruce tops. A new two-way pickup system was offered, with piezo sensors both in the bridge and inside the guitar, and stereo or mono output, depending on the model. In 1995 some APX guitars began to be equipped with three-band EQ systems.

While these models were being offered to the world at large, as usual, Yamaha was creating some arguably more interesting items for the Japanese market. These

included some deluxe APX models with six-tuners-in-line headstocks, plus the handmade series with a food deal more pearl than generally available, including elaborately engraved headstock inlays.

In 1996 Yamaha expanded the APX line with the Travel Series in either steel or nylon-string versions. These had full-scale necks but small bodies about two-thirds the normal size, and piezo electronics. The following year Yamaha celebrated a decade of the APX line with a beautiful APX-97LTD, a limited edition in white-finished spruce and sycamore with abalone top trim, a Japanese cherry blossom inlaid on the head, and snowflake clusters on the fingerboard.

Yamaha took a fairly conservative approach to its classical line, which remained all-acoustic far longer than many other manufacturers. In 1992 Yamaha introduced the GD series, beginner classicals but with solid tops. By 1994 the first piezo pickup systems began to appear, and around 1995 the first cutaway acoustic-electric classicals debuted. At least through 1996 Yamaha continued to produce acoustics in Japan and Taiwan. At about this time, like most other companies before it, Yamaha also began to source some less expensive models from Indonesia.

In 1996 Yamaha introduced yet another line of solid-topped dreadnoughts, the DW

series, all with bound fingerboards, plus a budget version of the semi-jumbo LS in the FS-311. By 1998 the DWs were joined by pickup-and-EQ models and cutaway versions, as was Yamaha's traditional FG series, the new models dubbed FGX.

The next significant development from Yamaha was the debut of the new CPX Compass Series of acoustic-electrics in 1998. The Compass guitars appear to have been made in response to Takamine's successful Santa Fe series, with decorations inspired by Southwestern Native American themes. Essentially variants of the APX guitars, CPXs combined some technological advances with decorative themes. Central to the theme was a tribute to the discovery of new worlds, thus the elaborate compass inlay on the head. The top-of-the-line CPX-50 was decorated with inlays of colorful nautical flags like those seen on tall ships. Their pickup systems employed a new floating bridge designed to reduce unwanted noise and feedback, coupled with a flexible three-band EQ system.

Later that year the Compass line expanded to include a model with a Western theme, with belt buckle inlays and bullhorn rosette – not exactly linked to discovering new worlds, but pretty cool nonetheless. In 1999 two other models debuted. One was an Eastern tribute to the ancient mysteries of Egypt, with hieroglyphic inlays of

Yamaha CPX55-TMB 2003 (center) *This model from the Handcrafted Series (telltale 'compass' headstock inlay) has a cutaway jumbo body and built-in electronics.*

Yamaha FS-720S 2007 (far right) *A small-body flat-top with solid spruce top and non-scalloped bracing.*

Yamaha ad 2005 (right) *Promo for the Dave Navarro LLX6DN model.*

Yamaha FG-423-TBS 2002 (above) *A sunburst dreadnought from the long-running FG line with solid spruce top and laminated nato body.*

various woods and a sort of Egyptian-fabric-design rosette. The other was a Southern tribute, with starfish and fish inlays and a Caribbean style rosette.

As Yamaha entered the 21st Century its lines had consolidated around its 1990s developments. The FG/FGX and DW/DWX models anchored the production steel-string acoustics, with fine handmades limited but still available. Classicals came in a full range of solid-topped models and included cutaway acoustic-electrics. The APX and CPX Compass series made up the principal acoustic-electrics.

In 2002, Yamaha joined the trend toward smaller guitars and began producing CSF parlor guitars. Unlike many of this neo breed, the Yamahas were wisely made with reduced bracing to improve their response. Also in 2002, Yamaha introduce its highly innovative SLG Silent Guitar, an acoustic-electric classical that could be used for practice or performing. Four years later, the company introduced its ART (Acoustic Resonance Transducer) pickup system for electro-acoustics, plus in 2009 a new classical line, the NX series, and in 2011/2014 two new steel-string lines, the A and L series. A further acoustic introduction came with the revised FG series in 2016.

Throughout its many decades of guitar-making, Yamaha has consistently pursued its vision of creating a full range of guitars that balance art, playability and value.

ZEMAITIS

Tony Zemaitis, born in 1935, was an English cabinet-maker turned luthier who built some of the most over-the-top guitars ever. Best known are his engraved metal-front electrics, but it was his individual acoustics that first caught attention. They were solidly built but delicately inlaid acoustics, often with soundholes in the shape of a heart, crescent moon, or even a sunflower, and with elaborate pearl and metal inlays.

Zemaitis acoustics initially became popular among British folk and rock artists of the 1960s such as Donovan and Ralph McTell. His unique guitars later found their way to rock's aristocracy in the hands of Jimi Hendrix, Eric Clapton, David Gilmour, Ron Wood, Bob Dylan, and George Harrison. For Ronnie Lane of Small Faces, Zemaitis built a huge acoustic bass guitar long before such instruments were commonplace. He built only six to ten guitars per year, retired in 2000, and died in 2002. Even though the builder himself never capitalized on the cult surrounding his name, Zemaitis guitars are today sought-after collectors' items, often fetching large sums, and there are a number of Zemaitis owners' clubs in Europe, the United States, and Japan. A new Zemaitis Guitars firm based in Japan today offers instruments made in collaboration with Tony's relatives.

Donovan 2002 *The folk-popster brings his rare Zemaitis acoustic back into view in the UK on the Glastonbury Festival stage.*

Yamaha LSX36C 2008 (far left) *Yamaha's 36 series were high-end models with the company's new ART pickup system.*

Yamaha LJ56 Custom ARE 2016 (left) *The 56 models were the flagship instruments of Yamaha's L series, introduced in 2014, with the J here indicating a Jumbo body size.*

ACKNOWLEDGEMENTS

AUTHORS & EDITORS

This book was written by Walter Carter (WC), Ben Elder (BE), Teja Gerken (TG), Dave Hunter (DH), Mikael Jansson (MJ), Richard Johnston (RJ), John Morrish (JM), Michael Simmons (MS), Jerry Uwins (JU), and Michael Wright (MW). It was edited by Dave Hunter and Tony Bacon. It was updated by Nigel Osborne and Tony Bacon in 2017. The following key indicates who wrote which entries. Alvarez MW; Alvarez-Yairi MW; Andersen MS; Aria MW; Art & Lutherie MW; Ashborn MW; Avalon JU; Ayers JU; Aylward MS; Beltona MS; Benedetto WC; Bernabé JM; Bohmann MW; Bolin MJ; Bourgeois MJ; Bozo MS; Breedlove MJ; Brink BE; Brook JU; Campellone MJ; Carvin MJ; Collings RJ; Contreras JM; Cort MW; Crafter JU; Cromwell WC; DAngelico WC; DAquisto WC; De Jonge MS; Del Vecchio MJ; DellArte MS; Di Mauro MS; Ditson MW; Dobro WC; Dunn MS; Dupont MS; Dyer MW; EKO MW; Epiphone MW; España MJ; Esteso JM; Euphonon MW; Favino MS; Fender DH; Fleta JM; Framus MW; Franklin TG; Froggy Bottom TG; Furch JU; Fylde JU; Gallgher TG; Garrison TG; Gay BE; Giannini MW; Gibson WC; Gilbert JM; Goodall MS; Grammer MJ; Greenfield BE; Gretsch BE; Grimes TG; Grimshaw MJ; Guild RJ; Gurian MS; Hagström MJ; Harmony MW; Harptone MW; Hauser JM; Heritage MS; Hilo BE; Hodson MS; Höfner MJ; Humphrey JM; Ibanez MW; Jones WC; Kalamazoo WC; Kay MW; Klein TG; Koontz MW; Kramer MW; Lakewood JU; Landola MJ; La Patrie MW; Larrivée TG; Levin MJ; Lowden DH; Maccaferri MW; Maingard DH; Manson JU; Manzer MS; Martin RJ; Maton MS; Maurer MW; McPherson MJ; Monteleone TG; Morgan JU; Mossman MW; Mozzani MS; National WC; Norman JU; Oahu BE; Old Kraftsman MW; Olson TG; Ovation MW; Paramount DH; Park MS; Peavey JU; Prairie State MW; Rainsong JU; Ramírez JM; Regal MW; Ribbecke TG; Rickenbacker MJ; Roger MJ; Romanillos JM; Ruck JM; Samick MW; Santa Cruz MS; Scheerhorn WC; Schoenberg BE; Seagull MW; Selmer MS; Silvertone MW; Simon & Patrick MW; Slingerland MW; Smallman JM; Sobell MJ; Somogyi MS; Stahl MW; Stella MW; Stromberg WC; Tacoma JU; Takamine MW; Taylor MS; Torres JM; Traugott TG; Turner TG; Vanden MJ; Vega MW; Washburn RJ; Wechter MJ; Weissenborn BE; Wilkanowski MJ; Yamaha MW; Zemaitis MJ.

GUITAR PHOTOGRAPHS

Most of the guitar pictures in this book come from the Balafon Image Bank, a unique archive of thousands of guitar images managed by Backbeat UK. Principal photography was by Miki Slingsby. We are grateful to the various owners who allowed us to photograph their fabulous instruments. Some photos were supplied by Guitar Magazine (UK), and a small number of additional images were supplied by manufacturers. Michael Wright also kindly photographed guitars from his own collection for use in this book.

MEMORABILIA

The catalogs, photographs, record sleeves et cetera reproduced in this book came from the collections of Tony Bacon, Balafon Image Bank, Ben Elder, Paul Day, Alan Rogan, and Steve Soest. Original advertisements came from the pages of Acoustic Guitar, Beat Instrumental, Guitarist, The Guitar Magazine, Guitar Player, Guitar World, The Music Trades.

ARTIST PICTURES

Many artist pictures in this book come from the Balafon Image Bank, while of the others, more were supplied by Redferns than by any other single agency.

Redferns photographers are indicated by the following key: AE Amanda Edwards; AL Andrew Lepley; AP Andrew Putler; BE Brigitte Engl; BS Barbara Steinwehe; DP David Peabody; DR David Redfern; EL Elliott Landy; ER Ebet Roberts; GT Gai Terrell; HH Harry Herd; HM Hayley Madden; KM Keith Morris; LM Leon Morris; MH Mick Hutson; MOA Michael Ochs Archive; NJS Nicky J. Sims; PF Patrick Ford; RP Roberta Parkin; TF Tabatha Fireman; TH Tim Hall; VW Val Wilmer.

Page key: 11 Smithers DR; 12 Flaming Lips HM; 16 Starr & Bolan KM; 27 Eitzel HM; 31 Lovett LM; 33 Griffin AE; 53 Clapton ER; 54 Hedges ER; 63 Bolan KM; 67 Bowie MOA; 71 Kinks DR; 77 Doves TF; 77 Hitchcock ER; 79 Lowe BS; 84 Ellington MOA; 125 Renbourne VW; 128 Adams HM; 129 Cash ER; 132 Williams VW; 134 Neil MOA; 145 Blackwell MOA; 151 Mead HM; 151 Robertson ER; 155 Bensusan AL; 169 Anderson GT; 211 Martin AP; 214 Clapton ER; 223 Neil Finn PF; 235 Eurythmics MH; 237 Harris BE; 243 Campbell DR; 244 Cope; 249 Fuller VW; 261 Paxton RP; 262 Baez DP; 265 Poe ER; 275 The Band EL; 279 Mtukudzi BE; 286 Vega ST; 289 Albarn MH; 290 Griffith HH; 294 Dixie Chicks NJS; 306 Williams TH; 308 McLaughlin AP; 310 Jansch NJS; 313 Springsteen ER.

Key to artist photos supplied by other agencies: Retna – BW/R Baron Wolman, CH/R Christian Him, JA/R John Atashian; DC David Corio; FD Frank Driggs; GM Gems; HD Howard Denner; JP Jan Persson; SP Sylvia Pitcher; TB/CJ Teri Bloom – Concord Jazz; TC Terry Cryer; TR Tony Russel.

Page key: 19 Alden TB/CJ; 49 Betts GM; 58 Five Spirits Of Rhythm FD; 60 Nat King Cole FD; 78 Watson SP; 82 Broonzy FD; 118 Green JP; 123 Buckley JP; 126 Havens JP; 176 Mound City FD; 178 Rodgers FD; 183 Autry FD; 188 Snow FD; 190 Johnson FD; 191 Monroe FD; 195 Presley FD; 196 Broonzy (hands) SP; 197 Broonzy TC; 199 Seeger BW/R; 201 Mitchell TR; 203 Young JP; 204 Crosby & Nash JP; 205 Nelson HD; 213 Odetta DC; 216 Frisell CH/R; 230 White JP; 237 Taylor HD; 241 McCartney JP; 246 DiMeola JA/R; 273 Estes JP; 280 Scofield JP; 305 Hiatt JP; 315 Donovan JP.

THANKS

In addition to those named elsewhere in this section, we would sincerely like to thank: Bob and Cindy Benedetto, Brook Guitars, Guitar Village in Farnham, Barry Moorhouse and all at House Music in London, Ervin Somogyi, James Laney at Headstock Distribution.

TRADEMARKS

Trademarked names are used throughout this book. Rather than put a TM trademark symbol next to every occurrence, we state here that we are using the names only in an editorial fashion, primarily as references to industry standard designs, and that we do not intend to infringe any trademarks.

Out of the air a voice without a face. W.H. Auden